John Drinkwater

A History of the Late Siege of Gibraltar

With a description and account of that garrison, from the earliest periods

John Drinkwater

A History of the Late Siege of Gibraltar
With a description and account of that garrison, from the earliest periods

ISBN/EAN: 9783337318109

Printed in Europe, USA, Canada, Australia, Japan

Cover: Foto ©ninafisch / pixelio.de

More available books at **www.hansebooks.com**

A

HISTORY

OF THE LATE

SIEGE of GIBRALTAR.

WITH

A DESCRIPTION and ACCOUNT of that GARRISON,

FROM THE EARLIEST PERIODS.

BY

JOHN DRINKWATER,

CAPTAIN IN THE LATE SEVENTY-SECOND REGIMENT, OR ROYAL MANCHESTER VOLUNTEERS; AND AN
HONORARY MEMBER OF THE LITERARY AND PHILOSOPHICAL SOCIETY OF MANCHESTER.

THIRD EDITION.

———————————— VOLATILE FERRUM

SPARGITUR, ARVA NOVA NEPTUNIA CÆDE RUBESCUNT.

VIRG.

MONTIS INSIGNIA CALPE.

LONDON:

Printed by T. SPILSBURY, Snowhill;
And sold by J. JOHNSON, Nº 72, St. Paul's Church - Yard; T. and J. EGERTON,
Charing-Cross; and J. EDWARDS, Nº 102, Pall-Mall.

M,DCC,LXXXVI.

THE KING.

SIR,

WHEN I folicited the honor
of being permitted to place under Your
Majefty's protection the following Work,
I was not impreffed with the idea, that the
excellence of the compofition, but that the
importance of the fubject, might in fome
degree entitle it to that diftinction. The
Hiftory of an Event which reflects fo much
A 2 luftre

luftre on Your Majefty's Arms, could not, I apprehended, however feeble the execution, fo properly appear under any other aufpices.

THAT Your Majefty may never be lefs faithfully ferved, nor lefs fuccefsful againft the Enemies of your Crown and People, is the fincere and fervent wifh of

YOUR MAJESTY'S

much obliged and moft devoted

Subject and Servant,

John Drinkwater.

PREFACE.

THE following History (as I have prefumed to call it) is compiled from obfervations daily noted down upon the Spot, for my own fatisfaction and improvement; affifted by the information and remarks of feveral refpectable Characters, who alfo were Eye-witneffes of the tranfactions therein recorded.

DISAPPOINTED in my expectations of feeing this fubject undertaken by an abler Pen, nothing lefs than a conviction that an accurate detail of this extraordinary Siege might be ufeful, both in a military and hiftorical view, could have induced me, at this late period, to publifh.

IN the profecution of this defign, one principal difficulty has occurred. The work is addreffed to two claffes of Readers : thofe whofe principal object in the perufal of it was entertainment, I apprehended, might find the relation too minute and circumftantial ; and that,

that, from the infertion of many particulars, which thofe of the Military Profeffion would greatly blame an author for prefuming to curtail, or omit.

WITH the former, it is hoped that the neceffary connexion of fome Events (which at firft may appear trivial) with the great bufinefs of the Hiftory, will be fome apology; and I have endeavoured to diverfify the narrative, by fuch Anecdotes and Obfervations as will occafionally relieve or awaken the attention. To the latter I fhall not attempt any apology. The late Siege of Gibraltar afforded many inftances of very fingular exertions in the Art of Attack and Defence, the minutiæ of which cannot be without their utility to thofe Officers who make a fcience of their profeffion; and they muft be fenfible, that without pointed exactnefs, this Defign could not have been accomplifhed.—In fhort, it muft be remembered, that the Hiftory of this Siege is not that of a *Month*, or of a *Year*, but that it embraces a period of near FOUR YEARS, exhibiting a feries of operations perhaps unparallelled.

THE

THE Plans, I prefume, will be found tolerably cor-
rect; and, with the Views, are fuch as will be fufficiently illuftrative of the narration.

To MAJOR VALLOTTON, the Governor's Firft Aide-de-
Camp, and Lieut. HOLLOWAY, Aide-de-Camp to the
Chief Engineer, I have particular pleafure in this
opportunity of returning thanks for the favour of many
kind communications; alfo to other Officers of Rank,
whofe names I have not their permiffion to infert. I
muft alfo acknowledge having derived confiderable
affiftance, in the two introductory Chapters, from the
Hiftory of the Herculean Straits.——Great additions have
however been introduced; and I flatter myfelf upon
the whole, that thofe Chapters will not prove an unacceptable part of the Work, fince they will render it as
complete a GENERAL HISTORY OF GIBRALTAR as moft
Readers will require.

ADVER-

ADVERTISEMENT

TO THE

SECOND EDITION.

IT was my wish to render this Work as complete, at the first, as my abilities and information would permit: I omitted therefore no material circumstance, which, previous to the publication, came within my knowledge. Some improvements, however, have since occurred; and, though the omission of them in the former Edition by no means affects the general object of the History, I thought it my duty to insert them in this.

I AM chiefly indebted to the candid criticism of some respectable Friends, for whatever corrections in the style there may be in the present Volume; nor could I, without disrespect to them, and indeed to my Readers in general, neglect an opportunity of rendering the narrative more perfect and agreeable.

THE

THE kind reception with which this attempt has been favoured by the Public, was, I muſt confeſs, beyond my moſt ſanguine expectation. It is in compliance with their judgement, that I have been tempted to venture upon a Second Edition. I ſend it forth, however, with all that diffidence which a conſciouſneſs of my own powers ought to inſpire; and, however flattering ſuch ſucceſs may be to a young Author, I truſt, I ſhall not be found ſo ignorant of myſelf, as to be unreaſonably elated, or attribute to my own merits what I am certain is rather to be aſcribed to the intereſting nature of the ſubject.

DIRECTIONS for. placing the P L A T E S.

SUBSCRIBERS.

OFFICERS of the Old Garrison of GIBRALTAR,

WHO WERE PRESENT DURING THE LATE SIEGE.

THE Right Hon. GENERAL SIR G. A. ELIOTT, K. B. GOVERNOR   20 *copies*

    LIEUT. GEN. SIR R. BOYD, K. B. LIEUT. GOVERNOR   6 *copies*

    MAJOR GENERAL DE LA MOTHE

    MAJOR GEN. SIR WM. GREEN, BART. CHIEF ENGINEER 6 *copies*

    Lieut. Col. Hardy, Quarter-master General

    Major Horsbrugh, Adjutant General

    Major Vallotton, First Aide-de-Camp to the Governor

    Lieut. G. F. Koehler, Aide-de-Camp to the Governor   2 *copies*

    ———— Holloway, Aide-de-Camp to Gen. Green

    Capt. Foulis, (late) Town-Major

    —— Delhoste, (present) Town-Major

    —— S. Wood, (now 82d Regt.) Assistant Town-Major

ARTILLERY.

MAJOR Martin
———— Lloyd
Capt. Cuppage
—— Siward
—— Willington
—— Whitworth
—— Boag
Lieut. Burton

12th REGIMENT.

MAJOR GEN. PICTON   10 *copies*
Col. Trigge
Capt. Perryn
—— Spilsbury
—— Forch, (now 2d Regt.)
—— K. Wilson
Lieut. Sandby
—— Munro
Mr. Tate

39th REGIMENT.

Col. Kellet   2 *copies*
Major Vignoles
Lieut. Gerrard

56th REGIMENT.

Col. Craige
Major Moore
Capt. Price
—— Addison   5 *copies*
Mr. Chisholme

58th REGIMENT.

Lieut. Col. Horsfall

Major Duffe
Capt. Gledstanes, (now 57th Regt.)
Lieut. Littlehales
—— Gordon

72d REGIMENT.

MAJOR GEN. ROSS   2 *copies*
Col. Gledstanes
Major Aytoun
Major Tipping, (now 80th Regt.) 2 *copies*
William Clowes, Esq.
John Nangreave, Esq.
Capt. Græme
—— Burville
—— M'Cullock
—— Gordon
Lieut. Taylor
—— Reeves
—— Rollo
—— E. B. Frederick
—— C. Wilson
—— Harris
—— Nunns
Mr. Sutton
Mr. Henderson

2d BATTALION of the 73d REGIMENT.

Mr. Cairncrofs

97th REGIMENT.

Capt. Shewbridge, (now 3d Regt.)

MARINE BRIGADE.

SIR ROGER CURTIS, Kt.   3 *copies*
Capt. Bradshaw Smith
Mr. W. Maud

S U B S C R I B E R S.

OFFICERS of the prefent Garrifon of GIBRALTAR,

Whofe Names, not yet being received, cannot be individually noticed, 110 *copies*.

A.

HIS Grace the Duke of Atholl
The Hon. Lord Ankerville, Edinburgh
Sir W. Abdy, Bart. Surry
Mr. H. Ackers, Manchefter
Alex. Adair, Efq. Pall-Mall, London
R. Andrews, Efq. Rivington
J. P. Andrews, Efq. Brompton
Mr. T. Arrowfmith, Manchefter
Lieut. Armftrong, W. Norfolk Militia
N. Afhton, Efq. Liverpool
Mr. J. Afhworth, Manchefter
Rev. Mr. Aubrey

B.

The Right Hon. Lord Brownlow
Sir William Bowyer, Bart. Norwich
Wm. Bamford, Efq. Bamford, Lan-cafhire
S. Badcocks, Efq. London
Mrs. Bailey, Manchefter
Wm. Banks, Efq. Winftanley, Lanca-fhire
R. Bates, Efq.
Mr. W. Barrow, Salford
Mr. J. Barrow, ditto
Mr. E. Batterfbee, Manchefter
Mr. Beard, Derbyfhire
Mr. Robert Bent, Liverpool
Michael Bentley, Efq. Manchefter
R. Bickerton, Efq. Royal Navy
Peploe Birch, Efq. London
R. Birch, Efq. Cambridge
J. Bifcoe, Efq. London
J. Blakeney, Efq. Lythwood, Salop
J. G. Booth, Efq. Salford
Lieut. Bowker, (60th Regt.)
J. Bogle, Efq. London
Mr. Brandt, Manchefter
Salufbury Brereton, Efq. London
J. Brookes, Efq. Liverpool
Mr. Bull, Bath   .. 2 *copies*

Lieut. Col. Burton, Horfe Guards
G. Burges, Efq.

C.

His Grace the Duke of Chandos
Her Grace the Duchefs of Chandos
The Right Hon. the Earl of Chatham
Thomas Chadwick, Efq. Manchefter
Capt. Campbell (78th Regt.)
Mr. Carleton, London
Col. Chadwick, R. L. M. Healey-Hall
Charles Chadwick, Efq.   ditto
Lieut. Chesfhyre, Royal Navy, Salford
Mr. Edward Chesfhyre, ditto
Hon. Capt. Chetwynd, Navy
Major Clayton, Carr-Hall
Thomas Clayton, Efq. ditto
Samuel Clowes, jun. Efq. Broughton
Mr. James Cooke, Salford
Major Cooke
Mr. Thomas Cornell, London
Major Crofs, R. L. M.
Capt. W. Cunninghame

D.

Sir F. H. Drake, Bart.
Mr. E. Dakin, Warrington
J. Daintry, Efq. Leek
W. Davidfon, Efq. London
J. Davis, Efq.
Mr. Dickey, London
Mr. R. Downward, Liverpool
T. Dowdefwell, Efq. Salop
Charles d'Oyly, Efq. London
Robert Drummond, Efq. ditto
Henry Drummond, Efq. ditto
F. Duroure, Efq. Kenfington

E.

The Rt. Hon. the Earl of Exeter
Lieut. Col. Eliott, (6th Regt. Dragoons)
Mr. Eddleftone, Salford
Mr. Eubank, jun. York

SUBSCRIBERS.

F.

The Rt. Hon. Lord Fairfax
Lieut. Gen. Fawcett, Adjutant General
Sir Charles Frederick, K. B.
Mr. M. Falkner, Manchester
Mr. James Falkner, Manchester
J. Fanshawe, Esq. London
The Rev. Dr. Fairfax
Mr. H. A. Fellowes, London
R. Fisher, Esq.
M. Fletcher, Esq.
J. Flint, Esq. Salop
Mr. Duncan Forbes
Mr. Ford, London
Mr. Fox, Manchester
Rose Fuller, Esq. London

G.

The Rt. Hon. Lord Viscount Galway
The Right. Hon. Lord Grey de
 Wilton   5 *copies*
Rev. Mr. Gilbert, Yorkshire
R. Gregory, Esq. London
The Rev. Mr. Gregory, ditto   2 *copies*
B. R. Grieve, Esq.
Col. C. Gordon, (61st Regt.)
W. Gordon, Esq. Norwich
Mr. R. Gorton, Salford
Mr. Gough

H.

The Rt. Hon. Sir Richard Heron, Bt.
Mr. Hall, sen. Manchester
Peter Halsted, Esq. Lymme, Cheshire
W. Hale, Esq. London
H. Hamer, Esq. Liverpool
Capt. Hamilton
Mr. J. Hardman, Manchester
Mr. Hampp, Norwich,   2 *copies*
Mr. Harry
Mr. Harvey, London   5 *copies*
Rob. Harvey, Esq. Innisk. Dragoons
M. Haslingden, Manchester   5 *copies*
M. J. Haworth, ditto
Mr. Heath, ditto
Major Higginson, (50th Regt.)
Arthur Holdsworth, Esq. M.P.
Mr. T. Hodgson, Salford
Mr. W. Hodgson, ditto
Mr. J. Horne, Edinburgh

Mr. Houghton, Manchester
E. G. Hopwood, Esq. Hopwood
Hon. Lieut. Col. J. H. Hutchenson
W. Hulton, Esq. Hulton
H. Hulton, Esq. ditto
The Rev. Mr. Hunt, Cunde, Salop

I. J.

Sir W. Jernyngham, Bart.
Captain Imrie, (2d Battal. of the Royals)
Mr. J. Johnson, Congleton
J. L. Iselin, Esq. Norwich
J. Ives, jun. Esq. ditto

K.

Mr. Kearsley, Manchester
The Rev. Mr. R. Kenyon, Salford

L.

Sir Ashton Lever, Kt. Alkrington
Egerton Leigh, Esq.
Thomas Livesey, Esq. Lincolnshire
J. Lavie, Esq. London
G. Lloyd, Esq. Manchester
Mr. Lockhart, London

M.

Hon. Gen. Murray
Hon. Major Gen. Murray, M. P.
Major Gen. Sir Hector Munro, K. B.
Sir G. Massey, Kt. Dublin Castle
Capt. Mann, Navy
Mr. J. Mackay, Fludyer Street, West-
 minster
Mr. H. Mackay, ditto
Capt. M'Leod, Edinburgh
Mr. B. Markland, Blackburn, Lanca-
 shire
Manchester Circulating Library
Mr. Meredith, Manchester
Mess. Meyricks, London   3 *copies*
Mrs. Meyrick, Wigan, Lancashire
Colonel Morgan, (Coldst. Regt. Guards)
J. Moneypenny, Esq. Liverpool, 2 *copies*
Major Munro, London
Mr. Murdoch, ditto

N.

The Rt. Hon. Earl Nugent
Mr. Nicholson, Stockport.
Ensign Noel, (12th Regt.)

O.

The Right Hon. the Earl of Orford
2 *copies*

P.

Sir Richard Perryn, Kt. Baron of the Exchequer.
S. Townley Parker, Esq. Preston
B. Parker, Esq. Cuerdon
Colonel Patten, Bank, Warrington
J. Patteson, Esq. Norwich 2 *copies*
The Rev. Mr. H. Patteson, Suffolk
N. Pattison, Esq. Congleton
Capt. Paterson, (36th Regt.)
James Pettman, Esq.
Mr. F. Phillips, Manchester
Joseph Pickford, Esq. Royton
Domville Halsted Poole, Esq. Lymme, Cheshire
The Rev. Mr. G. Powell, Congleton
Mr. Poggi, London
Capt. Preston

R.

The Rt. Hon. Lord Rollo
W. T. Reade, Esq. Wimpole Street
Thomas Reed, Esq.
Mr. Walter Reed
Jacob Reynardson, Esq. London
W. Rigby, Esq. Manchester
Major Robertson (Engineers)
Capt. Robertson, (101st Regt.)
Capt. Rofs, (3d Regt. of Horse)

S.

General Severn
John Salkeld, Esq.
The Rev. Mr. Salmon, Hassal
The Rev. Mr. R. Sandford, Astbury
G. Secker, Esq. Cambridge
Mr. J. Sedgwick, Manchester
Miss Shaw, Derbyshire
Lieut. Shipley, (Engineers)
Mr. Thomas Slater, Manchester
J. C. Smith, Esq: London 3 *copies*
Capt. J. Smith, ditto
—— W. Smith, ditto
Robert Staniforth, Esq. Manchester

Mr. J. Stanton, Liverpool
Mr. R. Stewart
The Rev. Dr. Storer, Preb. of Canterb.
Lt. Col. Strickland, (1st Regt. of Guards)
Mr. R. Sullivan, London

T

James Taylor, Esq. Leigh
J. Tipping, Esq. Manchester
Ensign Thorley, (44th Regt.)
Capt. Trewan
Mr. Turnbull, London

W.

The Rev. Mr. Ward, Prebend of Ely and Chester
Mr. P. B. Wagner, Liverpool
Mr. R. Walker, Manchester
Mr. Walker, London
Capt. Walker, (R. L. M.)
Mr. G. Walker, Manchester
The Rev. Mr. Walcam, Ashton
Mr. A. Wall, London
Mr. Wallworth, Warrington
L. G. Watkin, Esq. London
Mr. G. Ward, ditto
Henry Lee Warner, Esq. London
Mr. H. Watson, Stockport
Mr. G. W. Watts, Liverpool
The Rev. Mr. Warton
The Rev. Mr. Welton, Somerby-Hall, Lincolnshire
Thomas Wetenhall, Esq.
Tho. Wharton, Esq. Edinburgh
Tho. Wilkinson, Esq. London
Mr. J. Wilkinson, Congleton, Cheshire
Henry Norton Willis, Esq. London
Mathew Winter, Esq. London
Mr. J. Withington, Manchester
Mr. Woodd, London
Capt. Woodford, (1st Regt. of Guards)
N. Wright, Esq. London

Y.

The Rt. Hon. Sir George Yonge, Bart. Secretary at War
Mr. Yvounet, London

GENERAL
TABLE OF CONTENTS.

CHAP. I.

The

C H A P. IV.

Description

C H A P. V.

c

Enemy's

Gallant

CHAP. VI.

C H A P.   VII.

Extraordinary

Governor

CHAP. VIII.

Governor

A
HISTORY
OF THE LATE
SIEGE of GIBRALTAR.

CHAPTER I.

General history of Gibraltar, since it was first noticed.—Fortified under the Saracen empire.—Reduction of the fortress by Ferdinand, of Castile.—Retaken by the Moors.—Finally recovered by the Christians.— Taken by the English.—Besieged by the Spaniards in 1705; afterwards in 1727.—Succession of Governors to the present time.

GIBRALTAR is situated in Andalusia, the most southern province of Spain. The Rock is seven miles in circumference, forming a promontory three miles long; and is joined to the continent by an isthmus of low sand: the southern extremity lies in 36° 2′ 30″ N. lat. and in 5° 15′ W. long. from the meridian of London.

HISTORIANS, from very early periods, have noticed Gibraltar, or *Mons Calpe*, by a well-known mythological fiction, denominating it, and *Mons Abyla*, on the opposite coast of Africa, the *Pillars of Hercules*. It does not however appear that the hill was ever inhabited by the Phœnicians, Carthaginians or Romans, who in the first ages of navigation visited the bay, and built cities in its neighbourhood; or that it ever engaged the attention of those intrepid and successful Barbarians who so violently subverted the Roman

B
empire,

empire, and eftablifhed a new government in Spain. The period, when it began to be remarkable for the natural ftrength of its fituation, feems well afcertained to be in the beginning of the eighth century, when the Saracens (then become a powerful nation in the eaft, and along the coaft of Africa) invaded Spain, and foon after made themfelves mafters of the whole country.

THE Gothic kingdom, which had exifted in Spain for 300 years, was, previous to the invafion of the Saracens, diftracted with inteftine divifions: the nation in general were become effeminate, totally neglecting the military difcipline of their anceftors: and their monarch Roderic, a profligate prince, not a little accelerated their ruin, by ravifhing the daughter of Count Julian, a nobleman of great wealth and influence, and governor of Ceuta, in Africa. Count Julian, to avenge the difhonour done to his family, combined with other difcontented chiefs, who had long complained, and were ripe for a revolt. The tyrant was however too powerful for whatever oppofition they alone could raife; the Count therefore fecretly retired with his family into Africa, and acquainting Moufa (the Saracen governor of the weftern provinces) with the divided ftate of the empire, promifed, if he would attempt to dethrone Roderic, to affift him with his own intereft, and that of his friends.

MOUSA, cautious and prudent, communicated the project to his fovereign the Caliph Al Walid Ebn Abdalmalic, who agreed to try the practicability of it, and to infpect more accurately the ftate of affairs, by fending over a fmall detachment. One hundred horfe, and four hundred foot, were accordingly embarked in the year 711, under the command of Tarif Ebn Zarca, attended by Count Julian, and other Gothic noblemen: this fmall force foon paffed the Herculean Straits, and landed on the coaft near the prefent town of Algeziras, where finding no oppofition, and the country almoft defencelefs, the

Saracen

Saracen general ravaged the neighbouring towns, and returned laden with fpoils, to report the fuccefs of his firſt expedition.

Mousa, elated with the flattering profpect, the following year affembled an army of 12,000 men, and Tarif was appointed to the chief command. Having fupplied himfelf with provifions and ſtores, Tarif once more embarked on the rapid Strait, and landed on the iſthmus between *Mons Calpe* and the continent. The object of this invafion being of a more ferious nature than that of the former, he determined to fecure an intercourfe with Africa, by eſtabliſhing a poſt on the coaſt; and, preferring the ſtrong natural fituation of *Mons Calpe*, gave orders to erect a caſtle on the face of the hill, which might anfwer the original purpofe, and alfo cover his retreat, in cafe he ſhould be unfortunate in his future operations. The fuperior part of this once magnificent pile at prefent remains; and, from an infcription difcovered over the principal gate, before it was pulled down, the period of its being finiſhed is afcertained to be about the year 725.

Tarif, leaving a garrifon at the foot of *Mons Calpe* (which was now called by the Saracens, in compliment to their general, *Gibel-Tarif*, or the mountain of Tarif, and thence Gibraltar) marched into the country, and furprifed many towns, amongſt which was Heraclea, or Carteia, fituated on the coaſt of the bay, about four miles diſtant from *Gibel-Tarif*.

King Roderic, receiving intelligence of Tarif's approach, affembled a numerous body of troops to oppofe his progrefs. Both armies met, after feveral ſkirmiſhes, near Xeres, in Andalufia, and a bloody conflict enfued. The victory was for a long time doubtful; but the Gothic army being raw and undifciplined, and part difaffected and joining the Saracens, Tarif at length prevailed, and by this victory was left in poffeffion of the whole kingdom.

THE

The Goths, or Spaniards as we will now call them, were driven by the rapid conquests of the invaders into the provinces of Afturias, Bifcay, &c. where, like the ancient Britons, they maintained a ftrenuous and refpectable oppofition. By degrees they re-affumed their former difcipline and valour, while their conquerors declined into luxury and effeminacy : they made feveral excurfions from the mountains, recovering, after many obftinate actions, great part of the northern provinces. This fuccefs encouraged them to attempt the total rejection of the Arabic yoke. Meafures were concerted among the chiefs, to act with union and with vigour. The Infidels were attacked and routed in fucceffive engagements ; and the kingdoms of Afturias, Galicia, Leon, Navarre, and Caftile, erected under different monarchs.

Gibraltar, during thefe tranfactions, increafed in importance, though not in an equal degree with the neighbouring city of Algeziras, which had been built, pofterior to Gibraltar, on the oppofite fhore of the bay, and was then become a fortrefs of great magnificence and ftrength. This celebrated city feems totally to have obfcured Gibraltar in the hiftories of thofe times, fince very trifling mention is made of the latter, till the beginning of the fourteenth century, when we learn, that Ferdinand, king of Caftile, in the courfe of his conquefts, firft took it (with a fmall detachment) from the Infidels.

Gibraltar could not at this period be very ftrong, as it fell fo eafy a prey to the Chriftians, whofe army had been, and at that time was employed in the fiege of Algeziras. It does not however appear that Ferdinand was equally fuccefsful in his operations againft that city ; for we find, in the year 1316, the Moors of Grenada applying to the Emperor of Fez for fuccour : and, to facilitate their reception,

reception, Algeziras, and other cities on the coaſt, were put into the hands of the Africans. We may therefore conclude, that Ferdinand was obliged to withdraw from before Algeziras, and that he afterwards directed his force againſt the Infidels in a more vulnerable part, which induced them to apply for the aſſiſtance juſt mentioned.

GIBRALTAR continued in the poſſeſſion of the Spaniards till 1333, when Abomelique, ſon of the Emperor of Fez, was diſpatched with further aſſiſtance to the Mooriſh king of Grenada, and landing, at Algeziras, immediately laid ſiege to Gibraltar, whilſt the Grenadians were making diverſions elſewhere. Alonzo XI was then on the throne of Caſtile; and intelligence was immediately ſent to inform him of the deſcent of the Africans. He was, however, prevented from marching to the relief of Gibraltar by a rebellion in his kingdom, and by the approach of Mahomet, king of Grenada, towards his frontiers. Abomelique commenced his attack on the caſtle with great judgement and bravery, and the Spaniſh Governor Vaſco Perez de Meyra defended it with equal obſtinacy; but Perez having embezzled the money which was advanced to victual the garriſon, the troops and inhabitants ſuffered great diſtreſs; and no proſpect of relief offering, he was compelled, after five months ſiege, to ſurrender.

ALONZO having quelled the rebellion, and obliged Mahomet to retire, was then marching to his aſſiſtance, and was advanced within a ſhort diſtance of Gibraltar, when he was informed of the capitulation. He was reſolved, nevertheleſs, to attempt its recovery before the Moors could victual and repair it : he accordingly proceeded on his route, and encamped before the town five days after it had ſurrendered. Alonzo parted his army into three diviſions ; the main body occupied the iſthmus, the ſecond he ſent by boats to the red ſands, and the third climbed up the north of the hill above the town. Several ſerious attacks had been made on the caſtle, when Mahomet,

king

king of Grenada, joining Abomelique's forces, their combined army encamped in the rear of the Spaniards, extending across the isthmus from the bay to the Mediterranean. This position hemmed in the besiegers, debarred them from foraging, and cut off their communication with the country. Alonzo, though thus critically situated, still maintained the siege; but at length, driven to great difficulties for want of provisions, and hearing that some of his disaffected subjects, taking advantage of his absence, were again in arms, he hearkened to an accommodation, and was permitted to retire with his army.

To BE thus disgracefully compelled to raise the siege, did not agree with the ambitious and impatient temper of Alonzo: he secretly meditated a new attack, whenever an opportunity should occur; and this intention was not a little strengthened by his success in the year 1343-4, when Algeziras was taken, after a most memorable siege. In 1349, the tumults and civil wars in Africa afforded him the opportunity he waited for: great preparations were therefore made for this expedition, which was not esteemed of inferior consequence to the preceding siege of Algeziras, as the Moors, since the loss of that city, had paid great attention to the completion of the works, and to the rendering of the place considerably stronger, by additional fortifications: the garrison was also numerous and well provided, and of their choicest troops.

ALONZO encamped before Gibraltar in the beginning of 1349, and immediately laid waste the delightful groves, gardens, and houses of pleasure, which were erected in its neighbourhood. The siege was commenced with great bravery; and though the camp of the Castilians was much harrassed by the flying squadrons of Grenadian horse, yet the castle, in the course of several months, was almost reduced to a capitulation. At this critical period, a pestilential disorder fwept away numbers of the befiegers, and, among the reft, Alonzo, who died, much lamented, on the 26th of March, 1350; and the Spaniards immediately afterwards raifed the fiege.

THE defcendants of Abomelique continued in quiet poffeffion of Gibraltar till 1410, when Jufaf III, king of Grenada, availing himfelf of the inteftine divifions which prevailed among the African Moors, took poffeffion of the place. The inhabitants, however, not relifhing the government of their new mafters, unanimoufly revolted the following year againft the Grenadian Alcaide, drove him with his garrifon out of the town, and wrote to the Emperor of Morocco, to be taken again under his protection. The Emperor difpatched his brother Sayd, with 1000 horfe and 2000 foot, to their affiftance. The king of Grenada, being informed that Sayd had garrifoned the caftle, marched with an army, and fending his fleet round to the bay, appeared before the place in 1411. Sayd advanced to meet him, but, being worfted in feveral fkirmifhes, was obliged to retreat within the caftle, and being clofely befieged, and reduced to great diftrefs for want of provifions, was at laft compelled to fubmit.

IN 1435, Henry de Guzman Count de Niebla formed a defign of attacking Gibraltar by land and fea; but, imprudently fkirmifhing with the garrifon, from his gallies, before his fon John de Guzman arrived with the land-forces, he was defeated, and forced to a preci-pitate retreat; in which confufion he himfelf loft his life, and many of his followers were killed and drowned.

IN 1442, a civil war breaking out in Grenada, great part of the garrifon of Gibraltar was withdrawn, to affift one of the competitors for the crown: the governor of Tarifa had intelligence of this by a Moor, who had left the town, and embraced the Chriftian faith.

An

An army was accordingly affembled from the neighbouring garrifons, and Gibraltar was befieged. The inhabitants defended it with great refolution; but frefh troops joining the befiegers, the garrifon furrendered to John de Guzman, Duke de Medina Sidonia (fon of the unfortunate Count de Niebla) who, hearing that the place was reduced to great diftrefs, hafted to the camp, and arrived juft in time to be prefent when the Moors capitulated. From this period it has remained in the hands of the Chriftians, after having been in the poffeffion of the Mahometans 748 years. The news of this conqueft was fo acceptable to Henry IV, of Caftile and Leon, that he added it to his royal titles, and gave it for arms, * *Gules*, a caftle, *proper*, with a key pendent to the gate, *or*, (alluding to its being the key to the Mediterranean); which arms have ever fince been continued. Pedro de Porras was appointed governor; but the fucceeding year King Henry made a journey to Gibraltar, and fuperfeded him, giving the command to Don Bertrand de la Cueva, Count Lederma, who placed the truft in the hands of Stephano Villacreces : the Duke de Medina Sidonia, however, afterwards recovered, and enjoyed it, till the reign of Ferdinand and Ifabella in 1502, when it was annexed to the crown.

In the year 1540, Piali Hamet, one of Barbaroffa's captains, furprifed and pillaged Gibraltar, making prifoners many of the principal inhabitants; but being met on his return by fome gallies from Sicily, the Corfairs were all killed, or taken, and the prifoners redeemed.

In the reign of Charles V, the fortifications of the town were modernifed, and feveral additions made by Daniel Speckel, the Emperor's engineer; after which the garrifon was thought to be impregnable.—From this time there appears a chafm in the hiftory

of

* See the vignette in the title-page.

of the garrifon till the year 1704, when Gibraltar was wrefted (moft probably for ever) from the dominion of Spain, by the Englifh, under Sir George Rooke. This Admiral had been fent into the Mediterranean, with a ftrong fleet, in the fpring of 1704, to affift Charles arch-duke of Auftria in obtaining the crown of Spain; but, his inftrudtions being limited, nothing of importance was done. Senfible of the reflexions that would fall on him, for being inadtive with fo powerful a fleet, he held a council of war, on the 17th of July, 1704, near Tetuan, where feveral fchemes were propofed, particularly a fecond attack upon Cadiz, which however was found impradticable for want of a fufficient body of land-forces. At length it was refolved to make a fudden and vigorous attempt on Gibraltar.

The 21ft of the fame month, the fleet arrived in the Bay; and 1800 men, Englifh and Dutch, commanded by the Prince of Heffe D'Armftadt, were landed on the ifthmus. The Prince then fummoned the garrifon; but the Governor refufing to furrender, preparations were made for the attack. By day-break on the 23d, the fhips appointed to cannonade the town, under Admirals Byng and Vanderduffen, with thofe that were deftined to batter the new mole, commanded by Captain Hicks, were at their feveral ftations. The Admiral made the fignal to begin the cannonade, which was performed with great vivacity and effedt, fo that the enemy, in five or fix hours, were driven from their guns, efpecially from the new-mole head. The Admiral confidering, that by gaining that fortification the town might fooner be reduced, ordered Captain Whitaker, with the armed boats, to poffefs himfelf of it; but Captains Hicks and Jumper, who lay next the mole, pufhed afhore with their pinnaces, before the reft came up; whereupon the Spaniards fprung a mine, which blew up the fortifications, killed 2 lieutenants and 40 men, and wounded 60. The affailants neverthelefs kept poffeffion

of

of the work, and being joined by Captain Whitaker, advanced and took a finall baftion*, half-way between the mole and the town. The Marquis de Salines, who was governor, being again fummoned, thought proper to capitulate : hoftages were therefore exchanged, and the Prince of Heffe, on the 24th, took poffeffion of the gates.

NOTWITHSTANDING the works were very ftrong, mounting 100 pieces of ordnance, well appointed with ammunition and ftores ; yet the Garrifon, at moft, confifted only of 150 men, exclufive of the inhabitants. The Marquis marched out with all the honours of war, and the Spaniards who chofe to remain were allowed the fame privileges they had enjoyed under King Charles II. The lofs of the Englifh in this attack was, 2 lieutenants, 1 mafter, 57 failors, killed; 1 captain, 7 lieutenants, 1 boatfwain, 207 failors, wounded.

THE Prince of Heffe remained governor, and as many men as could well be fpared from the fleet, were left as a garrifon. Sir George afterwards failed for Tetuan, to wood and water. This being performed, he fteered up the Mediterranean, and on the 13th of Auguft, off Malaga, engaged the French fleet, under the command of Count de Touloufe. The action was long and warm ; but many of the Englifh fhips, having expended a great quantity of ammunition in taking Gibraltar, were foon obliged to quit the line; which gave the enemy a decided fuperiority. The engagement ended in a drawn battle ; and Sir George returned to Gibraltar, where he ftayed eight days to refit ; and then fupplying the Prince with what men and provifions he could fpare, failed thence on the 4th of September, N. S. on his way home, leaving 18 men of war, under the command of Sir John Leake, at Lifbon, to be in readinefs to fuccour the garrifon, if there fhould be occafion.

THE

* The prefent eight-gun battery.

THE courts of Madrid and Paris were greatly concerned at the lofs of fo important a fortrefs as Gibraltar, and, confidering its recovery of the laft confequence to the caufe, the Marquis de Villa-darias, a grandee of Spain, was ordered to befiege, and endeavour to retake it. The Prince, apprifed of their intentions, and being further informed that they were to be affifted by a naval force from Toulon, fent advice to Sir John Leake, requefting affiftance and fupplies. Sir John prepared for this duty; but in the mean time a fleet of French fhips arrived, and landed fix battalions, which joined the Spanifh army. After difembarking their reinforcements, the French fquadron proceeded to the weftward, leaving only fix frigates in the bay.

ON the 11th of October, the Marquis opened his trenches againft the town; and foon after, Sir John arrived with 20 fail of Englifh and Dutch fhips: hearing, however, that the Enemy were preparing to attack him with a fuperior force, he thought it moft eligible immediately to return and refit, that he might be in a better con-dition to fupply and affift the garrifon, in a fecond expedition, for which he had very prudently directed preparations to be made at Lifbon in his abfence. The 25th Sir John again put to fea; and on the 29th unexpectedly entering the bay, furprifed three frigates, a fire-fhip, two Englifh prizes, a tartan, and a ftore-fhip. He then landed the reinforcements, and fupplied the garrifon with fix months provifions and ammunition, at the fame time detaching on fhore a body of 500 failors to affift in repairing the breaches which had been made by the enemy's fire. The arrival of the Admiral was very opportune and critical; for that very night the Marquis had refolved to attack the place by fea and land at five different points; for which purpofe he had affembled 200 boats from Cadiz, &c.

THOUGH difappointed in their defigns, the Spaniards ftill enter-tained hopes of taking the fortrefs; and fuppofing the troops would

be

be lefs on their guard while the fleet was in the Bay, they formed the defperate fcheme of furprifing the garrifon, though the Britifh Admiral was before the town. The 31ft of October, 500 volunteers took the facrament, never to return till they had taken Gibraltar. This forlorn party was conducted by a goat-herd to the fouth fide of the rock, near the cave-guard, (at that time called the pafs of locuft-trees.) Fortune, in the beginning, fo far favoured the enterprife, that they mounted the rock, and lodged themfelves unperceived the firft night in St. Michael's cave; the fucceeding night they fcaled Charles the Vth's wall; furprifed and maffacred the guard at Middle-hill, where afterwards, by ropes and ladders, they got up feveral hundreds of the party who had been ordered to fuftain them; but being difco-vered, a ftrong detachment of grenadiers marched up immediately from the town, and attacked them with fuch fpirit, that 160 of them were killed, or driven over the precipice, and a colonel and 30 officers, with the remainder, taken prifoners. Thefe brave, but unfortunate adventurers, were to have been fupported by a body of French troops, and fome feints were to have been made below to engage the attention of the garrifon; but the commanding officers difagreeing, they were left to their fortune.

SIR JOHN LEAKE was not idle whilft he remained in the Bay, but was continually alarming the enemy on their coafts. The 22d of November he had information, by one of his cruifers, that a ftrong fquadron was fitting out at Cadiz, which would be foon ready for fea; and receiving further intelligence, that a convoy, fitted out from Lifbon for the relief of Gibraltar, was on their way, he prepared to join them off Lagos, in order to protect them paft Cadiz; but was confined within the Straits by a wefterly wind. The Prince, in the mean time, redoubled his exertions to prevent the enemy's defigns, who flattered themfelves, that on the arrival of their fleet from Cadiz, Sir John would be obliged to retire, and the garrifon fur-

render

render to their united attacks. Their fire was continued with additional vivacity, many cannon in the place were difmounted, and the works were materially injured in different parts.

AFFAIRS were in this fituation, when part of the long-wifhed-for fuccours arrived on the 7th of September; and two days following, the remainder came in with near 2000 men, with proportionable ammunition and provifions. They failed from Lifbon under convoy of four frigates, and thought themfelves fafe on difcovering, off Cape Spartel, a fleet of men of war, under Englifh and Dutch colours: expecting to meet Sir John, with the combined fleet, at the entrance of the Straits, they endeavoured to join them, but fortunately were becalmed : they then hoifted out their boats to tow the fhips, when, perceiving the men of war extend themfelves in form of a half-moon, in order to furround them, they began to fufpect fome deception, and accordingly made a private fignal, which totally fruftrated the Enemy's meafures, who were thereby difcovered, and, ftriking their falfe colours, endeavoured to fall upon the tranfports; but thefe latter, being lighter veffels, efcaped by their oars, and, night coming on, fteered for the bay, with the lofs only of two tranfports. It was now thought no longer neceffary to detain the fleet in the bay, or on the coaft; efpecially when Monfieur Pointis was fo near, with a fuperior force. Sir John accordingly arrived at Lifbon the latter end of the year.

THE Spanifh General being reinforced with a confiderable body of infantry, on the 11th of January 1705, made an attack with 60 grenadiers on the works at the extremity of the King's lines; but, two officers, and feveral others being killed, the reft retreated. This repulfe did not, however, difcourage him; for early the fucceeding day, the attack was renewed by 5 or 600 grenadiers, French and Walons, fupported by 1000 Spaniards, under Lieut. Gen. Tuy.

Their

Their difpofition was to ftorm a breach which had been made in the Round tower, at the extremity of the King's lines, and another in the intrenchment on the hill. The retrenchment which covered the latter breach, with part of the intrenchment joining the precipice of the rock, was defended at night by a captain, three fubalterns, and 90 men ; but it was cuftomary for the captain to withdraw, with two fubalterns, and 60 men, at day-break. The Roun tower was defended by 180 men, commanded by a lieutenant-colonel. The Marquis, by deferters from the garrifon, had obtained intelligence of the ftrength of thefe pofts, and concerted his attack accordingly. The detachment for the upper breach mounted the rock at dead of night, and concealed themfelves in the clefts till the captain had withdrawn. They then advanced to the point of the intrenchment, and, throwing grenades on the fubaltern and his party, obliged them to retreat. At the fame time 300 men ftormed the Round tower, where Lieut. Col. Barr made a vigorous defence, though the enemy, having paffed the breach above, annoyed him on the flank with great ftones and grenades : obferving, however, the Spaniards marching down to cut off his retreat from the town, he retired, and by getting over the parapet of the King's lines, defcended into the covert way, where the Englifh guards were pofted. By this time the garrifon was alarmed; all the regiments affembled at their proper pofts ; and Captain Fifher endeavoured to ftop the progrefs of the enemy with 17 men, but was repulfed, and himfelf taken prifoner. Lieut. Col. Moncal, at laft, with 4 or 500 men, charged them with fuch bravery, that they were repulfed, and the tower was retaken after it had been in their poffeffion upwards of an hour. Soon after this attack, fix companies of Dutch troops, and 200 Englifh foldiers, were received by the garrifon, with provifions and ftores.

THE Spaniards and French were ftill obftinately bent on the recovery of Gibraltar. The Marquis de Villadarias was fuperfeded by the
Marfhal

Marſhal Teſſé, a French general ; and Monſieur Pointis was directed to co-operate with the Marſhal, in blocking up the port with his fleet. The Marſhal joined the army with four freſh battalions, beſides eight companies which had been ſent before. The ordnance, which from conſtant uſe had been greatly injured, were totally exchanged ; and the works, as they then ſtood, were put in the beſt repair.

The Engliſh Miniſtry had been informed of the enemy's new arrangements ; and, ſenſible of the importance of Gibraltar, ordered a reinforcement under Sir Thomas Dilkes, and Sir John Hardy, to join Admiral Sir John Leake at Liſbon. The junction being effected, and his own fleet refitted, Sir John, on the 6th of March, ſailed with 28 Engliſh, 4 Dutch, and 8 Portugueſe men of war, having on board two battalions. Happily for the beſieged, the inceſſant rains about this period had retarded the Marſhal's operations, and greatly diſtreſſed Monſieur Pointis, eight of whoſe ſhips were forced from their anchors by the ſtrong weſterly wind, and obliged, on the 9th, to drive aloft. Thus were they ſituated when the Britiſh Admiral entered the Straits, and about half paſt five, on the morning of the 10th, was almoſt abreaſt of Cabrita Point. The few remaining ſhips of the French fleet on his approach put to ſea ; and Sir John, diſcovering five ſail making out of the bay, and a gun fired at them from the garriſon, concluded that the town was ſafe, and immediately gave chace. Three French ſhips of the line were taken, and the Admiral's ſhip, and another, run aſhore and burnt. Sir John afterwards looked into Malaga, where the ſhips that had been driven from the harbour had taken ſhelter ; but, hearing the report of the guns, they had made the beſt of their way to Toulon. Sir John, finding the purſuit of them in vain, returned to Gibraltar, which was now ſo well ſupplied, that Marſhal Teſſé withdrew his troops from the trenches, and formed a blockade ; drawing an intrenchment acroſs the iſthmus, to prevent the garriſon from ravaging the country.

In

In the course of this fiege, the enemy did not lofe fewer than 10,000 men, including thofe who died of ficknefs, &c. The gar-rifon loft about 400.

The Prince of Heffe remained in the place while the batteries were repaired : he made alfo fome additions to the fortifications, and left the garrifon much ftronger than it was before the fiege. The Prince then joined the Arch-duke Charles at Lifbon, where the combined fleet of England and Holland were affembled, to fupport that Prince in obtaining the crown of Spain.

As the Arch-duke was refolved to try his fortune with the Earl of Peterborough, in Valencia and Catalcnia, the Prince of Heffe was fent back to Gibraltar, to prepare part of the garrifon to embark, and foon after was followed by the fleet; upon whofe arrival, the Arch-duke was received by the garrifon as lawful fovereign of Spain. Having taken on board the Englifh guards, and three old regiments, leaving only two new battalions in the town (as there was no danger to be apprehended from the enemy), they proceeded, on the 5th of Auguft, for Valencia. His Majefty then appointed Major-general Ramos, who had been prefent during the fiege, governor of Gibraltar; and fent with him about 400 men for its greater fecurity. General Ramos afterwards refigned his government, and was fucceeded by Colonel Roger Elliot; during whofe government, Gibraltar was made a free port, by a fpecial order from her Majefty, Queen Anne.

The following was the Governor's Manifefto on the occafion.

" By the Hon. Roger Elliot, Colonel of one of her Majefty's regiments of foot, and Governor of the city and garrifon of Gi-braltar.

" Whereas

" WHEREAS Her Majefty of Great-Britain, &c. hath been gracioufly pleafed, by Her warrant to me, dated 19th February laft, to
confirm Her former declarations for the freedom of this port, and
to regulate and command me, not to permit any duty or impofition
whatfoever to be laid or received for any fhip or veffel, or for any
goods, wares, merchandife, or provifions, imported or exported
out of this port ; but that the fame be free and open for
all fhips and veffels, goods, wares, merchandife, and provifions :
Thefe are to make known and publifh Her faid Majefty's Royal
will and pleafure ; and all perfons concerned are hereby ftrictly
required to take notice thereof, not prefuming to demand or receive
any duty or impofition whatfoever for any fhip or veffel, or for any
goods, wares, merchandife, or provifions, as they will anfwer the
contrary at their peril.

" GIVEN at Gibraltar, April 1706."

COLONEL CONGREVE was governor before 1714. He was fucceeded by Colonel Cotton. In 1720 Gibraltar feems to have been
threatened by the Spaniards. Ceuta, a Spanifh fortrefs in Barbary,
had then been befieged many years by the Moors ; and a formidable force, commanded by the Marquis de Leda, was affembled
in Gibraltar bay, under pretence of relieving it, but with a fecret
intention of firft furprifing Gibraltar ; for which purpofe they had
procured fcaling-ladders, &c. &c. This armament was not fitted
out fo fecretly, but the Britifh Miniftry had timely notice, and,
fufpecting fome fineffe, difpatched orders to Colonel Kane, governor
of Minorca, immediately to embark a part of his Garrifon, and
repair to Gibraltar, under convoy of the fleet in the Mediterranean.
On his arrival he found Gibraltar in a very critical fituation ; the
garrifon confifting only of three weak battalions, commanded by
Major Hetherington, who, except Major Batteroux, was the only
D   field-

field-officer in the place. Many officers were abſent, only fourteen days proviſions in the ſtores, and many Spaniards in the town, with a fleet before its walls. Such was the feeble poſture of affairs when he opportunely arrived with 500 men, proviſions, and ammunition. The Britiſh Commodore acted afterwards in ſo ſpirited a manner, that the Marquis de Leda was obliged to ſail for Ceuta, though he continued of opinion that the garriſon might have been taken by a general aſſault.

This ſcheme proving abortive, Gibraltar remained unmoleſted till the latter end of the year 1726, when the Spaniards, who had kept a watchful eye on the garriſon, aſſembled an army in the neighbourhood of Algeziras. The 20th of January following, they encamped on the plain below St. Roque, and began to erect a battery on the beach to protect their camp. Admiral Hopſon was then at anchor in the bay, with a very formidable fleet ; but, as he had not received any intelligence of hoſtilities having commenced between the courts of Great-Britain and Madrid, he was with reluctance compelled to overlook the tranſporting of proviſions, artillery, and ammunition, from Algeziras, (where they had formed their dépôts,) to the camp. Brigadier Kane, who had been a ſecond time ordered from Minorca to Gibraltar, lay alſo under ſimilar embarraſſments with the Admiral. The operations of the enemy, however, tending towards a direct attack upon the garriſon, he thought it prudent to order the Spaniards out of the town, and forbid their gallies anchoring under his guns.

It muſt be underſtood that Gibraltar had undergone conſiderable alterations ſince the ſiege of 1705 : ſeveral works had been erected on the heights above the lines, which were diſtinguiſhed by the name of Willis's batteries ; the Prince's lines were extended to the extremity of the rock ; and an inundation was formed out of the moraſs which was in front of the grand battery.

THE

THE Count de Las Torres commanded the Spanish forces, amounting to near 20,000 men ; and soon after his camp was formed, he advanced within reach of the garrison. The Brigadier thereupon difpatched a parley, to defire " That he would withdraw " from the range of his guns, otherwife he fhould do his utmoft " to force him." The Count anfwered, " That, as the garrifon " could command no more than they had power to maintain, he " fhould obey his Catholic Majefty's orders, and encroach as far as " he was able." The Brigadier ftill waved commencing hoftilities, till the Spaniards, by their proceedings, fhould oblige him, in defence of his command.

IN the beginning of February, Brigadier Clayton, the lieutenant-governor, arrived with reinforcements, on board Sir Charles Wager's fleet ; and a council of war was immediately fummoned, but the refult was a determination not to fire upon the Spaniards. The 10th of February, the enemy brought materials for batteries, to the old wind-mill, on the neutral ground ; upon which the Lieutenant-governor again collected the fenfe of the Admirals and Field-officers ; when in the fecond council it was unanimoufly agreed, that the Spanifh General had made open war, in encroaching fo far on the liberties of the garrifon. This being their opinion, Brigadier Clayton fent a parley to the Count, to know the reafon of his breaking ground : to which the Count replied, that " he was on " his Mafter's ground, and was not anfwerable to any other perfon " for his conduct." As this anfwer in fome meafure indicated the hoftile intentions of the Spaniards, the Lieutenant-governor, in the evening, withdrew the out-guard, and, the fucceeding day in the afternoon, opened the Old mole, and Willis's, on their workmen. They perfifted, neverthelefs, in carrying on the work ; and at night a large party marched down to the Devil's tower, where they immediately broke ground, and began a communication with their other

D 2 work.

work. This party were greatly annoyed in marching to their post, but were soon under cover of the rock, where the guns could not be depressed to bear upon them.

Numbers of the enemy deserted to the garrison, by whom, on the 17th, the Lieutenant-governor was informed that they were constructing a mine, in a cave under Willis's, with an intention, if possible, to blow up that battery. The engineers, on this intelligence, reconnoitred the cave; which, after some difficulty, they discovered, with a sentry at the entrance; and a party was immediately stationed to annoy the communication with musquetry. On the morning of the 22d, the Count opened on the garrison, with 17 pieces of cannon, besides mortars. The day following, Brigadier Kane left the garrison, to detach a reinforcement from Minorca. In the mean time Sir Charles Wager and Admiral Hopson, with the fleet under their command, were constantly distressing the enemy, by intercepting their homeward-bound ships; and the prizes, which were brought into the bay, greatly benefited the besieged. The 3d of March, the enemy opened a new battery of 22 guns on the Old mole, and town; and on the 8th, another of 15 guns, bearing also upon the Old mole, which, it seems, proved a troublesome battery to the western flank of their approaches.

The Lieutenant-governor continued a constant and well-directed fire from all the batteries that bore upon their works: but the ordnance in general, being old, were bursting daily on the batteries; by which accidents the garrison experienced more casualties, than from all the fire of the enemy. The 27th, Col. Middleton's regiment arrived, also six companies and a half of Col. Hay's, with two engineers, a captain of artillery, and several bombardiers, gunners, and matrosses; with 140 recruits for the other regiments.

THE

THE Admirals, the 2d of April, formed the defign of bombarding Algeziras, whence the enemy were conftantly fupplied with various articles of ammunition; but the fhips, after getting under way, were becalmed, and obliged to come to anchor; after which the navy never gave themfelves any further concern about annoying them in that quarter. On the 10th, Colonel Cofby arrived in the Solebay, with 500 men, from Minorca; and two days following, the Admirals failed to the weftward, leaving Commodore Davies behind, with fix men of war and the floops. Sir Charles did not return during the fiege. The 16th, the Lieutenant-governor ordered two ferjeants, with ten men each, to advance from the fpur-guard, under the rock, and along the caufeway, and alarm the enemy in the trenches; giving them directions to retire when they found their guards fufficiently alarmed, when he intended to falute them with grape, &c. from Willis's, and the lines. Thefe orders were executed, and the enemy inftantly beat to arms; but the bombardier appointed to give the fignal to the batteries, firing too foon, the enemy faw through the defign, and retired without any confiderable lofs.

LORD PORTMORE, the governor, arrived, the 21ft, with a battalion of guards, and another of the line; alfo Colonel Watfon, of the artillery, with feveral Noblemen as volunteers. The 26th, the Count opened a new battery, againft Willis's, and the extremity of Prince's lines. Their batteries now mounted 60 cannon, befides mortars. In the beginning of May, the garrifon had intelligence that the enemy defigned an affault: precautions were accordingly taken, and the guns on the lower defences loaded with grape. The Spaniards added ftill to their approaches, and raifed various communications to and from their advanced batteries. Towards the 16th and 20th, their firing abated; but their engineers proceeded in advancing their trenches. On the 31ft, a veffel arrived
with

with 375 barrels of powder from Lisbon. June the 3d, the Solebay came in, with a further supply of 980 barrels of powder, and
500 thirteen-inch shells, from Mahon. The firing continued till
the 12th, when, about ten at night, Colonel Fitzgerald, of the
Irish brigade, beat a parley, and, being admitted into the garrison,
delivered letters to Lord Portmore, from the Dutch minister at
the court of Madrid, with a copy of the preliminaries of a general
peace; whereupon a suspension of arms took place, and all hostilities
ceased on both sides.

THE garrison lost, in the whole, about 300 killed and wounded;
and 70 cannon, with 30 mortars, burst during the siege. The
enemy's casuals could never be ascertained. In killed, wounded, &c.
it was computed they lost near 3000 men.

WHEN Lord Portmore and the Count agreed to a cessation,
the Spaniards of course were compelled to forsake the mine under
Willis's : their parties, however, taking possession of it a second
time, his Lordship considered it as a breach of the articles of
cessation, and represented it accordingly. The Count afterwards
withdrew : the works were dismantled and levelled, and the troops
retreated to their different cantonments.

THE Spaniards during this siege never made the least attempt
to cut off the communication by sea ; so that the garrison was
regularly supplied with provisions and fascines from Barbary, and
had a regular correspondence with England.

IN 1728, the Parliament of Great-Britain addressed his Majesty
King George II, to take effectual care, in the treaty then pending,
to preserve his undoubted right to Gibraltar, and the Island of
Minorca. Overtures had been made by his Majesty George I, to
restore

reſtore the former to Spain, if the Parliament would have conſented to ſuch reſtitution; but the Miniſter, finding an oppoſition, declined the buſineſs. In 1730, Lieutenant-general Sabine was governor of Gibraltar. The Spaniards in his government erected the forts and lines acroſs the iſthmus, about a mile from the garriſon: theſe effectually prevent any communication with the country, and, as we have experienced, are of conſiderable advantage in caſe of a ſiege. The weſtern fort, called St. Philip's, entirely commands the beſt anchorage on the ſide of the bay next the garriſon. General Colum-bine ſucceeded General Sabine, and he was ſucceeded by General Hargrave.

GENERAL BLAND was appointed governor in 1749, at which time a general relief of troops took place. The eſtabliſhment at that period was, four battalions of infantry, and a company of artil-lery. Lord George Beauclerk, and the Hon. General Herbert, were ſeverally commandants in the abſence of General Bland; and in 1753 General Fowkes was deputed governor. Lord Tyrawley ſucceeded him, in whoſe abſence the Earl of Panmure was comman-dant. Earl Home was afterwards governor, and died there in 1761. During the government of this nobleman, about the year 1760, an incident occurred, which, as it alarmed the garriſon very much at that time, is deſerving of notice. Two Britiſh regiments had been a very conſiderable time on that ſtation, and, from the continuance of the war, ſaw little proſpect of being relieved. Amongſt theſe a conſpiracy was formed, by ſome diſaffected perſons, to ſurpriſe, plunder, and maſſacre the officers, and in ſhort, all whom they judged to be averſe to their deſigns. After ſecuring the money which was intended for the payment of the troops, they meant to purchaſe for themſelves a ſecure retreat, by ſurrendering this ſo much wiſhed-for fortreſs into the hands of Spain. The numbers who joined the conſpirators were not fewer than 730. An accidental quarrel, in a

wine-houſe,

wine-houfe, defeated this dangerous project, and produced a difco-
very. Reed, a private in the feventh regiment, was executed on the
grand parade, as the ringleader; and ten others were condemned.
After the death of Lord Home, Colonel Tovey and General Parflow
were each commandants, till the Hon. General Cornwallis was
appointed governor. During this General's abfence from the garrifon, Colonel Irwin was commandant; and on General Cornwallis
leaving Gibraltar a fecond time, Major General Boyd, lieutenant-
governor, commanded. In this General's government, the garrifon
was confiderably ftrengthened with three new baftions on the fea-
line, and additional improvements at the fouthward.

In 1776, the Right Hon. General George Augustus
Eliott was appointed Governor of that important fortrefs, and
joined his command in 1777.

CHAP-

CHAPTER II.

Description of the Rock, with the fortifications and town of Gi-braltar.—Remains of Moorish architecture.—Natural Curiosities.—Climate.—Vegetation.—Fish; and whence supplied with cattle, &c.—Military establishment.—Description of the Bay.—Algeziras.—Some accounts of the ancient city of Carteia.—St. Roque.—Con-clusive remarks.

As the History which is to be the subject of the following pages, will be more in detail than the preceding narrative, it may on some accounts be necessary, and cannot on any, I flatter myself, be dis-agreeable, to present the reader with a short description of this celebrated Rock, and the fortifications which have been erected for its defence.

The Promontory, or rock, at the foot of which stands the town, is upwards of 1300 feet in height; projecting into the sea several miles from the continent, to which it is connected by an isthmus of low sand. This appearance makes it not improbable that *Mons Calpe* has, in former ages, been totally surrounded by the sea. The north front of the peninsula, which presents itself to the main land, is of various heights. The breadth of the isthmus, at the foot of the rock, is about 900 yards; but it grows considerably wider towards the country. Across this Isthmus, (which, with Gibraltar and the opposite coast, forms the bay) the Spaniards have drawn a fortified line at about a mile's distance from the garrison, extending 1700 yards, and embracing both shores: a fort of masonry is erected at each extremity, mounting 23 or 24 guns each; they are of different

E   forms,

forms, and are called St. Philip and St. Barbara. The former of
these forts commands the best and the usual anchoring-place of
our shipping and small craft, and by forming a cross-fire with fort
St. Barbara on the neutral ground, prevents all communication
between the garrison and the country.

THE Rock, as I have mentioned before, is upwards of 1300
feet perpendicular, above the level of the sea; and is separated by
a ridge from north to south, dividing it into two unequal parts.
The western front or division is a gradual slope, interspersed with
precipices; but the opposite side, looking to the Mediterranean, and
the north front, facing the Spanish lines, are both naturally very
steep, and totally inaccessible. It is this peculiar circumstance,
which forms the chief strength of Gibraltar.

THE Town is built at the foot of the north-west face of the hill,
and is fortified in an irregular manner. The communication with it
from the isthmus, is by a long narrow causeway, (serving as a dam
to an inundation) which is defended by a curtain, with two bastions,
mounting 26 pieces of cannon, a dry ditch, covered way, and glacis
well mined. These, with the causeway, are warmly flanked by the
King's, Queen's, and Prince's lines; works cut in the rock with
immense labour, and scarped to be almost inaccessible. Above the
lines are the batteries at Willis's, and others at different heights,
until they crown the summit of the rock, where several batteries
are erected for cannon and mortars. These batteries, the lowest of
which is upwards of 400 feet above the neutral ground, mount
between 50 and 60 pieces of heavy ordnance, and entirely command the isthmus below. Exclusive of what are here mentioned,
additional works of a singular nature were projected in 1782, and
partly executed the year following, which, when finished, will
render Gibraltar (almost) impregnable in that quarter. The Old

mole,

mole, to the weft of the grand battery, forms alfo a very formidable flank, and, with the lines, a crofs-fire on the caufeway and neutral ground. This battery has been found fo great an annoyance to the befiegers, that, by way of diftinction, it has long been known under the appellation of the Devil's tongue. Indeed, the ordnance in the lines, upon the Grand battery, and the Old mole, all together, exhibit fo formidable an appearance to a fpectator on the caufeway, that the entrance into the garrifon is called by the Spaniards, the *Mouth of fire.*

From the Grand battery, along the fea-line, looking towards the bay, the town is defended by the North, Montague's, Prince of Orange's, King's, and South baftions; the line-wall or curtains between which, mount many cannon and mortars. Montague's, Prince of Orange's, and King's baftions, have been erected lately. The latter is a very complete piece of fortification, commanding the bay from New to Old mole heads, and mounting twelve thirty-two pounders, and four ten-inch howitzers in front, ten guns and howitzers on its flanks, and has cafemates for 800 men, with kitchens and ovens for cooking. Montague's is much fmaller, mounts only 12 pieces of cannon, but has a cafemate for 200 men, communicating with the Old mole. In 1782 the engineers began a cavalier upon this baftion for two guns; but it was not finifhed till after the grand attack in September. Another work of this nature was likewife erected in the beginning of the blockade, for five guns, on the north baftion of the Grand battery. The town on the fea-line is not lefs protected by natural defences, than by fortifications. A fhoal of fharp rocks extends along the front far into the bay, and prevents fhips of large burthen from approaching very near the walls.

From the South baftion (which is confiderably higher than the reft of the works, in order to protect the town from the eminences

E 2   on

on the red fands) a curtain extends up the face of the hill, and con-
cludes, at an inacceffible precipice, the works of the town. In
this curtain is the South port gate, before which, and the fouth
baftion, is a dry ditch, with a covered way and glacis. At the eaft
end, on the declivity of the hill, above the gate, is a large flat
baftion, connected with the curtain, and mounting 13 guns, bearing
on the bay, &c. This work is covered by a demi-baltion that joins
the precipice. Above the precipice, an old Moorifh wall is continued to the ridge of the rock ; in the front of which a curtain
with loop-holes and redans (built in the reign of the Emperor
Charles V, and called after his name) extends to the top, effectually
cutting off all communication in that quarter. Between the
Moorifh and Charles the Vth's walls, is the fignal-houfe ; whence
the guard, on a ferene and clear day, have almoft an unbounded
view of the Mediterranean, and can juft obferve a part of the
Atlantic ocean over the Spanifh mountains. Signals formerly were
made at this poft, on the appearance of top-fail veffels from eaft
and weft ; but foon after the commencement of the late war, we
difcovered that the Spanifh cruifers were more frequently informed
of the approach of our friends by our fignals, than by their own.
The fignals were therefore difcontinued.

THE above comprehends a general defcription of the fortifications
of the town, avoiding too minute a detail of each work. I fhall
therefore proceed in defcribing, in the fame general manner, the
works to the fouthward.

FROM the South baftion a line-wall is continued along the beach
to the New mole, where an irregular fort is erected, mounting 26
guns. This line-wall is divided by a fmall baftion of eight guns; and
in its rear is a retired work, called the Princefs of Wales's lines ; in
which are feveral ftrong batteries for the fea. Near the South baftion,
though

though without the town, is a wharf called Ragged Staff, where the supplies for the garrison are usually landed, being convenient from its vicinity to the victualling-office and stores. The communication to this quay, is by spiral wooden stairs, and a draw-bridge opening into the covert-way; in front of which is a small work of masonry, mounting two guns. At the foot of the stairs is the bason; where shipping take in water. Two tanks are also appropriated to this purpose, near the Eight-gun bastion, having a connexion with the grand aqueduct.

In the new Mole there is depth of water sufficient for a ship of the line to lie along-side the wharf, and heave down. At the mole-head is a circular battery for heavy metal, joined to the New-mole fort by a strong wall, fraised; having a banquet for musquetry, with two embrasures opening towards the bay. This mole, with the old mole at Waterport, were built for the accommodation of trading-vessels: the former however is generally occupied by men of war; and the latter, not having more than six feet at low water, only admits small craft to the wharfs: merchantmen of large burthen are obliged therefore to anchor about half or three quarters of a mile from Waterport, in seven or eight fathoms. But in time of war this anchorage is commanded by the Spanish forts: they are consequently, in case of a rupture with Spain, under the necessity of removing to the southward of the New mole, where the ground is so rocky and foul, that they are often in imminent danger during the strong southerly winds. From the New-mole fort, to the north end of Rosia bay, the rock is difficult of access; nevertheless a parapet is continued, and batteries are erected, as situations dictate. The works at Rosia are strong, and act as flanks to each other. They are close along the beach, which is low, and have a retired battery of eight guns in their rear.

THE

THE Rock continues to afcend from the fouth point of Rofia Bay, by Parfon's Lodge (behind which, upon an eminence, is a new battery, *en barbet*, on traverfing carriages) to Camp-guard, and Buena Vifta; fo called from the beautiful profpect of the bay, and neighbouring kingdoms of Barbary and Spain, which is there prefented to a fpectator. A line wall is raifed, notwithstanding the rock being inacceffible, with cannon at different diftances. At Buena Vifta there are feveral guns *en barbet*, which have great command; and the hill towards Europa is flightly fortified, which gives it the appearance, at a diftance, of an old caftle repaired. The rock then defcends by the Devil's Bowling-green, fo named from the irregularity of its furface, to Little Bay. At this poft, which is totally furrounded with precipices, there is a barbet battery, flanking the works to the New mole : thence the rock continues naturally fteep for a confiderable diftance, when the line-wall and batteries recommence, and extend in an irregular manner to Europa Point, the fouthern extremity of the garrifon, though not the fouthern point of Europe. The rock from this point is regularly perpendicular to Europa advance, where a few batteries, and a poft at the Cave-guard, terminate the works. The fortifications along the fea-line at Europa do not however conftitute the principal ftrength of that part of the garrifon. The retired and inacceffible lines of Windmill Hill have great command, and being fituated within mufquet-fhot of the fea, are very formidable, and of great confequence in that quarter.

The preceding defcription, it is hoped, will be fufficiently explanatory, with the affiftance of the annexed Engravings; which, though the fcale of the garrifon-plan, for obvious reafons, is very minute, will yet point out the improvements that have been made within thefe few years. The new baftions on the fea-line were planned, and executed, by and under the direction of the prefent

Chief

Chief Engineer, Major-general Green. Lieutenant-general Sir Robert Boyd, K. B.[*] laid the foundation-ftone of the King's baftion, in the abfence of General Cornwallis, the governor. The garrifon alfo underwent confiderable alterations whilft he commanded: Windmill Hill was fortified, and other changes were effected at the fouthward. The improvements on the northern front were carried on under the direction of Sir George Auguftus Eliott, K. B. fince he was appointed to the government. The communication, or gallery leading to St. George's Hall, above Farringdon's battery; Queen's-lines battery, and communication; two works of the fame nature, which extend under the Queen's battery, Willis's, and in the rock above Prince of Heffe's baftion; are all fo fingularly contrived, and of fo formidable a nature, that all *direct* attacks by land, henceforward, may be confidered as quixotifm and infanity.

BEFORE the interior part of the place is defcribed, it will not be improper to conclude the defcription of its outer works, by inferting an abftract of the guns, howitzers, and mortars, mounted upon the different batteries. The original, from which this was copied, was taken in the beginning of March, 1783.

Nature of Ordnance.	Cannon.						Mortars.				Howitzers.		
	Prs. 24. 32 & 26	18	12	9	6	4 & 3	Inch 13	10	8	5½ 4½	Inch 10	8	5½
Serviceable Ordnance, *mounted*,	77	122	104	70	16	25 38	29	1	6	34	19	9	.
Field Artillery,	.	.	.	.	4	6 8	.	.	.	.	.	.	4
Serviceable Ordnance, *difmounted*,	.	27	9	.	.	15	.	2	7	31	.	.	.
	77.149.113.74.16.31.61						29.3.13.65				19.9.4		

Total ferviceable in the garrifon, 663 pieces of artillery.

THE Town is built on a bed of red fand, fimilar to thofe emininences without South port, which originally extended from Landport to the foot of the afcent to the fouth barracks. The buildings, before

before the town was deftroyed in the late fiege, were compofed of
different materials, principally of tapia ;* though, fince the Englifh
have been in poffeffion of Gibraltar, many have been built of the
rock-ftone, plaftered, and painted on the outfide, to break the
powerful rays of the fun, which otherwife would be too glaring,
and prejudicial to the eyes. The modern houfes were in general
covered with tiles; but the flat terraced roofs remained in thofe
erected by the Spaniards, and in fome, the mirandas or towers,
whence the inhabitants, without removing from home, had a beautiful and extenfive profpect of the neighbouring coafts.

Of the buildings that are moft deferving notice, the old Moorifh
caftle is the moft confpicuous. This antique ftructure is fituated
on the north-weft fide of the hill, and originally confifted of a triple
wall, the outer inclofure defcending to the water's edge : but the
lower parts have long fince been removed, and the Grand Battery
and Water-port fortifications erected on their ruins; and the firft,
or upper wall, would long ago have fhared the fame fate, had it not
been found of fervice in covering the town from the Ifthmus, in cafe
of a fiege. The walls ftanding at prefent form an oblong fquare,
afcending the hill, at the upper angle of which is the principal tower,
where the Governor or Alcaide formerly refided. The ruins of a
Moorifh mofque, or place of worfhip, can be traced within the
walls; as alfo a neat morifque court, and refervoir for water : but
the latter cannot, without great difficulty, be difcovered by a ftranger.
A large tower on the fouth-eaft wall has long been converted into a
magazine for powder; and in different places quarters were fitted up,
before the late fiege, for officers and two companies of foldiers. This
caftle was erected, as I have mentioned before, by the Saracens or
Moors,

---

* A cement confifting of mortar made of fand, lime, and fmall pebbles, which being well
tempered, and wrought together in a frame, acquires great ftrength and folidity.

Moors, on their firſt invading Spain; and the preſent venerable remains are inconteſtable proofs of its magnificence, whilſt it continued in their poſſeſſion.

The other principal buildings are the Convent, or Governor's quarters; the Lieut. Governor's houſe, which is a modern ſtructure; the Admiralty-houſe, formerly a monaſtery of white friars; the Soldiers barracks, Victualling-office, and Store-houſe. Beſides theſe, there are the Spaniſh church, the Atarafana, or galley-houſe, and ſome other buildings, formerly of note, but now in ruins from the fire of the Spaniards during the late ſiege.

At the ſouthward, are the South Barracks and the Navy Hoſpital. The former a ſtately building, delightfully ſituated, with a parade in front, and two pavilions detached; the whole capable of quartering 1200 men, and officers proportionate. The latter a capacious pile, well adapted to the purpoſe for which it was intended: it has an area in the center, with piazzas and a gallery above, by which the ſick may enjoy the ſun, or ſhade, as they think proper: there are apartments for 1000 men, with pavilions at each wing for the accommodation and convenience of the ſurgeons and their attendants. This hoſpital was originally erected for the navy, in caſe a Britiſh fleet ſhould be ſtationed in the Mediterranean; but, on the Spaniards bombarding the town in 1781, the Governor removed into it the ſick of the garriſon. At ſome diſtance, in the front of the barracks, are two powder-magazines, in which the ſupplies from England are uſually depoſited, before they are diſtributed to the other magazines. Theſe laſt conclude the chief, I might ſay almoſt the only buildings remaining on the rock after the late ſiege; and their preſervation was owing to their being kept in conſtant repair by workmen purpoſely appointed for that duty.

F

BESIDES

BESIDES the remains of Moorish architecture which have already been mentioned, the following have been esteemed not unworthy of notice. Within the town we find the Galley-house, and part of the Spanish church; also the Bomb-house, adjoining the line-wall : and at the southward, ruins of Moorish buildings are discernible on Windmill-hill, and at Europa. The former are situated on an eminence, but no antiquarian can determine to what use they were appropriated: some are of opinion they were burying-vaults for persons of rank; others suppose them a prison; whilst, in the garrison, the whole is generally known by the name of the Inquisition. At Europa, opposite the guard-house, may be traced the remains of a building erected by the Moors, but used by the Spaniards as a chapel, and called Nuestra Senora del Europa. Along the water's edge, without the fortification, are also several ruins of Moorish walls; and towards Europa advance is a Moorish bath, called by the garrison, the Nuns well. It is sunk eight feet deep in the rock, is 72 feet long, and 42 feet broad, and, to preserve the water, has an arched roof, supported by pillars. To the left of this bath is a cave, under Windmill-hill, known by the name of Beef-steak cave; which was a common residence for many of the inhabitants, during the late siege.

THE hill abounds in cavities, that serve as receptacles for the rain. None, however, is so singular and worthy of notice as St. George's cave, on the side of the hill, in a line with the south barracks, about 1100 feet above the level of the sea. At the entrance are the remains of a strong wall. The mouth is only five feet wide; but on descending a slope of earth, it widens considerably; and, with the assistance of torches, the openings of several smaller caves are discovered. The outer cave is about 200 feet long, and 90 broad. The top appears to be supported by pillars of vast magnitude, formed by the perpetual droppings of petrifying water,

the

rhe whole bearing great refemblance to the infide of a gloomy Gothic cathedral.

The feveral gradations in the progrefs of thefe petrifactions are eafily difcovered. In fome may be obferved fmall capitals, defcending from the roof, whilft proportionable bafes rife underneath : others again are formed of very fmall diameter ; and a third clafs, immenfely large, feem to fupport the roof of this wonderful cavern. Few ftrangers vifit Gibraltar but are conducted to view this cave ; and numbers, with the affiftance of ropes and torches, have attempted to explore the depth ; however, after defcending about 500 feet, they have been obliged to return, by the grofs vapours which iffued from beneath. It was in this cave that the Spaniards concealed themfelves in the fiege of 1727, when a party of them, unperceived, got into the garrifon, at the Cave-guard, near Europa advance, but afterwards failed in their enterprife.

There are feveral other caves on different parts of the hill, in which the water poffeffes the fame petrifying qualities. One under Middle-hill, called Pocoroca, was fitted up, previous to the bombardment, for the Governor's reception ; but was afterwards converted into a powder-magazine, being very convenient for the batteries on the heights.

Amongst the natural curiofities of Gibraltar, the petrified bones, found in the cavities of the rocks, have greatly attracted the attention of the curious. Thefe bones are not found in one particular part, but have been difcovered in various places at a confiderable diftance from each other. From the rocks near Rofia bay, (without the line-wall) great quantities of this curious petrifaction have been collected, and fent home for the infpection of naturalifts. Some of the bones are of large diameter ;

and,

and, being broken with the rock, the marrow is eafily to be diftin-guifhed. Colonel James, in his defcription of Gibraltar, mentions an entire human fkeleton being difcovered in the folid rock, at the Prince's lines; which the miner blew to 'pieces: and in the beginning of the late blockade, a party of miners, forming a cave at Upper All's-well, in the lines, produced feveral bones that were petrified to the rock, and appeared to have belonged to a large bird : being prefent at the time, I procured feveral fragments; but in the bombardment of 1781, they were deftroyed with other fimilar curiofities.

THE hill is remarkable for the number of apes about its fummit, which are faid not to be found in any other part of Spain. They breed in inacceffible places, and frequently appear in large droves, with their young on their backs, on the weftern face of the hill. It is imagined they were originally brought from Barbary by the Moors, as a fimilar fpecies inhabit *Mons Abyla*, which, on that account, is generally called Ape's-hill. Red-legged partridges are often found in coveys: woodcocks and teal are fometimes feen; and wild rabbits are caught about Europa and Windmill-hill. The garrifon-orders forbid officers to fhoot on the weftern fide of the rock; parties however often go in boats round Europa point to kill wild pigeons, which are numerous in the caves.

EAGLES and vultures annually vifit Gibraltar from Barbary, in their way to the interior parts of Spain. The former breed in the craggy parts of the rock, and, with the hawk, are often feen towering round its fummit. Mofchetoes are exceedingly trouble-fome towards the clofe of fummer; and locufts are fometimes found. The fcorpion, centipes, and other venomous reptiles, abound amongft the rocks and old buildings; and the harmlefs

green

green lizard, and fnake, are frequently caught by the foldiers, who, after drawing their teeth, treat them with every mark of fondnefs.

WITH regard to the climate of Gibraltar, the inhabitants breathe a temperate and wholefome air, for moft part of the year. The fummer months of June, July, and Auguft, are exceffively warm, with a perpetual ferene and clear fky : the heat is however allayed, in a great meafure, by a conftant refrefhing breeze from the fea, which ufually fets in about ten in the forenoon, continuing till almoft fun-fet ; and, from its invigorating and agreeable coolnefs, is emphatically called the Doctor. The cold in winter is not fo exceffive as in the neighbouring parts of the country. Snow falls but feldom, and ice is a rarity : yet the Grenadian mountains in Spain, and the lofty mountains in Africa, have fnow lying on them for feveral months. Heavy rains, high winds, and moft tremendous thunder, with dreadfully-vivid lightning, are the attendants on December and January. The rain then pours down in torrents from the hill, and, defcending with great rapidity, often choaks up the drains with large ftones and rubbifh, and fometimes does great injury to the works; but thefe ftorms never are of long duration : the fky foon clears up ; the heavy clouds difperfe ; the chearing fun appears, and fufficiently compenfates for the horrors of the preceding night. It is during this feafon that the water that ferves the garrifon for the enfuing fummer is collected. The aqueduct, which conducts it to the Fountain in the centre of the town, is extremely well executed; and was conftructed by a Jefuit, when the Spaniards were in poffeffion of Gibraltar. It is erected againft the bank of fand, without South port, beginning to the fouthward of the eight-gun baftion, and, collecting the rain-water that filters through the fand, conducts it to the South port, and thence to the

Fountain.

Fountain. The water, thus ftrained and pprified, is remarkably clear and wholefome.

THE appearance of the rock is barren and forbidding; as few trees or fhrubs, excepting palmettos, are to be feen on the face of the hill: yet it is not entirely deftitute of vegetation; wild herbs, of different kinds, fpring up in the interftices of the rocks, when the periodical rains fet in, and afford fome trifling nourifhment to the bullocks, fheep, and goats, that browfe upon the hill. The firft rains generally fall in September, or October, and continue at intervals, to refrefh the garrifon till April or May. When they ceafe, and the powerful rays of the fun have withered the little verdure that appeared on the hill, nothing offers to the eye but fharp uncouth rocks, and dried palmetto bufhes. The foil collected in the low ground is however extremely rich and fertile, producing variety of fruits and vegetables. Colonel James, in his elaborate hiftory of Gibraltar, enumerates no lefs than 300 different herbs, which are to be found on various parts of the rock. Gibraltar confequently muft be an excellent field of amufement to a botanift.

THE garrifon, before the blockade of 1779, was chiefly fupplied with roots and garden-ftuff from the gardens on the neutral ground, which, being on a flat, could almoft conftantly (even in fummer) be kept in a ftate of vegetation. The proprietors of thefe gardens were obliged totally to relinquifh them when the Spaniards erected their advanced works: from that period General Eliott encouraged cultivation within his own limits, by every poffible indulgence. Many plots at the fouthward were inclofed with walls, the ground cleared of ftones and rubbifh, and foil collected from other parts: fo that with affiduity and perfeverance, after fome time, the produce, during the winter feafon, was fo increafed as to be almoft equal to the confumption; and probably, in the fpace of a few years, the

garrifon

garrifon may be totally independent, in this article, of any affiftance from the neighbourhood.

GIBRALTAR, by being nearly furrounded by the fea, is exceedingly well fupplied with fifh : the John-doree, turbot, foal, falmon, hake, rock-cod, mullet, and ranger, with great variety of lefs note, are caught along the Spanifh fhore, and in different parts of the bay. Mackarel are alfo taken in vaft numbers during the feafon, and fhell-fifh are fometimes brought from the neighbouring parts.—The Moors, in time of peace, fupply the garrifon with ox-beef, mutton, veal, and poultry, on moderate terms ; and from Spain they procure pork, which is remarkable for its fweetnefs and flavour. Fruits of all kinds, fuch as melons, oranges, green figs, grapes, pomegranates, &c. are brought in abundance from Barbary and Portugal : and the beft wines are drank at very reafonable prices.

THE prefent military eftablifhment* of Gibraltar confifts of fix companies of artillery, eight regiments of the line, and a company of artificers, commanded by engineers ; compofing an army of near 4000 men, officers included. Before the late bombardment, the troops were quartered in the barracks at the fouthward, and in quarters fitted up out of the old Spanifh buildings in town. The officers were diftributed in the fame manner ; but in cafe of reinforcements, and that government quarters were not fufficient for their accommodation, billet-money was allowed in proportion to rank, and the officers hired lodgings from the inhabitants.

THE regiments, on their arrival in the garrifon, are entitled to falt provifions from the ftores, in the following proportion. One ration for each ferjeant, corporal, drummer and private, confifting

* 1ft of January, 1785.

ing of 7lb. of bread, delivered twice a week, beef 2lb. 8 oz. pork
1 lb. butter 10 oz. peafe half a gallon, and groats 3 pints: every
commiffioned and warrant officer, under a Captain, receives two
rations, a Captain three, a Major and Lieutenant-Colonel four, a
Colonel fix. In times of profound peace, officers generally receive
a compenfation in money for their provifions, or difpofe of them
to the Jews, of whom there are great numbers in the garrifon,
who are always ready to purchafe, or take them in barter. The
troops are paid in currency, which, let the exchange of the garrifon be above or below *par*, never varies to the non-commiffioned
and privates. A ferjeant receives weekly, as full garrifon-pay, one
dollar, fix reals, equal to nine-pence fterling, *per diem*; a corporal,
and drummer, one dollar, one real, and five quartils, in fterling
about fix-pence, *per diem*; and a private, feven reals, or four-pence
half-penny fterling, *per diem*. Officers receive their fubfiftence
according to the currency: thirty-fix pence *per* dollar is *par*. During
the late bombardment, the exchange, for a confiderable time, was
as high as forty-two pence, by which thofe gentlemen who were
under the neceffity of drawing for their pay, loft fix-pence in every
three fhillings; and it feldom was lower than forty pence whilft the
fiege continued. The coins current in Gibraltar are thofe ufed in
Spain. All accounts are kept in dollars, reals, and quartils: the
two former, like the pound fterling, are imaginary; the latter is a
copper coin.

THE Bay of Gibraltar, formed by the headlands of Cabrita and
Europa Points, is 'commodious, and feems intended by nature to
command the Straits: there are opportunities, however, when a
fleet-may pafs unobferved by the garrifon; for fuch is the impene-
trable thicknefs of the mifts, which ufually prevail during the
eafterly winds, that many fhips have baffled the vigilance of the
cruifers, and gone through unnoticed: the fouth-wefterly winds,

particularly

particularly at the equinox, are alfo often attended with fuch thick and rainy weather, that veffels have paffed through and got into the Bay without being feen.

SINCE Gibraltar has been in the poffeffion of the Englifh, the Spaniards have erected, in different parts of the Bay, feveral batteries and forts for the protection of their fmall craft in war, and to prevent their coaft from being annoyed. At Cabrita, which is a bold rocky point, are a barbet-battery and watch-tower, whence, during the blockade, fignals of flags by day, and lights at night, were made to inform the Spanifh cruifers at Algeziras, &c. of the approach of any veffel towards the Bay. Thefe watch-towers are diftributed, at fhort diftances, along the coaft for a confiderable extent, to alarm the country, in cafe of a vifit from the Algerines, or when any other extraordinary circumftance happens. To the northward of Cabrita are two others, with a fort at the northern-moft tower, which is called San Garcia : the point on which the latter are erected, projects, with a long reef of dangerous fhoals and rocks, confiderably into the Bay. The town and ifland of Algeziras, with their batteries, then appear in view.

ALGEZIRAS lies oppofite to Gibraltar, about 5¼ miles acrofs the Bay; and, fince the late fiege, has greatly increafed in confequence and wealth. The town was built and fortified by the Saracens about the year 714, two years after their eftablifhment at Gibraltar. It is remarkable for being the place where thofe invaders firft dif-embarked, when they fo rapidly overturned the Gothic empire in Spain; and, as well as Gibraltar, was erected to preferve a com-munication with Africa. Whilft the Moors maintained their conquefts, it confequently became a city of great importance and ftrength. We find, during the fucceffive wars which took place between the Moors and the Spaniards, Algeziras was frequently

G   befieged

befieged by the kings of Caftile; and, when Gibraltar fo cafily fell into the hands of the Chriftians in 1310, this city refifted all their efforts. At length, after a moft obftinate fiege in 1344, Algeziras was compelled to furrender to the victorious arms of Alonzo XI. The fiege continued twenty months, and moft of the potentates in Europe interefted themfelves in the event, by fending fuccours to the Chriftian befiegers. The Englifh, under the Duke of Lan-cafter, the Earls of Derby, Leicefter, Salifbury, and Lincoln, particularly diftinguifhed themfelves by their gallantry and conduct during this memorable conteft. It is worthy of remark, that cannon are faid to have been firft made ufe of in this fiege, by the Moors againft the affailants; and the Englifh, profiting by the knowledge gained on this occafion, afterwards ufed them at the glorious battle of Creffy. The Spaniards continued mafters of the town till 1369, when the Moors of Grenada furprifed the city; but being unable to retain it, they demolifhed the works, and carried away the inhabitants captives.

Whilst the Moors kept poffeffion of Gibraltar, which was now in its turn become a city of importance, the Spaniards never attempted to rebuild Algeziras; and ftill lefs did they efteem it an object worthy their attention, after Gibraltar fell into their hands. The town, therefore, remained in ruins and defolate, excepting a few fifhermen's huts, till the Spaniards, in the beginning of the prefent century, thought proper, after the ceffion of Gibraltar to Great-Britain, to repeople and fecure it by a few batteries towards the fea, which alfo might occafionally protect their cruifers in time of war. Since that period, from the conftant intercourfe and trade between it and Gibraltar, Algeziras is become a town of fome confequence and wealth; and, as a late writer has juftly expreffed, "like a phœnix, has rifen out of its own afhes, after " being for ages in ruins."

THE

THE New Town is built to the northward of the old city, (whose venerable ruins still remain) and is defended to the south-ward by a battery of nine or ten guns, erected on an island some distance from the shore. To the northward of the town is another battery of six guns, and a little farther, on an eminence, one of 22, which was raised by Admiral Barcelo, when he was apprehensive of an attack from Sir George Rodney in 1780. Between the island and the town, small craft find tolerable shel-ter; but ships of war, or of large burthen, anchor to the north-ward. The lands round the town are of late much cultivated, and, with the shipping, form, in the spring, a pleasantly-variegated and beautiful prospect to a spectator at Gibraltar. A detachment or regiment of infantry is constantly on duty here, who, with those of the Spanish lines and neighbourhood, are under the command of the commandant at St. Roque.

To THE northward of Algeziras are the rivers Palmones and Gua-daranque : the former is the broader and deeper of the two, and was the principal retreat of the Spanish gun and mortar boats, when they wanted repairs, after bombarding the garrison. Admiral Barcelo in this river also prepared the fire-ships he sent over in June 1780. On the east banks of the Guadaranque, near Rocadillo Point, where there is a small fort and tower, are the venerable ruins of the once famous city of CARTEIA. This celebrated place, scarcely a stone of which is now left to inform posterity where it stood, is reported to have been built by the Phenicians, in the first ages of navigation, when those adventurers visited the extreme parts of the then known world. Historians mention it under the names of Carteia, Heraclia, and Calpe Carteia. When the Carthaginians became a powerful nation, and aimed at the sovereignty of Spain, Carteia maintained its independence for some time, till Hannibal, according to Livy, stormed the city, and demolished most of its

G 2   works.

works.   When Scipio obliged the Carthaginians to quit Spain,
Carteia was a place of little importance; but the Romans finding
it a convenient station for their navy, the city was increased with
a Roman colony, and once more began to rise into splendor and
magnificence.   After the memorable battle of Munda, Cneius
Pompey fled to Carteia, but, being pursued, was obliged to leave
it precipitately.   As the Roman Empire declined, so did Carteia;
and probably, soon after the irruption of the Goths and Vandals,
it became almost desolate and waste.   On the invasion of Spain by
the Saracens, that nation undoubtedly dismantled the buildings of
this famous city for materials to erect Gibraltar and Algeziras.   The
remains of a quay are still visible, with some few ruins of public
buildings, apparently Roman; and the country peasants, in tilling the
ground, often find various antique coins, which curious antiquarians
have not thought unworthy of a place in their cabinets.

HALF way between the Guadaranque and the garrison, is another
fort and tower, called Point Mala, or Negro Point, to the northward of which is the inland village of St. Roque.   This is a small
insignificant town, though delightfully situated, at about five miles
distance from Gibraltar.   It was built by the Spaniards, in the beginning of the present century, when the garrison of Gibraltar
surrendered to Sir George Rooke.   The Spanish Commandant of
the Lines generally makes it his residence; and during the late
siege, under the Duke de Crillon, the Count d'Artois, and the
Duke de Bourbon, had apartments in the town.   Previous to the
war of 1779 it was often frequented by the officers from Gibraltar;
and in the spring and summer seasons, British families resided there
for several months, some for the benefit of their health, others
for pleasure.   The combined army, during the late siege, encamped
on the plains below St. Roque, and landed all their ordnance,
and military stores, a little to the westward of Point Mala, near
the Orange-grove.

I CAN-

I CANNOT help remarking in this place, that, among the evils of the late fiege, the Garrifon have to regret the interruption of that friendly intercourfe, which before fubfifted between them and the neighbourhood, and which is now prohibited by the Spanifh government. When the communication was free and unlimited (except in point of introducing a contraband traffic in Spain) the ftricteft intimacy fubfifted between the Britifh military, and the Spaniards refident in the adjacent villages. Parties were reciprocally vifiting each other, and the officers conftantly making excurfions into the country. Thefe excurfions, with others to the coaft of Barbary, (which in the feafon fuperabounds with various fpecies of game) were pleafing relaxations from the duties of the garrifon, and rendered Gibraltar as eligible a ftation as any to which a foldier could be ordered.

ON the whole—Whether we confider Gibraltar as commanding the entrance of the Mediterranean, and confequently as capable of controuling the commerce of the Europeans with the Levant; or whether we confider it as almoft impregnable by nature, and confequently as moft fufceptible of the improvements of art; its fituation is, perhaps, more fingular and curious than that of any fortrefs in the world. Thefe circumftances, and the degree of confequence which it confers on its poffeffor, in the opinion of the Barbary ftates, have not failed to excite the attention, and alarm the interefts, of moft maritime nations in Europe; and, with the multitude at leaft, it has always been an object of political importance. Politicians, however, there have been, of no inferior rank, who have thought very differently of its value and utility. On this delicate fubject I will frankly confefs my inability to decide. I fhall therefore, without further apology, leave thefe fpeculations to men of more leifure and experience; and proceed to matters better adapted to my capacity and information.

CHAP-

CHAPTER III.

*Commencement of the war in 1779, between Great-Britain and Spain.
—State of the garrison of Gibraltar at that period.—Ambiguous conduct of the Spaniards.—Enemy encamp before the garrison.—Form
a blockade.—Many Inhabitants leave the place.—Motions of the
enemy.—Erect additional batteries in their lines.—Fired upon from the
garrison.—Continue their operations.—Loss of the Peace and Plenty
privateer.—Provisions extremely scarce in the garrison.—Spirited
behaviour of the Buck cutter privateer.—Description of the Straits.
—Fidelity of a Moor.—Great distress in the garrison.—Relieved
by some fortunate occurrences.—Arrival of Sir George Rodney, and
the British fleet.—Tetuan.—Anecdote of Prince William-Henry.—
Ceuta.—Departure of the fleet.*

ALTHOUGH the Spaniards had been thrice defeated in their
attempts to recover Gibraltar, they continued to view that garrison
with a jealous eye, determined, if we may judge from their late
conduct, to seize the first eligible opportunity of wresting it, if
possible, from the dominion of Great-Britain.

THE war of 1762 was too unexpected on the part of Spain, and
conducted with too great success by the British Minister, to admit
of such an enterprise as the siege of Gibraltar. The period was not
however far distant, when the contest between Great-Britain and
her Colonies, seemed to promise as favourable an opportunity as
their warmest wishes could have anticipated; particularly when, in
addition to the civil war, they found hostilities taking place between
Great-Britain and France. The close of the year 1777, when the

news

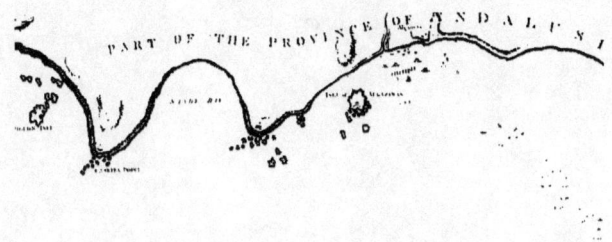

news of the convention of Saratoga firft arrived in Europe, was the period which they embraced, to introduce themfelves into the difpute. Hoftilities had then been carried on for near fix months between Great-Britain and France: Spain therefore judged the opportunity favourable to offer her mediation, propofing fuch an arrangement as fhe muft be affured would not be agreeable to the principal belligerent powers. Great-Britain had no fooner refufed her acquiefcence, than the Court of Madrid efpoufed the part of France; and, on the 16th of June, 1779, the Spanifh Ambaffador, the Marquis d'Almodovar, prefented to the Court of London his hoftile manifefto.

1779. June.

THE principal defign of the Court of Madrid, in entering into this war, was evidently the recovery of Gibraltar. Before any reply was given by the Britifh Miniftry to their propofals for a pacification, overtures had been privately made to the Emperor of Morocco, to farm his ports at Tetuan, Tangier, and Larache; by which means Gibraltar might be cut off from its principal fupplies. This conduct feemed to argue a confidence that her terms in the mediation would be refufed; and the confiderable dépôts of military ftores, which were collected in her arfenals, undoubtedly pointed out, that the fiege of that garrifon was her firft and immediate object. On the 21ft of June, 1779, the communication between Spain and Gibraltar was clofed, by an order from Madrid.

Two days previous to this event, General ELIOTT, the Governor, accompanied by many Field-officers of the garrifon, paid a vifit to General Mendoza, the Commandant of the Spanifh lines, to congratulate him on his promotion. Their reception at St. Roque was far from agreeable; and it was remarked that the Spanifh General appeared embarraffed during their ftay, which might proceed

ceed from his knowledge of what was to follow. The vifit was fhort, and the Governor had fcarcely returned to the garrifon, when Mr. Logie, his Majefty's Conful in Barbary, arrived from Tangier in a Swedifh frigate, with certain intelligence of the intended rupture between Great-Britain and Spain. Mr. Logie's information proceeded from a Swedifh brig, which on her paffage to Tangier had fallen in with the French fleet, of about 28 fail of the line, off Cape Finifterre, when the mafter being ordered on board the Admiral, M. d'Orvilliers, he learned that they had been cruifing for fome time in that latitude, expecting the junction of the Spanifh fleet from Cadiz. From the amicable affurances held out by the Spaniards, we could not perfuade ourfelves in the garrifon that a rupture was fo near; but the mail from the garrifon being refufed on the 21ft of June, and being acquainted at the fame time that the intercourfe between Gibraltar and the neighbourhood was no longer to be permitted, we had fufficient confirmation of Mr. Logie's intelligence. We afterwards learned, that the courier, who brought from Madrid the order to fhut up the communication, had been detained by accidents on the road; otherwife it was not impoffible that he might have arrived during General Eliott's vifit at St. Roque.

As the Fortrefs of Gibraltar after this event became a little world of itfelf, it may not be unacceptable, to commence the Hiftory of the Siege with a ftate of the troops in garrifon at that period, and the commanding officers of the different corps.

General G. A. ELIOTT, Governor.

Lieutenant-General R. BOYD, Lieutenant-Governor.

Major-General DE LA MOTTE, commanding the Hanoverian Brigade.

	Off.	Staff.	S.	D.	Rank & File	
Artillery . . .	25 .	0 .	17 .	15 .	428	Col. Godwin, Commandant of Artillery.
12th Regiment	26 .	3 .	29 .	22 .	519	Lieutenant-Colonel Trigge.
39th ————	25 .	4 .	29 .	22 .	506	Lieutenant-General Boyd, Major Kellet.
56th ————	23 .	4 .	30 .	22 .	508	Major Fancourt.
58th ————	25 .	3 .	29 .	22 .	526	Lieutenant-Colonel Cochrane.
72d, or R. M. V.	29 .	4 .	47 .	22 .	944	Lieutenant-Colonel Gledstanes.
Hanoverians { Hardenberg's	16 .	13 .	42 .	14 .	367	Lieutenant-Colonel Hugo.
{ Reden's . .	15 .	12 .	42 .	14 .	361	Lieutenant-Colonel Dachenhaufen.
{ De La Motte's	17 .	16 .	42 .	14 .	367	M. G. De La Motte, L. Col. Sclippergill.
Engineers with a Company of Artificers	8 .	0 .	6 .	2 .	106	Colonel Green, Chief Engineer.

Total 209 . 59 . 313 . 169 . 4632

Making an army of 5382 men.

ON the communication being clofed, a council of war was immediately fummoned, to advife concerning the meafures to be purfued on the occafion. Preparations had been privately made for the defence of the garrifon, when intelligence was firft received of the probability of a war: the objects therefore at this time to be confidered were, how to procure conftant fupplies of provifions from Barbary, and in what manner the correfpondence between England and Gibraltar was to be conducted. Mr. Logie's prefence in Barbary was very effential to both thefe points: he confequently returned to Tangier on the 22d, having concerted with the Governor proper fignals, by which he might communicate intelligence acrofs the Straits. Admiral Duff alfo, on the 22d, removed the men of war under his command from their ufual anchorage, off Waterport (where they were liable to be annoyed by the enemy's forts), to the fouthward, off the New Mole. His force at that time confifted of the Panther, of 60 guns, Capt. Harvey, on board of which was

H

. the

the flag; three frigates, two of which were on a cruife; and a floop of war.

It is natural to fuppofe that the garrifon were not a little alarmed at this unexpected procedure of the Spaniards. The Northern guards were reinforced, and the piquets cautioned to be alert, in cafe of alarm. Land-port barriers were fhut; and an artillery officer ordered to Willis's batteries, to obferve the movements of the *Enemy*, and protect the Devil's-tower guard, which was ordered to be very circumfpect and vigilant.

Whilst the friendly intercourfe fubfifted between the garrifon and the neighbourhood, feveral Britifh families and officers had per-miffion to refide at St. Roque, Los Varios, and other fmall villages a few miles diftant; but immediately on the communication being clofed, General Mendoza fent them peremptory orders to remove; and the time limited for their departure was fo fhort, that fome of them were obliged to leave moft of their effects behind. Thofe officers whofe curiofity had led them into the interior parts of the country, were pofitively refufed liberty to return to the garrifon; they were therefore conducted to Cadiz, and had paffports granted them to leave the kingdom by other routes. Col. Rofs and Capt. Vignoles, of the 39th, with Capt. Lefanue, of the 56th, never-thelefs contrived to join their corps, by affuming difguifes, and rifking the paffage in a row-boat from Faro (a port in Portugal) to Gibraltar: others alfo attempted, but unfortunately were taken in their voyage.

The Childers floop of war, on the 24th, brought in two prizes from the Weft, one of which (an American) Capt. Peacock captured in the midft of the Spanifh fleet, then at fea. The conduct of the Spaniards on this occafion was extremely ambiguous. Every cir-cumftance that fell under our immediate obfervation, convinced us that they now intended hoftilities againft Great-Britain; and from Mr. Logie's intelligence we had every caufe to think, that this fleet was out to join the French Admiral. Their permitting our cruifers, therefore, to capture a friend, (as they might then call the Americans) under the protection of their fleet, we muft either confider as a fineffe, or fuppofe that they had not received orders to act offenfively.—The Childers left two of our frigates watching the motions of the Spanifh fleet. It was fomewhat fingular, that a Mr. Suafé (an American Major, who had been prifoner in the garrifon a little time before, along with others of his countrymen, but had made his efcape) and two deferters from Gibraltar, fhould be recognifed through their difguifes, on board the American prize: the Major was remanded to his old confinement, in the Navy-hofpital, and the latter were punifhed according to their deferts.

THOUGH the motions of the enemy did not indicate any immediate defign of attacking the garrifon, and the clofing of the communication might be only in confequence of hoftilities having commenced between Great-Britain and Spain; yet our intelligence, and their late deceitful conduct, gave us great reafon to fuppofe that they intended fome attempt on Gibraltar. Dépôts of earth, &c. were therefore collected, in various places; empty hogfheads and cafks were bought from the inhabitants, for the purpofe of filling them with earth, to ftrengthen and repair the fortifications; and other precautions were taken for the defence of the place. On the other hand, the enemy employed what troops they had then on duty, in the lines and neighbourhood, in drawing down cannon from St. Roque, &c. to *animate* the forts, (in which few ordnance were mounted during the peace) and in arranging matters to ftrengthen and fupport their pofts.

H 2

IN

IN the beginning of July, the Enterprife frigate, Sir Thomas
Rich, Bart. returned with a fleet of fmall craft, laden with live
ftock and fruit, from Tangier; in confequence of which fourteen
days frefh provifions were iffued to the troops.   The engineers continued preparing materials in their departments, towards completing
the works of the garrifon; for which purpofe ftrong parties from
the line were granted them daily, under the command of overfeers.
About 300 Jews and Genoefe were alfo employed in levelling heaps
of fand, near the gardens, on the neutral ground, in order that, if
the enemy fhould approach, they might not receive any protection
and cover from our lower batteries.   The picquets of the garrifon
were ready, on the Grand parade, to fupport thefe parties in cafe
they had been molefted; but though they were at work within half
mufket-fhot of the enemy's advanced guards in the Micquelet-huts,
yet not the leaft attempt was made to difturb them.

THE 3d of July, a detachment of about 180 men from the
Britifh line was ordered to join the artillery, to be taught the practice
of the great guns.   The artillery in garrifon were only five companies; a number not adequate to the different duties in cafe of a
fiege : this reinforcement was therefore added, and proved afterwards
of great fervice in that department.   Three Englifh failors came in
an open boat, on the 4th, from Cadiz, and brought intelligence that
an embargo was laid on all Englifh veffels in that port.   In the
evening we obferved the Spaniards relieve the guards in their lines.

THE Spaniards, in time of peace, always ftationed a regiment of
cavalry at St. Roque, with another regiment, or detachment of
infantry, at Algeziras; parties from which did duty at their lines;
and no additional body of troops, or fhips of war, had yet appeared
near the garrifon.   On the 5th, however, in the afternoon, a Spanifh
fquadron of two feventy-fours, five frigates, and other veffels, to the
number

number of eleven, hove in fight from the weft, and lay-to fome time off the garrifon. Whilft they remained in this fituation, the Governor thought it prudent to make fome new difpofition of the ordnance at the fouthward, and to caution the regiments in the South barracks, the 12th, and 72d, to be alert. The Captain of Europa guard, who before ufually joined at retreat-beating, was alfo ordered to his command. In the afternoon, three privateer cutters arrived from the weftward. A fchooner, under Portuguefe colours, ftood acrofs from the enemy to reconnoitre the firft that came in, and on her return was fired upon from Europa batteries, which was the firft hoftile fhot from the garrifon. The enemy's fquadron in the evening drove to the eaftward; and at night the Enterprife frigate arrived from Tetuan with Mr. Logie, the conful. In the interval of this Gentleman's departure from the garrifon, a fhip of the Emperor's had arrived at Gibraltar to be repaired; but Admiral Duff being backward in granting the ftores, the Governor thought proper to fend for Mr. Logie to explain to the Admiral the neceffity there was of complying with the Emperor's requeft. To refufe fuch trifling affiftance at that important time, he confidered, might be productive of ferious confequences to the garrifon. The Enterprife frigate accordingly failed to Tetuan to bring over the Conful. About fun-fet, the evening of the 5th, the frigate left Tetuan to return, and was difcovered by the enemy's fquadron, part of which immediately gave chace. Sir Thomas, however, from his fuperior knowledge of the tides, efcaped, though the wind was contrary. When he arrived within view of the garrifon, not making the concerted night-fignals, for fear of being difcovered by the purfuers, the officer at Europa faluted him with feveral fhot; but fortunately they did not take effect.

THE following day, the 6th of July, a packet was received from England, by way of Lifbon and Faro, informing the Governor that hoftilities had commenced between Great-Britain and Spain. A
proclamation

proclamation in confequence was publifhed in the evening, for capturing all Spanifh veffels, &c. and letters of marque were granted for that purpofe to the privateers in the bay. Early on the morning of the 8th, a foldier of Reden's deferted from the Devil's-tower guard, and fome time afterwards was followed by a ferjeant of the 39th, who was one of the overfeers attending the inhabitants employed beyond the Gardens. In the evening, General Mendoza, with feveral officers, advanced from the lines, as far as the Micquelet-huts, and, after reconnoitring about an hour, returned.

The Spanifh Commodore continued cruifing in our neighbour-hood till the 8th, when he ftood, under an eafy fail, for the weft-ward. Before they quitted the Mediterranean, they brought-to a Portuguefe fchooner, bound from Tetuan to the garrifon, and made very earneft enquiries concerning the ftate of our provifions. The 9th, the American prifoners were diftributed amongft the privateers; and the following day, in company with the Childers floop of war, they brought in four fmall prizes.

Admiral Duff having received intelligence that a large fleet of fmall veffels was to fail from Malaga, with wine and provifions for the Spanifh grand fleet, the Childers was ordered, on the 11th, to cruife to the eaftward, and give information, by fignal, when they appeared, with the ftrength of their convoy. Whilft fhe was on the look-out, her boat gave chace to a fettee, and was fired at from Fort St. Barbara, which was the firft hoftile fhot from the enemy. About eleven o'clock, the fignals were made of the expected Spanifh convoy being in fight, and foon after, of their force. Our Admiral, however, only cautioned the Navy to be ready, and went to Windmill-hill to reconnoitre them perfonally. About four in the afternoon, the convoy, confifting of about fixty fail of different burthens, under charge of five xebeques, from twenty to thirty

guns

guns each, were abreaſt of Europa point. The privateers, which had accompanied the Childers in the morning, were then towing in a prize taken from the midſt of their fleet; and they, as well as the Childers, kept up a ſmart running fire on the Spaniſh Commodore; which was ſeconded at the ſame time from the garriſon batteries at Europa point and Europa advance. The Panther, (the Admiral's ſhip, with the flag on board) and the Enterpriſe, were ſtill at anchor; but at ſun-ſet Sir Thomas Rich had permiſſion to ſlip, and the Panther ſoon after got under way. On the appearance of the frigate, the enemy were confuſed, and inſtantly ſteered for Ceuta. The Childers and privateers purſued, followed by the frigate, and ſoon after by the Panther. Night was now advancing apace, and in a ſhort time we loſt ſight of the ſhips. A few broadſides, now and then, gave us hopes that our friends had come up with them; and we could not help flattering ourſelves, from the inferior force of the convoy, that day-light would exhibit the majority of them in our poſſeſſion. In the morning, however, we diſcovered the Admiral, ſtanding towards the bay with five or ſix ſmall prizes, and not one other of the enemy in ſight: whence we concluded that they had worked back to their own coaſt, or eſcaped through the Straits in the night, whilſt our ſhips were off Ceuta. We afterwards learned, that the ſquadron which appeared on the 5th, was ſent to convoy this valuable fleet paſt Gibraltar, leſt the Britiſh Admiral ſhould intercept them, and prevent their grand fleet from receiving theſe much-wanted ſupplies; but the convoy being by ſome unforeſeen delays detained, the Spaniſh Commodore quitted the ſtation on the 8th.

Two line-of-battle ſhips were obſerved cruiſing behind the rock on the 13th, and at night they went into Ceuta. The 16th, the Enemy blocked up the *port* with a ſquadron of men of war, conſiſting of two ſeventy-fours, two frigates, five xebeques, and a number

ber

ber of gallies, half-gallies, and armed fettees : they anchored in the bay, off Algeziras, and being judiciously arranged, and keeping a vigilant look-out, the garrifon became clofely blockaded. This was the firft motion of the enemy, that difcovered any direct intentions of diftreffing, or attacking Gibraltar. At night, Water-port-guard was reinforced with a Captain and ten privates. Till the 18th of this month, nothing material occurred, when a fmall convoy of fettees, &c. arrived at the Orange-grove, laden with military ftores, which the enemy began foon afterwards to difembark.

MR. LOGIE having prevailed on the Admiral to grant the ftores neceffary for repairing the Emperor's fhip, and his prefence in Barbary being abfolutely neceffary, as well to procure provifions, as to conduct the correfpondence between Great-Britain and the garrifon ; he returned on the 19th, on board a Moorifh row-galley, which had arrived from the Emperor with difpatches relative to the fhip under repair. The galley was interrupted in her return, by the enemy's cruifers, and detained from feven in the morning till five in the afternoon, when fhe was permitted to proceed to Tangier. During the embargo, Mr. Logie was concealed in a fmall fkuttle, down the run of the galley, having previoufly made up the Governor's difpatches, and concerted fignals, in a loaf, which was entrufted to a Moor, to be delivered at Mr. Logie's houfe in Tangier, in cafe he himfelf fhould be difcovered, with an order for the Moor to receive a gratuity, if he delivered it fafe.

EARLY in the morning of the 20th, a Portuguefe boat arrived with fowls and charcoal from Tangier. Another, attempting to come in, was taken by a half-galley, and carried to Algeziras. Sixty pounds of frefh beef were delivered, the fame day, to each regiment, for the ufe of the officers : the artillery and engineers received in proportion, and the navy were included in the diftribution. The
following

following day, orders were iſſued for the troops to mount guard with their hair unpowdered; a circumſtance trifling in appearance, but which our ſituation afterwards proved to be of great importance, and which evinced our Governor's great attention and prudent foreſight in the management of the ſtores.

So SUPERIOR a naval force as the enemy now had in our neighbourhood, alarmed Admiral Duff, who was apprehenſive that they would make ſome attempts on the King's ſhips. Signals were therefore agreed upon between the fleet and the garriſon, that, in caſe the enemy ſhould make an attack in the night, the latter might afford the ſhips every aſſiſtance and protection. Three lights in a triangle were fixed upon by the navy, to diſtinguiſh them from the enemy. The 22d, the navy manned their boats, and captured a ſettee, within a ſhort diſtance of the Enemy's xebeques: ſhe proved of little value, but the exploit reflected great credit on the party employed. The ſame day arrived a boat, with cattle, &c. from Tangier. In the courſe of the 22d, ſeveral officers, attended by a party of men, were obſerved tracing out ground on the plain below St. Roque, apparently for a camp; and it was remarked, that the Micquelets in the advanced huts on the neutral ground, were relieved by regular troops. Theſe Micquelets are of the ſame deſcription with our revenue-officers, and were ſtationed to prevent the ſmuggling of tobacco from the garriſon into Spain.

A PORTUGUESE boat, with letters, arrived early in the morning of the 24th; alſo a ſchooner, with charcoal and fruit from Tangier. Between 2 and 300 men landed, the ſame day, at the Orange-grove, with an intention, as we conjectured, of taking charge of the ſtores which the enemy were diſembarking there. The 25th, they pitched a tent on the plain, for the working party employed in clearing the ground. I ſhould have mentioned, that on the 12th an Hanoverian

I   ſoldier

foldier deferted, and this day two of the fame brigade followed his example. The enemy, the 26th, began to form a camp on the plain below St. Roque, about half a mile from Point Mala, and three miles from the garrifon. Fifty tents were pitched, and a detachment of cavalry and infantry foon after took poffeffion. The fame day the Illerim, a Swedifh frigate, which had been in the Bay fome weeks before, arrived, though oppofed by the enemy. The Swedifh captain politely brought-to on their firing a gun ; but being told he muft not anchor under the walls of the garrifon, he refumed his courfe, telling them he muft go to Gibraltar, and they fhould not prevent him. Some fhots were exchanged, but none took place.

THE Spanifh camp being daily reinforced with additional regiments of cavalry and infantry, and large parties being ftill employed in landing ordnance and military ftores at Point Mala, the Governor thought proper, on the 29th, to eftablifh the following ftaff officers ; namely, Captains, Vallotton, of the 56th regiment,—Patterfon, of the artillery,—Forch, of the 12th regiment, and Eveleigh, of the engineers, to be Aide-de-camps to himfelf, as Commander in Chief ; Captain Wilfon and Lieutenant Buckeridge, of the 39th regiment, Aide-de-camps to Lieutenant-general Boyd ; Lieutenant Weinzey, of the Hanoverian Brigade, Aide-de-camp to Major-general De La Motte ; Major Hardy, of the 56th regiment, Quarter-Mafter General ; Captain Horfburgh, of the 39th regiment, who was Town-Major, Adjutant-General ; Captain Burke, of the 58th regiment, Town-Major ; and Lieutenant S. Wood, of the 56th regiment, Affiftant Town-Major. At the fame time all the horfes, except thofe belonging to field and ftaff officers, were ordered to be turned out of the garrifon, unlefs the owners, on infpection, had 1000 lb. of feed for each horfe ; and, to enforce the latter order by example, the Governor directed that one of his own horfes fhould be fhot.

In

IN the afternoon of the 30th, one of the enemy's xebeques manned her yards, and fired a falute. Immediately afterwards we obferved fhe had hoifted a flag at the mizen top-maft head, inftead of a broad pendant; from which ceremony we concluded that the naval commandant had been promoted, or that he was fuperfeded by an admiral.

IN the beginning of Auguft, the corps in garrifon were ordered to give in returns of their beft markfmen, and alfo of thofe men who had ever been employed in making fafcines. Thofe officers unmarried, or without families, who drew double rations for two commiffions, were ordered at the fame time to draw rations only for one commiffion. Two Dutchmen came in, the 2d, unperceived by the enemy's cruifers, laden with rice and dried fruits: the rice, and a part of the fruit, the Governor purchafed, for the ufe of the troops. The enemy's camp by this time was confiderably increafed, and we numbered 26 cannon behind the fort at Point Mala.

A VENETIAN arrived on the 5th, though fired at by the enemy. She (with the Dutchmen) remained no longer than was neceffary to take on board fome of the inhabitants, who, apprehenfive that the garrifon would be befieged, thought it eligible to feek an afylum in time. Indeed about this time fcarcely a boat or veffel left the port without being crowded with Jews or Genoefe, who preferred a refidence in Barbary, or Portugal, to remaining in Gibraltar, where the neceffaries of life became every day more fcarce. Early on the 6th came in a Portuguefe fchooner, from Tangier, with 44 bullocks, 27 fheep, and a few fowls; and two days following, another arrived with onions, fruit, and eggs: the latter brought letters for the Governor, but no news from England. From this day, nothing material occurred till the 10th, when the enemy's cruifers captured a boat belonging to the garrifon.

As

As AFFAIRS began to wear a more serious aspect, a general activity reigned throughout the garrison, promoted not a little by the
example of the Governor, who was usually present when the workmen paraded at dawn of day.   The engineers were busily employed
in putting the works at Willis's in the best repair, and in erecting
new batteries on the heights of the North front.   A considerable
extent of ground above the Town was cleared and levelled, to
encamp the different regiments, in case the enemy should fire upon
the Town.   Parties were likewise detached to collect shrubs, &c.
from the face of the hill, for fascines; and the artillery were daily
engaged in completing the expence magazines with powder, ranging
the different ordnance, and preparing every thing for immediate
use in their department.   The navy were not less diligent.   A new
battery for 22 guns was begun in the Navy-yard, as a resource in
case the enemy's operations should make it necessary to lay up the
ships; and the stores were removed from the New mole to the Navy
hospital.

Towards the middle of August, the motions of the enemy were
no longer mysterious; every succeeding day confirmed us in the
opinion, that their object was to distress the garrison as much as
possible.   The blockade became more strict and severe, their army
was in force before the place, and their present plan seemed to be
to reduce Gibraltar by famine.   Our stock of provisions, they concluded, was small; and their squadron under Admiral Barcelo, who
commanded in the bay, could prevent succours being thrown in by
neutral vessels; whilst their grand fleet, united with that of France,
would be superior to any which Great-Britain could equip, in her
then critical situation.   This scheme, every circumstance considered,
was specious; and, had not the garrison fortunately received a supply
of provisions, &c. in April, 1779, the troops undoubtedly would have
been reduced to the greatest distress, and the place might probably
have

have been in imminent danger, before the Miniſtry could diſpatch a fleet to its relief. . The ſituation of the garriſon was becoming every day more intereſting : only forty head of cattle were now in the place; and from the vigilance of the enemy, there was little proſpect of conſtant ſupplies from Barbary : two bullocks were ordered, therefore, to be killed daily for the uſe of the ſick. The inhabitants had been warned in time to provide againſt the calamities which now impended : the ſtanding orders of the garriſon ſpecified, that every inhabitant, even in time of peace, ſhould have in ſtore ſix months proviſions; yet by far the greater number had neglected this precaution. Theſe unfortunate people, as they could not expect to be ſupplied from the garriſon ſtores, were in general compelled to ſeek ſubſiſtence by quitting the place : ſome, however, were induced to weather out the ſtorm, by the property they had in the garriſon, which was probably their all, and which they could not remove with themſelves. Thoſe of this deſcription, on application, obtained leave to erect wooden huts and ſheds at the ſouthward, above the Navy hoſpital, whither they removed their principal papers, &c. that they might be ſecure from the annoyance of the enemy, in caſe the town ſhould be bombarded.

FIFTEEN or ſixteen covered carts, on the 15th, arrived at the enemy's camp, and unloaded timber, planks, &c. at their laboratory-tents. They continued landing ſtores on the beach, which employed a great number of carts to convey them to their dépôts : and at night we generally obſerved a number of lights, and frequently heard a noiſe like that of men employed on ſome laborious duty : this might proceed from dragging cannon, as we obſerved, on the 17th, they had *animated* all the embraſures in fort St. Philip.

EARLY on the 17th, the enemy attempted to cut out a polacre, which was anchored off the Old mole; but retired on a gun being
fired

fired at them from the garriſon. The ſmall craft, after this circum-ſtance, removed to the New mole, as the men of war had done ſome time before. The 18th, in the morning, two parties of workmen came from the camp, and were employed at Forts St. Philip and St. Barbara: covered carts continued conſtantly going from Point Mala to the laboratory-tents, ſuppoſed to be laden with ſhot. The following morning, a Spaniard came in an open boat to Waterport, with onions and fruit, having a paſs for Ceuta: he was examined by the quarter-maſter general, and allowed to ſell his cargo, and purchaſe tobacco, but was not permitted to land: at night he was ordered to return, which he did about eight o'clock. He informed us the camp conſiſted of between 5 and 6000 men, which were to be immediately completed to 15,000. The 20th, the enemy formed a new camp, to the left of the ſtone quarry, under the Queen of Spain's chair: we imagined it to be intended for the Catalonian troops, as they are uſually encamped ſeparate from the reſt of the Spaniſh forces. The ſame day, our markſmen were embodied into a company of two non-commiſſioned officers, and 64 men; and the command was given to Lieutenant Burleigh, of the 39th regiment.

THE enemy, on the 21ſt, had more men than uſual employed in making faſcines: they likewiſe were very buſy in piling ſhot, and had a party at work in the covert-way of Fort St. Philip. A number of carts daily brought ſhot (as we imagined) to the lines, parti-cularly to Fort St. Barbara. The 23d, the corps of engineers were formed into three diviſions, and ſeveral officers of the line appointed to join them as aſſiſtant engineers and overſeers. The ſame day ſome experiments were made with *red-hot ſhot:* this practice was continued on the 25th, when ſome carcaſſes were alſo thrown, and much approved. The 27th, we obſerved a faſcine-work begun upon the glacis, north of Fort St. Philip, which afterwards proved

to

to be a mortar-battery. A great number of carts continued to be employed in the enemy's camp, and vaſt quantities of ſtores were conſtantly landing beyond Point Mala. In the courſe of the 30th, the Childers, and an armed ſchooner, attempted to cut off two half-gallies becalmed in the Bay; but the enemy's xebeques, getting under way, obliged them to deſiſt. At night upwards of 80 covered carts came down to the enemy's lines.

FROM the time the enemy firſt appeared encamped before the gar-riſon, troops had been continually joining them from all quarters. Their camp conſiſted of two lines, (independent of the Catalonians) extending from Point Mala, in an oblique direction, into the country, towards the Queen of Spain's chair. The ſtreets were in a direction nearly parallel to the bottom of the Bay. The guards in their lines and advanced poſts were, as the camp increaſed, propor-tionably reinforced; but no act of hoſtility had yet taken place in that quarter, though the Governor continued the garriſon-guard at the Devil's tower. The forts were repaired, and put in the beſt order of defence. Laboratory-tents for the artillery were pitched in front of their camp, and magazines erected for military ſtores, which were frequently brought by fleets of ſmall craft, convoyed by men of war from Cadiz, Malaga, and other ports in the neigh-bourhood.

ON the 5th of September, a ſoldier of Hardenberg's deſerted from a working party employed in ſcarping the rock, under the lines. He was fired upon from Willis's, but got off. Beſides the party engaged in rendering the lines inacceſſible, our engineers were daily ſtrengthening them with paliſades, &c. Traverſes were alſo erected along the covered way, grand battery, and line-wall above Waterport, where a ſtrong boom of maſts was laid, from Old-mole head, to the foot of Landport glacis. About this time

time the regiments began to practife grenade exercife. The day
on which the Hanoverian deferted, a Moorifh galley came over
from Algeziras, where fhe had been detained ten days. The crew
reported that the Spanifh camp was very fickly. It is fuppofed
this veffel came to order home the fhip which had been fome time
repairing in the New mole, as the following day both of them left
the garrifon for Tangier : a xebeque however fpeaking them off
Cabrita Point, the Moors were conducted to the Spanifh Admiral.

THE enemy's workmen in the lines appeared at this time to be
about 500. They were principally engaged in filling up with fand
the north part of the ditch of Fort St. Philip, completing the
mortar-battery before mentioned, and raifing the creft of the glacis
of their lines in different places. From the noife often heard
during the night, and the number of lights feen, we judged that
they worked without intermiffion. Two waggons, drawn each by
twelve mules or horfes, arrived at the lines on the 8th, which we
conjectured brought fixed ammunition. The 11th, we obferved
that they had begun feveral fafcine-works on the creft of their lines,
apparently for mortar-batteries ; and had raifed feveral traverfes for
the protection of their guard-houfes. Waggons and carts continued bringing fafcines and other materials to the lines from the
camp. The fame day, a row-boat, fitted out by the Jews, brought
in a Dutch dogger laden with wheat ; a very valuable fupply in
our fituation.

THE operations of the enemy now began to engage our attention. They had been permitted to pafs and repafs unmolefted for
fome time ; but the Governor did not think it prudent to allow
them to proceed any longer with impunity. A council of war was
confequently fummoned on the 11th, to confer on the meafures
to be purfued. The council confifted of the following officers : the

Governor ;

Governor; the Lieutenant-governor; Vice-admiral Duff; Major-general De la Motte; Colonels, Rofs, Green, and Godwin; with Sir Thomas Rich, Bart. In the evening it was reported that their opinion was, not to open on the enemy, whilft they continued within their lines : but this rumour was only propagated to deceive the public ; for on the fucceeding morning, being Sunday the 12th of September, the artillery officers were ordered to the batteries on the heights; and the Devil's-tower guard being withdrawn, the Governor opened on the enemy from Green's lodge, (a battery made fince the blockade commenced) Willis's, and Queen Charlotte's batteries. Their advanced guards in the Micquelet-huts, and in the ftone guard-houfes, were in a fhort time compelled to retire, and the workmen affembled in the lines obliged to difperfe. The covered waggons returned to the camp without depofiting their ladings; and fo general a panic feized the Enemy at this unexpected attack, that their cavalry galloped off towards the camp, and for fome hours fcarce a perfon was to be feen within the range of our guns. The forts were too diftant to be materially damaged; and the Governor's intention being only to difturb their workmen, the firing after a few hours flackened, and a fhot was only difcharged as the enemy prefented themfelves. A brafs gun in the Queen's battery (Willis's) run with eight rounds.

The mortar-batteries that had been difcovered in the Enemy's lines, fome few days previous to our firing, had caufed no fmall alarm amongft the inhabitants : thofe, therefore, who had huts in Hardy town at the fouthward, immediately removed their moft valuable effects, fully convinced that the Spaniards at night would return the fire.

That the duty of the batteries might be performed with fpirit, in cafe the Enemy perfifted in carrying on their works, a Captain,

K   three

three fubalterns, and 52 men of the artillery, were ordered to take in charge Green's lodge, Willis's, and other batteries on the heights. The firing was continued the fubfequent days, as circum-ftances directed. The 16th, the artillery made three attempts to reach the enemy's laboratory-tents, or artillery-park, (as henceforward they will be called) from a fea-mortar at Willis's. The firft and fecond fhell burft immediately on leaving the mortar : the third went its range, but fell a little fhort of the *fafcine*-park. The artillery at this period ufed the old fhells, the fufes of which were in general faulty; and this was the caufe that the experiment did not anfwer on the firft and fecond trials. We obferved, the fame day, that the Spaniards had pitched fome additional tents a little beyond Point Mala : they alfo began to erect a pier, or wharf, for the convenience of landing their ftores and fupplies.

WHILST the Governor kept a watchful eye on the enemy's operations, molefting their workmen as much as poffible from Willis's; proper precautions were taken in the town, to render a bombardment lefs diftreffing, in cafe they retaliated, which, indeed, their preparations gave us reafon to think, would not be long deferred. The pavement of the ftreets, in the north part of the town, was ploughed up; the towers of the moft confpicuous buildings were taken down, and traverfes raifed in different places, to render the communications more fecure. The enemy appeared to bear our fire very patiently in their lines : their parties continued working on the mortar-batteries : the ftone fentry-boxes were pulled down, and the guard-houfes unroofed : a boyau, or covered way, was likewife begun, to make a fafe communication from the lines to their camp.

OUR firing was ftill continued; but their parties were at too con-fiderable a diftance (being near a mile) to be materially annoyed by our fhot; and the works being furrounded with fand, the large
fhells

shells sunk so deep, that the splinters seldom rose to the surface. An experiment was therefore recommended by Captain (now Major) Mercier, of the 39th regiment; namely, to fire out of guns, 5-¼ inch shells, with short fuses; which were tried on the 25th, and found to answer extremely well. These small shells, according to Capt. Mercier's method, were dispatched with such precision, and the fuses calculated to such exactness, that the shell often burst over their heads, and wounded them before they could get under cover. This mode* of annoyance was eligible on several other accounts. Less powder was used, and the enemy were more seriously molested: the former was an advantage of no small consequence, since it enabled the Governor to reserve, at this period, what might be probably expended to the greater benefit of the service on some future occasion. It will also account for the extraordinary number of shells which, the reader will observe in the Appendix, were discharged from the garrison.

In the afternoon of the 26th, a soldier of the 72d regiment deserted from a working party out at Landport. He took refuge behind one of the Micquelet-huts, and, notwithstanding our endeavours to dislodge him, remained there till night, when it is imagined he proceeded to the lines. Our firing was now very trifling. The enemy continued making additions to their boyau, and the works in the lines; but the latter were chiefly done in the night. Indeed, since our firing, their operations within our reach had been principally carried on during the night, at which time, or very late in the evening, they also relieved their guards.

In the beginning of October, the enemy's army, according to our intelligence, consisted of sixteen battalions of infantry, and twelve squadrons of horse, which, if the regiments were complete, would

K 2

amount

---

* The Enemy, we were informed, attempted this practice, but never could bring it to perfection.

amount to about 14,000 men. Lieutenant-general Don Martin Alvarez de Sota Mayor was commander in chief. We continued our fire, varying as objects presented themselves.

THE great command we had over the Enemy's operations from Green's lodge, induced the engineers to mount still higher, and endeavour to erect a battery on the summit of the northern front: a place therefore was levelled, and a road for wheeled carriages begun at Middle-hill. The 4th, a soldier of the 58th attempted to desert from Middle-hill guard, but was dashed to pieces in his descent. The artillery were too impatient to have a gun mounted on the summit of the rock, to wait till the new road was finished: they accordingly determined to drag a twenty-four-pounder up the steep craggy face of the rock; and in a few days, with great difficulty and prodigious exertions, they were so successful as to get it to the top. The 9th, a party of the Navy attempted to cut off two Spanish polacres, becalmed between Algeziras and their camp. Our seamen spiritedly boarded one, and were on their return with the other, when two gallies from Point Mala gave chace, maintaining a smart and well-directed fire as they advanced; and gained so considerably on the prizes, that the captors were reluctantly obliged to quit them, and betake themselves to their boats. The Childers sloop of war was ordered out, to protect them, and fortunately was in time to stop the progress of the gallies. The tiller of one of our barges was carried away by a shot, but no other damage was received.

THE platform on the summit of the rock was completed on the 12th; and, the gun being mounted, the succeeding day we saluted the enemy's forts with a few rounds of shot and shells. This gun was mounted on a traversing carriage, and was distinguished by the name of the Rock-gun. From that post we had nearly a bird's-

eye

eye view of the enemy's lines, and, with the affiftance of glaffes, could diftinctly obferve every operation in their camp. In the afternoon of the 16th, a fervant of Mr. Davies (the agent-victualler of the Garrifon) under pretence of looking for a ftrayed goat, obtained leave to pafs Landport barrier, and immediately went over to the enemy. The defertion of this man gave us fome concern, as probably, to enfure a favourable reception, he might have taken with him fome memorandums of the ftate of our provifions.

THE Enemy's parties had not been remarkably active in the beginning of the month ; but about the 17th and 18th, their workmen in the lines were more numerous than ufual, which produced a more animated fire from our batteries. As our artillery by this time were accuftomed to fire from heights, the fmall fhot did confiderable execution amongft their workmen, many of whom we obferved were carried off. On the evening of the 19th, the Governor was at Willis's, to fee an experiment of a light ball, invented by Lieut. Whitham, of the artillery. It was made of lead, and, when filled with compofition, weighed 14 lb. 10 oz. This ball, with 4 lb. of powder, was fired, at fix degrees of elevation, out of a thirty-two-pounder, upon the glacis of their lines : it burnt well ; and the experiment would have been repeated, had not a thick fog fuddenly arifen. The Governor was at Willis's the fucceeding morning, to fee a fecond ; when, the fog being totally difperfed, the light ball anfwered his expectation. The Enemy, during the night, had been uncommonly noify ; but when the light balls were fired, no parties were difcovered at work. Neverthelefs, at day-break, to our great furprife, we obferved 35 embrafures opened in their lines, forming three batteries; two of 14 each, bearing on our lines and Willis's, and one of feven, apparently for the Town and Waterport. They were cut through the parapet of their glacis, and fituated between the barrier of the lines, and Fort St. Philip. The embrafures

fures were all maſked, and many of the merlons were in an unfi-
niſhed ſtate : the Governor ordered the artillery to direct their fire
on theſe works, and on the ſeven-gun battery in particular, where
they had a party finiſhing what was left imperfect in the night.*
In the afternoon, a Venetian was brought-to by a gun from
Europa, and came in : two gallies attempted to cut her off, but
in vain.

Our workmen now became exceedingly diligent ; new communications and works were raiſed in the lines, which were reinforced
at night, with a ſubaltern and 43 men ; the alarm-poſts of the regiments were alſo changed, and other arrangements took place.   On
the night of the 20th, we imagined, from the noiſe in the enemy's
lines, that their carpenters were platforming the new batteries, the
merlons of which they had caſed and capped with faſcines.   Their
boyau now extended from the faſcine-park, almoſt to the barrier of
the lines.   The 23d, a prize ſettee, laden with rice, was ſent in
from the eaſtward : ſhe was taken by a privateer belonging to Mr.
Anderſon, of the garriſon, the Captain of which thought the cargo
would be uſeful to the inhabitants ; and indeed this ſupply was truly
ſeaſonable.   No veſſel or boat had arrived for ſix weeks (excepting
the Venetian, on the 20th inſtant), and every article in the garriſon
began to ſell at a moſt exorbitant price : this trifling addition of proviſions was therefore well received by the miſerable Jews and Genoeſe,
though the rice ſold for 21 dollars 6 reals per cwt. which at 40 d.
ſterling the dollar, is 3 l. 12 s. 6 d.

The Enemy's artillery, on the 26th, decamped from their old
ground, before the right wing of their front line, and took poſt
near the Catalonians, where they were reinforced with a detachment

---

* From the diſtance of theſe batteries; we did not imagine they would ever materially
injure the garriſon: but the cannonade and bombardment of 1781, convinced us of our
error.

ment that had lately joined. The following night, the Dutch dogger, which had brought us the supply of wheat some weeks before, sailed for Malaga : she took 73 Genoese and Spanish passengers. The next day our artillery got up to Middle-hill two twenty-four-pounders, to be in readiness for a new battery, which was erecting below the rock-gun. Another twenty-four-pounder was taken to the same place, on the morning of the 25th. Our firing still continued, as the Enemy's parties were daily bringing down timber and other materials for their new batteries.

THE 30th, an English privateer, called the Peace and Plenty, 18 six-pounders, ——— M'Kenzie master, attempting to get in from the eastward, ran ashore, half-way between Fort Barbara and the Devil's tower. Some of the crew came on shore on the neutral ground; the remainder, with the master, were brought off by the Admiral's boats : and on the night of the 31st she was burnt. As there was something extraordinary and unaccountable in the circumstances attending the loss of this vessel, I cannot resist the temptation of relating them more at large. In the morning, she was bearing down, under a fine sail and leading wind, for Europa advance-guard, as two xebeques were cruising off Europa Point. One of the xebeques, about nine, got within shot of her : a few rounds were exchanged, and the privateer was apparently resolved to fight her way in ; but on a sudden she altered her course, and ran ashore under the enemy's guns, about 4 or 500 yards from the garrison. The boatswain was killed, and several others wounded from the fort, before our boats arrived to their relief.

TOWARDS the conclusion of the month, the small-pox was discovered in the garrison, amongst the Jews. The Governor, apprehensive that it might spread amongst the troops, and be attended with dangerous consequences, ordered those who had never been
affected

1779,
Oct.

affected with that diforder, to be quarfered at the fouthward till the infection fhould difappear; and every precaution was taken to prevent its communicating. In the evening of the 31ft, the new battery below the rock-gun was finifhed: it mounted four twenty-four-pounders, and was called the Royal battery.

Nov.

NOVEMBER was not introduced by any remarkable event. The fire from our batteries was variable, as their workmen were employed. Confiderable depofits of fafcines, with planks and pieces of timber, were formed in the Spanifh lines; and other parts of their glacis were raifed with fafcines and fand for additional mortar-batteries. The 3d, the Enemy began to form merlons at Fort Tonara, on the Eaftern fhore, which, joined with the circumftances of their erecting two fafcine-batteries on the beach, between Fort St. Philip and Point Mala, and one near the magazine at the Orange-grove, gave us reafon to fuppofe that they expected a fleet in their neighbourhood. Few workmen were at this time to be feen in their lines; a party was trimming up the boyau; and numbers were employed about the landing-place in difembarking ftores; which appeared to be their chief employment.

PROVISIONS of every kind were now becoming very fcarce and exorbitantly dear in the garrifon; mutton 3s. and 3s. 6d. per pound; veal 4s. pork 2s. and 2s. 6d. a pig's head 19s. ducks from 14s. to 18s. a couple; and a goofe, a guinea. Fifh was equally high, and vegetables were with difficulty to be got for any money; but bread, the great effential of life and health, was the article moft wanted. It was about this period, that the Governor made trial what quantity of rice would fuffice a fingle perfon for twenty-four hours; and actually lived himfelf eight days on four ounces of rice per day. Sir George is remarkable for an abftemious mode of living, feldom tafting any thing but vegetables, fimple puddings, and water; and

yet

yet is very hale, and ufes conftant exercife: but the fmall portion juft mentioned would be far from fufficient for a working man kept continually employed, and in a climate where the heat neceffarily demands very refrefhing nourifhment to fupport nature under fatigue.

Two deferters came in, with their arms, on the night of the 11th. They belonged to the Walon guards, a corps in the Spanifh fervice, compofed principally, if not entirely, of foreigners. The following morning they were conducted to Willis's, whence they had a view of the enemy's works, which they defcribed to the Governor. The Spanifh army were under arms on the 12th, in the front of their camp, and were difmiffed by corps as the General paffed.

The 14th, arrived the Buck cutter privateer, Captain Fagg, carrying twenty-four nine-pounders. The abilities and bravery of a Britifh Sailor were fo eminently confpicuous in the Captain's conduct previous to his arrival, that even our enemies could not help beftowing on him the encomiums to which his merit entitled him. About eight in the morning, the privateer was difcovered in the Gut, with a wefterly breeze. The ufual fignal for feeing an enemy was made by the Spaniards at Cabrita Point; and Admiral Barcelo, with a fhip of the line, one of fifty guns, a frigate of forty, two xebeques, a fettee of fourteen guns, with half-gallies, &c. &c. to the number of twenty-one, got under way to intercept her. On the firft alarm a xebeque at anchor off Cabrita had weighed, and ftood out into the Straits: the cutter neverthelefs continued her courfe; but obferving the whole Spanifh fquadron turning the point, fhe fuddenly tacked, and ftood towards the Barbary fhore: the xebeques, frigate, and lighter veffels purfued, but were carried down to leeward by the irrefiftible rapidity of the current, whilft the cutter in a great degree maintained her ftation. As it may appear

L   very

very extraordinary to readers unacquainted with nautical affairs, that the privateer should not be equally affected by the current, it may be necessary to inform them, that a cutter, or any vessel rigged in the same manner, from the formation of her sails can go some points nearer the wind than a square-rigged vessel; which advantage, on this occasion, enabled Captain Fagg to turn better to windward, by stemming the current, whilst the Spaniards, by opposing their broadsides, were carried away to the eastward. But, to resume the narrative; Barcelo, who had his flag on board the seventy-four, was the last in the chace, and, perceiving his squadron driving to leeward, prudently returned to the Point, to be in readiness to intercept her in the Bay. The fifty-gun ship also laid her head to the current, and keeping that position, drove very little in comparison with her friends. Affairs were thus situated when Captain Fagg, persuaded that the danger was over, boldly steered for the garrison. The fifty-gun ship endeavoured to cut her off from the eastward, but was compelled to retire by our batteries at Europa: and Barcelo got under way to intercept her from the Point; but finding his efforts ineffectual, he was obliged to haul his wind, and giving her two irregular broadsides, of grape and round, followed his unsuccessful squadron to the eastward. The Cutter insultingly returned the Spanish Admiral's fire with her stern-chace, and soon after anchored under our guns.

The expectations of the troops and inhabitants, who were spectators of the action, had been raised to the highest pitch: few doubted but she was a King's vessel; and as no intelligence had been received from England for many weeks, their flattering fancies painted her the messenger of good news; probably, the forerunner of a fleet to their relief. But what was their despondency and disappointment, when they were informed that she was only a privateer, had been a considerable time at sea, and put in for provisions?

Though.

Though our condition in the victualling-office became weekly more and more ferious, yet the Governor generoufly promifed Captain Fagg affiftance. What indeed could be refufed to a man by whofe manœuvres the Port was once more open, and the Bay and Straits again under the command of a Britifh Admiral ? Only two or three half-gallies returned to Cabrita Point; the reft of their fquadron were driven far to leeward of the rock.

Assuming the liberty of a fhort digreffion in this place, it may be neceffary to inform the Reader, of the extent and breadth of the Straits of Gibraltar, and acquaint him, at the fame time, with the opinions of different writers concerning the perpetual current that fets into the Mediterranean Sea, from the great Atlantic Ocean, which has fo long engaged the attention of many celebrated natural philofophers.

The Straits of Gibraltar (formerly known by the name of the Herculean Straits) are about twelve leagues in extent, from Cape Spartel to Ceuta Point, on the African coaft; and from Cape Trafalgar to Europa Point, on the coaft of Spain. At the weftern entrance, they are in breadth about eight leagues, but diminifh confiderably about the middle, oppofite Tarifa (a fmall fifhing-town on the Spanifh coaft, originally a place of great confequence and ftrength) though they widen again between Gibraltar and Ceuta, where they are about five leagues broad.

Philosophers, who have communicated their fentiments on the extraordinary phænomenon of a conftant current, differ widely in accounting for the difpofition of that continual influx of waters, which, it is natural to fuppofe, would, without fome confumption or return, foon overflow the boundaries of the Mediterranean Sea. The late ingenious Dr. Halley was of opinion, that this perpetual

L 2
supply

supply of water from the vaft Atlantic Ocean was intended by
nature to recruit what was daily exhaled in vapour : others again
think, the waters that roll in with the center current are returned,
by two counter-ftreams, along the African and Spanifh fhores. That
there are two counter-ftreams is without doubt ; but their rapidity
and breadth bear little proportion to the principal current. A third
clafs fuppofe a counter-current beneath, and of equal ftrength with
the upper ftream ; and this opinion appears confirmed by a circumftance related by Colonel James, in his defcription of the Herculean
Straits, of a Dutch fhip being funk in action by a French privateer
off Tarifa, which fome time afterwards was caft up near Tangier,
four leagues to the *weftward* of the place where fhe difappeared, and
directly againft the upper current. This hypothefis receives alfo
additional fupport from the repeated difappointments which have
been experienced by many naval officers, in attempting to found the
depth of the Straits with the longeft lines : for the oppofition between
the currents might carry the line in fuch directions as to defeat the
intention of this experiment.

THESE facts feem ftrongly to indicate a recurrency to the weftward ; which, though it may not be fo rapid as the upper ftream,
yet, with the affiftance of the currents along the Spanifh and Barbary
fhores, and the neceffary exhalations, may account for the Mediterranean Sea never increafing by the conftant fupply received from
the Atlantic Ocean. The rapidity of the fuperior current renders
the paffage from the Mediterranean to the weftward very precarious
and uncertain, as fhips never can ftem the ftream without a brifk
Levanter, or eafterly wind. Veffels, therefore, are often detained
weeks, and fometimes months, waiting for a favourable breeze ; in
which cafe they find a comfortable birth in the bay of Gibraltar.—
To return to my narrative.

TWO

Two frigates, on the night of the 14th, joined the enemy's small craft in the Bay, from the weft. It was thought, from some preparations that were made on board the men of war the succeeding evening, that the Admiral intended an attempt to cut out or deftroy thefe fhips : a council was held in the navy, and the practicability of fuch an enterprife debated ; but nothing was done.

The Bay being again open, the night of the 19th, a Moorifh fettee came in, with 39 bullocks and a few fheep : the former were fo weak and poor, that many of them died on the beach as foon as they were landed : they were, however, a moft acceptable fupply. The patron informed us, that a veffel had failed, the preceding night, for the Garrifon, with 40 bullocks, 50 fheep, and 30 goats ; which we imagined was taken by the gallies at the Point. The following day, a Swede ftood in for the Garrifon, with a fignal at her fore-top-gallant maft-head, by which fhe was known to be laden with provifions, and confignd to an inhabitant. Off the Point fhe was boarded by a row-boat, and conducted immediately to Algeziras. The 23d, the Governor proportioned the fuel to the officers. This article was now become fcarce and important. The coals in the Garrifon were few : what fuel, therefore, was iffued at this period, was wood from fhips bought by Government, and broken up for that purpofe, but which had fo ftrongly imbibed the falt water, that it was with the utmoft difficulty we could make it take fire.

A SMALL boat arrived on the 24th, with a packet from Mr. Logie : this packet was landed at Mogadore in South Barbary, by the Fortune floop of war, Captain Squires. If I rightly recollect, it was upon this occafion that the following fuccefsful ftratagem was effected, through the fidelity of a Moor entrufted by Mr. Logie to carry the difpatches to that part of the coaft, whence, to prevent interception, he thought it prudent to send them to Gibraltar. The Spaniards, acquainted with the importance of these dispatches, wished to prevent them coming to our hands; and accordingly offered a thousand Cobs (about 225l. sterling) to the Moor, to induce him to betray his trust, and pretend he had been robbed on his way to the coast. The faithful Moor immediately acquainted the Consul with the offer, who directed him to promise that he would comply. In the interval Mr. Logie prepared false dispatches, in cyphers, signed and dated them St. James's, and affixed a seal from the cover of a letter of Lord Hilsborough's to himself: these were inclosed as usual, and directed to General Eliott. The Moor received part of the bribe, and delivered up the fictitious packet: Mr. Logie on his return appeared much distressed by the accident, and the next evening sent the real dispatches to Gibraltar.

THE wind veering round to the southward, on the 26th Admiral Barcelo returned from Ceuta to his old anchorage off Algeziras, and the port again became closely blockaded. A deserter came in, the morning of the 30th, from the lines; he belonged to the Walon guards: and about five in the afternoon, another Walon deserted to us. They fired several musquets at the latter, and he turned about and returned the shot: three horsemen then pursued him, but were driven back by our artillery. After first gun-fire, two more came in, of the same corps.

THE Enemy's operations continued to be confined to the completion of their batteries, and the finishing of their boyau. In their camp we observed them busily employed in erecting huts for the accommodation of their troops against the winter rains, which now had begun to set in. On the other hand, the Governor made every necessary addition to the works. Water-port covert-way was doubly palisaded, and a battery for three guns erected on the Quay;

a work

a work of mafonry, to mount two guns, was built at Ragged-ftaff; and traverfes of cafks and earth were raifed on the different roads, on the north front, to fecure the communications. Some improvements were alfo made in the batteries and works at Europa.

December commenced with the capture of a Genoefe polacre, becalmed off Europa. Our failors found about £. 220 in money on board, with fome letters, from which we learned that the Enemy fuftained fome lofs in the lines from our fire. The 4th, the Enemy beat a parley, and fent in a mule (belonging to Colonel Green, the chief engineer) which had ftrayed to their lines; an inftance of politenefs which we did not expect. The 8th, another deferter came in; he was purfued, but we protected him. The fubfequent day we obferved feveral men about the weftern and eaftern advanced ftone guard-houfes, which we imagined were pofted there to prevent defertion. Our artillery endeavoured to diflodge them with round fhot, but did not fucceed. The 10th, the Enemy fired feveral rounds, from Fort St. Philip, at our fifhing-boats in the Bay. Four foldiers of De la Motte's regiment, quartered on Windmill-hill, attempted, on the 13th, to defert: fearch was however immediately made for them, and two were retaken. Thofe who efcaped were fuppofed to have got down by a rope-ladder, left by the party employed in cutting brufh-wood for fafcines. The next day another of the enemy endeavoured to come over to us, but, being purfued by two horfemen, was cut down and fecured. One of the horfes belonging to the purfuers was killed by our fire, and the rider much bruifed with the fall. The fucceeding day, this unfortunate man was executed on a new gallows, erected near their artillery-park, and the body, according to cuftom, hung till fun-fet.

The Governor, on the 19th, ordered that no guns fhould be fired from the garrifon at the Enemy's fhipping, if the diftance

required

required more than 6° elevation; except when ſhips were chaſing, or engaged. On the 20th, the Buck, having refitted, failed on a cruiſe to the eaſtward. We were afterwards informed that ſhe unfortunately fell in with a French frigate, which, after a few broadſides, captured the Buck; but before ſhe could be got into port, ſhe ſunk from the damage received in the action. On the night of the 26th, we had a moſt violent ſtorm of rain, with dreadful thunder and lightning. The ſucceeding morning a vaſt quantity of wood, cork, &c. was floating under our walls: the rain had waſhed it from the banks of the Palmones and Gua-daranque, and it was wafted by the wind over to our ſide of the Bay. Fuel had long been a ſcarce article: this ſupply was therefore confidered as a miraculous interference of Providence in our favour.

THE Enemy, the 27th, fired four guns from Fort St. Philip: one of the ſhot ſtruck the extremity of Prince's lines. Whether theſe were fired to frighten our fiſhermen, who were dragging their nets near the farther gardens, without Land-port, or only as an experiment, we could not ſay, as they immediately ceaſed on our returning the fire from Willis's. The day following, came in three deſerters; and the ſame morning the Fly packet-boat arrived from Tangier, with 40 goats, fowls and eggs, but no mail: this cargo, though trifling, was highly acceptable. The deſerters informed us that the enemy were almoſt overflowed in their lines, from the late exceſſive rains: in ſome places, particularly near the new batteries, the water was two and three feet deep; and their efforts to drain it off had hitherto been ineffectual. The 28th, a ſoldier of Hardenberg's deſerted down the back of the rock.

JANUARY, 1780, did not commence with any very intereſting events. A ſquadron of men of war paſſed through to the weſt on
the

the 2d: it being hazy, we could not diftinguifh of what nation they were; but many thought them Spaniards from Carthagena. On the evening of the 5th, a fire broke out in the enemy's camp, which, we afterwards learned, deftroyed four officers marquees, and fix or feven huts. The following day, after gun-fire, two Walons deferted to us: they brought information that upwards of forty mortars were mounted in the lines, and that all their batteries were completed with cannon.

A NEAPOLITAN polacre was luckily driven under our guns on the 8th, and obliged to come in. On board we found about 6000 bufhels of barley, a cargo (circumftanced as we were) of ineftimable value. The bakers had long been limited to the quantity of bread daily to be iffued to the inhabitants, and fentries were placed at the wickets where it was delivered, to prevent confufion and riot. The ftrongeft neverthelefs had the advantage; fo that numbers of women, children, and infirm perfons, returned to their miferable habitations, frequently without tafting, for fome days, that chief, and perhaps neceffary fupport of life. The inhabitants were not the only fufferers in this fcene of diftrefs; many officers and foldiers had families to fupport out of the pittance received from the victualling-office. A foldier, with his wife and three children, would inevitably have been ftarved to death, had not the generous contribution of his corps relieved his family: one woman actually died through want; and many were fo enfeebled, that it was not without great attention they recovered: thiftles, dandelion, wild leeks, &c. were for fome time the daily nourifhment of numbers. Few fupplies arriving from Barbary, and there appearing little profpect of relief from England, famine began to prefent itfelf with its attendant horrors: had there been a glimmering hope of affiftance from home, it would have enabled many to fupport

M themfelves

themſelves under this accumulation of diſtreſs; but, alas! we ſeemed entirely abandoned to our fortune.

Not only bread, but every article neceſſary to the ſupport of life, was hard to be procured, and only to be purchaſed at exorbitant prices. Veal, mutton, and beef, ſold from two ſhillings and ſix-pence, to four ſhillings per pound; freſh pork, from two to three ſhillings; ſalt beef and pork, one ſhilling and three-pence per pound; fowls, eighteen ſhillings per couple; ducks, a guinea; fire-wood, five ſhillings per hundred weight; a pint of milk and water, one ſhilling and three-pence. Vegetables were extremely ſcarce: a ſmall cabbage coſt one ſhilling and ſix-pence, and a ſmall bunch of the outward leaves ſold for five-pence: Iriſh butter, two ſhillings and ſix-pence per pound; eggs, ſix-pence each; and candles, two ſhillings and ſix-pence per pound. The beſt fiſh was moſt exorbitantly dear, conſidering on what terms the garriſon had been formerly ſupplied. It is natural to ſuppoſe, from the rock being almoſt ſurrounded with the ſea, that we ſhould have a conſtant reſource in this article; the contrary was however the caſe: our fiſhermen were foreigners, and being under no regulation, they exacted, by degrees, moſt extravagant ſums for what ſome months before we ſhould have looked upon with diſguſt.

This extreme ſcarcity of proviſions, it may well be imagined, could not fail to exerciſe the invention of individuals. A ſingular mode of hatching chickens was about this time ſucceſsfully practiſed by the Hanoverians; and, as it may be acceptable to ſome readers, the proceſs, as communicated by a friend, is here inſerted. The eggs were placed, with ſome cotton, wool or other warm ſub-ſtance, in a tin caſe of ſuch conſtruction as to be heated either by a lamp or hot water; and, by a proper attention to the tempera-ture of heat, the eggs were commonly hatched in the uſual time

of

of a hen's fitting. A capon (however ftrange it may appear) was then taught to rear them : to reconcile him to this truft, the feathers were plucked from his breaft and belly; he was then gently fcourged with a bunch of nettles, and placed upon the young hatch, whofe downy warmth afforded fuch comfort to the bared and fmarting parts, that he, from that period, reared them up, with equal care and tendernefs as if they had been his own offspring.

EARLY in the morning of the 10th, a fquadron of fhips was feen to the eaft, which had paffed through in the night; five were of the line, and one under jury-mafts : fuppofed to be Count D'Ef-taing's fleet from the Weft Indies. The fame day a foldier of the 58th regiment was executed for ftealing : he was the firft man who had fuffered fince General Eliott had been Governor. The day following, the enemy fired, from Fort St. Barbara, on a clergyman performing the laft office over the corpfe of a foldier of the 72d regiment, at the burial-ground near the Governor's meadow. The party immediately retired, though not before they had depofited their charge. As this conduct convinced us that the enemy would not permit us to bury our dead without the garrifon, a part of the red fands behind the Princefs of Wales's lines was appropriated to that purpofe.

THE 12th, they furprifed us again with ten fhot from Fort St. Philip : feveral came into town, and did fome trifling damage amongft the buildings. The inhabitants, whofe alarms had not totally fubfided fince the middle of September, when the Governor opened upon the enemy, were now perfectly convinced they meant to return our fire; and accordingly began, on the firft report of their guns, to remove themfelves to the fouthward. Some in the greateft confufion endeavoured to fecure their valuables in

town;

1780,
Jan.

town; but the firing ceasing, the fugitives, before night, summoned up sufficient courage to return. A woman, passing near one of the houses, was slightly hurt. It was singular that a female should be the first person wounded at this remarkable siege. In the evening, the commanding officers had orders to inform their corps, that the Governor was under the necessity of curtailing the weekly allowance of provisions. Disagreeable as this intelligence was, and particularly when we consider the distress which many experienced even with the full allowance, the men received it without the smallest appearance of discontent. Convinced of the necessity, they acquiesced with cheerfulness: indeed, to do them justice, in all the vicissitudes of this trying period, the garrison submitted, without murmuring, to every necessary regulation, however unpleasing. It was fortunate for many, that this substraction of provisions did not continue long: nay, it remains a doubt with some, whether, at the time, the Governor was not apprised of a relief being near; and did not enact this regulation, solely to make trial of the disposition of his troops. If so, how satisfactory a circumstance must it have been, to find the army under his command accord, with so much good-humour, to what might be considered as a real hardship, however indispensable!

ADMIRAL DUFF, on the 13th, gave orders to the men of war and armed vessels, to be prepared, in case a convoy was near, to afford every protection to any straggling ships that might attempt the Port before the main body arrived. This caution confirmed us in the opinion of a convoy being expected; and a general joy was diffused throughout the garrison, at the flattering, though probably distant prospect. Two days after, an ordnance-brig, which with other vessels seemed to be going through to the east, suddenly altered her course, and, notwithstanding she was opposed by the enemy, anchored under our walls. A ship with the British flag,

entering

entering the Bay, was so uncommon a sight, that almost the whole garrison were assembled at the southward to welcome her in; but words are insufficient to describe their transports on being informed that she was one of a large convoy which had sailed the latter end of the preceding month for our relief. The distressed Jews, and other inhabitants, were frantic with joy; and the repeated huzzas from all quarters, for some time prevented further enquiries. We afterwards learned, that she had parted company with the convoy in the Bay of Biscay, and off Cadiz had discovered nine sail of large ships, which the master concluded were Spaniards stationed there to oppose their entrance. The latter part of their information gave us much uneasiness. The enemy, we concluded, would have good intelligence of the force of the British convoy. If, therefore, any opposition was intended, a superior squadron would consequently be stationed at the entrance of the Straits. These reflections damped, in a great degree, the pleasure we before experienced, and made us apprehensive that the relief was not so near as we at first expected. The prospect of it had however a very visible effect on the price of provisions, which immediately fell more than two thirds.

SINCE it was probable that straggling ships might attempt the Port before the body of the convoy approached, the Childers sloop of war, and armed vessels, were ordered to cruise in the Bay, to protect them from the Enemy's small-craft. Previous to the arrival of the brig, a soldier of the 58th regiment deserted from a party employed behind the Rock in gathering shrubs, &c. for fascines. The 16th, a Walon deserted to us, by whom we were informed, that the Enemy had every thing prepared in their lines to bombard the Town. - At another time we should have been greatly alarmed at this intelligence; but our thoughts were too much engaged with the pleasing, though uncertain hopes of relief, to reflect on the
consequences

1780,
Jan.

confequences of a bombardment. In the evening, our apprehenfions concerning the convoy were totally difpelled, by the arrival of a brig laden with flour, which communicated the joyful news that Admiral Sir George Brydges Rodney had captured, off the coaft of Portugal, a Spanifh 64 gun fhip, five of 32 and 28 guns, with feventeen merchantmen, belonging to the Caracca Company, going from Bilboa to Cadiz ; and that, with a FLEET of TWENTY-ONE fail of the line, and a large convoy of merchant-fhips and tranfports, he was proceeding to our relief. Every idea of oppofition at this information immediately vanifhed ; and we once more anticipated the flattering profpect of feeing the Britifh flag again triumphantly difplayed in the Mediterranean.

THE weather, on the 17th, was very hazy ; but clearing up the fucceeding day, one of the prizes arrived without any oppofition from the Enemy. The midfhipman who brought her in informed us, that when he parted with the fleet on the 16th, Sir George was engaged with a Spanifh fquadron off Cape St. Mary's ; and that, juft before they loft fight of them, a fhip of the line blew up ; but he was at too great a diftance to diftinguifh whether fhe was friend or foe. In the evening, one of the armed Caracca prizes came in, but no further particulars of the engagement could be learned. Our anxiety concerning the event of the action was however removed, a few hours afterwards, by the appearance of the convoy off Europa. The wind, at that critical time, unfortunately failed them ; and the vivid flafhes of lightning, by which we had difcovered the fleet at the firft, only ferved to exhibit them to us, driving with the current to the eaftward of the rock. The Apollo frigate, Capt. Pownall, with one or two merchantmen, neverthelefs got in about eleven ; and by the former, the Governor and Garrifon were acquainted with the agreeable tidings of a complete VICTORY over the Spanifh Admiral, who, with three others of his fquadron,

was

was taken; one was run a{hore, another blown up in the engagement, and the re{t di{per{ed.

WE now found, that the plan for relieving Gibraltar had been
conducted at home with {uch {ecrecy and prudence, that the Enemy
never {u{pected that Sir George meant to convoy the tran{ports to
the Straits, with {o {trong a fleet. By their intelligence from Bre{t,
they under{tood he was to {eparate in a certain latitude, and proceed,
with the main body of the men of war, to the We{t-Indies.
Thus deceived, they concluded that the tran{ports with their convoy
would fall an ea{y prey to their {quadron, which confi{ted of eleven
men of war, all cho{en {hips from their grand fleet.

AT day-break, on the morning of the 19th, the Enemy unma{ked
one of their fourteen-gun batteries. The guns, with tho{e in the
fort, were all elevated, and the lines reinforced with two regiments
of infantry. The Governor, notwith{tanding the{e appearances,
ordered a royal {alute to be fired at {ix o'clock from Willis's. The
Panther man of war was decorated, and al{o fired a {alute on
account of this victory. About {even the Edgar arrived, with the
Phœnix prize of 80 guns, having on board the Spani{h Admiral,
Don Juan de Langara y Huarte. This {hip had lo{t her mizen
and main top-ma{ts, but {eemed little injured in the hull. The
Admiral, who was wounded in the engagement, was conducted
on {hore in the evening to lodgings in town, and had every attention and compliment paid him, which were due to his rank. At
night, Admiral Digby, in the Prince George, worked round Europa
with eleven or twelve {hips; but Sir George remained with the
crippled prizes, and with the main body of the fleet, off Marbella,
a Spani{h town, formerly of note, {ixteen leagues to the ea{tward
of Gibraltar.

THE

THE 20th, being the anniverſary of the King of Spain's birth-day, Admiral Barcelo's ſhips were decorated according to cuſtom. When the colours were ſtruck in the evening, the flag-ſhip, with her conſort of 50 guns, was hauled cloſe in land; and the next day a large party began to erect a battery on the ſhore for their protection; being apprehenſive, probably, of an attack from the Britiſh fleet. The night of the 21ſt, the Enemy unmaſked the other batteries in the lines, which again cauſed a general diſturbance amongſt the inhabitants. Every thing ſeemed now prepared to fire upon the town. The convoy continued beating up; but the prizes were ſo damaged in their rigging, that they could not be expected to make the Bay till the wind veered round to the eaſt. Early on the 22d, ſeveral men of war, in coming into the Bay, were carried down under the Enemy's batteries, near Point Mala, which occaſioned a general alarm in their camp. Drums beat to arms, and their artillery opened in an inſtant. The boats of the fleet, however, were ordered to their aſſiſtance, and the ſhips were towed back without receiving much damage. One man was killed, and two wounded, on board the Terrible; all of them Spaniſh priſoners.

SIR GEORGE, on his arrival off the coaſt of Barbary, had ſent intelligence to Mr. Logie, to prepare ſupplies for the garriſon. Three veſſels, therefore, ſailed in the courſe of the 22d for Tetuan, to bring over what was at hand. The Conſul had provided cattle, faſcines, pickets, &c. in readineſs for the ſhips when they arrived; but, to his ſurpriſe, the ſhips ſent in the hurry of buſineſs, under convoy of the Bedford, were tranſports, fitted up for the reception of troops, with many weeks proviſions on board; and before the births could be removed to admit the ſupplies, the wind came eaſterly, and the ſhips were obliged to return without them. This overſight was of great detriment to the garriſon, as at this period we might have procured freſh proviſions, which with economy would have

ſerved

ferved for fome months. The garrifon veffels were afterwards fent for thefe articles; but after Sir George Rodney's departure, moft of them were detained by the vigilance of the Enemy's cruifers.

WE learned by the Childers, on the 23d, that Sir George was at anchor, with the prizes, in Tetuan Road; and waited only a favourable wind to join the remainder of the fleet in the Bay. As the town of Tetuan has frequently been mentioned in the preceding pages, and probably will as often occur in the courfe of the fubfequent; the reader will perhaps not be difpleafed to find in this place a fhort defcription of it. Tetuan is a very ancient town in Barbary, fituated to the fouth-eaft of Ceuta, about fix miles from the fea, on a river which meanders beautifully through a pleafant country; but which has a bar at the entrance, that renders it unnavigable for large fhips. Small veffels get up about two miles, as far as Marteen, which is the quay and port of Tetuan. The town is walled round with fquare towers at different diftances, to flank the curtains. It is built on the gentle flope of a hill; and the houfes being white, with flat roofs, have the appearance at a diftance of an encampment. The buildings are fo contrived, that a perfon may go from one end of the town to the other, without defcending into the ftreets; and in this manner their women, by occupying the upper ftories, vifit each other without being expofed to the fight of the male fex in the ftreets below.

THE Town has a manufactory, and carries on a confiderable trade, principally in barter: the road is, however, fo expofed towards the eaft, that fhips cannot remain there during the Levant winds. The Moors exchange cattle, poultry, and fruit, for other articles; and when there is a truce between the powers, fupply feveral parts of Spain with provifions. The oranges of Tetuan are efteemed the largeft and beft-flavoured of any in that part of the globe.

THE Enemy, we imagined, were not a little alarmed by the casual appearance of our ships on the morning of the 22d; as, for several days after, they were busy in removing cannon from their artillery-park to the different batteries along the coast. At Algeziras, the top-masts and yards of the men of war were struck, and the ships hauled as close in land, under the protection of the new battery, as the depth of water would admit. Several Spanish officers were now permitted to return on their parole to Spain. The 24th, the Childers sailed back to Tetuan; and soon after, arrived a British letter of marque from Newfoundland, laden with salt-fish.

WHILST the fleet remained in the Bay, the Governor and Garrison were often honoured with the presence of the Royal Midshipman, Prince William-Henry; and when that youthful hero, on his return, laid his early laurels at the feet of his Royal Father, he presented, at the same time, a plan of the garrison, in the relief of which he had made his first naval essay. In that plan were delineated the improvements which the place had undergone, and the new batteries erected on the heights since the commencement of the blockade.

THE mention of his Royal Highnefs brings to my recollection an anecdote of him, which occurred whilst the fleet was in the Bay. The Spanish Admiral, Don Juan Langara, one morning visited Admiral Digby, to whose charge the Prince was intrusted; and Don Langara was of course introduced to his Royal Highnefs. During the conference between the Admirals, Prince William retired; and when it was intimated that Don Juan wished to return, His Royal Highnefs appeared in his character of midshipman, and respectfully informed the Admiral, that the boat was ready. The

Spaniard,

Spaniard, aſtoniſhed to ſee the ſon of a Monarch acting as a petty officer, could not help exclaiming, " Well does Great-Britain merit " the empire of the ſea, when the humbleſt ſtations in her Navy " are ſupported by Princes of the Blood."

THREE of the enemy, on the 25th, deſerted to the garriſon ; a fourth, attempting to deſert, was retaken, and another was ſhot by the purſuers within muſket-ſhot of our lines. We fired from Willis's at the horſemen who followed them, and wounded two of their horſes. The deſerters ſaid it was reported, that the Enemy intended bombarding the town the ſucceeding day. For ſeveral preceding months we had reaſon, from their operations, to think ſuch an event not improbable. Seven or eight mortar-batteries had been diſtributed along their lines, in which, according to our intelligence, were upwards of forty mortars : theſe, with the cannon bearing on the garriſon from their gun-batteries, amounted in all to upwards of 100 pieces of ordnance. They therefore were not unprepared for ſuch ſervice ; but whether the circumſtance of the Spaniſh Admiral and officers being lodged in town might not at that time in ſome degree influence their conduct, or whether they were over-awed by the ſtrong naval force in their neighbourhood, they deferred the bombardment to a more diſtant period.

SIR GEORGE arrived in the Sandwich from Tetuan on the 25th ; and the following day, the prizes, and remaining men of war, were all at anchor in the Bay. A council of war wa. immediately held on the Admiral's arrival ; but the ſubject of their debates was not made public. Late in the evening of the ſame day, a Newfoundland veſſel with fiſh, coming in, approached ſo cloſe to the oppoſite coaſt, that our guard-boats were obliged to bring her to her proper birth.

1780,
Jan.

THE Fortune floop carried over to Point Mala, on the 26th, the Spanifh wounded prifoners: Admiral Langara, with his fuite, ftill remained in town. Admiral Sir George Brydges Rodney landed on the 27th at Ragged-ftaff, and, after vifiting the Spanifh Admiral, dined with the Governor. Prince William, with Admiral Digby, &c. likewife dined at the Convent. The fame day, the Governor ordered thofe foldiers wives and children, who were not provided with twelve months provifions, to prepare to leave the garrifon with the fleet: 250 lb. of flour, or 360 lb. of bifcuit, was ftated as fufficient for one perfon. By this regulation many ufelefs hands were fent home, which would have been a vaft burthen on the garrifon, circumftanced as we afterwards were. The evening of the 28th, the Childers failed for England with difpatches from the Admiral; but meeting with a gale of wind at weft, fhe was compelled to return, after lofing her fore-yard, and throwing four guns over-board. At night came in a deferter from the Walon guards.

ABOUT noon, on the 29th, a large fhip appeared from the weftward: on doubling Cabrita Point fhe was difcovered to be an enemy. Signals were inftantly made for the Edgar and two frigates to attack her. In the mean time the Spaniard feemed greatly confufed, but at laft worked clofe in land, between two barbet batteries at the Point. Several broadfides were exchanged between her and the Edgar, whilft the frigates attacked the batteries. They were however after fome time recalled, the Admiral being apprehenfive that they might fuftain greater damage from the land, than the object in action would excufe. The fame day the fecond battalion of the 73d regiment, or Lord M'Leod's High-landers, commanded by Lieut. Col. George M'Kenzie, difembarked from on board the fleet at the New mole, and took poffeffion of the cafemates in the King's baftion, &c. This regiment was intended for Minorca; but General Eliott thought proper, with the advice

of

of the Admirals, &c. to detain them. Their strength at this time was 30 officers, 6 staff officers, 50 serjeants, 22 drummers, and 944 rank and file : an excellent reinforcement in our situation, since the scurvy had already begun to appear among us. Colonels Picton and Mawhood, with many other officers, joined their corps also by this fleet. On the night of the 29th, came in three more Walons. The Minorca convoy sailed on the 31st, under the Marlborough, Invincible, &c. The wind changing to the east in the evening, the Childers made another attempt to pass the Straits; which she effected, and carried home dispatches giving authentic accounts of the preceding victory.

Sir George, when he captured the Caracca fleet, judged that the cargoes of several would be useful to the garrison : he therefore brought with him what ships he thought would be serviceable, and landed their freights along with the supplies which Government had sent out. A great number of guns of heavy metal, and some hundred barrels of powder, were also purchased from the Spanish prizes by the Governor, notwithstanding he had received a large supply of the latter by the convoy. The artillery (whose constant practice it was to try the strength of powder on the batteries) afterwards compared the quality and strength of the British and Spanish powder, and found the former greatly superior.

In the beginning of February, the wind from the S. W. blew a strong gale, which, from the foulness of the anchorage off Rosia Bay, &c. involved the fleet in great distress. Some of them were in very imminent danger of being forced upon the rocks, particularly one of the Spanish prizes, which without doubt would have experienced that fate, if seasonable assistance had not been sent her, and the wind had not abated. The 3d, Admiral Barcelo again hoisted his flag and ensign, having secured his ships by a strong boom, and completed the battery on the land, which mounted
22 guns.

22 guns.   Merlons were also added to the Fort on the Island, which before was *en barbet*.

THREE deserters came in on the 5th: they were immediately sent on board the fleet, where the others had been ordered the preceding day, to take their passage for England. These men gave dismal accounts of the Enemy's sufferings in camp, where universal discontent prevailed on account of the great scarcity and dearness of provisions. We little doubted the truth of this intelligence: the neighbourhood of their camp, from our own knowledge of the country, was not capable of subsisting so large an army; consequently they were obliged to be supplied with provisions, &c. from places at a distance; and these resources, since Admiral Rodney's arrival, had been cut off. Our cruisers, in truth, not only obstructed these supplies, but also prevented the garrison of Ceuta from receiving the refreshments from Spain which their situation made necessary; and our intelligence from Barbary mentioned that that garrison was in a similar, if not worse condition than their opposite friends. If Sir George therefore had continued some time longer in the Mediterranean, our enemies probably would have been reduced to greater difficulties than we ourselves had experienced.

As THIS fortress is in some degree connected with the subject of the present narrative, it may not be improper to relieve the reader's attention by a brief description of it. The town of Ceuta is situated on the coast of Barbary, about 15 miles to the southward of Gibraltar. In the æra of the Romans it was a town of some note, but on the decline of that empire fell, like others, to the dominion of the Goths and Moors. Ceuta remained in the possession of the latter till the year 1414, when John I. King of Portugal, with a formidable force, surprised and took it. The Moors afterwards made many attempts to recover it, but in vain; and ever since,

it

it has remained in the poffeffion of the Chriftians. Upon the demife of Henry of Portugal, in 1578, that crown was feized upon by the Spaniards ; Ceuta confequently became a Spanifh garrifon : and when the Portuguefe revolted, under John Duke of Braganza, in 1640, and again eftablifhed themfelves into a diftinct kingdom, Ceuta did not, with the reft of the Empire, return to its natural allegiance, but continued in the hands of the Spaniards, by whom it has been held ever fince.

BEING a promontory projecting into the fea, the fituation of Ceuta is not much different from that of Gibraltar. The town, which is built on the neck of land that joins it to the Continent, is ftrongly fortified in the modern manner. The fuburbs are at fome diftance, in order to be more out of reach of the fhells, in cafe of an attack from the land ; and they extend to the foot of a mountain, at the extremity of the peninfula, on which are erected a watch-tower and caftle, furrounded with a fortified wall, about a league in circumference. The fortifications are kept in good repair by flaves, who are fentenced to this punifhment from the different prifons in Spain ; and a ftrong garrifon is kept in the fortrefs, to prevent a furprife from the Moors, who, like the Spaniards with refpect to Gibraltar, have a watchful eye over it. The city is regularly furnifhed with provifions from the oppofite ports in Spain ; and being deftitute of water, which was formerly conducted by an aqueduct from the neighbourhood, is fupplied with that article from Eftepona, a fmall Spanifh fifhing-town about nine leagues to the eaftward of Gibraltar.

ANOTHER deferter came in on the 10th of February. The day following, the invalids and women embarked on board the fleet. By the 12th the fupplies were all landed, and the rigging of the Spanifh prizes being repaired, the fleet prepared to return. The fame day a flag of truce brought over fome Englifh prifoners : one

of

of them, the mafter of a merchantman, which had been taken in
her voyage to the Garrifon, informed us that the boom at Algeziras
was a twenty-two-inch cable-rope, buoyed up by cafks, to prevent
our fending fire-fhips among their fhipping.

THE Spanifh Admiral, having regulated with Sir George Rodney
every thing concerning the exchange and releafe of prifoners, was
permitted, on the 13th, to return upon his parole into Spain. · He
was conducted, with part of his fuite, in the Governor's carriage,
to the Spanifh lines, where he was received by his friends, and with
them proceeded on to the camp.   The fucceeding day, the remainder
of the Spanifh officers were taken by the Fortune floop, and landed
at the Orange-grove.   Lieut. Williams, of the navy, (who, after
taking poffeffion of one of the Spanifh prizes in the action off St.
Mary's, was obliged to run her afhore near Cadiz, and furrender
himfelf prifoner,) returned, with another officer, on board the floop,
to the Garrifon.   The liberal and polite behaviour of the Navy and
the Governor to Don Langara and his countrymen, made a fenfible
and lafting impreffion on their minds, and was, confeffedly, of great
advantage to the Englifh prifoners in Spain ; particularly to thofe
taken in our neighbourhood, who ever afterwards were treated with
great attention and humanity.

IN the evening of the 13th, the Britifh fleet got under way,
excepting the Edgar and the Panther fhips of the line, the Enterprife and Porcupine frigates, which were left behind, as great part
of their crews had been removed to man the prizes.   The enemy,
on their appearing in motion, immediately gave the alarm, which
was communicated by fignals from their towers along the coafts
towards Cadiz.   At dufk, few of our fhips were in fight from the
upper part of the hill.

CHAP-

CHAPTER IV.

*The Spaniards renew the blockade.—Attempt to burn our shipping by nine
fire-ships, but miscarry.—Gun-boats.—Garrison again distressed.—
Enemy effectually cut off the supplies from Barbary.—Break ground
in advance from their lines.—Scurvy very prevalent.—Greatly
relieved by the use of lemons.—Mode of using this vegetable acid.—
Garrison obtain a few supplies from Minorca.—Enemy retarded in
their operations.—Spirited action between the Enemy and an English
polacre.—Garrison obliged to quit the gardens on the neutral ground.
—Tangier.—Speedwell cutter arrives after a spirited engagement.—
A spy discovered.—Mr. Logie, the British Consul in Barbary,
expelled the Emperor's dominions.—Cruel treatment which he and
the other British subjects experienced.—Cause of this event.—A
memorial from the Officers of the Garrison.—Great distress of the
troops.—The Kite cutter, Captain Trollop, arrives with intelligence
that the British fleet is at the entrance of the Straits.*

THE Garrison might now be considered in a very perfect state
of defence.   The scurvy indeed had begun to affect many, and
threatened to become more general; but we flattered ourselves that
the Enemy would give up their intention of starving us to a surrender,
and, by relaxing in their vigilance at sea, might afford us an opportunity of receiving constant supplies of those articles most essential
to health. Our stores and magazines were full; a reinforcement had
joined the garrison; and new spirits were infused into the troops,
since they were convinced, from the powerful force sent to their
relief, that they were not forgotten in the multiplicity of objects
which necessarily engaged the attention of our friends at home.

1780,
Feb.

O   ADMIRAL

ADMIRAL DUFF having returned on board the fleet to England, the command of the squadron that remained in the Bay, consequently devolved on Captain Eliott of the Edgar, who, on the 14th of February, hoisted his broad pendant as Commodore.

THE 16th of the same month, Admiral Barcelo removed the boom at Algeziras, and warped out to his former anchorage, immediately detaching his small craft to Cabrita Point, to intercept any ships that might attempt coming in. In the afternoon, the Enemy executed two men in camp, who, it was imagined, had been retaken in attempting to defert: their bodies were not cut down until the 20th. This punishment feemed however to have little effect; for at night three others came in, having swum round Fort Barbara. The multitude of deserters from the Spanish lines during the whole of the siege, is one of the circumstances least capable of a satisfactory explanation. What could these unhappy men expect in a confined and blockaded garrison, and even at a time when they could not fail to be acquainted with the distress and difficulties under which we laboured? The very act of escaping was attended with innumerable dangers; and, should the Garrison afterwards fall into the hands of the Enemy, they were certain to meet with the severest punishment. There is, however, a kind of heroism in the passions: disgust, or resentment, will prompt men to overlook dangers and difficulties, which, in the line of their duty, would be esteemed infurmountable.

A VENETIAN came in from the west, on the 21st: she spoke the British fleet all well to the west of Cape St. Vincent. The subsequent day, a Dutch prize, laden with flour, was sent in by the Maidstone privateer, which arrived herself on the 23d. Several other vessels came in during the intermediate time to the 27th: when a Spanish squadron of four line-of-battle ships, two frigates, and

and a xebeque joined Admiral Barcelo from the weſt, and again blocked up the port. From the patched and diſorderly appearance of their ſails and rigging, it was conjectured that they were fitted up in haſte, and ſolely for the duty of the blockade: it gave us however ſome uneaſineſs to find them again likely to adopt their former ſyſtem.

At day-break, on the preceding day, we diſcovered a veſſel at anchor off Waterport, which we fired upon, ſuppoſing her to be a Spaniard: ſhe immediately ſent her boat to Ragged-ſtaff, and informed us that ſhe was of Naples, and bound to London ; that ſhe had touched at Minorca, and had on board two Engliſh diſcharged ſoldiers, and two women paſſengers. The boat returned, and ſoon after went on ſhore at Fort St. Philip, where it remained about half an hour. In the evening the Enemy fired a ſhot at the veſſel ; upon which ſhe ſent her boat a ſecond time aſhore : we anſwered the ſhot from Willis's ; nevertheleſs at night ſhe went over unperceived to Algeziras.

In the beginning of March, three regiments decamped from the Enemy's army, and took different routes. On the night of the 2d, two Genoeſe ſailors, who had formerly belonged to a privateer of the garriſon, came over to us in a ſmall boat from Algeziras. The following day a Spaniſh convoy under a Commodore arrived in the Bay, from the weſt. The Governor, on the 11th, ordered the Garriſon to be victualled monthly (bread excepted) in the following proportion: for a ſoldier, each firſt and third week, 1 lb. of pork, 2¼ lb. of ſalt fiſh, which had been purchaſed from the Newfoundland ſhip ; 2 pints of peaſe ; 1 lb. of flour ; ¼ lb. of raiſins ; 1 lb. of rice ; 5 oz. of butter ; 1½ pint of oatmeal. Second and fourth week, 1¼ lb. of beef, 2 lb. of fiſh, 2 pints of peaſe, 1 lb. of rice, 5 oz. of butter, 1¼ lb. of wheat, ¼ lb. of raiſins. The ſalt cod

O 2   being

being indifferent of its kind, and the foldiers not having proper
vegetables to drefs with it, proved very pernicious. This article
continued to be delivered for near feven months ; and undoubtedly, in
a great degree, promoted that dreadful diforder, the fcurvy, which,
before Sir George Rodney arrived, had made its appearance, and
aftewards became very general and fatal. The Governor, however,
in this new diftribution, confidered the hofpital, whofe proportion
of falt meat was lefs, and more nourifhing articles iffued in ftead.

Notwithstanding the repeated affurances from the Spaniards,
that the Englifh prifoners in our neighbourhood fhould be exchanged
for thofe taken with Admiral Langara, none were yet fent in agreeably
to that Admiral's promife : Commodore Eliott was therefore under
the neceffity of making a formal demand, and to enforce it told them,
if they did not comply, he fhould expect the Spanifh Admiral would
return with the officers then upon their parole. This convinced
them the Commodore was no longer to be trifled with : accordingly,
on the 12th, about 390 Britifh feamen were received on-board the
Fortune floop, and diftributed amongft the men of war, whofe
crews, as I have mentioned before, were fent to man the Spanifh
prizes. The fame day a Moorifh floop came in from Malaga, and
brought intelligence that the Enemy had fitted up feveral fire-fhips
in the Bay. In the evening, three of the 72d abfented themfelves
from their corps : fearch was made the fucceeding day, and two of
them were difcovered afleep in a cave, behind the Sugar-Loaf Point.
They had cut up their working-dreffes into fhreds, which were tied
together to favour their defcent down the rock ; and it is imagined
the following night they would have repeated their attempt to get off.
One of thefe men was afterwards executed, but the other was
pardoned.

THE

THE Fly packet arrived the 14th, with an Englifh mail. In the afternoon the Maidftone came in, with a fettee prize, which the Captain had cut out of Malaga road. A privateer, called the Alert, beat in from the Weft on the 15th, notwithftanding an eafterly wind. A prize following her was taken off Cabrita Point. . The 17th, the Enemy fent in 41 Britifh feamen, who were diftributed as before.

THE Enemy at this time were not particularly employed. Some new arrangements were made in their artillery-park ; and in their camp they were bufy, collecting brufh-wood for fafcines, which caufed various conjectures in the Garrifon concerning their future operations. A falute and feu-de-joie were fired in their camp on the 19th, fuppofed to be occafioned by the birth of a fon to the Princefs of Afturias.. The night of the 23d, the Alert failed with difpatches for England ; and on the 29th we received from the Enemy more Englifh prifoners. In the courfe of the month the Garrifon loft four men by defertion.

APRIL was not remarkable for any events of moment. On the 2d, the Porcupine frigate, Sir Charles Knowles, Bart. failed to the eaftward on a cruife. The 5th, arrived the Fly packet: fhe reported that a merchantman, bound to the Garrifon, had been obliged, by a north wind, when fhe was almoft arrived in the Bay, to pafs to the eaftward, and put into Tetuan, where fhe waited a favourable opportunity to renew her attempt. The Fortune floop, on the 6th, took over to the enemy 300 Spaniards, who had been confined as prifoners for fome time in our Navy-hofpital. She returned with nine Britifh, and two days after took over 280 prifoners. The night of the 12th a floop, with two fettees, came in from Tangier: the former brought a packet from Mr. Logic ; and the latter, cattle, and other acceptable articles. The following day we we observed the Enemy forming a bridge of pontons acrofs the mouth of the river Guadaranque.   At night, the Hyena frigate, Capt. Thompfon, arrived in thirteen days from England.   She was chafed by the Enemy's cruifers, and fired at, but received very little damage.   The 20th, the Edgar, Commodore Eliott, and the Hyena, with a privateer, failed to the weft, notwithftanding the Enemy's fuperiority in the Bay.   Admiral Barcelo feemed to fufpeft their intentions ; for inftantly on their appearing under fail, he made a fignal for his fquadron to purfue.   The Edgar and her confort were, however, out of fight before the Spaniards got abreaft of Cabrita Point.

Towards the conclufion of the month, the Enemy were more aftive in their camp, and fometimes in the lines ; to which place they brought down a great quantity of fafcines.   They were chiefly employed in raifing the boyau, and making repairs, which were however fo trifling, that our artillery did not difturb them.   Befides the arrivals already noted, we received fupplies by two or three boats from the Barbary coaft ; and in the courfe of the month, three deferters came over from the Enemy, one of whom fwam from Teffé's battery to Landport.

May.   May was not lefs barren of interefting occurrences than the preceding month.   Several deferters attempted to get in, but fome were fo unfortunate as to be overtaken by the purfuers.   Thefe wretches were generally executed the fucceeding day, but the example did not deter others from fimilar attempts.

The 4th, the Fly returned with fowls, leather, and fruit.   Two days following, the Enemy's army were under arms in two divifions, and performed a fham-engagement.   One divifion took poft on the eminence above the Stone-quarry, under the Queen of Spain's chair, and was attacked by the other from below.   After a fmart cannonade,

and

and brisk discharge of musquetry, the party above gave way; but the night prevented our observing the conclusion. The succeeding day, the Fortune received from a Spanish flag of truce 47 prisoners, very few of whom were British. At night small arms were discharged on the neutral ground, supposed to be at some deserters who were coming off. One Walon reached the barrier, and informed us that several of his comrades agreed to follow him. The 10th, two men were executed in the Spanish camp; probably, the same who were retaken.

ANOTHER deserter, belonging to the regiment of Estremadura, came in on the 11th, and was remarkable for being the first native of Spain who deserted. The Spanish infantry in general is raised upon a local establishment. Each district is required, by an ancient law called the *Quinta*, to furnish a certain proportion of troops; and the men are enrolled for about seven or eight years service, after which time they are permitted to return to their respective provinces: and, as the Spaniards are all strongly attached to their native spot, desertion is consequently less common with them than with any other troops. Most of the men who deserted to us, came from those regiments in their service which are composed of foreigners.

A SWEDE was brought-to from Europa, the 15th, and obliged to come in. We were much disappointed in her lading, which was salt. We had a few days before received some supplies from Tangier; and on the 18th two boats arrived from Tetuan, with fowls and oil: the latter reported that the Fly packet, which had left us on the 11th, was driven ashore on the Barbary coast by the Enemy's cruisers, who, after the crew had quitted her, took possession. We were much concerned at this intelligence; for the Fly was a fast sailer, and had been very fortunate in frequently
passing

paſſing in and out unobſerved. The 20th, came in a Mooriſh ſloop from Malaga, with butter, raiſins, and leather : the latter article was much wanted; indeed, ſo ſcarce was it become in the garriſon, that ſeveral officers, and moſt of the men, had been neceſſitated to wear ſhoes made of canvas, with ſoles of ſpun yarn.

A Letter of Marque arrived on the 25th from Leghorn, with wine, oil, and other articles : a very valuable cargo to the Garriſon. On the 30th the Enemy's army were again under arms. Their manœuvres on that day, were the attack and defence of a convoy. Their parties, as in the laſt month, continued arranging the ordnance in their artillery-park, and bringing down to the lines, materials for the repair of their works. Our artillery, however, took little notice of them.

June. In the beginning of June we received ſome ſeaſonable ſupplies, by the arrival of three boats from Tetuan, and one from Tangier. By the latter we had intelligence, that the Fox packet, from Faro, and a ſloop, were at that place, waiting an opportunity to get in ; and by this, or one of the former veſſels, Mr. Logie gave information that the Enemy had prepared ſeveral fire-ſhips, to burn our ſhipping in the Bay. Two months before, he had intimated to Commodore Eliott, that the Spaniards had five fire-ſhips in readineſs for immediate uſe ; and that they had once made an attempt to ſend them over, but the wind failed. Repeating the intelligence, therefore, at this time, was peculiarly fortunate, as the next night they attempted to put in execution their deſign. The ſame day, a Spaniſh ſhip of the line ſailed from Algeziras, to the eaſtward.

Our naval force, at this period, conſiſted of the Panther of 60 guns, Captain Harvey, (who, ſince Commodore Eliott's departure, commanded

commanded in the Mediterranean) ; the Enterprife frigate, Captain Lefley; two armed veffels commanded by lieutenants, with feveral armed tranfports; and other fhips, belonging to merchants. On the morning of the 7th, a little after midnight, the Enterprife, which was anchored to the northward, off the New-mole head, difcovered feveral fail approaching her from the oppofite fide of the Bay: they were hailed ; but before fatisfactory anfwers could be received, feveral fireworks and inflammable fubftances were thrown on board, and fix fire-fhips fuddenly appeared in the form of a crefcent, bearing down upon her and the ordnance-fhips in the New mole. Captain Lefley, with immediate prefence of mind, inftantly fired three guns to alarm his friends, and cutting his cable, drove clofer in fhore. The Panther and fhipping, on the appearance of the enemy, immediately commenced a brifk cannonade to retard their progrefs ; and, manning their boats, the officers and feamen, with their ufual intrepidity, grappled the fhips ; and, notwithftanding the fiercenefs of the flames, towed them clear of our veffels under the walls, where they were afterwards extinguifhed. Befides thefe fix, which were intended for the New mole, three others were lighted, and directed towards the Panther, at anchor off Buena-Vifta : but one was towed off by the boats, and the other two were at fo great a diftance that they drove out to fea to the eaftward.

The Garrifon was as early alarmed as the Navy. The drums beat to arms ; the guards were all upon the defence ; and the picquets, with the different regiments, affembled at their pofts, and continued under arms till day-break. The artillery from the batteries feconded the fire from the fhips ; but the darknefs of the night prevented any certain knowledge of the effect. The wind, which was favourable for their purpofe in the beginning of the night, fortunately grew ftill when they were moft in need of it. The largeft of them, neverthelefs, would certainly have got into the New mole amongft

P   the

the ordnance-tranfports, had not a few bar-fhot, from a thirty-two-pounder at the Mole-head, turned her round, and the current carried her into Rofia Bay.

THE Navy, on this occafion, cannot be too highly commended for their courage, conduct, and alertnefs. Their intrepidity overcame every obftacle; and though three of the fhips were linked with chains and ftrong cables, and every. precaution was taken to render them fuccefsful, yet, with uncommon refolution and activity, the Britifh feamen feparated, and towed afhore the veffels, with no other injury to themfelves than a few bruifes. The defign all together, to do juftice to the ingenuity of Don Barcelo, was well projected; and his fquadron judicioufly ftationed at the entrance of the Bay, to intercept our men of war in cafe they had attempted to efcape from the fire-fhips*. We afterwards were informed, that Admiral Barcelo propofed to Don Alvarez, to draw off our attention from the fouthward by opening his land-batteries on the Town. Without doubt fuch a proceeding would have diverted the attention of the Garrifon in fome meafure from the fhipping: but, as the Navy had the principal, nay, I may fay the fole honour of oppofing the fire-fhips, their endeavours would not have been lefs ftrenuous, nor of courfe lefs fuccefsful.

THE hulls of the fire-fhips were foon after broke up and fold to the inhabitants for fewel, and proved a moft feafonable relief. Firing was become a more important article than before; which may appear very extraordinary to the reader, when he looks back to the fhort time which had elapfed fince the departure of Sir George Rodney's fleet; but it is neceffary to inform him, that the colliers intended for the Garrifon were too late, in coming round from the

Downs,

* This occurrence is introduced in the Chart of the Bay.

Downs, to join at Spithead: Sir George Rodney therefore failed without them.

THE morning of the 8th, arrived the Fox packet, and another vessel from Faro; and in the course of the 10th and 12th, four boats came in from Tetuan and Tangier, with various cargoes: the *Patrons* reported it was current at Tangier, that we killed 14 or 15 men in the attack of the fire-ships, and that the Spaniards had several more fire-ships ready in the Bay, with which it was not improbable they might make a second attempt. Our Navy were consequently very vigilant, and kept a good look-out. For some weeks past we had been remarkably successful in receiving these small, and very acceptable supplies. Their cruisers, however, now began to be more alert, and appeared to be stationed with better judgement. On the 15th, a boat was taken coming in, but her consort escaped; and on the 20th, another arrived from Tangier, which brought intelligence, that a large ship, with coals and butter, bound to the Garrison, was captured by the Spaniards, two days before, under the guns of Tangier. The 24th, several broadsides were exchanged between four of the Enemy's ships, passing to Algeziras, and our shipping and batteries at the southward. Some few shot came ashore, but no particular damage was received. The Enterprise had eighteen sailors burnt by the explosion of some powder.

EARLY on the 27th, four Spanish gun-boats, with a xebeque and two gallies, approached under cover of the night, and fired upon the Panther. A brisk discharge was however returned, and they soon retired. One shot struck the south pavilion, and three were fired through the Panther. This mode of annoyance the Enemy afterwards greatly improved upon. These boats were strongly built, but ill finished: they had a small mast inclining forward from the center of the boat, almost over the bow; upon which was

hoisted

hoifted a latine yard and fail, which, at anchor, ferved as an
awning to the men on board. They rowed aftonifhingly fwift, and
each carried a twenty-fix-pounder in the bow. We never had a
good opportunity of making any fatisfactory obfervations on them,
but judged from their fize, that they were about 70 feet long, and
20 broad.*

In the beginning of July, the Panther man of war receiving
upwards of 100 Englifh prifoners from the Enemy, Captain
Harvey failed for England. Some alterations and additions took
place the fame day in the Garrifon detail. The 4th, the Fortune
brought over more Britifh prifoners. We had received fome fupplies in the courfe of a few days by two Moorifh boats; and they
were followed, on the 11th of July, by one from Tangier, which
informed us of a fleet having been feen off that coaft, and that two
boats had been taken, coming into the Bay. The fleet here mentioned was the combined fleet of France and Spain, which foon
after captured our outward-bound Eaft and Weft India fleets, and
carried them into Cadiz.

The recent attempt of the Enemy to burn the fhipping and
ftore-houfes at the fouthward, added to the intelligence which the
Governor had received of the Enemy's fleet being off Cadiz, caufed
him to direct particular attention towards that quarter of the Garrifon. Batteries for heavy metal were made on the rock above
Parfon's Lodge, at Rofia; and directions were given for the New
mole to be cleared of fhipping, that the ordnance might have
more liberty to play. Other alterations alfo took place in that
neighbourhood. Early on the morning of the 17th, five gun-boats
and four gallies fired upon the Enterprife, and fhipping in the New
mole.

* A reprefentation of them is introduced in the Weft View of Gibraltar.

1780,
July.

Auguſt.

mole. One of the frigate's forecastle-guns was difmounted, and
her fore-ftay cut : fome fhot came alfo on fhore.

DURING the remainder of the month, our firing, which had
been continued at intervals, was brifker on their parties, who were
principally employed in forming confiderable dépôts of fafcines,
cafks, and timber, in the lines, and in collecting brufh-wood from
the country : they were likewife very bufy in difembarking ftores
which had lately arrived. Several empty tranfport-veffels, in the
courfe of this month, left the Garrifon for England. A man of
the 58th regiment deferted to the Enemy : one alfo came in from
the lines.

IN Auguft few incidents occurred on either fide. Our provifions began to be bad, and extremely offenfive. What few fupplies
we received, were rather luxuries than fubftantials : wine, fugar,
oil, honey, onions, and articles of the like kind, compofed chiefly
the cargoes of thofe craft which arrived. Sugar was rifen to two
fhillings and fix-pence per pound, and every thing elfe fold in
proportion.

ABOUT ten in the forenoon of the 3d, a fettee, coming in from
the weft, was chafed by the Enemy, and taken into Algeziras.
We imagined it was the Fox packet, which we then anxioufly
expected with an Englifh mail ; and our conjectures afterwards
were confirmed. The 10th, we obferved the Enemy laying a bridge
of boats acrofs the river Palmones. Two days following, a brig
was boarded almoft under our guns, and conducted to Algeziras.
It was thought to be the fame, of which we had intelligence fome
time before, and was laden with variety of articles much wanted :
her capture was therefore greatly lamented. The night of the 15th,
fix failors deferted, in a boat, from the New mole. The fucceeding

ing day, the Fortune ſloop received from the Enemy 64 priſoners. Enſign Bradſhaw, of the 56th regiment, and ſeveral who were paſſengers in the brig taken on the 12th, were of the number. At night, five more ſailors, who were rowing guard, went over to the Enemy. In the night of the 25th, a Minorquin boat came in with wine, tea, and ſugar, in eight days. The 27th and 29th, a ſoldier and four ſailors deſerted to the Enemy. It was imagined the ſailors forced with them the midſhipman who commanded the boat. Colonel Mawhood, of the 72d regiment, died on the 29th.

A SMALL boat arrived from Barbary on the 30th, with information that the Moors permitted the Spaniards to capture every Engliſh veſſel which took refuge under the protection of their guns ; that the Spaniards would not allow any boats to leave the Bay of Tangier, and only waited for orders from Admiral Barcelo to burn and deſtroy what remained. This intelligence very ſenſibly affected us. To be cut off from what we had always conſidered our domeſtic market, was a ſtroke we little expected. We waited, however, more authentic proofs of this extraordinary conduct, before we could implicitly believe the defection of thoſe whom during the preſent conteſt we had conſidered as our firm friends.

SEPTEMBER was as barren with reſpect to material incidents, as the preceding months. The Enemy finiſhed their ponton bridge over the river Palmones on the 2d. About a week afterwards, two ſoldiers of the 56th deſerted. On the 23d, a flag of truce brought over the midſhipman carried off by the ſailors who deſerted the latter end of Auguſt. The 29th, a deſerter came in in the habit of a peaſant : he ſpoke ſeveral languages fluently, and ſaid he had been a ſerjeant in their ſervice. Some ſuſpicions ariſing, he was charged to remain with part of the 58th regiment at Wind-mill-hill. The following day we remarked, that the Enemy's

guards

guards in the lines, at the hour of relieving, amounted to about 300 infantry, and 70 artillery, befides cavalry.

THE fituation of the Garrifon by this time was again become very interefting. The blockade was, if poffible, more ftrict and vigilant than before. Chains of fmall cruifers were ftationed acrofs the Straits, at the entrance of the Bay, and on every fide of the rock ; and the late difagreeable intelligence from Tangier feemed now confirmed, by our having never heard from that quarter during the month. What little affiftance we therefore received, came from Minorca; but the fupplies from that place were fo trifling, and fold at fuch enormous prices, that few were able to purchafe them. We had not been favoured with a cargo of cattle for a long period, and the fcurvy began to gain confiderable afcendency over the efforts of our furgeons. Our diftreffes, in fhort, promifed to be more acute and fatal than thofe we had already experienced.

The Enemy's operations on the land fide had been for many months fo unimportant, as fcarcely to merit our attention. However, on the morning of the 1ft of October, we obferved they had raifed an epaulement, about 6 or 700 yards advanced from their lines. The preceding night, our out-guards had been alarmed with an unufual noife on the neutral ground, like that of men at work : feveral large fires alfo appeared, and fome attempts were made to burn our advanced barriers with devils, and other combuftibles, which were foon thrown off without taking effect ; and notice was given to the Lines, Land-port, and other guards. This alarm, however, was not general in the Garrifon. As the morning advanced, the noife ceafed ; and we difcovered that they had fet fire to the fifhermen's huts in the gardens : but when the day permitted us to examine further, we obferved the above-mentioned work.

THE

THE epaulement was about thirty yards in extent, of a fimple conftruction, compofed of chandeliers, fafcines, and a few fand-bags ;
and was erected near the windmill or tower on the neutral ground,
diftant about 1100 yards from our grand battery. The Enemy's
guns were elevated, and batteries manned; which, with other
preparations in the lines, feemed to argue that they expected we
fhould fire, and were determined to oppofe it. Thefe appearances,
probably, induced the Governor not to take any particular notice
of their work in the day: but at night, orders were fent to
throw a few light balls, to difcover if they were making any
additions. The inhabitants immediately took the alarm, upon being
told that the Enemy had thrown up an advanced work, and that
their batteries were manned ; and at night very few remained at the
north end of the town.

IT now feemed evident, the Enemy had determined on a more
ferious attack, in cafe the fecond blockade was unfuccefsful : but
we were at a lofs to imagine what motives could influence them
to act fo oppofite to the eftablifhed mode of approaching a befieged
garrifon, by erecting a work fo diftant, and which had no connection with their eftablifhed lines.

THE Enemy's batteries continued to be manned till the 2d ; and
in the afternoon of that day, Don Alvarez, accompanied by an
officer, fuppofed to be the Count d'Eftaing, who was expected
in the Spanifh camp when the laft deferter came in, vifited the
lines. They remained three quarters of an hour at Fort St. Barbara,
viewing the rock with glaffes. On their return they were faluted
from Point Mala ; and as they paffed the front line of the camp, the
regiments turned out without arms. On the night of the 3d, a
fmart engagement was heard off Cabrita Point, fuppofed to be
between fome veffel attempting to come in, and the Enemy's
cruifers ;

70ᵉ Reg.ᵗ del.

A South View of Gibraltar

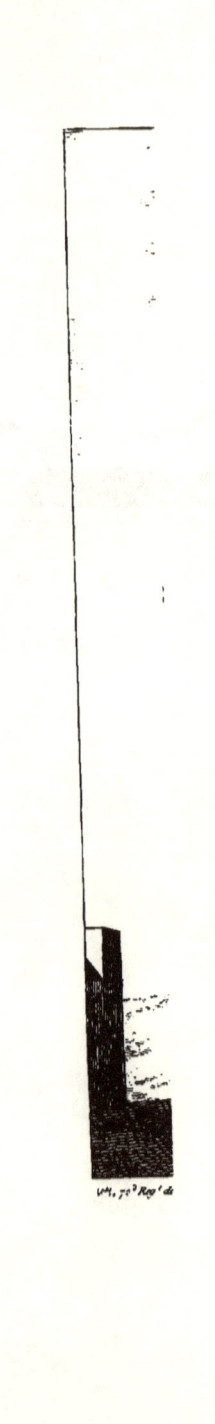

cruisers; and the next morning, a sloop, with English colours reversed, was observed at Algeziras.

EARLY on the 4th, our advanced guards discovered the Enemy endeavouring, a second time, to fix fire-faggots on our barriers. A smart discharge of musquetry was immediately directed from these posts, and from the Queen's lines; on which they retired. At day-break we observed they had carried away vast quantities of vegetables from the gardens, and trampled others under foot: but little, if any, addition was made to the epaulement. A parley came in on the 5th; and soon after, the Fortune sloop received upwards of forty British prisoners, many of whom had been taken going from the Garrison. In the evening of the 6th, the Spanish General came to the lines, at the head of the relieving guards. Soon after he arrived, the guns were again elevated, and every preparation made, as if they had resolved to open on the Garrison. The 8th, the Town-major, Captain Burke, went out with a parley, intending to proceed to the Tower, the place appointed by custom for the officers to give and receive packets. When he got abreast of the new work, the sentries by motions informed him he must not advance. He pointed to the Tower; but they continued inflexible: on his turning round however to return, one of them came up with his arms, and proceeded with him to the Tower, whilst another ran to acquaint the officer in the lines. The messenger after some time came back, and both remained apparently as a guard over Major Burke, till the officer arrived; when, delivering his packet, the Major returned to the Garrison.

THE Enemy did not appear very anxious to complete the epaulement; their parties were employed in raising and finishing the merlons of the batteries in the lines, raising the merlons of Fort St. Philip with fascines, and erecting a new battery near the guard-house on

Q   the

the beach. The 11th, a ſmall ſettee arrived from Minorca : the
patron informing us that two others were ﬆanding for the Rock,
the Navy manned their boats to aſſiﬆ them, in caſe the Enemy
oppoſed their entrance; but on getting round Europa Point, no
ſuch veſſels appeared. A Dutch convoy was however paſſing: the
boats therefore boldly advanced, and boarded a dogger which had
got, during the fog, pretty near the Rock. She was a Dane from
Malaga, laden with lemons and oranges, which the Governor
immediately purchaſed, and diﬆributed to the Garriſon.

Few articles ever arrived more ſeaſonably than this cargo of
fruit. The ſcurvy had made dreadful ravages in our hoſpitals, and
more were daily confined : many, however, unwilling to yield to the
firﬆ attacks, perſevered in their duty to its more advanced ﬆages.
It was therefore not uncommon, at this period, to ſee men,
who ſome months before were hale, and equal to any fatigue,
ſupporting themſelves to their poﬆs upon crutches, and even
with that aſſiﬆance ſcarcely able to move along. The moﬆ fatal
conſequences, in ſhort, to the Garriſon, were to be apprehended
from this terrible diſorder, when this Dane was happily directed to
our relief. The lemons were immediately adminiﬆered to the ſick,
who devoured them with the greateﬆ avidity. The ſalutary effects
were almoﬆ inﬆantaneous : in a few days, men who had been conſidered as irrecoverable, left their beds to congratulate their comrades on the proſpect of once more becoming uſeful to their country.

Mr. Cairncross, a ſurgeon of great eminence, who was preſent at this time and the remaining part of the ſiege, has favoured
me with the following information relative to the ſcurvy, and the
mode of uſing this vegetable acid; which, with his permiſſion, I
inſert for the benefit of thoſe who may hereafter be under ſimilar
circumﬆances.

"The

" THE Scurvy which attacked the Garrifon of Gibraltar, differed
" in no refpect from that difeafe ufually contracted by failors in long
" voyages; and of which the immediate caufe feemed to be the
" fubfifting for a length of time upon falted provifions only, without
" a fufficient quantity of vegetables, or other acefcent foods. The
" circumftance related in the Voyage of that celebrated circum-
" navigator, the late Lord Anfon, of confolidated fractures difuniting,
" and the callofity of the bone being perfectly diffolved, occurred
" frequently in our hofpitals: and old fores and wounds opened anew
" from the nature of the diforder.

" VARIOUS antifcorbutics were ufed without fuccefs, fuch as acid
" of vitriol, four crout, extract of malt, effence of fpruce, &c. but
" the only fpecific was frefh lemons and oranges, given liberally;
" or when they could not be procured, the preferved juice in fuch
" quantities, from one, to four ounces *per diem*, as the patient
" could bear. Whilft the lemons were found, from one to three
" were adminiftered each day as circumftances directed. The juice
" given to thofe in the moft malignant ftate, was fometimes diluted
" with fugar, wine, or fpirits; but the convalefcents took it
" without dilution. Women and children were equally affected;
" nor were the officers exempted from this alarming diftemper. It
" became almoft general at the commencement of the winter feafon,
" owing to the cold and moifture; and in the beginning of fpring,
" when vegetables were fcarce.

" THE juice was preferved by adding to fixty gallons of expreffed
" liquor, about five or ten gallons of brandy, which kept it in fo
" wholefome a ftate, that feveral cafks were opened in good con-
" dition at the clofe of the fiege. The old juice was not however
" fo fpeedily efficacious as the fruit, though, by perfevering longer
" in its ufe, it feldom failed."

THE

THE same day that the dogger was brought in, a parley came from Don Alvarez, to inform the Governor that all intercourse or correspondence betwixt them, in future, was to be conducted by flags of truce in the Bay; which regulation continued till the peace was notified in 1783. The 14th, two gun-boats, from the Orange-grove, ranged along the front of the Garrison, and drove in our fishing-boats; and on the 16th they again ranged off the Mackarel-bank, and forced our fishermen to retire. We did not much approve of this conduct, as the boats, by this means, were prevented from bringing any fish to our market. They continued, however, this practice at intervals for some time.

THE 21st, the gun-boats fired upon the Enterprise and town. Captain Lesley, not choosing to remain the object of their fire, withdrew the frigate into the New mole; where the Navy, under the direction of the engineers, had begun to lay a boom of masts from the New-mole head to the watering-tank. This boom, though it was considered a difficult operation on account of the swell of the sea, was soon completed.

IT was not till the night of the 21st, that the Enemy threw sand in the front of their epaulement, to cover it against our fire-balls and carcasses; and on the 26th they lengthened it to the west about 30 yards, and strengthened it in front with sand. The night of the 28th, they erected two large traverses in the rear for magazines. It now presented a very compact appearance; whence we concluded that it was intended for a mortar-battery.

THOUGH it was generally imagined in England, that the Garrison had been amply provided with every article and necessary of life, when Sir George Rodney arrived with the transports and relief from England, our wants, in reality, were far from being supplied.

In

In the articles of ammunition and falt provifions, the Garrifon had
probably as much as they could difpenfe with; but of frefh provifions, wine, fpirits, fugar, &c. we began to find a great fcarcity;
and the price of what remained was confequently much enhanced.
The affiftance we received formerly from Barbary had now been
fufpended for feveral months; the Enemy feemed determined to
prevent our deriving fupport from the element that almoft furrounded us; and their cruifers were too numerous and vigilant
to expect any thing from the weft. Thus fituated, the Garrifon
turned their eyes on the ifland of Minorca, whence we had already
received fome very acceptable fupplies, and whofe fituation, from
the great fcope of fea-room, afforded a flattering probability of the
boats being oftener able to efcape the Enemy's cruifers. The pro-
ductions of that ifland are various; and thofe articles which it did
not afford, could be purchafed from the prizes that were daily carried
thither by the privateers. Several Garrifon-boats were therefore
fent to Minorca, fome of which returned, in the courfe of October,
laden with the wine of that ifland, fugar, (an article become exceedingly fcarce) and cheefe; with fometimes a few live ftock. Thefe
articles were all fold by auction, according to a regulation eftablifhed
by the Governor; and, though they feldom were purchafed by the
lower ranks, yet afforded upon the whole a temporary relief to the
Garrifon.

THE 30th, we obferved that the Enemy had pofted an officer's
guard in the Mill-battery, which was the name we gave to the
new work. Montague's baftion was therefore opened on it in the
evening, and, by forming a crofs-fire with the batteries on the
heights, confiderably annoyed them, and much retarded their operations. The fame night, two foldiers of the 56th and 72d deferted
from Upper All's-well, in the lines: they were fentries at the fame
poft, and got down by means of a rope; but, previous to their
defcent,

descent, had the precaution to wet the priming of their firelocks. We also lost another man by desertion in the course of the month.

THE Governor, in the beginning of November, made an arrangement of the troops, that in case the Enemy bombarded the Garrison, each regiment might know the quarters and stations which they were to take up. The 1st of the month was rather unpropitious to us: an English snow was taken to the east of the rock: at night, a soldier of the 56th regiment deserted, during a heavy shower of rain; and the following evening, two others, of the 12th and 56th, attempted to get off by swimming round the Old-mole head; but a few days afterwards, the body of the former was washed ashore near the King's bastion: we therefore concluded his comrade had shared the same fate. In the evening of the 7th, a smart cannonade was heard in the Straits: after it had continued for some time, a sudden flash appeared, and a report was heard, like the blowing-up of powder. The next morning, we observed that the Enemy had captured an English vessel, and were at that time towing in a gun-boat; which accounted for the firing and explosion.

OUR fire, about the 7th and 8th, became more animated; yet the Enemy, almost every night, made some interior additions. We had observed, for several preceding mornings, deep ruts in the sand, leading from the principal barrier to the Mill-battery; which led us to imagine that they brought at night, heavy timber, and other materials, from their dépôts in the lines. The artillery were therefore ordered to direct a *ricochetting* fire of small shells along this track. In the evening of the 10th, a large party, followed by a number of carts and mules, laden with different materials, advanced along the beach, from the sally-port of the ditch of Fort St. Philip, to the Mill-battery. They were perceived by the artillery at Willis's, before they had proceeded half-way; and a brisk
fire

fire was directed towards their route, which threw the mules into
confusion, and obliged some to return, after having left their
burthens on the beach. The batteries being reinforced, the firing
was continued with great vivacity the whole night. The subsequent evening our artillery were prepared, and, immediately on
the party's appearing, saluted them with a warm discharge of shot
and shells, which seemed to have greater effect than the fire of the
preceding evening. This circumstance convinced us of the effect
of the *ricochetting* fire from the lower batteries, along the track
from the barrier : but the Enemy were not so soon driven from the
new track as from the former ; and continued, notwithstanding our
fire, (which must have killed and wounded many of them) to bring
materials in this exposed manner, till a line of communication was
finished from the lines. .

1780;
Nov.

An English armed polacre, called the Young Sabine, arrived on
the 12th, after a spirited engagement in the Bay with several armed
vessels and three gun-boats. The Enemy attempted to board her,
but were as often repulsed by musquetry : at length she beat them
off, and anchored under our guns. Her cargo was cheese, hams,
and potatoes ; the latter of which sold at forty-three dollars per
cwt. which, according to forty-two pence per dollar, (the exchange
at that time) are equal to 7l. 10s. 6d. sterling. Other articles sold
in proportion. In the afternoon, a Minorquin settee arrived with
the usual cargo : a Spanish gun-boat boarded her on her passage; but
the patron shewing papers from Majorca to the camp, the Spaniard
took no further notice than keeping her company as a convoy.
The Minorquin afterwards seized a convenient opportunity, and
slipped in.

In the course of the 14th, a Minorquin tartan, bound for the
Garrison, was taken by the Enemy : the crew however quitted
her,

her, and got aſhore. The Enemy the ſame day mounted twelve guns *en barbet*, in the battery near the Guard-houſe, in the vicinity of Fort St. Philip; which we had ſuppoſed was intended for mortars; and about a week afterwards they erected merlons to this work, admitting the embraſures to open upon the Garriſon. Two nights following, the gun-boats, which were now increaſed in number, fired upon the town and ſhipping. Three, that directed their fire on the former, were ſtationed off the Old-mole head, and threw ſeveral ſhots into the town. Several men were wounded in the Enterpriſe frigate.

THE night of the 17th, the Enemy threw up two *places d'armes* for muſquetry, on the flanks of the Mill-battery: the parapets formed ſemicircles joining the battery, but afterwards extended in an oblique direction towards the lines. Theſe additions appeared very ſlight, being only a row of caſks or gabions, ſtrengthened with half-chandeliers, and ſand in front; covered on the top with ſand-bags. The 18th, we were viſited again by the gun-boats: in returning their cannonade one of the thirty-two-pounders on the King's baſtion burſt, killed an artillery-man on the ſpot, and wounded three others. The man who fired the gun eſcaped, but was a little ſcorched with the powder.

A GREAT number of mules were employed on the 22d, bringing forward caſks, chandeliers, and other materials, from the camp. The night of the 23d, the Enemy began an approach from the lines, to the Mill-battery: it conſiſted of faſcines, with ſand banked up in front, and commenced near the weſt angle of the weſtern fourteen-gun battery, extending about 120 feet towards the advanced Guard-houſe in front of Fort St. Philip: the following night, notwithſtanding our fire, they lengthened it about 100 feet, with chandeliers placed in a trench and filled with faſcines. The Enemy

endeavoured

endeavoured to draw our attention from this quarter by another
falute from the gun-boats, but in vain.   As it was not improbable
that the gun-boats were directed in their firing by the lights in the
houfes along the line-wall, and thofe looking towards the Bay;
orders were iffued " that no lights in future fhould appear in any
" houfe, barrack, or guard-houfe, towards the Bay, after feven
" o'clock in the evening."

We had hitherto derived occafional affiftance from the gardens
on the neutral ground, though vaft quantities of vegetables had
been removed from thence by the Enemy.   On the 25th, however,
they determined to expel our people altogether from the gardens;
which in the courfe of a few days they accomplifhed, notwithftanding the markfmen under Lieut. Burleigh were ftationed at
Willis's, and in the Lines, in order to prevent them.

From this period, our refources in refpect to vegetables depended
entirely upon our own attention to cultivation; which, happily for
the Garrifon, was crowned with tolerable fuccefs, efpecially during
the winter months, at which time the produce was increafed to be
almoft equal to the confumption.   The fupplies from the gardens
had indeed begun to fail for fome time before; and we foon had
little reafon to regret their lofs.   We had, befides, the additional
fatisfaction of reflecting that the Enemy were now cut off from a
channel, through which it was not improbable they had been
informed of every occurrence which happened in the Garrifon.

The 26th, a Frenchman, one of the crew of the Young Sabine,
deferted in a boat to the Enemy.   The night of the 27th, the
Danifh dogger, which brought us the cargo of lemons, failed; and
the next morning we obferved her at anchor off Algeziras.   By
the 29th, the Enemy had finifhed the fecond branch of the line
of approach, and begun the return for the third towards the weftern

R   beach.

beach. Our fire, as they advanced, became more fpirited than ever, and muft have been feverely felt by the Enemy in this expofed duty. The 30th was only diftinguifhed by the arrival of a polacre from Algiers with foap, oil, wine, and candles—a very valuable cargo.

DECEMBER was introduced with bad weather. The 1ft, arrived the Anglicana privateer from Smyrna; and two nights after, fhe continued her voyage towards England: Lieutenant Gage, of the Enterprife, went home paffenger with difpatches. The 2d was particularly ftormy, with thunder and lightning, which happily did not continue long, or the works of the Garrifon might have materially fuffered. The rain poured down with fuch violence from the heights, forcing with it vaft quantities of rubbifh, ftones, and loofe earth, that the ftreets leading from the hill were inftantly choaked up, and confiderable damage was done to the buildings. The Enemy, notwithftanding the ftorm, completed their third branch, and raifed the return towards the eaft. Though the ftorm did not retard their finifhing what they had begun in the evening, yet the chandeliers were very much funk in many places, which employed their parties five or fix of the following evenings to repair. They alfo made fome alterations in the direction of the fecond branch, and repaired the batteries in the lines. A brig arrived from Leghorn on the 10th; alfo three fettees from Minorca.

FROM the 10th, the Enemy added every night fo confiderably to the fourth branch of the approach, that on the 14th at night they joined the extremity of the eaftern *place d'armes*; and two nights following, began a fifth branch, which on the 19th was extended to the eaft flank of the Mill-battery. Their operations had not been wholly confined to completing this line of communication: a mortar-battery for the fea was erected to the north of Fort St. Barbara; and large and fmall traverfes were raifed within both forts, to protect their men from our upper batteries.

ABOUT

ABOUT noon on the 17th, a cannonade was heard towards the 1780, weſt. A cloud of ſmoke was obſerved near Tangier, and we after- Dec. wards learned that the Moors were firing a ſalute on account of the arrival of their Emperor. Three hundred and ninety rounds were numbered, and it was repeated the next day. The reader will probably recollect, that the Garriſon of Tangier is to us an object of ſome curioſity, as having formerly been in the poſſeſſion of the Engliſh. It was ceded by the Portugueſe (who had been maſters of it for ſome time) to King Charles II. as part of the dowry of the Princeſs Catharine of Portugal, and remained under the Engliſh dominion till 1684, when, the nation refuſing to pay the heavy expence attending its maintenance againſt the repeated attacks of the Moors, the fortifications were blown up, and the Garriſon ordered to abandon the Town. The Moors, after the place was deſerted, returned ; and it has ever ſince continued in their poſſeſſion. When the Engliſh were maſters of Tangier, the works on the land ſide were conſidered as almoſt impregnable ; and, for the accommo- dation of ſhipping, a mole of conſiderable extent was advanced into the ſea.

THE preſent town is built at the bottom of a bay, on the ſide of a hill, overlooking the ſea. The Moors have, in ſome meaſure, repaired the moles, and endeavoured to reſtore the city to its former importance ; but their efforts go ſlowly on towards accompliſhing that work. Tangier was the reſidence of a Britiſh conſul, and, in conjunction with Tetuan, in times of peace, ſupplies Gibraltar Cadiz, Liſbon, and other ports on the coaſts of Spain and Portugal, with fowls, beef, mutton, and fruit : it was about this time the ſcene of ſome intereſting tranſactions, which will ſhortly be related.

THE Enemy, on the 20th, began to erect ſmall traverſes in the rear of their approach. On the 21ſt, the Speedwell cutter, Lieutenant

R 2   Gibſon,

Gibſon, arrived with Government diſpatches, after a warm engagement with the Enemy off Ceuta, in which the Spaniards attempted
to board the cutter, but were repulſed. Lieutenant Gibſon was
dangerouſly wounded in the action; which was the only caſualty on
board. The 23d, arrived a privateer brig, called the Hannah,
Captain Venture, laſt from Liſbon. She brought ſome excellent
ſupplies; and the day following, two other veſſels from Liverpool
got in with variety of proviſions: the cargoes of theſe ſhips were
ſold by auction for 300 *per cent.* profit.

IT was about this period, ſome letters of a curious tenor were
diſcovered in the poſſeſſion of the deſerter who came in, the 29th
of September, in the dreſs of a peaſant, and ſaid he was a ſerjeant.
They were directed to Colonel Nugent, of the Hibernian corps, in
the Spaniſh ſervice; and the purport of them was, " that Europa
" was the moſt eligible place to attack the Garriſon: acknow-
" ledging having received ſeveral ſums of money, and concluding
" with expreſſing his fears leſt he ſhould be diſcovered; therefore
" deſired the Colonel would concert ſome meaſures for his eſcape."
The man was immediately ordered into cloſe confinement, and
remained a priſoner for ſome time, till, an opportunity offering, he
was ſent away from the Garriſon. We were afterwards informed by
other deſerters, that he was ſent in as a ſpy, and liberally rewarded
for this hazardous ſervice.

THE Enemy, having completed their approach to the Mill-battery,
were employed in dreſſing the communication, and raiſing faſcine-
traverſes in the rear, for their greater protection. The 26th, and
following nights, their carpenters braced with head-rails the chandeliers, which, owing to the late rains, had given way in ſeveral
places. They were ſo very noiſy in this duty, as to induce a briſk
fire from our batteries. The 30th, a ſettee, going from Algeziras

to

to the eaftward, was becalmed off Europa, and was boarded and brought in by our boats.   Many private letters were found on board, which mentioned the confiderable lofs the Enemy had fuftained from our fire.   There were alfo a quantity of clothes, and fome money. The next day a fettee got in from Minorca.

Our carpenters, in the beginning of January, were very bufy in erecting ftages and temporary cranes, in Camp and Rofia bays, and upon the Line-wall, above the Navy-yard; which led us to imagine, that the Governor had received intelligence by the Speed-well, that a convoy might foon be expected.   The reafon for erecting thefe machines fo far to the fouth, and at fuch a diftance from the Garrifon ftore-houfes, was the apprehenfion of being annoyed in difembarking the provifions at Ragged-ftaff, &c. from the Enemy's advanced battery, which was now finifhed, and reported to mount eight thirteen-inch mortars.   Thefe precautions will appear to be very prudent and effential, when the reader, on a farther perufal, is informed of the range and effect of the Enemy's fire.   Some altera-tions were alfo made in the works at the New mole.

The 11th, a Spanifh flag of truce, with two Moorifh gallies, came over from the Orange-grove, having on board Conful Logie, his Lady, and all the Britifh fubjects who had been refident in Barbary.   We had long complained of a neglect in that quarter, but were now convinced, to our forrow, that fuch accufations were premature and ungenerous.   The mercenary and avaricious difpo-fition of the Emperor had been bribed by the Spanifh Miniftry, with a prefent of one hundred thoufand cobs, (about £.7500 fterling) and a promife of the fame fum annually, with the redemp-tion of a hundred African prifoners; on condition that he fhould deliver up, for a certain period, the ports of Tangier and Tetuan, and banifh from his dominions the Conful and fubjects of Great-Britain.

1781,
Jan.

Britain. Befides the prefent of money, and the redemption of a hundred prifoners, the Emperor had permiffion to import from Spain, grain, which was fo remarkably fcarce in Barbary, that a famine was apprehended. Without this circumftance to urge as a palliative for entering into a treaty with this avowed and natural enemy, the Emperor would probably have found it a difficult tafk to perfuade his fubjects to defert their old Allies.

As THIS defection of the Moorifh Monarch was of much importance to the Garrifon, and was in itfelf an object not undeferving political remark, I fhall fubjoin a fhort relation of fome tranfactions previous to this event; with an account of the injurious treatment which Mr. Logie and the Britifh fubjects experienced before they quitted that country.

I HAD formerly occafion to mention, that in the early part of 1779, overtures were made by the Spaniards to the Moors, to farm the ports of Tangier, Tetuan, and Larache. Of this General Eliott received immediate information, by a confidential meffage from the Emperor of Morocco. It did not appear that the Emperor, in this inftance, was actuated by any other impulfe than friendfhip. But fince, by refufing to accede to their offers, he might fubject his coafts to be infulted, it would of confequence be prudent to arm his cruifers, in order to enable him to act on the defenfive: he therefore requefted that the Englifh would fupply him with naval ftores for three new veffels which he had lately built, the value of which, on calculation, did not amount to fifteen hundred pounds.

SUCH apparent difintereftednefs, and fo modeft a demand, had a proper effect with the Governor, who, confidering the Emperor's alliance of the firft confequence to the welfare of the Garrifon, recommended to Government to double the quantity of ftores,

that

that they might fecure his friendſhip.   Miniſters at home, however,
did not confider his alliance in the fame light with the Governor and
Conful, as Sir George Rodney arrived the January following without
ſtores, or as much as an anſwer : and the Spaniards, (having then
declared war) increaſing in their propoſals, the Emperor, after
repeated applications to Mr. Logie, to know when he might expect
the ſupplies he had given him to underſtand were coming from
England, at length, by degrees, permitted the Spaniards to capture
all Britiſh veſſels under the protection of his guns.   The Conful
remonſtrated againſt fuch proceedings, but in vain : the anſwer
generally received was, that the Spaniards had the Emperor's leave ;
and if they chofe to take *him* from his own houſe, the Emperor
would not oppofe them.

THESE indignities Mr. Logie was neceſſitated to overlook.   He
found the Spaniſh influence daily gaining ground : he had therefore
no alternative, but tacitly to fubmit to the evils of his ſituation.
He contrived, neverthelefs, to acquaint General Eliott with this
change in their affairs.

THOUGH there appeared little profpect of doing further fervice
to the Garriſon of Gibraltar by remaining in Barbary, Mr. Logie
ſtill continued to refide at Tangier.   The natives were partial
to the Engliſh, and perſonally attached to him ; and thefe circumſtances he imagined might probably be improved to fome advantage.

THUS matters proceeded till the beginning of October, 1780,
when a party of the Emperor's black troops, which were quartered
in the neighbourhood of Tangier, came to Mr. Logie's houſe, and,
being introduced, informed him they had orders from their Maſter
to abuſe and infult him in the groſſeſt manner ; which they immediately

diately put in execution, by fpitting in his face, feizing him by the collar, and threatening to ftab him with their daggers.

Two days after this tranfaction, Mr. Logie was ordered to attend the Emperor near Sallee. The 13th, he began his journey, guarded by one of the Emperor's chamberlains, and a party of horfe. They arrived at the camp on the 20th; and the fame evening Mr. Logie was ordered into the Emperor's prefence. After various queftions relative to Gibraltar, to which fuch anfwers were given as were leaft likely to pleafe, the Emperor addreffed himfelf to his troops, and a great mob that were affembled on the occafion, faying, " the " Englifh were an avaricious, proud, and headftrong people; they " always attacked the head : but when people came to beg, they " ought to crawl up by the feet. He had however deprived them " of every benefit they formerly derived from his country ;" concluding with ordering the Conful to be taken to Sallee. Mr. Logie objected to this mandate, informing the Emperor he was ready to attend his camp; but that his Sovereign's fervice did not permit his trifling away his time in vifiting towns.

The Emperor, after this interview, feemed to relax in his feverity to the Conful; allowing him to return to Tangier, and confoling him with the promife that the Britifh fubjects fhould not be molefted by the Spaniards. The 26th of October, Mr. Logie arrived at Tangier, and found the Emperor had not deceived him.

Affairs remained quiet till the 26th of November, when an order came to fit up all the Britifh boats, at the Emperor's expence, as he was determined to fend the Englifh away fatisfied. The Conful however anticipated his intention, by getting them completed himfelf by the fucceeding evening. The night of the 28th, the Spaniards, informed of the Emperor's refolution, fent a party on
fhore

shore to burn the boats. They were discovered by the guards, and confined; but in consideration of a sum of money, they were the next day liberated. Two days following, the Consuls attended to hear the Emperor's orders, which were brought by two of his secretaries: they expressed, that the Emperor had sold the port of Tangier to the King of Spain; in consequence of which, every Christian, except of that nation, was to quit the Town and Bay; awarding slavery as the punishment of those who remained after the 1st of January, 1781.

Mr. Logie was no sooner acquainted with this order, than he departed for the Emperor's camp, then near Tetuan, in order to represent the impossibility of removing their property on so short a notice. He arrived on the 2d of December, but could not procure an audience. The 4th, he had intelligence from Tangier, that a second order had compelled the British subjects instantly to remove to Marteen. Mr. Logie made several attempts to have this cruel order reversed, but in vain. He at length procured a friend to mention this delicate point to the Emperor, who apparently relented, saying, the English should have permission to remain twenty days to collect their effects; and so far flattered them, as to make them believe they were not to be removed till the British fleet arrived, if it might be expected soon. Mr. Logie was however afterwards convinced, that the Emperor at this time was informed his orders had been executed, as the British subjects, amounting to 109, arrived at Marteen, a few miles from Tetuan, the subsequent evening; having been forced to abandon their vessels, houses, and all their property; and compelled to submit to the greatest imposition, for the use of camels and mules, to remove their bedding and wearing-apparel. The value of the effects left behind, Mr. Logie computed to amount to upwards of sixty thousand pounds.

S

THE

THE heavy expence attending their removal from Tangier, with their ftay at Marteen, to their arrival at Gibraltar, Mr. Logie was obliged to difburfe; the Emperor's order on the 26th of November, having fo much impofed upon them, that they had laid out what money they were poffeffed of, in purchafing fuch articles as they judged would be ufeful at Gibraltar, imagining they were to be conducted immediately to that Garrifon.

THE Emperor removed on the 17th of December to Tangier; whence he ufually fent, once or twice every week, fome infulting meffage to the Conful, charging the Englifh with having cheated his Ambaffador, and being indebted to him feveral thoufand cobs for maintaining the garrifon of Gibraltar; with others equally falfe and abufive.

MR. LOGIE, on the 26th of December, was informed that the Emperor had given up all the Britifh fubjects as prifoners to the Spaniards, and that the fucceeding day they were to be removed to Algeziras. Being affured of the truth of this intelligence by one of the Emperor's fervants, he burnt all his public papers, to prevent their falling into the Enemy's hands. The 28th, the Conful embarked with Mrs. Logie (who had attended him through all thefe troubles) and about twenty more, on board a fchooner, without being allowed time to take in any refrefhment for their voyage. Others, under fimilar circumftances, were put on board other veffels. They were guarded by two Spanifh cruifers, and for the firft night put into Ceuta Bay: the next morning they proceeded acrofs the Straits, and about noon anchored off the Orange-grove, but foon after were ordered by Admiral Barcelo to moor at the entrance of the river Palmones. Here the Conful was detained till the 11th of January following, by which time an anfwer arrived from Madrid concerning their future deftination.

DURING

DURING this period, no offer was made to supply them with provifions or neceffaries, though the Moors were permitted to purchafe whatever they wanted. Mr. Logie therefore applied to the French *Chargé des affaires* at Algeziras, who very generoufly difpatched fuch articles as he judged would be moft acceptable. The 11th, they were conducted to Gibraltar.

THE removal, or rather expulfion, of the Britifh fubjects from Barbary, was attended with other unfortunate confequences befides depriving us of provifions : our connection with Portugal became afterwards more precarious ; and the Governor was cut off from a fource of information, by which he was acquainted with the Enemy's operations both in camp and at Cadiz. Mr. Logie had always contrived to procure pretty certain intelligence of the Enemy's motions, by thofe Moors who were in his intereft ; for, the Spaniards allowing them to bring various articles to the army before Gibraltar, and the fleet at Cadiz, and Mr. Logie lending them money to carry on this advantageous trade, they faithfully communicated to him whatever came to their knowledge. The laft information Mr. Logie himfelf was the bearer of to the Governor, which was, that the Enemy had a great number of fire-fhips in the rivers, ready for immediate ufe.

THE 16th of January, a brig came in from Madeira, in four days, with feventy butts of wine. The mafter had left London with a cargo to exchange at Madeira ; but a violent gale of wind had driven him to fea with his cargo incomplete, and half his crew afhore. The fame day, the Moorifh veffels which brought over Conful Logie, returned to Algeziras. Two days following, the Tartar privateer arrived with various articles from England : fhe brought His Majefty's manifefto for commencing hoftilities againft the Dutch.

ON

ON the 19th, some experiments were made at Algeziras, from two new Spanish boats, with mortars on board. We had some time before learned that they were preparing such vessels, and that they intended soon to try them against the Garrison. Their construction was upon a plan similar to that of the gun-boats: the mortars were fixed in a solid bed of timber, in the centre of the boat; and the only apparent distinction was, that they had long prows, and braced their yards more athwart the boat when they fired.

THE 21st, the serjeant commanding one of our out-guards, deserted to the Enemy: he went towards the Devil's tower, and once stopped, as if undetermined to proceed or not. He belonged to the 56th regiment, and left a wife and family behind: he had always been esteemed of good character, and was much confided in by his officers. Some pecuniary matters were supposed to be the reason of his deserting. This was the fourth man which we had lost in this way within the course of a month. The 28th, a ship arrived from Leghorn with various articles. In her passage she picked up at sea the long-boat of the Brilliant frigate, Captain Curtis, which we had been anxiously expecting for some time with dispatches from England. On the 25th and 27th, three of Hardenberg's brigade had deserted; and this day a rope was found near the Signal-house, by which we imagined the last two of them had escaped. The 29th and 30th, two or three settees arrived, from aloft, with the produce of Minorca. By them we were informed that the Brilliant was got safe into Mahon, having been chased through the Straits by the Enemy's cruisers in the night.

THE Enemy's working parties had for several weeks been less numerous: their occupation was principally confined to repairing the damages done by the weather; securing themselves against the
effects

effects of our firing, by fplinter-proofs and traverfes; and collecting
dépôts of different materials, in various parts of their lines. Their
advanced patroles frequently approached very near our out-pofts;
but feldom waited a fecond difcharge from the fentries. On our
fide the engineers were indefatigable in putting every thing in the
beft ftate of defence. The Enemy, it muft be confeffed, dealt
openly in warning us, fo long before-hand, of their intentions; and
the Governor was exceedingly active and diligent in preparing
againft whatever circumftances might occur.

THE 1ft of February we found, behind the rock, the bodies of
two deferters, who, in attempting to efcape from the Garrifon, had
been dafhed to pieces. One of them was a man of the 56th, who
was miffing the day preceding; the other, a ferjeant of the 73d, who
had deferted fome months before. The 3d, we obferved the Enemy's artillery examining the ordnance in their lines. The morning
of the 8th, a deferter from a Catalonian regiment came in, and
reported, that the Enemy pofted every night a chain of fentries
along the fkirts of the Governor's meadow, which were conftantly
vifited by patroles of cavalry, to keep them alert; and that a
captain's guard, befides artillery, mounted in the St. Carlos's
battery, as they called the advanced work. He faid the camp
was well fupplied with provifions, &c. but that the men were fickly,
and numbers of them deferted.

IT was about this period, that the Officers in Gibraltar pré-
fented a memorial, through the commanding officers of the different
regiments, to the Governor, requefting his Excellency, as he muft
be convinced of the truth of the contents, to fupport it with his
approbation and intereft.

THE

The memorial ftated, "That the Officers of his Majefty's feveral
"regiments of foot, ferving under his Excellency's command, had
"been neceffarily expofed to a great variety of inconveniences fince
"the commencement of the blockade, independent of the addi-
"tional duties which they had been required to difcharge: That,
"in particular, their pay, which conftituted their chief, if not
"their fole fupport, had, at different times, fuffered a great dimi-
"nution by the exorbitant rate of exchange;" which they ftated to
have fluctuated, during a certain period, between 40 and 42 pence
per dollar, Gibraltar currency: "That every article of clothing,
"and ftill more, thofe effential to life and health, were fo advanced
"in price, that, with the ftricteft economy, their pay was totally
"inadequate to the expences abfolutely indifpenfable in their
"prefent fituation; a fituation which, they apprehended, pre-
"cluded them, in a great meafure, from participating with the
"officers at home in the extenfive promotions which had of late
"taken place in the army. They therefore appealed to the paternal
"feelings, the juftice, and the humanity of his Excellency; truft-
"ing that, through his recommendation and interceffion, fuch
"affiftance and protection might be granted them, as their fituation
"and fervices deferved:" Concluding with a requeft, "that His
"Excellency would be pleafed to lay their prayer, with all humi-
"lity on their part, at His Majefty's feet." This memorial was
feconded by another of a fimilar import; but no official anfwer was
received to either.

It muft be confeffed, that under thefe circumftances, the fituation
of the officers was by no means flattering. Whatever obftacles
might be in the way of their promotion, they could not help
feeling the peculiar hardfhip of their fituation: nor was the
inactive and tedious fervice of a blockaded Garrifon at all calculated

to

to divert their minds, or to foothe them into an acquiefcence with their fortune. They reflected, with no very agreeable fenfations, upon the preferment which had been liberally beftowed upon young officers in England ; while many fubalterns in Gibraltar had ten or twelve years, or upwards, of ftrict duty and fervices to plead. Nay, the fituation of fome of them was peculiarly difcouraging : for their friends had repeatedly offered to raife companies to fecure their rank ; but of fuch confequence was the fafety of Gibraltar efteemed by the Miniftry, that orders were fent to forbid any officers leaving the Garrifon, unlefs replaced by others from England. It is but juftice to them, however, to obferve, that they in general fubmitted to the evils of their fituation without murmur or repining ; and that, preferring their country's good to every partial confideration, they never publickly teftified their difcontent, except in the two refpectful memorials which they prefented to their Governor.

A PRIVATEER, on the 9th of February, arrived from Mahon : fhe ran through ten cruifers, befides fix gun-boats, and was chafed by a xebeque, but efcaped them all. The 17th, fhe continued her courfe for England. Mr. Logie, who carried home difpatches, was a paffenger, with feveral others. The 19th, and 20th, arrived two polacre fhips from aloft.

OUR fupplies from the eaftward were now pretty regular, and the boats and veffels in general very fuccefsful in their voyages. When the reader confiders the variety of difficulties and dangers attending this intercourfe, he cannot but admire the perfeverance of thefe foreigners. Their veffels were generally of light burthen, and open, excepting a fmall fcuttle abaft, which, with the other parts of the veffel, was ufually filled with part of their cargo. Their paffage
was

was feldom performed in lefs than five days; and fometimes it exceeded ten, and fourteen. Their courfe was all the way along the Enemy's coaft; and even when arrived within fight of the Port, the danger was greater than before, from the number and vigilance of the Enemy's cruifers : the horrors of a Spanifh gaol ftared them in the face, with the chance of lofing probably their ALL. One circumftance indeed was in their favour; their veffels, in the rigging, refembled thofe of the Enemy. To the chance of deceiving them they were neverthelefs unwilling entirely to truft : it was their cuftom therefore to make the Rock, if poffible, about fun-fet; then ftrike fail, and lie-to, and at night pufh for the Bay. By manœuvring in this manner they frequently arrived fafe; and in that cafe, it muft be confeffed, they were amply recompenfed.

THE 26th, the regiments in Garrifon began to be reviewed : after the review, each regiment marched to its alarm-poft, and difcharged feveral rounds of *parapet* firing. The 28th, a brig under Genoefe colours came over from Algeziras : the crew reported, they had injured their maft, and put into Algeziras for another, but that the Spaniards had ill-treated them; they therefore came over to remedy their lofs. To this ftory the Governor did not give implicit credit : a guard of a fubaltern and twelve men was fent on board; and after being for fome time detained, her cargo, which was fruit, was fold.

March.
THE want of bread in the beginning of March began again to be feverely felt : many families had not tafted any for feveral days. The poor foldiers, and ftill more the inhabitants, whofe finances would not allow them to purchafe articles from the Minorquin veffels (the cargoes of which, by the way, were chiefly luxuries,) were in intolerable diftrefs. Bifcuit-crumbs fold for 10d. and 1s. *per lb.*
The

The allowance of the troops was also curtailed, and many Portuguese fishermen left the Garrison for want of this article.   Towards
the conclusion of the month, the invalids of the Garrison embarked
on board the Enterprise frigate, and St. Fermin armed ship.   The
27th, the former, with the Fortune sloop, sailed for Minorca;
and the St. Fermin was to have accompanied them, but in getting
out of the New mole some accident befell her, by which she was
detained.   In the course of the month, several small craft arrived
from Minorca; and we lost two men by desertion.

THE beginning of April, the Spanish Admiral called in all his   April.
cruisers, and some movements took place in their disposition, which
seemed to indicate the expectation of a superior force.   The 2d,
we observed their artillery laying the mortars in the Mill-battery;
which confirmed us in the conjecture.   The succeeding day, a
British cutter, called the Resolution, arrived with rum, coals,
and sugar, in twenty-nine days from Plymouth.   The master
informed us, that he left A FLEET, which was coming to our
relief, at anchor in Torbay.   Our joy at this news was greater,
if possible, than when we were told of our former relief.   The
exigencies of the Garrison, since Admiral Rodney's departure, had
been as severe, if not more so than before.   Since the soldier, for
himself, only received weekly 5¾ lb. of bread; 13 oz. of salt beef,
18 oz. of pork, both of them almost in a state of putrescence;
2¼ oz. of butter, which was little better than rancid congealed oil;
12 oz. of raisins; ½ a pint of pease; 1 pint of Spanish beans; 1 pint
of wheat, which they ground into flour for puddings; 4 oz. of
rice, and ¼ of a pint of oil: what then must be the sufferings of
those who had a family of small children to support out of this
pittance! or what must be the distress of the inhabitants, who had
no assistance from the stores!

T

THE

THE night of the 3d, the St. Fermin, with the Brilliant's tender, which had been forced by a gale of wind to put into Gibraltar, failed for Mahon : two xebeques immediately gave chace, and, we afterwards learned, captured the former.

IT being obferved that the Enemy had ftationed at Cabrita Point, (though at fome diftance from the land) a floop and two light brigs, fuppofed to be fire-fhips, the Captains of the privateers propofed cutting out the floop, and burning the other veffels : the plan was mentioned to the Governor by an officer of the Garrifon, who had permiffion to take with him a party of volunteers from the different corps, and join in the expedition. About eleven o'clock on the night of the 4th, they proceeded in four boats. When they fet out, the night was very favourable for the enterprife ; but before they reached the veffels, the moon fuddenly fhone forth, and they reluctantly returned. Whether the Spaniards difcovered the boats or not, is a matter of doubt ; it is probable they did, as the next morning four gun-boats joined them from Algeziras, and the floop removed farther to the fouthward.

THE Enemy, on the 5th, fcaled feveral of their ordnance in the batteries round the Bay ; two frigates were alfo placed in front of eight veffels, fuppofed to be fire-fhips : thefe motions convinced us that the Enemy were aware of the fleet which was expected. The evening of the 7th, the Eagle privateer, of fourteen guns, arrived in fourteen days from Glafgow : a xebeque, a floop of fourteen guns, a galliot, and eleven gun-boats, engaged her in the Bay ; but by warm fighting, and good feamanfhip, fhe efcaped. The Captain informed us that the fleet had failed, and he was much furprifed in not finding them arrived. The following day, the Spanifh General vifited the lines and advanced works. The 9th, only two
xebeques

xebcques and the gun-boats were at Algeziras, the reft of their cruifers having left the ftation. The 11th, a felucca came round Cabrita, with oars, and with a prefs of fail : immediately upon entering the Bay, fhe made a fignal, which was anfwered at Alge-ziras by an Englifh enfign at the main-top-gallant maft-head. Soon after, a boat went over to Ceuta, and the xebeque which was ftationed at the point was called in with the gun-boats. In the evening many fignals were made from the weft; and about midnight arrived the Kite cutter, Captain Trollop, with the joyful news that the Convoy was at the entrance of the Straits, under charge of ADMIRAL DARBY, with the BRITISH GRAND FLEET.

T 2   CHAPTER

CHAPTER V.

Admiral Darby relieves Gibraltar.—Spaniards bombard the Town.—
Soldiers guilty of irregularities.—Town frequently on fire, and
greatly injured.—Gun and mortar boats very troublesome to the
Navy.—Admiral Darby returns to England.—Captain Curtis
arrives with a convoy of victuallers.—Town in ruins.—Gun-boats
renew their attacks on the Garrison : fatal effects.—Inhabitants
much alarmed by their attacks.—One of the Enemy's magazines
blown up.—General Eliott adopts a mode of annoying the Enemy's
camp, and constructs prames to oppose the gun-boats.—Bombard-
ment abates.—The Helena sloop of war arrives, after a warm
action with the Enemy.—Singular system of firing, from the Enemy.
—Melancholy fate of a matross.—Enemy make additions to their
works.—Firing increases on both sides.—Death of Major Burke.—
Gallant behaviour of a working party.—A conspiracy discovered in
the Navy.—Enemy, by their operations, demonstrate their intention
of besieging the Garrison in form.—Ineffectual attempt to destroy
their batteries.—Several cutters taken.—Enemy finish their bat-
teries.—General Eliott projects a sally, which proves successful.

1781,
April.

AT day-break, on the 12th of April, the much-expected fleet,
under the command of Admiral Darby, was in sight from our
signal-house, but was not discernible from below, being obscured
by a thick mist in the Gut. As the sun, however, became more
powerful, the fog gradually rose, like the curtain of a vast theatre,
discovering to the anxious Garrison one of the most beautiful and
pleasing scenes it is possible to conceive. The Convoy, consisting of
near a hundred vessels, were in a compact body, led by several men
of

1781,
April.

Wm 7ᵗʰ Reg.ᵗ del.ᵗ

A View of the Straits of G.

A View of the Straits of Gibraltar with the Coast of Barbary from Cape Spartel to Ceuta Point

of war: their fails juſt enough filled for ſteerage, whilſt the majority of the line-of-battle ſhips lay-to under the Barbary ſhore, having orders not to enter the Bay, leſt the Enemy ſhould moleſt them with their fire-ſhips.* The ecſtaſies of the inhabitants at this grand and exhilarating ſight are not to be deſcribed. Their expreſſions of joy far exceeded their former exultations. But, alas! they little dreamed of the tremendous blow that impended, which was to annihilate their property, and reduce many of them to indigence and beggary.

As THE convoy approached the Bay, fifteen gun-boats advanced from Algeziras, and forming in regular order under the batteries at Cabrita Point, began a ſmart cannonade on the neareſt ſhips, ſeconded by the gun and mortar batteries on the land. A line-of-battle ſhip and two frigates, however, ſoon obliged them to a precipitate retreat; and, continuing to purſue them, the crews of ſeveral deſerted their boats, and took refuge amongſt the rocks. Had our ſhips advanced at this critical juncture, and manned their boats, the whole might probably have been deſtroyed, and the Garriſon by that means been rid of thoſe diſagreeable neighbours which afterwards ſo haraſſed and annoyed us; but the frigates, having diſperſed them, thought no more of the *bum-boats*, as ſome Naval officers contemptuouſly called them, and left them to be repoſſeſſed by the fugitives.

THE Enemy, on the land ſide, were far from being idle ſpectators of this relief. On the firſt intimation of Admiral Darby's approach, preparations, it is imagined, were made in the lines, and a reinforcement of artillery ordered down from the camp; as at day-break, before the fleet was well in ſight, we remarked that their cannon were elevated, and the ſpunges and rammers reared againſt the merlons.

* The diſpoſition of the whole is introduced in the annexed View of the Straits.

merlons.   Thefe, with other appearances, indicated an intention of opening on the Garrifon.

OUR private letters had, for fome time before, mentioned that the Spaniards propofed to bombard Gibraltar, if the Garrifon was a fecond time relieved : but the truth of this intelligence was doubted, it being conceived that no beneficial confequences could arife to them from fuch a cruel proceeding.   We however overlooked the predominant characteriftic of the nation, which, particularly in this inftance, feems to have influenced them more than any other motive, and even to have carried them beyond that line of prudence and caution, which in military affairs ought to be ftrictly attended to.

ABOUT three quarters paft ten o'clock, the van of the convoy came to an anchor off the New mole and Rofia bay; and, as if this was the fignal for the Enemy to open, a fmart fire immediately commenced from Fort St. Philip, followed by all the batteries which bore upon the Garrifon.   The number of ordnance bearing on the place was as follows: the King's, or Black battery, mounting 14 guns, 12 bearing on the Garrifon; Fort St. Philip, 27 guns, 11 bearing on the Garrifon; Infanta's battery, of 7 guns; Prince's and Princefs's batteries, of 14 guns each; Fort St. Barbara, 23 guns, 6 bearing on the Garrifon: thefe, with about 50 mortars, mounted in the lines, and in St. Carlos's battery, amount to 114 pieces of artillery; all of heavy metal, being twenty-fix-pounders, and thirteen-inch mortars.

THE Enemy's cannonade was inftantly returned from the Garrifon; but our artillery had orders to difregard their lines, and notice only the St. Carlos's battery, which confequently foon flackened its fire.   The miferable and terrified inhabitants, who juft before were congratulating each other on the arrival of the fleet, now

now changed their exultation to forrow, and flocked, old and young, men, women, and children, in the greateſt confuſion, to the ſouth-ward, leaving their property, unſecured, to the mercy of the ſoldiers. The ſhells from the St. Carlos's battery were directed towards the New mole : the Convoy, however, had been warned not to anchor within the range of their fire : the ſhipping, therefore, were not in the leaſt moleſted. A ſettee was ſunk near the watering-tank, and numbers of ſhells fell on the red-ſands, and in the neighbourhood of South-Port, which added no little to the alarm of the fugitives from town. The Enemy's other batteries were chiefly directed to Willis's, the Lines, and particularly the ground upon which the troops were intended to have been encamped. Between one and two o'clock their firing abated, and in a ſhort time ceaſed. Of this favourable ceſſation the Inhabitants availed themſelves, to ſecure ſuch valuable property as could be expeditiouſly removed ; but the heavier articles, which the avaricious and hard-hearted huckſters had kept concealed in their ſtores, to bring forth in ſmall quantities when the prices ſuited, were all deſtroyed in the courſe of the bombardment.

ABOUT five o'clock, the batteries of the Enemy again opened, and the firing continued, without intermiſſion, the remainder of the day, and the ſucceeding night. It did not, however, interrupt the diſem-barkation of the ſupplies. Five hundred men, with a proportion of officers, were ordered for that duty : they were afterwards confi-derably augmented ; and ſuch was the labour and diligence of the Garriſon, that the ſtores were landed, with the aſſiſtance of the Navy, in nine or ten days. Our caſualties, on the 12th, were but few : Lieut. Boag, of the artillery, was wounded ; alſo ſeveral non-com-miſſioned officers and privates.

THE bombardment was continued the 13th, and ſeveral ſoldiers were killed and wounded in their quarters. In the courſe of the day, a hundred and fifty men were ordered to remove ammunition to the

magazines

magazines on the hill, and an additional number to join the party employed in landing the supplies. The 14th, the gun and mortar-boats fired upon the shipping, but were soon obliged to retire. Several barges attended, having officers in them, who seemed to give directions how to point their cannon. Our batteries ceased firing this day, but the Enemy's ordnance were kept going with great vivacity. They appeared to have got the exact range of the heights ; even the Royal battery did not escape their shells. Ensign Martin was slightly wounded with splinters of stones. No arrangement of the troops was yet known ; and the former distribution, given out in November, was totally overthrown by the extensive range of the Enemy's fire. Officers, however, whose quarters were damaged, received marquees from the public stores, to encamp at the southward ; and the distressed inhabitants were accommodated with tents.

It being remarked that the Enemy's fire considerably abated about noon, the Governor ordered the town-guards to assemble at twelve o'clock ; by which regulation less danger was apprehended in relieving the men on duty. The night picquets were likewise ordered to occupy the casemates under the Grand battery, that they might be at hand to reinforce the northern guards, in case of alarm. The total strength of the picquets, at this period, was two captains, nine subalterns, nine serjeants, nine drummers, and three hundred and ninety-one rank and file. The cause of the cessation in the Enemy's fire at noon, arose from a custom, pretty general in Spain, and common, I believe, in most warm climates, that of indulging themselves with a meridian nap. This luxury the Spaniards could not refuse themselves, even in war ; and it was invariably attended to during their future operations against Gibraltar.*

VICE-

---

* This will not appear so extraordinary when the Reader is informed that, during the insurrection at Madrid, in 1766, the insurgents, as mentioned by Major Dalrymple, in his Travels through Spain, regularly indulged themselves with their *siesta*, and then returned to their different places of rendezvous. Government did the same ; so that there seemed to be a sleepy convention, for a few hours, every day, between administration and the mob.

Vice-Admiral Darby, with the ſhips of war, continued cruiſing in ſight of the Rock: the ſervice however requiring diſpatch in landing the ſupplies, he detached Rear-Admiral Sir John Lockart Roſs to ſuperintend that duty in the Bay; and the Garriſon party was augmented to upwards of a thouſand men, beſides officers. The evening of the 14th, the Enemy's ſhells were very profuſely diſtributed: ſome that did not burſt we examined, and on drawing the fuſe, found inflammable matter mixed with the powder: theſe combuſtibles ſet fire to a wine-houſe in the green-market, near the Spaniſh church; and before the fire could be extinguiſhed, four or five houſes were burnt to the ground. Detachments from the regiments and guards in town were immediately ordered to quench the flames; but the Enemy's cannonade became ſo briſk, that great confuſion enſued. From this moment, we may date the commencement of the irregularities into which, through reſentment and intoxication, the ſoldiers were betrayed. Some died of immediate intoxication, and ſeveral were with difficulty recovered, by oils, and tobacco water, from a dangerous ſtate of ebriety.

Though riot and violence are moſt contrary to that ſpirit of regular diſcipline which ſhould always prevail in military affairs, ſomething may yet be urged in extenuation of the conduct of the troops, which has been ſo much the ſubject of reprehenſion amongſt the people intereſted. The extreme diſtreſs, to which the ſoldiers had been reduced by the mercenary conduct of the huckſters and liquor-dealers, in hoarding, or rather concealing their ſtocks, to enhance the price of what was expoſed for ſale, raiſed amongſt the troops (when they diſcovered the great quantities of various articles in the private ſtores) a ſpirit of revenge. The firſt and ſecond days, they conducted themſelves with great propriety; but on the eve of the third day, their diſcipline was overpowered by their inebriation; and from that inſtant, regardleſs of puniſhment, or the intreaties of

U   their

their officers, they were guilty of many, and great exceſſes. The
Enemy's ſhells ſoon forced open the ſecret receſſes of the merchants ;
and the ſoldiers inſtantly availed themſelves of the opportunity to
ſeize upon the liquors, which they conveyed to haunts of their own.
Here, in parties, they barricaded their quarters againſt all oppoſers,
and, inſenſible of their danger, regaled themſelves with the ſpoils.
Several ſkirmiſhes occurred amongſt them, which, if not ſeaſonably
put a ſtop to by the interference of officers, might have ended in
ſerious conſequences.

IT did not appear, through all their intemperance, that theſe irregularities aroſe from any cauſe ſo much as a ſpirit of revenge againſt
the merchants. A great quantity of liquor, &c. was wantonly
deſtroyed ; and, in ſome caſes, incredible profuſion prevailed. Among
other inſtances of caprice and extravagance, I recollect that of roaſt-
ing a pig by a fire made of cinnamon. The offenders were at firſt
confined and reprimanded, which the Governor judged would have
a greater effect than puniſhment ; but relapſing a ſecond time, he
was convinced his lenity was diſregarded ; and he was therefore compelled to uſe more rigorous meaſures.

I HAVE thought proper to digreſs a little upon this ſubject, not
in juſtification of the ſoldiers, but to acquaint the world with the
truth ; as ſome, who have related the occurrences of this period to
their friends, have omitted doing the Garriſon the juſtice to annex
the account of their former hardſhips. Beſides, had the troops been
in the higheſt degree abſtemious, the Enemy's fire would ſoon have
deſtroyed what was only the ſooner conſumed by their extravagance ;
for the inhabitants were too much alarmed for the ſafety of their
own perſons, to attend to the ſecurity of their effects.

I FORGOT to mention in its place, that, previous to the bombardment, the ſick in town had received orders to remove when
the

the firing commenced: on the 13th, therefore, the men were conveyed to the Naval hofpital at the fouthward.

THE 15th, the bombardment was continued with greater vivacity. Not content with difcharging their ordnance regularly, they faluted us almoft every inftant with a volley of eight or ten cannon, befides mortars. Our batteries remained filent, and the guns at Willis's were drawn behind the merlons, to fecure them againft the Enemy's fhot. It was obferved, they directed a great number of fhells towards the Working-parade, and about the Victualling-office. In the morning, the gun-boats again attacked the fhips of war and tranfports; and the Navy returned a fmart fire. About noon, Lieut. Budworth, of the 72d regiment, and Surgeon Chefholme, of the 56th, were wounded by a fplinter of a fhell at the door of a northern cafemate in the King's baftion. The former was dangeroufly fcalped, and the latter had one foot taken off, and the other leg broken, befides a wound in the knee. The troops in town, in the afternoon began to encamp at the fouthward, and to be regularly diftributed amongft the cafemates in town. The following was the arrangement. To the Hanoverians were allotted the bomb-proofs under the Grand battery, occupied by the picquets, which in confequence removed to Land-port gateway, and Prince of Heffe's cafemate. The 12th, 39th, and 56th regiments, were ordered to poffefs Montague's cafemate with the Galley-houfe, and Water-port gateway : thofe who could not be accommodated in thefe quarters, encamped above the South barracks, and Navy hofpital on the declivity of the hill : the 72d regiment totally withdrew into the King's baftion, and the 58th and 73d regiments remained in the South barracks : the artillery and engineers were difpofed of on the fame plan. Several days elapfed before the troops were properly fettled. The ground on which they encamped, was very fteep and rugged : it was neceffary therefore to level it into terraces, for

U 2   the

the men to pitch their tents. The regimental ſtores were alſo to be removed, and other duties of a ſimilar nature executed, before the troops could be conſidered as properly eſtabliſhed.

THE gun-boats attacked the ſhipping on the 16th, and endeavoured to moleſt the parties employed in landing the proviſions: but a line-of-battle ſhip, and two frigates, ſoon obliged them to retire. In the courſe of the day, the women and children who had taken refuge with their huſbands and friends in the caſemates in town, were ordered to remove, and encamp at the ſouthward. Though this order, from motives of humanity, was not ſtrictly enforced, yet it greatly relieved the men, and in a meaſure removed our apprehenſions of ſome infectious diſorder being generated from their crowded and confined ſituation.   The officers were under the neceſſity of participating with the men in theſe unpleaſant accommodations: their preſence, however, produced this beneficial conſequence, that they often prevented the men from indulging in thoſe exceſſes, into which, otherwiſe, they undoubtedly would have entered. The ſame day, the Queen's-lines, Main, New-mole, and Roſia guards, were ordered to be Captain's guards.

THE Enemy, on the 17th, firſt reached the Rock-gun with ſhot from the ſeven-gun battery. Colonels Roſs, Green, and Picton, were appointed the ſame day to rank as Brigadiers; and Captain Wilſon of the 72d regiment, Lieutenant Holloway of the engineers, and Captain Picton of the 12th regiment, were appointed their brigade-majors.   Two field-officers, with a captain from each regiment, and one ſubaltern for every fifty men, were ordered alſo to ſuperintend the diſembarkation of proviſions.   In the afternoon, the ſhells of the beſiegers ſet fire to the ſtores in the Spaniſh church. Parties were inſtantly detached from the main guard, 72d regiment, and other corps in town, to remove the proviſions. The Lieutenant-Governor

Governor with his Aide-de-camps was prefent, encouraging the men to perform this duty with expedition. The Enemy's fire at this time was remarkably fpirited; nevertheless, the greater part was faved by the activity of the parties. Many cafks of flour were brought into the King's baftion, and piled as temporary traverfes before the doors of the fouthern cafemates, in which feveral perfons had been killed and wounded in bed. Thefe traverfes, however, did not continue long; for the men, when the fpoils in the town became fcarce, confidered thofe barrels which the Enemy's fhot had pierced, as lawful prizes. The contents were foon fcooped out and fried into pancakes, a difh which they were very expert in cooking; and the upper cafks, wanting fupport from below, gave way, and the whole came to the ground. Though the flour by this means was in a great meafure loft to Government, yet the number of accidents which thefe traverfes prevented, greatly overbalanced the value of the article. Traverfes of another nature were afterwards erected in their room.

THE gun-boats, on the 18th, fired again upon the fhipping and men of war cruifing in the Bay. The Minerva and Monfieur, frigates, had feveral men dangeroufly wounded; and the Nonfuch had a maft crippled. The Navy, after this attack, no longer confidered thefe boats in the fame defpicable light as on their firft entrance into the Bay. In the courfe of the day, a fhell fell through the arch of the galley-houfe, where part of the 39th, and fome of the 12th regiments, were quartered: it killed two, and wounded four privates. In confequence of this unexpected cafualty, the troops removed thence, and joined their regiments at the fouth-ward.

OUR batteries, efpecially at Willis's, by this time exhibited a very diforderly and ruinous appearance. The ordnance had been
withdrawn

withdrawn when the artillery ceafed to fire : but the merlons were :now :confiderably damaged, and fome of the cannon difmounted and injured. The Lines were alfo nearly choaked up with loofe ftones and rubbifh, brought down by the fhot from the rock above; the traverfes along the line-wall were greatly injured ; and the town, particularly at the northward, approached every day towards a final demolition. The engineers, however, were ordered to prepare materials for repairing the Queen's battery at Willis's ; and parties of workmen were employed in carrying up, from below, fand-bags, and other requifites for that purpofe. New traverfes were likewife begun along the different communications, higher, ftronger, and at fhorter diftances, than the old ones.

The gun-boats renewed their attack, the 19th, on the fhipping, but were foon obliged to retreat. In the courfe of the day, the terrace ftore-houfe was fet on fire. The camp-equipage of the Garrifon being in an adjacent houfe, parties from the regiments in town were ordered to remove them with the greateft expedition. The men generally received fome gratuity from the Governor for thefe hazardous duties. The following day, the fupplies being landed, the Fleet in the evening prepared to return to the weftward. Before they weighed, their good friends the gun-boats gave them a parting falute, and did fome damage. By fix o'clock the whole were under way. Many merchantmen, freighted with merchandize, and articles much wanted in the Garrifon, returned with their cargoes ; the merchants refufing to take them, on account of the bombardment. Great numbers of the inhabitants, and officers ladies, likewife embraced this opportunity of leaving the Garrifon.

The impatience of the Britifh Admiral to difembark the fupplies, that he might not lofe the opportunity of the eafterly wind to return from the Mediterranean, had prevented the Garrifon from
unloading

unloading the colliers that had arrived with the fleet: thefe fhips
were therefore fkuttled in the New mole, to be difcharged at leifure. The ordnance-tranfports were alfo ordered within the boom for the fame purpofe. In the courfe of the 20th, the Victualling-office was on fire for a fhort time; and at night, the Town was on fire in four. different places; but the public ftores being fafe, no attempts were made to extinguifh the flames.

THE Enemy's cannonade and bombardment continued ftill very brifk. The 21ft, forty-two rounds were numbered in two minutes, between fix and eight o'clock. The Garrifon flag-ftaff on the Grand battery was fo much injured by their fire, that the upper part was obliged to be cut off; and the colours, or rather the glorious remains, were nailed to the ftump. The evening of the 22d, the combuftible matter in their fhells fetting fire to fome fafcines at Waterport, Lieut. Cunningham, of the 39th regiment, was wounded in extinguifhing them. The fate of this young gentleman may be confidered as extraordinary. On examining the wound, which was in the head, it appeared fo trifling, that the furgeon judged his fkull unhurt; and his feeming recovery confirmed the opinion. Something more than a fortnight elapfed, when he complained of a pain in his head: he immediately took to his bed, and in a fhort time expired. After his deceafe, a confiderable fracture was difcovered, with a quantity of extravafated blood. encircling the brain.

THE gun and mortar boats, on the 23d, fired upon our parties ranging the provifions at the fout.hward. Two hundred and fixty fhot and forty fhells were difcharged, feveral of which fell about the camp, and powder-magazines. The wife of a foldier of the 58th regiment was killed behind the South barracks, and feveral men wounded. The bombardment from the lines was now in fome degree :

degree abated, in consequence of their batteries being shaken and injured by their own constant cannor de. We observed, during this day, a number of mules, with carts, bringing materials to the lines to repair them. Our artillery, at night, annoyed them with a few rounds from the batteries above Willis's.

THE 24th, a shell fell at the door of a casemate, under the south flank of the King's bastion, and wounded four men within the bomb-proof. This casemate had been appropriated as a magazine for the bastion, and the powder had only been removed to the opposite casemate a few days previous to this accident. In the afternoon, a soldier of the 12th regiment deserted from Land-port guard; in consequence of which, the town-guards were ordered to assemble, the subsequent day, at two o'clock P. M. The Enemy, however, not increasing their fire as was expected, the guards afterwards mounted as before.

THE Garrison-orders of the 26th expressed, that any soldier, convicted of being drunk or asleep upon his post, or found maraud-ing, should be immediately executed. These measures, rigorous as they may appear, were become absolutely necessary, and, in reality, had been too long deferred. The soldiers were now arrived at so high a pitch of licentiousness, that no respect was paid to their officers, and scarcely obedience to them even when on duty. Such behaviour, if not curbed in time, too commonly induces very serious consequences. At the same time that this order was issued, the regiments quartered at the southward were commanded, in case of alarm, to assemble, in two lines, on the Red sands, the British in front, and the Hanoverian brigade in the rear. The troops in town had their stations likewise allotted them.

IN the afternoon of the 27th, a convoy of twenty victuallers, under charge of four frigates and the Fortune sloop, arrived in thirteen

days

days from Minorca. It now appeared that the Governor did not
entirely depend on receiving fuccours from England, but thought
it prudent to obtain fupplies from other quarters, left any accident
fhould prevent the Britifh fleet arriving in time to his relief. Thus
determined to provide againft fortuitous events, he had fecretly
ordered provifions to be purchafed from the prizes taken aloft, and
fhipped on board veffels that were hired for that purpofe. Captain
Curtis, of the Brilliant frigate, had the charge of this valuable
Convoy, and the fuccefs attending the enterprife demonftrates with
what fecrecy it had been conducted. They were ignorant of Admiral
Darby having been in the Mediterranean, and were agreeably furprifed to find from the Enemy no oppofition to their entrance.

THE provifions thrown in by the Britifh Admiral were not yet
ftored; nor had they any further protection againft the weather, than
a covering of canvas, formed from the fails of the colliers that were
run afhore in the New mole. Under thefe unavoidable circumftances, it was peculiarly unfortunate, that the rains at this period
fhould be unufually heavy, and of long continuance. The troops
alfo were very material fufferers from this inclemency of the
weather. The rain, that poured down in torrents from the face
of the hill, foon broke down the loofe banks of earth raifed to
cover their tents, which, being pitched on the declivity of the
hill, were fwept away by the force of the ftream; and thus the
fatigued foldier, who fcarcely was one night out of three in bed, was
frequently expofed, at midnight, to a deluge of rain. Thefe misfortunes, however, taught them to provide againft fuch future accidents; and in a few months, after fome labour and attention, their
quarters were more comfortable and fecure.

THE remainder of the month was remarkable for exceffive rains,
attended with moft dreadful thunder and lightning, which, during

X   the

1781,
April.
the night, in addition to the fire from the Enemy, had an awful and tremendous effect. The bombardment continued warm and well fupported; but the Enemy did not appear to have any particular object. In the early part of the day, they in general fired pretty fmartly: about noon their batteries flackened, and from twelve till two o'clock almoft totally ceafed: after two they recommenced, and perfevered till the fucceeding meridian. During the night they directed their fire principally to the heights and lines, as probably they had information, by the laft deferter, that we employed, every night, parties to clear and repair thofe works.

THE morning of the 30th, we difcovered the gun and mortar boats approaching the Garrifon: they took their ftations off the town, to avoid the fire from the frigates, and varied very little from their former attacks. Five fhot landed on Windmill-hill, which was efteemed a remarkable long range. We returned a brifk and well-directed fire; and they retired. It was remarked that the land-batteries were in a meafure filent during their ftay. In the evening, an Hanoverian, with fome others, was detected marauding in a ftore: the party was given in charge to a fentry, but the former attempted to efcape: the fentry called to him to ftop, otherwife he would fire; which he not complying with, the fentry fhot him dead on the fpot. A general return of cafualties, &c. for every month, is inferted at the conclufion.

May.   EARLY on the 2d of May, two fettees arrived from Algiers, laden with fheep, wine, and brandy. The Enemy now feemed to have given up the idea of blockading us to a furrender. No cruifers had been obferved out fince the departure of Admiral Darby. In the evening a fhell from the Garrifon fell upon the eaftern traverfe, in the St. Carlos's battery, under which was their magazine, and, communicating with the powder, blew it up. The explofion

was

was not loud; but the damage was so very confiderable, that the
ordnance were filent for feveral days. Our artillery annoyed the
Enemy greatly during their confufion, though they kept up a brifk
difcharge from the lines, at the rate of two hundred and fifty rounds
an hour. The day following, Lieut. Willington, of the artillery, was
wounded at Willis's. The 5th, a foldier of the 58th regiment was
executed on the Grand parade, at the door of the ftore where he was
detected plundering. His body hung till fun-fet, as an example to
other offenders.

THE Enemy's cannonade and bombardment continued to be wide
and fcattered, apparently having no particular object. Shells were
yet lavifhly expended; and, what was very finglar, many of thofe
which fell blind, contained, on examination, a vaft quantity of fand
mixed with the powder. We could not otherwife account for this
unufual circumftance, than by fuppofing the powder was ftolen by
their people in the laboratories. Other fhells ftill diffufed, on
their explofion, combuftible matter, which, fetting fire to the loofe
timber and wood difperfed amongft the ruins of the town, greatly
endangered the King's ftores and magazines. This induced the
Governor, on the 6th, to publifh a placart, fignifying to the inhabitants, that fuch materials, of this nature, as were not removed out
of the reach of the Enemy's fire, would be converted to the King's
ufe. The morning of the 7th, the gun and mortar boats fired upon
the Town and the New mole: they ftayed about an hour, and then
retired. We returned upwards of four hundred rounds with great
vivacity; which greatly difpleafed the Governor : " There would
" be no end," he faid, " of expending ammunition, if we fired every
" time they came, and while they were at fo great a diftance : in
" future," he ordered, " no notice to be taken of the gun-boats,
" unlefs they approached within the diftance of grape." The 8th,
Captain Fowlis, of the 73d, was wounded in the lines.

X 2   THE

THE Enemy's fire was now more regular: we no longer experienced the fudden fits that had induced them to difcharge a whole
battery at a volley : it amounted, about this time, upon an average,
to fifteen hundred rounds in the twenty-four hours.   The 9th,
Lieut. Lowe, of the 12th regiment, a fuperintendant of the working-parties, loft his leg by a fhot, on the flope of the hill under
the Caftle.   He faw the fhot before the fatal effect, but was fafcinated
to the fpot.   This fudden arreft of the faculties was not uncommon :
feveral inftances occurred to my own obfervation, where men,
totally free, have had their fenfes fo engaged by a fhell in its defcent,
that, though fenfible of their danger, even fo far as to cry for
affiftance, they have been immediately fixed to the place.   But what
is more remarkable, thefe men have fo inftantaneoufly recovered
themfelves on its fall to the ground, as to remove to a place of fafety
before the fhell burft.   The gun and mortar boats repeated their
vifit on the 11th, but fired from fo refpectful a diftance, that fcarcely
a fhot came afhore.   Our batteries were manned ; neverthelefs, not
a gun was returned.   Lieutenant Thornton, of the 12th regiment,
was wounded the fame day with fplinters of ftones, thrown up by
a fhot which grazed betwixt his legs.

THE buildings in town, at this time, exhibited a moft dreadful
picture of the effects of fo animated a bombardment.   Scarce a
houfe, north of the Grand parade, was tenantable; all of them were
deferted.   Some few, near South port, continued to be inhabited
by foldiers families ; but, in general, the floors and roofs were
deftroyed, and the bare fhell only was left ftanding.   The Governor
and Lieutenant-Governor, however, maintained their quarters, having
parties conftantly employed in repairing the damage.   Both had
bomb-proofs; and the former afterwards had a large tent, pitched
on a rifing fituation fouth of the Red fands, where, with his fuite,
he generally remained during the day, returning at night to town;
but

but the Lieutenant-Governor conftantly refided in town, having accommodations in the King's baftion.

THE evening of the 12th, the gun and mortar boats fired upon. the Garrifon from off the Old mole, feconded by a very warm fire from their land-batteries. Several fhells from the former ranged as. high as the Signal-houfe, and fome fell over the rock. They difcharged a hundred and eighty fhot and forty-fix fhells, and then retired, throwing up the ufual fignal of a rocket from each boat.. Though our batteries were manned, the Garrifon remained filent. About the 13th, and for a few fucceeding days, the Enemy's fhells were directed for an unufual long range. One fell on the forecaftle of a collier in the New mole, and pierced both decks, but did not burft.. Two fell amongft the provifions on the New-mole parade, and another in the middle yard of the South barracks: a fplinter of the latter flew to the Navy-hofpital. The 14th, a fhell fell into the Small armoury, near South port, but fortunately did little injury. The 17th, the Jews fynagogue and other buildings were. burnt down. The following day, a fhell from our upper batteries · blew up the Guard-room in the *place d'armes* of Fort Barbara. Our engineers were at this time employed every night in clearing the. works, filling up fhell-holes, and repairing the glacis and traverfes at Water port. The Enemy's fire feldom exceeded a thoufand. rounds in the courfe of twenty-four hours: their batteries were much fhaken with the firing, and parties were conftantly bringing. fupplies of ammunition to the lines, and different materials for the. repair of their works.

AN attempt was made by the navy, on the 19th, to cut off a polacre. becalmed near Europa point ; but, a breeze fpringing up, fhe efcaped.. The gun-boats foon after came out, apparently with an intention

of.

of avenging this affront; but, the wind freſhening, they returned. The cannonade from the Enemy was now principally directed at our upper batteries. The rock-gun, mounted on the ſummit of the northern front, was become as warm, if not warmer than any other battery; and ſcarcely a day paſſed without ſome caſualties at that poſt. The gun and mortar boats, early in the morning of the 20th, repeated their attack on the Garriſon and ſhipping. They were arranged in two diviſions, thoſe to the northward directing their fire towards the King's baſtion and South port, but moſt of their ſhells broke on the face of the rock; whilſt the ſouthward diviſion annoyed the ſhipping and camp. Their uſual ſignal for retiring was made about a quarter paſt three o'clock. On this occaſion we returned a few ſhots from the town-batteries.

AT the commencement of the bombardment, the out-guards of Bay-ſide and Lower Forbes's had been withdrawn from thoſe barriers, and an officer's guard ſtationed every night in the Flêche, a work erected near the Inundation at the foot of Land-port glacis. On the morning of the 21ſt, the ſentries at this poſt obſerved a man advancing, with great circumſpection, along the cauſeway: inſtead of anſwering when challenged, he immediately dropped. Lieut. Wetham, of the 58th regiment, the officer on duty, ſuſpecting he came to reconnoitre, inſtantly, with the ſerjeant, went out to ſeize him; but the man riſing, he purſued, and was within a very ſhort diſtance of ſecuring him, when he fell into a ſhell-hole near Bay-ſide, and the man eſcaped. It was imagined that curioſity had prompted him to make trial of the alertneſs of our ſentries. His hat, which fell off in his retreat, his firelock with bayonet, and pouch filled with twenty-nine rounds of ammunition, were hung on the paliſades of the barrier, and were afterwards brought in.

EARLY

EARLY on the morning of the 22d, a fplinter of a fhell, which fell and burft on the Church-battery, ranged upwards of two hundred yards, and cutting the apron of the morning-gun on the South baftion, fired it off. This fingular circumftance, happening fome hours before day-break, not a little furprifed thofe who heard the report, and were ignorant of the caufe. Our fire was now increafed to about a hundred and fifty rounds in the twenty-four hours, the Enemy's parties being repairing the lines of approach. Their cannonade, on the contrary, was reduced, upon an average, to near fix hundred and fifty rounds.

THE night of the 23d, the gun and mortar boats renewed their attack upon the camp, which, in its confequences, was more dreadful than any we had hitherto experienced. The filence obferved by the Garrifon during their preceding vifits, emboldened them, on this occafion, to advance fo near, that we could diftinctly hear their officers give orders to the men, who frequently cried out to us, in Spanifh, to "take care." During the firft and fecond rounds, the fhells fell over Windmill-hill into the fea; but this miftake they foon rectified, and the attack became exceffively fmart. Two fhells fell within the Hofpital-wall, and a fhot paffed through the roof of one of the pavilions. A fhell fell in a houfe in Hardy-town, and killed Mr. Ifrael, a very refpectable Jew, with Mrs. Tourale, a female relation, and his clerk. Another, from the St. Carlos's battery, fell into a houfe near South fhed, in which were fifteen or fixteen perfons: the fhell burft; but all efcaped, except a child, whofe mother had experienced a fimilar fate fome time before. A foldier of the 73d regiment was killed in his bed by a fhot; and a Jew butcher was equally unfortunate. In all, feven were killed, and twelve or thirteen wounded. A fplinter of the fhell which was fo fatal amongft Mr. Ifrael's family, is now exhibited, as a curiofity worthy of notice, in Sir Afhton Lever's valuable mufeum, where this
affecting

affecting story is also related. The silence of the Garrison, when the deftructive effects of this attack were publicly known, caused great fecret difcontent amongft the foldiers; and fuch reprefentations were made to the Governor, that he ordered the artillery to return their fire when they repeated their vifit.

THE evening of the 27th, the engineers, with a ftrong party, repaired the Queen's battery, (Willis's.) The new merlons were raifed with fand-bags on the bafe of the old ones, and the whole was completed before morning gun-fire. The following day, a fquadron of Ruffian men of war paffed through the Straits to the weft. Whilft they remained in fight, the Enemy increafed their fire upon the Garrifon. The fame day arrived the General Murray privateer and a polacre from Minorca, with wine, brandy, lemons, and falt; and in the evening, the Enterprife frigate, with feventeen ordnance-fhips and tranfports, failed for England. The Enemy difcovered them before they quitted the Bay, and repeated their fignals towards Cadiz. The Garrifon flag-ftaff, on the Grand battery, was now fo mutilated, and the flag fo much torn by the Enemy's fhot, that it became neceffary to erect a new one, which was done the night of the 28th; and it ferved to engage the attention of the Enemy in the fucceeding day's firing.

THE morning of the 29th, two Britifh frigates, the Flora and Crefcent, which had conveyed the Minorca ordnance-fhips to Mahon, appeared from the eaft. Captain Peere Williams, in the former, ftood towards the Bay, and being informed by Captain Curtis, that the Enterprife had failed the preceding evening, put about, and followed his confort, the Crefcent, which was then chafing two veffels, apparently Dutchmen, under the Barbary fhore: and foon after they difappeared, we heard a cannonade to the weft; which

which moſt likely proceeded from the enſuing engagement, as we afterwards learned that the ſhips chaſed were Dutch frigates.* At noon the ſame day, two artificers were executed at the White Convent in Iriſh Town for marauding ; and the following day, one of the 58th ſuffered for the ſame offence. The 31ſt, in the evening, a ſhip under Raguſan colours, attempting to get round Europa Point to proceed to Algeziras, was driven under our guns, and obliged to come in. She was laden with wheat and barley, bound from Barcelona to Cadiz ; and her cargo was condemned as a lawful prize.

THE Enemy's bombardment was conſiderably abated towards the cloſe of the month. Their objects for ſome time were the upper batteries, and particularly the Royal battery, whence they were greatly incommoded. They often attempted to reach Land port and the lines with grape from the advanced mortars ; but it ſeldom ranged farther than the Inundation. Our engineers, notwithſtanding their fire, continued making ſuch repairs as their cannonade rendered neceſſary.

ABOUT two o'clock, on the morning of the 1ſt of June, the gun and mortar boats ſaluted us as uſual, and wounded three or four men : they were in three diviſions. We returned the fire from different batteries between King's baſtion and Buena-Viſta. During this attack, an incident happened, which I will beg leave to inſert. A ſoldier, rambling about the town, accidentally found, in the ruins of a houſe, ſeveral watches and other articles of value, which he immediately made prize of ; but how to ſecrete them afterwards, was a ſubject that required the utmoſt reach of his

Y   invention.

---

* Captain Williams, in this action, took his opponent ; but the Creſcent, from ſome unfortunate accidents, was compelled to ſurrender to her adverſary. The Creſcent was however retaken by the Flora ; but being greatly damaged, both ſhe and the Flora's prize afterwards fell a prey to ſome French cruiſers.

invention. He was fenfible he could not fecure them in his quarters, as every foldier of his regiment was examined on his return from duty to his bomb-proof. He refolved, therefore, on a fingular expedient. Taking out the wad which ferved as a tompion to a gun on the King's baftion, he lodged his prize, which was tied in his handkerchief, as far as he could reach within the gun, and put the wad in its former place. In times of peace, he could not have devifed a better repofitory; but unfortunately the gun-boats coming the fame evening, (whilft he was faft afleep in his cafemate, not apprehending any danger to his fecreted treafure) this richly-loaded gun was one of the firft that was difcharged at the Enemy, and the foundation of his future greatnefs was difperfed in an inftant.

THE Enemy's cannonade, in the beginning of June, decreafed to about five hundred rounds in the twenty-four hours : the King's, or Black battery, (as it was called by the Garrifon,) with the two fourteen-gun batteries in their lines, were now filent.

THE morning of the 3d, the gun-boats repeated their vifit about the fame time as before. In this attack two ferjeants, of the 12th and 58th regiments, were killed, and two privates wounded: many fhells fell among the tents of the different regiments, and two fhot in the hofpital-yard. A corporal, going with the relief at Land port, had the muzzle of his firelock clofed, and the barrel twifted like a french-horn, by a fhell, without injury to his perfon. We returned the fire from the town-batteries, hoping by that means to engage their attention from our camp. The 4th, the Governor commemorated the anniverfary of His Majefty's birth-day, by a falute at noon of twenty-three cannon, and forty-three mortars, being the number of ordnance that bore on the St. Carlos's battery. The fire began at the Rock-mortar, feconded by the Old mole,

and

and fo on from right to left till the whole were difcharged : the Enemy, indulging themfelves as ufual with a *fiefta*, did not imme- diately return our fire; but in the early part of the day, they had made the town pretty warm, and fired twice or thrice through the royal ftandard.

IN the courfe of the 4th, a Tartan was taken coming in from the eaft : the crew, however, efcaped to the Garrifon in their boat. A Spanifh fquadron of two line-of-battle fhips, three xebeques, and two bomb-ketches, alfo arrived the fame day at Algeziras, from aloft. With this reinforcement, their naval force before Gibraltar amounted to two fhips of the line, five xebeques, two ketches, feveral half-gallies and armed veffels, with fifteen or fixteen gun and mortar boats. Thefe latter were become fo active, that we could never promife ourfelves a night's repofe without being difturbed by a cannonade; and their attacks were more vexatious from the impoffiblity of being able to retaliate, becaufe they prefented to us fo minute an object. Whenever the alarm was given of their approach, which was generally a little after midnight, the fouthern part of the rock was in immediate commotion. Their effects had been found fo deftructive, that all were upon the look-out : the troops were ordered from their tents, to places where they were covered from the fhot; but the fhells were directed into the moft fequeftered receffes. Such was the terror of the miferable inhabitants, that many of them fled nearly naked to the remote parts of the rock; and even here they could fcarcely deem themfelves fecure : in fhort, no fcene could be more deplorable than their diftrefs on thefe occafions.

THE Enemy's bombardment from the land was ftill continued with little variation : they appeared indeed to have no other object than the expenditure of ammunition. In their camp, large parties

were

were conſtantly bringing bruſh-wood for faſcines from the country; and others were employed in diſembarking ſtores, from ſmall veſſels which were daily arriving from all quarters.

THE 9th, we were alarmed with the blowing-up of one of the Enemy's magazines, ſituated at a ſmall diſtance from the Catalonian camp to the weſt of the Queen of Spain's chair. The different exploſions that ſucceeded the firſt, reſembled a continual roll of fire, like repeated vollies of muſquetry; from which circumſtance we conjectured, that it was their repoſitory for live ſhells, and fixed ammunition. Their drums immediately beat to arms; and the whole army, conſiſting of thirteen battalions beſides cavalry, aſſembled in front of the camp. Parties were inſtantly detached; but the ſplinters of the ſhells kept them for ſome time at a conſiderable diſtance. The ſhells however at length ceaſed to diſplode: they advanced, and removed powder, &c. from a neighbouring magazine, to a place ſouthward of the fire; where meeting afterwards in great numbers, our artillery endeavoured to reach them with a large ſhell from Willis's; but the diſtance was beyond the range of a ſea-mortar. From the long continuance and ſucceſſive loud reports, it was thought they muſt have ſuſtained great loſs; not only of ammunition, but of men; as the ſplinters were ſeen, with glaſſes, to range much farther than the ſpot where the detachment firſt aſſembled: and remarkable economy was afterwards obſerved in the article of ſhells.

THE following day, a line-of-battle ſhip, proceeding from Point Mala to the eaſtward, was fired upon from the Garriſon, and obliged to put about and anchor at Algeziras. A flag of truce came the day after to the New mole, to know the cauſe of our firing upon her, being a Neapolitan man of war. The Governor anſwered, that the firſt ſhot was to bring her to; which ſhe not
obeying,

obeying, every succeeding one was fired to sink her.   The night of
the 11th, the gun and mortar boats, according to custom, bombarded
the camp, killed a child, and wounded a woman.   They retired much
sooner than usual; which we attributed to their having received
some damage, as our grape was heard to strike them.   We returned
ninety-six rounds of various kinds.   Their land-batteries, during
the attack, directed their fire principally towards the King's bastion,
and along the line-wall in town, whence, they observed, we for
some time past generally fired when they came over.   The 14th,
being the anniversary of Corpus Christi, the festival was noticed by
the Enemy's shipping with the usual flags of decoration, and the
customary salutes : repeated vollies were likewise discharged from
the lines; which, being unexpected on our side,. killed and wounded
several.

1781,
June.

THOUGH their bombardment in general, at this period, scarcely
exceeded 450 rounds in twenty-four hours, yet the batteries at Willis's, notwithstanding the recent repairs, were again greatly damaged.
The Enemy's shot, though fired at so great a distance, frequently
pierced seven solid feet of sand-bag work.   To obviate this, strong
wooden frames, called *caissons*, were constructed of the same dimen-
sions as the merlons; which, when well rammed with clay, and
covered in front and on the top with junk cut in lengths for the
purpose, were expected to resist better than the temporary repairs
that had been done during the severity of the Enemy's fire.   The
Enemy also adopted the same mode in capping the merlons of Fort
St. Barbara.

A FLAG of truce, on the 15th, informed us that two ships had
been captured leaving the Garrison, and that the prisoners were
ready to be sent in.   The Fortune sloop, in consequence, the next
day, brought over 141 English and Jews, men, women, and children.

dren. It was remarked, that the Enemy the preceding day continued their bombardment during the flag of truce; but a ftrict
ceffation was obferved this day, owing, as we imagined, to fome
reprefentations. We obferved, on the 20th, a new camp of 112
tents in the rear of Barcelo's battery, north of Algeziras. The day
following, Montague's baftion was opened on the Enemy, as parties
were repairing the St. Carlos's battery.

THE bombardment now decreafed daily. The fire of the Enemy
was chiefly directed to our upper batteries, for the town was almoft
a heap of ruins: they fometimes threw a long-ranger; but thefe
fhells feldom did any injury. The night of the 24th, the gun-
boats fired upon the camp, but at fuch a diftance, that little
damage was received, though they expended four hundred fhot, and
feventy fhells. We returned eighty-eight rounds, principally fmall
fhells, whofe fufes were fo accurately cut, as to break juft over the
boats. The 27th, we obferved another encampment (capable of
quartering two battalions) at the Tower between the river Palmones
and Algeziras. Many were of opinion that this camp, with that at
Barcelo's battery, was occupied by militia. The gun and mortar
boats again bombarded our camp about midnight for two hours:
they then made their ufual fignal, and, as we imagined, were gone
back; but foon after, they returned, and re-commenced a brifker fire
than before; killed and wounded twelve or fourteen, the greateft
number of which were of the 39th regiment. This was the moft
important lofs which our troops had yet experienced from the gun-
boats; but we concluded ourfelves in fome degree fortunate in not
fuffering more confiderably; as moft of the regiments, imagining the
bombardment over for the night, were in bed when they returned.

THE difagreeable and frequent repetition of thefe attacks
prompted the Governor to adopt, if poffible, fome expedients to
annoy

annoy their camp in return. The diftance was conceived to be within the range of fhells from the Old-mole head : accordingly a thirteen-inch fea-mortar was removed to the extremity; and fix cannon, five thirty-two-pounders, and one eighteen-pounder, were at the fame time funk in the fand behind the Old mole, and then fecured with timber, &c. at different degrees of elevation.. Thefe arrangements had been for fome time in agitation; and being now completed, he determined to make the experiment. About ten o'clock in the forenoon of the 28th, fix rounds were difcharged from each : three of the fhells burft in the Enemy's camp, and one over it. The other two difploded in their paffage : all the fhot went home. A battalion of Spanifh guards, happening to be under arms, were greatly alarmed, and difperfed three different times : at length they were affembled, and marched off towards the left. This being only intended as an experiment, the artillery foon ceafed firing; but it is fcarcely poffible to exprefs the general fatisfaction which this fuccefs diffufed through the Garrifon. The mortar was loaded with from 30 lb. to 28½ lb. of powder at the ufual elevation; the thirty-two-pounder with 14, and the eighteen with 9 lb. of powder; the latter, all at forty-two degrees.

The Governor, befides this plan of retaliation, devifed other fchemes to cover and protect his camp, if poffible, from future attacks. Two brigs were ordered to be cut down and converted into *prames*, each to carry four or five heavy cannon; which were to be moored between the New mole and Ragged-ftaff, at fuch diftance from the works as to be eafily protected, and yet far enough out to keep their boats at a refpectful diftance. Artificers from the Garrifon affifted the Navy in fitting out thefe veffels. One of them, being finifhed previous to the before-mentioned experiment, was moored at the diftance of about half mufquet-fhot from the New-mole head.. She was named the Vanguard, mounted two Spanifh

twenty-

twenty-fix-pounders, and two twelves, and was rigged like a fettee.
The Enemy's fquadron, on the 29th, was reinforced with five
xebeques and two gallies, from the eaft.   At night failed a packet
for Faro, in Portugal.

July.
THE 2d of July, additional tents were pitched at the new camp
near the Tower, north of Algeziras.   About one in the morning
of the 4th, the gun-boats repeated their attack ; but, contrary to
their former cuftom, numbers of their fhot and fhells fell amongft
the fhipping.   The Porcupine frigate, Sir Charles Knowles, Bart.
and an Indiaman, each received a fhot; and the Brilliant's bottom
was ftruck with a fplinter of a fhell, which burft under her; but
no particular damage was received in the Garrifon, except two
men being flightly wounded.   The Governor retaliated by ordering
fix rounds of fhot and fhells to be fired into their camp, from the
guns and fea-mortars at the Old mole : the cannon were pointed
indifcriminately for the camp; but the mortars were laid for the
fafcine and artillery parks.   One of the fhells fet fire to a hut, and
alarmed them exceedingly.   As the Governor now determined
to retaliate in this manner, we were in hopes it would deter them
from fo frequently difturbing us.

THE Enemy continued making gabions, and bringing much wood
into the camp : on the other hand, our people were employed in
repairs, and additions to the works.   Traverfes were erected at the
Royal battery, and parties were employed on the north front, from
the Rock-gun, to the Old-mole head.   The 10th, a brig coming
in from the eaft was taken by the Enemy's cruifers, which for fome
weeks paft had again kept a very vigilant look-out.   The crew
however efcaped to the rock; and they had thrown the letters
over-board, before they abandoned the veffel.

THE

THE bombardment, which, by almoſt imperceptible degrees, had been decreaſing, on the 12th nearly ceaſed. The cannon in their ſeven and fourteen-gun batteries were all drawn back, to facilitate, as we imagined, the repairing of the platforms, and inner part of the batteries. The 13th, ſome troops at the tower decamped, and in a few days afterwards a regiment marched away from the Algeziras camp. The 15th, two ſettees and a brig failed from Point Mala, with gabions, to the weſt. One veſſel had failed thence on the 13th. Theſe materials, we conjectured, were for ſome new works in the neighbourhood; but we were afterwards informed that they were taken to Minorca, and were uſed in the approaches carried on againſt St. Philip's. Their firing was now confined to the night, and, unleſs we provoked them, ſcarcely ever exceeded thirty rounds.

THE Spaniſh General viſited the Lines on the 18th; but a fire breaking out in his camp, he returned immediately on its appearance. In the evening, the caiſſons for the Queen's battery being carried up to Willis's, and the ſand-bags brought from Pocoroca clay-pit, the engineers at duſk, with a party of three hundred and eighty men, began to re-eſtabliſh the merlons; and by the morning gun-fire of the 19th, the old ſand-bags were removed, the caiſſons placed, and filled with clay, ſand, and junk, and the battery made fit for the reception of artillery. The Governor was preſent the whole time, and expreſſed the higheſt approbation of the diligence and activity of the party. The caiſſons were made of oak timber, joined by ſtrong iron bolts. Whilſt they were at work, the gunboats fired upon the camp, and were ſeconded by the land-batteries on the town: a hundred and thirty-two rounds were returned on the boats, and ſixteen ſhells thrown into the Enemy's camp. One of the artillery and one of the 73d regiment were wounded.

THE

THE morning of the 20th, the Enemy fired a salute from the Lines, followed by a feu-de-joie from the army drawn up in two lines in front of their camp, concluding with a grand discharge from their shipping and small craft at Algeziras. The troops in garrison changed quarters on the 21st: the 39th and Hardenberg's regiments relieved the 72d, and other detachments in King's and Montague's bastions, Waterport-casemate, and Picquet-yard. The 58th, 72d, and 73d regiments encamped; the 12th regiment remained on their ground; and the 56th, Reden's, and La Motte's, occupied the South barracks, and other quarters. The Enemy, on the same day, decamped from the ground north of Algeziras. Brigadier Rofs failed, on the night of the 22d, in a boat to Faro, in his route to England; and the following day, a privateer arrived in eight days from Mahon, with a packet. Two days afterwards, a boat arrived from Portugal. The patron informed us, that the army at that time before Gibraltar principally consisted of militia regiments, the regular troops having embarked for the West-Indies : he further said, that the Spanish fleet had failed from Cadiz on a cruise. Soon after this boat arrived, a large fleet, of upwards of seventy sail, appeared from the west : when abreast of Europa, we discovered amongst them a ship of the line, two frigates, two cutters, a bomb-ketch, and several armed vessels : they did not display any colours.*

OUR camp was alarmed, on the 27th, with the report that the gun-boats were approaching. The batteries were manned, and the regiments assembled; but the Enemy not appearing, they returned to quarters. The signals for seeing the boats in future, were ordered to be a false fire, and two guns from the shipping.

Auguft.   AUGUST was introduced by an attack from the gun-boats. They came upon us by surprise; for we had no signal from our guard-boats.
                                                This

---

* This proved to be the fleet which afterwards blockaded Mahon.

This was afterwards accounted for, by the Enemy having taken a circle; by which means our guard-boats, when they began to fire, were without, and the gun-boats between them and the Garriſon. Our fire in return was well ſerved, and appeared to do ſome execution: twelve large ſhells and fifteen ſhot were likewiſe thrown into the camp from the Old mole: ſeveral of the former burſt juſt as they fell, conſequently promiſed to do miſchief. Their land-batteries ſeconded the fire from the ſea, but we did not experience any caſualties. Two days afterwards, the other prame, called the Repulſe, mounting five twenty-ſix-pounders, was moored about muſquet-ſhot to the ſouthward of the Vanguard, and the ſame diſtance from our batteries. Theſe veſſels were of ſuch annoyance to their boats, that whilſt they remained out, we never afterwards were ſo much diſturbed at the ſouthward.

The Artillery at Willis's endeavoured, on the 4th, to ſet fire to the canes and weeds in the gardens; but they were too full of ſap to take fire. This attempt attracted a briſk cannonade for ſome time from the Enemy. Early in the morning of the 6th, a ſhell fell into a tent behind General La Motte's quarters, at the ſouthward, in which were two men of the 58th, aſleep. They were not awakened by its fall; but a ſerjeant in an adjacent tent heard it, and ran near forty yards to a place of ſafety, when he recollected the ſituation of his friends. Thinking the ſhell had fallen blind, he returned and awakened them: both immediately roſe, but continued by the place, debating on the narrow eſcape they had had, when the ſhell exploded, and forced them with great violence againſt the garden-wall, but miraculouſly did no further miſchief than deſtroying every thing in the tent.

On the morning of the 7th, before the haze was quite diſpelled in the Gut, a ſignal for an enemy was made by the Spaniards at

Cabrita

Cabrita Point.. As the fog diſperſed, we diſcovered, at a conſiderable diſtance, a veſſel becalmed, but rowing towards the Garriſon
with the current. Fourteen gun-boats were then advancing from
Algeziras to intercept her; upon which Captain Curtis, of the
Brilliant, ordered out Sir Charles Knowles, with three barges, to
endeavour to get along-ſide, and receive any diſpatches the veſſel
might have on board, whilſt he attended the towing out of the
Vanguard and Repulſe prames, to cover them, and protect her. Sir
Charles perſonally executed his orders, and returned with a packet
for the Governor. The veſſel by this time was about a league and
a half from the Garriſon, and the headmoſt gun-boat within ſhot,.
advancing apparently with an intent to board: ſtopping, however, at
the diſtance of a few hundred yards, ſhe poured in a diſcharge of
round and grape ſhot, and was immediately ſeconded by her conſorts
aſtern. The veſſel, which we now diſcovered to be a King's ſloop
of war, returned the ſalute with a broadſide, and muſquetry from her
quarter-deck; and a ſpirited action commenced. Appearances at
this juncture were ſo greatly in favour of the Spaniards, that the Garriſon gave up the ſloop for loſt. Becalmed a league from the Rock,
and fourteen gun-boats, each carrying a twenty-ſix-pounder, full of
men, cannonading her on every ſide with grape and round ſhot; a
xebeque alſo bearing down with a gentle breeze; were circumſtances
which ſeemed to preclude the poſſibility of eſcape. After maintaining, however, a very warm, judicious, and well-ſerved fire, often
obliging the boats to retire, the weſterly breeze at laſt reached her;
and not long afterwards ſhe was ſafe under our guns. She proved to
be the Helena ſloop of war, fourteen ſmall guns, Captain Roberts, in
fourteen days from England. Her loſs during this action was much
leſs than could have been poſſibly imagined, when we conſidered the
ſhowers of grape and round ſhot that every inſtant ſurrounded her:
ſhe had only one killed and two wounded; but her upper rigging
and ſails were much cut and injured. We attributed the hull's being
                                                          ſcarcely

scarcely touched, to the construction of the gun-boats; for, being originally intended to annoy at a distance, their cannon could not be depressed. The Enemy however did not escape so well: numbers were seen to drop in the boats from the musquetry of the sloop, and several were towed off disabled; which were very convincing proofs that their loss was considerable.

A SETTEE was taken on the 12th by the Enemy's cruisers. The crew, excepting three Jew passengers, escaped to the Garrison: they informed us, that great preparations were making in the French and Spanish ports for some grand expedition: the object was however kept secret; but many at Minorca suspected St. Philip's to be the place.

THE Enemy's bombardment, if we may now call it by that name, scarcely exceeded, at this time, THREE shells in the twenty-four hours, which the soldiers (conjecturing that some allusion might be intended, by that superstitious nation, to the sacred Trinity) jocosely, though profanely termed, *Father, Son,* and *Holy Ghost.* It is not indeed altogether improbable, that the Spaniards might entertain some bigoted respect for that mystical number, and, considering the British in the light of heretics, might apprehend some efficacy from it, in the great work of *converting the Garrison to the Catholic faith :* at least it is difficult, on any more reasonable ground, to account for their exactly continuing to fire neither more nor less, for so considerable a period.

THE mention of this circumstance brings to my recollection another, of a ridiculous nature, which serves to demonstrate the thoughtlessness of the English soldiers, who can jest in the hour of danger, and indulge their prejudices at the expence of what other nations, however differing in sentiment, generally agree to hold in a degree of respect. It is first to be remembered, that, according to

the

the articles of capitulation, by which the Garriſon was ſurrendered to
Admiral Sir George Rooke, it was ſtipulated that the Inhabitants
ſhould be tolerated in their religion : the old Spaniſh church was
therefore continued as a place of worſhip for thoſe of the Roman-
Catholic perſuaſion, and, as is uſual in Roman-Catholic churches,
was decorated, amongſt others, with figures, as large as life, of our
Saviour and the Virgin Mary.

At the commencement of the firing, when the ſoldiers were
engaged in a ſucceſſion of irregularities, a party of them aſſembled in
the Spaniſh church, to carouſe and be merry.   In the midſt of their
jollity, the image of the Virgin Mary was obſerved in the ruins by
one of the party, who inſtantly propoſed, as a piece of fun, to place
her Ladyſhip in the whirligig.*   The ſcheme ſeemed to meet with
general approbation, till one, wiſer than the reſt, ſtopped them with
a remark, that it would ill become them, as military men, and particularly Engliſhmen, to puniſh any perſon without a trial.   A court
martial conſequently ſat, with mock ceremony ; and her Ladyſhip
was found guilty of drunkenneſs, debauchery, and other high crimes,
and condemned to the whirligig, whither ſhe was immediately carried
in proceſſion.   The Governor, (who, notwithſtanding the firing,
regularly attended the parade) at guard-mounting diſcovered the poor
Virgin in confinement ; but expreſſed his diſapprobation of the
action, and ordered her inſtantly to be removed to the White convent, where, by the bye, ſhe was by no means exempt from further inſult and diſgrace.   If a bigoted Spaniard could have beheld
this tranſaction, he probably would have thought the Engliſh worſe
than heretics ; and would have concluded, that their impiety could
not fail to attract the ſpecial vengeance of Heaven.

THE

* A machine erected at the bottom of the Grand parade, for the puniſhment of ſcolding-
women, or others guilty of trifling miſdemeanours.

1781,
Auguft.

THE night of the 15th, the gun and mortar boats bombarded our camp; their difpofition extending from off Little bay to the Old-mole head : their fire, as had been the cuftom for fome time before, was feconded by a brifk cannonade from the Lines, which was very judicioufly ferved. Many of their fhells burft in the air, over our fhipping ; but the fhips continued filent. Our artillery retaliated from the Old-mole head, and *fmall* fhells were difcharged from the elevated guns, which feemed to anfwer very well. One of the 72d regiment was killed ; two of the artillery, and two of the 73d, with a boy, an inhabitant, were wounded. In this attack, a fhell fell amongft fome naval ftores, in a ground-ward of the Naval Ho-fpital ; and the moft dreadful confequences might have been expected from this accident, if the fire had not been happily extinguifhed by the picquet, which the Governor had ordered, fome time before, to affemble here, to prevent, if poffible, fuch cafualties. The other picquet, which mounted at the fouthward, was ftationed for the fame purpofe at the New mole.

A SCHOONER arrived from Faro on the 17th, with fruit, onions, and falt. In the evening, a flag of truce came from the Enemy, in anfwer to ours of the preceding day. The day following, another boat arrived from Faro : fhe brought a packet, with fome private letters from Lifbon, which intimated the probability of our receiving a vifit from the Combined fleet, then cruifing off Cadiz. At night feveral guns were heard in the Gut, and a number of fignals made at the Point. The fucceeding morning, his Majefty's cutter the Kite arrived from England, with duplicates of the Helena's dif-patches. In her paffage fhe engaged a French cutter of twenty guns, and had three men killed and fix wounded. The Enemy's cruifers endeavoured to intercept her, but were driven to leeward. A boat alfo arrived about the fame time from Portugal.

THE

THE firing from the Garriſon now varied according as the Enemy's parties preſented themſelves: at this period they were buſy in repairing Fort St. Philip, and in ſecuring their works againſt the approaching rainy ſeaſon. Our Engineers were repairing the communications and batteries at Willis's, &c. A ſoldier of the 73d deſerted to the Enemy the 25th: he had been abſent from his corps five days, during which time he had concealed himſelf on the rock. Hunger probably preſſing him, he determined to make a bold attempt to get off: accordingly ſtuffing a ſand-bag with graſs, he came to Land port, and placing, unobſerved, the bag upon the ſpikes of the paliſades, jumped, unhurt, on the glacis; then running over the Cauſeway, he ſoon cleared Bay-ſide barrier, and, though many hundred rounds of muſquetry were fired from Land port and the Lines guards, he eſcaped. He was the fourth man loſt by deſertion in the courſe of ſix weeks.

EARLY the 27th, four men, who had been impreſſed from a privateer in the Bay, deſerted from the Repulſe prame. The next morning we were viſited again by the gun and mortar boats; but they ſcarcely ſtaid one third of their former time. We returned nine ſhot and fifty-eight ſhells, which, from the ſhrieks and piteous cries we heard, muſt have done execution. We annoyed them in camp from the Old mole, as uſual; and the artillery attempted to reach them from Willis's, but in vain. In this attack a wounded matroſs was killed by a ſhell in the Hoſpital. The circumſtances attending this man's caſe are ſo melancholy and affecting, that I cannot paſs them over in ſilence. Some time previous to this event, he had been ſo unlucky as to break his thigh: being a man of great ſpirits, he ill brooked the confinement which his caſe demanded, and exerted himſelf to get abroad, that he might enjoy the benefit of the freſh air in the court of the hoſpital: unfortunately, in one of his playful moments, he fell, and was obliged to take to his bed
again.

again. He was in this ſituation, when a ſhell from the mortar-boats fell into the ward, and rebounding lodged upon him. The convaleſcents and ſick, in the ſame room, inſtantly ſummed up ſtrength to crawl out on hands and knees, whilſt the fuſe was burning; but this wretched victim was kept down by the weight of the ſhell, which after ſome ſeconds burſt, took off both his legs, and ſcorched him in a dreadful manner: but, what was ſtill more horrid, he ſurvived the exploſion, and was ſenſible to the very moment that death relieved him from his miſery. His laſt words were expreſſive of regret that he had not been killed on the batteries.

THE Enemy's attention to the blockade ſeemed now to be revived. Their cruiſers were increaſed, and conſtantly on the watch. The force in the Bay at this time was one ſhip of the line, a xebeque having a broad pendant, a frigate, and five xebeques, with the gun and mortar boats, and ſmall armed craft. The arrangement of theſe veſſels for the purpoſe of blockading the Garriſon, appeared to be as follows. When the wind was weſt, two xebeques and four gun-boats anchored at Cabrita point, cruiſing at night at the entrance of the Bay and in the Straits: when eaſterly, the frigate, xebeques, and four gun-boats, cruiſed ſome between Ceuta and Europa, and others in the Gut: one xebeque was generally obſerved to lie-to off Europa point, at the entrance of the Bay. Though this diſpoſition apparently obſtructed all intercourſe between the Garriſon and our friends in Portugal and Minorca, yet opportunities ſometimes occurred, when boats ſlipped out unobſerved, and returned with the ſame ſucceſs.

THE evening of the 30th, the Enemy's cannonade, which, except when the boats fired on our camp, ſeldom exceeded three ſhells in the twenty-four hours, was pretty ſmart for an hour or two;

A a   occaſioned

occaſioned by our firing on their working-parties. Such ſtarts of retaliation they were often provoked to, by our annoying their workmen in the batteries.

Sept.　THE prames had been found ſo uſeful, that in the beginning of September, the Navy began to fit up the Fortune ſloop, in order to add her to their number. The 5th, a flag of truce from the Enemy brought over —— Pratts, an inhabitant of Gibraltar, who had been taken by the Spaniards in the Fox packet, about twelve months before, and whom, as it was ſaid, the Enemy for ſome time had objected to exchange. By this man we were informed that the Duke de Crillon, with ten thouſand men, had landed at Minorca, and that it was reported he was to be joined by a French army from Toulon. The evening of the 7th, the Captain at Willis's again endeavoured to ſet fire to the weeds, &c. in the gardens, which from their height afforded great cover to the Enemy's advanced ſentries; and in executing theſe orders a briſk cannonade was returned by the Enemy, which continued till day-break. Our carcaſſes and light balls frequently took effect; but the canes were too green to be burnt to any purpoſe. In the courſe of this firing, ſeveral ſhot from the Lines ranged as far as the South barracks and New mole. Great numbers of gabions were now obſerved in the Enemy's faſcine-park.

THE evening of the 12th, they fired a grand ſalute from their lines and ſhipping, and a feu-de-joie in camp. After the ſalute, they continued to cannonade from the lines, though for ſome days before they had only fired their myſtical number in the twenty-four hours. We imagined this ſalute to be on account of the Duke de Crillon's having gained ſome advantage at Minorca. In the courſe of their firing, on the 15th, a circumſtance happened,

similar

similar to one which occurred in May; and both of them may be considered as extraordinary. A shell from the Lines fell upon the rock, above the Red sands, and glanced off in a direction nearly at right angles with its range : it rolled to the bottom of the Princess of Wales's lines, burst on the platform of one of the thirty-two-pounders, and a splinter cutting the apron of the gun, fired it off : the shot took away the railing at the foot of the glacis, and lodged in the line-wall near Ragged-staff.

We observed, on the 16th, that the Enemy, during the preceding night, had thrown up three banks of sand in *zig-zags*, beginning at the centre of the fourth branch of approach, which seemed intended as a line of direction for a new communication to the St. Carlos's battery. In the evening, the Governor ordered the artillery to direct a brisk fire on this work, which was continued till day-break of the 17th. The Enemy returned the fire reluctantly, from a wish, as we imagined, not to increase ours. The next morning, we observed they had retained the sand thrown up the preceding night with casks; and from the materials seen in the vicinity of the works, other additions seemed intended to be made. At night, Crouchett's howitzer-battery and Montague's bastion were opened, and, with Willis's, &c. were kept constantly going. About mid-night the gun-boats, attended by a bomb-ketch, as we conjectured, came over, and, contrary to their former practice, directed their fire towards Willis's, the Lines, and north end of the Town. So determined were they to land their shells, that one went over the rock, and many fell on the hill ; and, in attempting to imitate us, in bursting their shells in the air, several disploded in their mor-tars. They staid two hours and a half, and expended a hundred and thirty shells and eighty-seven shot, and their land-batteries were not so sparing as the night before. We returned a smart fire on both sea and land, and retaliated on their camp, as usual.

A a 2

A SHELL,

A SHELL, during the above attack, fell in an embrasure oppofite the King's-lines bomb-proof, killed one of the 73d, and wounded another of the fame corps. The cafe of the latter was fingular, and will ferve to enforce the maxim, that even in the moft dangerous cafes, we fhould never defpair of a recovery whilft life remains. This unfortunate man was knocked down by the wind of the fhell, which, inftantly burfting, killed his companion, and mangled him in a moft dreadful manner. His head was terribly fractured, his left arm broken in two places, one of his legs fhattered, the fkin and mufcles torn off part of his right hand, the middle finger broken to pieces, and his whole body moft feverely bruifed, and marked with gun-powder. He prefented fo horrid an object to the furgeons, that they had not the fmalleft hopes of faving his life, and were at a lofs what part to attend to firft. He was that evening trepanned; a few days afterwards his leg was amputated, and other wounds and fractures dreffed. Being poffeffed of a moft excellent conftitution, nature performed wonders in his favour, and in eleven weeks the cure was completely effected. His name is Donald Rofs, and he now enjoys his Sovereign's bounty in a penfion of one fhilling a day for life. A non-commiffioned officer of artillery alfo loft his thigh on Montague's baftion; and a private of the 12th regiment, both his legs: the latter died foon after the amputation was performed.

THE morning of the 18th, a deferter from the Spanifh guards came in from the St. Carlos's battery. He was purfued by four of the Enemy, but in vain. He gave information of the Enemy's intention to erect fome new batteries. About ten o'clock in the evening, a fhell from the Lines fell into a houfe oppofite the King's baftion, where the Town-Major, Captain Burke, with Majors Mercier and Vignoles, of the 39th regiment, were fitting. The fhell took off Major Burke's thigh; afterwards fell through the

floor

floor into the cellar: there it burft, and forced the flooring, with the unfortunate Major, to the cieling.   When affiftance came, they found Major Burke almoft buried amongft the ruins of the room. He was inftantly conveyed to the Hofpital, where he died foon after. the wounded part was amputated, much lamented by his friends as an amiable and worthy member of fociety, and by the Governor as an indefatigable officer.   Majors Mercier and Vignoles had time to efcape before the fhell burft: they were neverthelefs flightly wounded by the fplinters; as were a ferjeant of the 39th, and his daughter, who were in the cellar underneath when the fhell entered. This houfe had efcaped almoft untouched during the warmeft period of the bombardment, till this unfortunate fhell fell in, which. deprived the Garrifon of this active and valuable officer.

THE Enemy did not increafe their works the fucceeding day, but *debouched* the fourth branch of the approach about the centre. In the evening, the Helena and Kite, with a privateer, left the Bay for England, and a fchooner for Portugal.   Lieut. Lowe, of the 12th, who had loft his leg, and the invalids, went home in the former. Our firing was increafed at night by the Catalan batteries; and Crouchett's was ftill kept open.   The 20th,. Capt. Fowlis, of the. 73d, was appointed Town-major.

OUR working-parties were employed by the engineers, on the 21ft, in repairing Princefs Caroline's battery, at Willis's,. which, owing to the fpirited behaviour and example of the officers, was cleared, the caiffons placed, filled, and the battery completed before night, under a moft heavy fire from the Enemy.   When the work, was finifhed, the party defired to give three cheers: but they were over-ruled by the Captain of artillery, who recommended to falute the Enemy with three rounds from each gun; which was immediately put in execution.   The party had not a man materially hurt
during

during the warm cannonade; but, in returning to be difmiffed, a ferjeant of La Motte's, who had braved the dangers of the day, was killed by a random-fhot below the artillery-guard.   Our firing continued with great vivacity on the 22d, particularly with fmall fhells from the Royal battery, Willis's, and Montague's baftion: thefe were kept going in the day; and at night thefe batteries, with the Catalans, Crouchett's, and batteries at the entrance of the Lines, were in action.   The Enemy in return were not fparing of ammunition : in the preceding twenty-four hours they fired feven hundred and feventy-five fhot, and fifty-feven fhells.   The Garrifon difcharged feven hundred and feventy-three rounds of different fpecies.

THE Enemy's new works were erected with cafks, covered and retained by fafcines, with fand in the front.   About two hundred men appeared to be employed in the day; but they were often compelled to retire, our ordnance was fo well ferved and directed.   The gun-boats, on the morning of the 24th, vifited us as ufual; and it was thought that a bomb-ketch again attended them. They pointed their fire principally towards the Victualling-office, in town, and Willis's: fome fhells fell in the New mole, but few afhore at the fouthward.   We returned their fire, and retaliated from the Old mole on their camp.

EARLY in the morning of the 25th, the fafcine-capping of the merlons of Fort Barbara took fire from the Enemy's guns, and burnt extremely fierce.   The officer at Willis's immediately directed a brifk fire on the Fort; which the Governor afterwards increafed, by opening the Grand battery.   The firing however from the latter did not anfwer fo well as was expected; owing perhaps to the unevennefs of the platforms, which are of ftone, and much worn: neverthelefs, the Enemy were obliged to evacuate the

Fort,

Fort, without extinguifhing the fire. At day-break we faw only
five fafcine-merlons ftanding : the other feven were all deftroyed,
with fome gun-carriages, traverfes on the rampart, and fafcine-
work in the ditch. We imagined that this accident would render
the Fort ufelefs for fome time; but they convinced us that our
conclufions were premature, by firing, probably out of bravado, a
few fhot in the courfe of the day; which killed one of the 58th,
and wounded another. In the morning, about feven, the Flying-
fifh cutter, of twenty guns, arrived with ordnance-ftores and in-
trenching tools : fhe informed us that Government had engaged
twenty cutters, of her force, for the fame purpofe. A xebeque and
four gun-boats oppofed her paffage, but in vain.

THE 26th, Lieut. Clarke, of the 56th, died of a decline. In
the courfe of the day, the Enemy began to clear Fort Barbara,
and in the evening to lay fafcines, (a great number of which were
in the neighbourhood of the Fort) towards repairing it. Our fire
continued to be well directed, and confiderably annoyed them. The
27th, a man was difcovered near Catalan bay, by the guard at
Middle-hill. A party of the Navy immediately went round, and
took him up. He proved to be a deferter from the 72d regiment;
but the wretch was fo famifhed with hunger, and fo bruifed in
getting down the rock, that his life was defpaired of. The 28th,
the Enemy capped two merlons of Fort Barbara. Their parties
were very diligent in making gabions and fafcines : the former we
imagined were removed, as they were finifhed, to the Lines and
advanced works, as we had obferved feveral behind the fourth
and fifth branches of the approach. This circumftance, with their
unufual activity in completing others, confirmed our late intelligence, that they intended additional batteries near the St. Carlos's.

THE firing from the Garrifon now exceeded feven hundred rounds
in the twenty-four hours; and the Enemy frequently return
ei

eight hundred, and sometimes more. Our casuals consequently began again to be pretty frequent, amongst our parties, which, in a great measure, was owing to the want of prudence in the men, who were become so habituated to the Enemy's fire, as scarcely to regard their shot. In fact, if a shell was at their feet, it was almost necessary for the officers to caution them to avoid its effects. It was really wonderful to behold with what undaunted coolness they persisted in their several occupations, though exposed to the Enemy's whole artillery: indeed the generality appeared totally callous to every sense of danger.

BOTH sides continued indefatigable in their operations. The Enemy finished two or three merlons in Fort Barbara, erected traverses near the Tower, in the rear of the new communication, and were continually bringing large quantities of fascines, &c. to the Lines. On the other hand, our engineers caissoned the terrace-batteries, replaced the sand-bags before the merlons of the Queen's battery, and had parties daily employed in repairs. The 30th, a soldier of the 72d lost his legs by a shot from Fort Barbara, from which they continued occasionally to fire. He bore amputation with prodigious firmness, but died soon after, through the loss of blood, previous to his being brought to the Hospital. This fact being represented to the Governor, the serjeants of the different regiments were ordered to attend the Hospital, to be taught by the surgeons how to apply the *tourniquets*; which was afterwards productive of very beneficial consequences. Tourniquets were also distributed to the different guards, to be at hand in case of necessity.

Oct.   THE Enemy, for several days, had made very little addition to the new communication, and the third return appeared still unfinished. A party of the Enemy was however discovered from Willis's, on the evening of the 1st of October, working to the west of the Mill-battery;

battery; and they perfifting in their labour, our fire was increafed from the batteries below; which brought on a warm return. At day-break we obferved, at the extremity of the new approach, a large epaulement, of forty-five gabions long, two in height, and four or five in breadth. On the top were feveral layers of fand-bags, and fand was banked up to protect it in front. It was fituated within the weftern *place d'armes* of the St. Carlos's battery, towards the beach, in a direction forming a very obtufe angle with the front of the Mill-battery. Our engineers immediately agreed that this epaulement was intended for mortars; which induced the Governor, in the courfe of the 2d, to order two embrafures (mafked at the Old-mole head, to cover the mortars which we ufually fired into their camp) to be opened, and two howitzers to be kept in action from thence. At night, our firing at intervals was fo aftonifhingly brifk, that the whole north front, from the Rock-gun to the Mole-head, was obfcured in fmoke. This fire was continued, with little intermiffion, till day-break; and though the Enemy did not return it warmly, they made up for their filence the fucceeding day. During the twenty-four hours they difcharged twelve hundred and fixty-three rounds, and the preceding day, one thoufand nine hundred and forty-eight; which to us was a proof that they were confiderably galled by our fire.

WE had obferved, for fome weeks, a party of the Enemy erecting a building upon an eminence, near the Stone quarry, under the Queen of Spain's chair, which at length turned out to be a fignal-tower; but no ufe was made of it till the beginning of this month, when we difcovered that it was intended to give information to their batteries in the lines, when our working-parties were going up the hill. On their marching up, the morning of the 3d, a fignal was made from the tower, and their batteries immediately increafed their fire on the heights: on their return in the evening, the fignal was

B b repeated.

repeated. This practice they continued for some time. At night, the body of a soldier of the 12th regiment, who attempted to swim to the Enemy from Water port, was discovered floating near the Repulse prame. The sailors on the watch, imagining some large fish had got foul of their cable, darted a harpoon into the body, but soon found out their mistake. The succeeding morning, we observed that the Enemy had thrown up a cover, from the eastern shoulder of the new battery, to the western magazine of the St. Carlos's: they also raised a shoulder on the western extremity, and erected five traverses in the rear.

OUR firing, on the 4th, was ordered to be diminished; only Montague's and the Hill batteries were kept going: few shot were now used, as the Enemy seemed to pay little attention to them; and we had ocular proofs daily of the annoyance from the small shells, which immediately made them desist, and get under cover. The same day a mutiny was discovered on board His Majesty's cutter the Speedwell, Lieut. Gibson; and four of the ringleaders were seized and confined. The plan of this conspiracy was, to murder the officers of the watch, cut the cable, and run away with the vessel to Algeziras, where they computed she would sell for a handsome sum, which was to be equally divided amongst the people interested, who were then to depart for England. Near half the crew were concerned; and the same evening, if the wind continued favourable, the scheme was to have been put in execution. Happily one of the party (I believe, a Spanish deserter) confessed in time to render the whole abortive. It was somewhat singular, that Mr. Gibson had been so unfortunate, when in England, as to have the cutter he then commanded run away with by the crew, into a French port, whilst he and his officers were ashore.

THE

THE Enemy, on the night of the 4th, threw up a line of casks and sand, extending upwards of sixty feet in a parallel line to the front of St. Carlos's. Some additions were also made to the new battery. The raising of the former work induced many to believe, that they were come at last to the determination of besieging the Garrison in form; and that this, with other works to be erected, would be the first parallel of attack. It was a lucky circumstance, in some respects, to have an enemy so tardy in their operations. Our troops were now accustomed, by six months bombardment, to the discharge and effect of heavy artillery: their firing had pointed out our weak places, which the Governor and engineers had been indefatigable in strengthening, so that the Garrison was now really in a better state of defence than at the commencement of the bombardment. In the nights of the 5th and 6th, the parallel, as we called the line to the east, was extended about a hundred feet, and the new mortar-battery raised with fascines. Small traverses were also made in the rear of the new approach from the fourth branch.

THE gun and mortar boats had now been absent some time; probably owing to the repairs which the mortar-boats necessarily demanded. On the evening of the 7th, they however renewed their visit, much earlier than was customary, and staid upwards of two hours. Their shot seemed all directed at our prames, whilst their shells, the fuses of which were remarkably dark, were thrown ashore. They fired about three hundred shot, and twenty-three shells, killed one of the 73d, and wounded two of the 12th. We returned forty-three shot, sixteen grape, and two hundred and seventy-nine shells. The 8th, two mortars were mounted in the new mortar-battery; and from the pickets marked for the platforms, we concluded it would mount eight mortars. In the afternoon, a shell fell into a house in town, in which Ensign

Stephens,

Stephens, of the 39th, was fitting: imagining himfelf not fafe where he was, he quitted the room to get to a more fecure place; but juft as he paffed the door, the fhell burft, and a fplinter mortally wounded him in the reins, and another took off his leg. He was conveyed to the Hofpital, and had fuffered amputation before the furgeons difcovered the mortal wound in his body. He died about feven o'clock, much regretted as a promifing young officer.

The Enemy's parties appearing numerous within the new works, our firing from the Garrifon was increafed on the 11th, and was as brifkly returned. The Governor however ordered the artillery to be lefs profufe in future, unlefs fome cafualty demanded an additional fire; for their lofs, he was of opinion, bore no proportion to our expenditure. Our fmall fhells were alfo decreafing very faft; and the Enemy appeared too well covered with traverfes in the new works, to be much annoyed by them. The fucceeding day our fire fcarcely exceeded a hundred rounds; and the Enemy's was equally diminifhed.

Their naval force before Gibraltar at this time was rather infignificant, though perfectly fufficient for the blockade. Moft of their xebeques had left the ftation, as we imagined, to block up Mahon; and only one line-of-battle fhip, one frigate, one xebeque, and two bomb-ketches, with the fmall craft and gun-boats, remained in the Bay. The 13th, the Governor ordered our lower batteries to be filent, in order to prove whether the Enemy could be diverted from firing on the Town, as their batteries, contrary to the ufual practice of befiegers, feemed to be guided in a great meafure by ours; and the manœuvre had the defired effect. Their parties were now employed chiefly in finifhing the interior part of the new mortar-battery.

THE

THE Garrison, on the 15th, fired only forty rounds; and the Enemy did not exceed double the number. The night of the 18th they were heard hard at work; but this circumstance produced no additional fire from us, as our artillery had been limited to a certain quantity since the Governor ordered the firing to decrease. The subsequent morning we observed they had erected a battery, of six embrasures, joining the second branch of the new communication, and bearing on Water port and the Town, about twelve hundred yards from the Grand battery: only four merlons appeared finished: the other three were in a rude state, with a number of fascines, pickets, and planks lying about the work, and at the *débouchure* of the fourth branch. The Governor, in the morning of the 19th, ordered a warm fire on the new battery, which the Enemy instantly returned. One of our carcasses set fire to the first branch of the new approach, and it burnt for some time. The following morning we found they had removed the sand to extinguish the fire, and displaced many of the fascines, which, with other materials, were lying in a confused manner in the vicinity of the breach.

THE night of the 20th, we were visited by the gun-boats; but their stay was much shorter than usual, owing to the springing-up of a brisk easterly wind: one of their shells slightly wounded Assistant-engineer Evans. This attack we imagined was intended to engage our attention from the land side, where the Enemy were heard busily at work: it had not however that effect, as our batteries directed an additional fire, and continued it the whole night. At day-break we found they had repaired the breach made by the fire, and strengthened the merlons of their gun-battery with gabions and sand heaped up in front.

THE situation of this battery afforded a more serious appearance than any operation yet undertaken by the Enemy. Colonel Tovey, the

the Commandant of artillery, therefore recommended to the Governor to open upon it, without loss of time, from such heavy guns
and howitzers as might be soon brought to bear upon it; assisted,
at the same time, with some thirteen-inch shells, and a few *red-hot*
shot from an eighteen-pounder or two. The following morning the
Enemy had almost completed the battery: the Governor was therefore induced to comply with the representation of Colonel Tovey,
and ordered the upper batteries, &c. to be opened on the Enemy's
works, and to continue to fire from his direction. About four
o'clock in the afternoon of the 22d, (a captain and two subalterns,
with the artillery picquet, manning the lower batteries) the firing
commenced, and was continued with unremitting spirit and regularity
the remainder of the evening and night. The Enemy, in return,
discharged repeated vollies from their lines; but to little purpose.
Our artillery soon drove them from the battery, which frequently
was set on fire by the carcasses, but extinguished. On the morning
of the 23d we had the mortification to find, that, notwithstanding
the heavy fire kept upon it in the night, five of the embrasures were
masked with sand-bags, to enable the whole better to resist the effect
of our shells. The work was nevertheless considerably damaged,
though not in a degree equal to our expence in ammunition. The
firing at noon was therefore ordered to cease, as we had expended
fifteen hundred and ninety-six shot, five hundred and thirty shells,
(most of a heavy nature,) ten carcasses, and two light balls.——It
must appear almost incredible, that a battery at such a distance should
be able to resist such heavy ordnance, without being levelled to the
ground; but indeed few works were ever erected so strong and compact. The St. Carlos's battery was silent the whole time; and from
the lines they returned a thousand and twelve shot, and three hundred
and two shells. Our loss was not very great; but on the Enemy's
side, many were observed to fall, and several to be carried into the
lines: their gallantry, we may therefore imagine, cost them dear.

THE

THE fucceeding night they repaired the damage done by our fire, and erected two traverfes in the rear of the gun-battery: it is probable they were working alfo on the platforms: and during the two following nights they ftrengthened it with other additions. The 25th the Enemy's fire was rather fingular. In the afternoon, about nine, their batteries, for near an hour and a half, difcharged repeated falvos from both cannon and mortars; not directing their fire to any particular object, but fcattering their fhot in every direction towards the Garrifon, and burfting the fhells principally in the air. In the afternoon, about three, this mode of firing was repeated, and continued nearly the fame time. The 26th, Lieut. Vicars, of the 56th, was flightly wounded in the Lines.

THE night of the 29th, a brifk cannonade was heard towards the weft; and foon after, by the moon, we difcovered a cutter engaging a frigate, a xebeque, and feveral gun-boats. The cutter anfwered a fignal made from the Brilliant at the commencement of the action, by which we knew her to be a friend. After the engagement had continued very warm for a confiderable time, the firing ceafed, and fhe was obliged to fubmit to fo fuperior a force. The fucceeding night, the Unicorn cutter arrived, and four boats from Faro: the former informed us, that fhe parted company with feveral cutters bound for Gibraltar. The fruit, &c. brought in the Portuguefe boats, was immediately purchafed by the Governor, for the ufe of the fick in the Hofpitals: and fome of the crew were confined, being fufpected to come as fpies. The 31ft, the Enemy's Engineers were obferved placing pickets to the weftward of the fix-gun battery; apparently with a view of extending that work. Since our laft attack upon it, the firing on both fides was much diminifhed. In the courfe of the month, three men deferted from the Garrifon.

THE

THE night of the 2d of November, the fignal was made for the
approach of the Enemy's gun and mortar boats, which for fome
time had not paid us the regular vifits they formerly did; owing, as
I have remarked before, to the repairs which the boats muft
neceffarily demand: but the Vanguard and Repulfe prames firing
feveral fhot, they retired. The 3d, the Fortune prame, mounting
five twenty-fix-pounders, was towed out, and moored to the
fouthward of the Vanguard. The next day, about feven in the
evening, thirteen gun and fix mortar-boats fired brifkly upon the
Garrifon, feconded by the Lines: they ftaid near an hour and a half,
and threw a vaft number of fhells; but few were directed towards
our camp. Lieut. John Frazer, of the 73d, had his leg fhot off on
Montague's baftion; and Lieut. Edgar, of the 56th, was wounded
with fplinters of ftones. Two of the 58th and 73d were likewife
wounded. The Enemy continued, on the 6th and 7th, to make
fome few alterations, and collect fafcines, gabions, and other materials at their lines, and various parts of the approaches. The parallel they alfo ftrengthened; but the fix-gun battery ftill remained
mafked with fand-bags.

As it appeared of greater confequence, at this period, to annoy
the Enemy from the Queen's battery at the Old-mole head, which
formed an excellent crofs-fire with the other batteries, than to fire into
their camp; the mortars ufed for the latter purpofe were removed,
and the mafked embrafures at the extremity, with two others adjoining, were ordered to be opened, and fo altered as to admit of four
howitzers bearing on the new battery. During the night of the 11th,
the Enemy erected an additional battery of fix embrafures, weftward
of the other, where the pickets were obferved at the clofe of laft
month. This work was retired a few yards, but joined the extremity of the fhoulder of the old battery, and extended almoft in
the fame direction towards the beach. It appeared very ftrong,
and

and feemed to be intended againft the Old-mole head, and Water port.

DURING the night of the 12th, many signals were made in the Gut and along the Coaft.   In the morning we obferved a cutter ftanding for the Bay : a xebeque and three gun-boats attempted to intercept her, but fhe got in without firing a gun.   She was called the Phœnix, and was laden, on government account, with ord-nance ftores.   Col. Rofs, who had left the Garrifon fome months before, was a paffenger, and returned to take the command of his regiment, the 72d, or Royal Manchefter Volunteers.   The Lieu-tenant who commanded the cutter, informed us that he parted company with two others, deftined for the Garrifon, on the 11th; at which time one of them was engaged with two of the Enemy's cruifers.   In the afternoon fome fignals were made at Algeziras; and a cutter was obferved ftanding in for the Bay, chafed by a frigate; whence we confequently concluded it muft be one of the two men-tioned by the Phœnix.   At this time feveral gun-boats were cruifing off Cabrita Point and at the entrance of the Bay, waiting to intercept her.   In the Straits the wind was W. but N. W. in the Bay, and not very ftrong.   About fix in the evening fhe came up with the gun-boats and an armed xebeque : a fmart engagement immediately commenced.   Whilft fhe was retarded by thefe, a fecond divifion of gun-boats from Algeziras cut her off from the Garrifon; and the frigate coming up, after a moft vigorous and refolute refiftance, fhe ftruck.   When fhe firft appeared, fix barges were ordered from our frigates to affift her, and a fignal was hoifted on board the Bril-liant, which fhe anfwered.   The boats rowed out a confiderable way, and, the evening being dark, found themfelves amongft the Enemy's gun-boats, from whom, with fome difficulty, they extricated them-felves.   The fubfequent morning we had the mortification to fee the

C c   cutter

cutter towed into Algeziras by five gun-boats, with colours flying, and other marks of exultation and triumph.

THE Enemy about this time adopted the mode of cutting the fuses of their shells, so that most of them which were fired for a long range burst in the air. They continued their practice of making signals at the tower above the Quarry, whenever our parties were assembled, or appeared at work: and the shot were in general better directed than before; but their effects against the works were considerably weakened by pieces of junk hung over the merlons of the batteries. Our workmen were chiefly employed at Willis's, in repairing the Tower-battery, &c. and at the Old mole. Other detachments were also engaged in various duties on the north front. The night of the 15th, the Enemy lengthened the parallel considerably, and, the succeeding night, made further additions. In the forenoon of the 16th, a long-ranged shell, from the St. Carlos's battery, burst in the air over Hardy town, and a splinter of it flew into the sea, beyond Buena-Vista, a distance of more than three miles. Another shell fell, in the course of the morning, at the foot of a wine-house, south of the barracks; and several burst high in the air over south shed. We attributed these uncommon long ranges to the force of the wind, which, blowing in the same direction in which the shells were thrown, undoubtedly increased their velocity. Mr. Tinling, assistant engineer, was wounded the same day at Willis's. A boat arrived on the 18th from Faro: the crew were separately examined, before they were permitted the liberty of the Garrison. The patron of this boat informed us, that seven cutters, destined for Gibraltar, had been taken by the Spaniards.

Two deserters came in, about seven in the evening of the 20th; one a corporal, the other a private in the Walon guards. The
former

former appeared to be very intelligent, and informed us of many circumftances with which we were not before acquainted. The new mortar-battery, he faid, was called St. Pafchal's; and corroborated our intelligence, that it mounted two mortars and fix elevated guns. The two fix-gun batteries were named St. Martin's. He further acquainted us, that the camp was principally compofed of militia regiments: that the men were much diffatisfied with their fituation, and greatly haraffed in raifing the additional batteries: that they had fuffered lately very fevere loffes from our fire; particularly inftancing the 22d and 23d of the preceding month, when feven officers and eighty men were killed and wounded. One of the latter was an engineer of rank, who died three days afterwards. We had remarked, in the courfe of the above firing, an officer to be particularly active, which we now found to be this engineer: he braved, for a confiderable time, the dangers of the day, but at length fell, and was carried off. This deferter gave the Governor further information, refpecting the ftrength and arrangement of their guards; and the next morning was conducted to Willis's, where he defcribed to him various parts of the Enemy's works and camp. It had always been cuftomary for the Governor to detain the deferters at the Convent a few days, till he was fufficiently informed of every particular; but thefe he immured fo clofe, that, excepting fome general information, the Garrifon had an opportunity of learning but few circumftances, till an event took place, which will prefently be related.

THE firing from both fides varied as objects offered. Many of the Enemy's fhells ranged as far as the South barracks; and others, agreeably to their newly-adopted plan, burft in the air. The morning of the 22d, a foldier of the 58th regiment, who had been miffing feveral days, was feen to go into Fort Barbara, from behind the rock. The following day the Enemy mounted guns in the

St.

St. Martin's battery; and a party was employed in completing the six eastern embrasures, which were now unmasked. We kept upon them our usual fire of small shells from Willis's and the upper batteries; but the lower ordnance were silent. In the course of the day the Governor reconnoitred the Enemy's works; and it was reported that all the batteries were to be again opened upon them, as soon as the four embrasures for the howitzers, at the Old-mole head, were completed.

The night of the 23d, the besiegers added to the parallel a return of cask-work to the west: it appeared very slight and trifling. The two succeeding days, their parties were very active in finishing the batteries, which, on the 26th, exhibited a perfect and formidable appearance. This was the crisis which the Governor considered as proper to frustrate all their views, by destroying these stupendous works, the construction of which had cost them such immense labour and expence. By the deserters who came in on the 20th instant, he was acquainted with the inactivity which prevailed throughout the Enemy's camp, and with the strength of their advanced guards. Lulled into security by their superiority of force, they never suspected the Garrison capable of attempting so bold and hazardous a *coup-de-main*. The Governor, however, secretly conceived this important design, and never imparted his intention till the evening in which it was put in execution.

The gates were no sooner shut, after first gun-firing, on the evening of the 26th, than he ordered a considerable detachment to assemble on the Red sands at midnight, with devils, fire-faggots, and working implements, to make a sortie on the Enemy's batteries. The General, Field, and other officers to be employed on this service, were convened in the interim, and the disposition of attack communicated: but, left some matters might have escaped him

him in the multiplicity of arrangements, the Governor defired every
perfon to propofe, without reftraint, whatever would, in his or
their opinion, further promote the fuccefs of the enterprife. The
following are the heads of the orders iffued on this occafion.

" EVENING GARRISON-ORDERS.

Gibraltar, Nov. 26, 1781.

" Counterfign, STEADY.

" ALL the grenadiers and light infantry of the Garrifon, and all
" the men of the 12th and Hardenberg's regiments, officers, and
" non-commiffioned officers now on duty, to be immediately
" relieved, and join their regiments : to form a detachment,
" confifting of the 12th and Hardenberg's regiments complete,
" the grenadiers and light-infantry of all the other regiments,
" .(which are to be completed to their full eftablifhment from the
" battalion companies ;) one captain, three lieutenants, ten non-
" commiffioned officers, and a hundred artillery ; and three en-
" gineers, feven officers, and twelve non-commiffioned officers
" overfeers ; with a hundred and fixty workmen from the Line,
" and forty workmen from the artificer company. Each man to
" have thirty-fix rounds of ammunition, with a good flint in his
" piece, and another in his pocket. No drums to go out, except-
" ing two with each of the regiments. No volunteers will be
" allowed. The whole to be commanded by Brigadier General
" Rofs ; and to affemble on the Red fands at twelve o'clock this
" night, to make a *Sortie* upon the Enemy's batteries. The 39th
" and 58th regiments to parade at the fame hour on the Grand
" parade, under the command of Brigadier General Picton, to
" fuftain the fortie if neceffary,".

THESE

1781, Nov.

THESE were the principal orders for forming the detachment. At midnight the whole were affembled ; and being joined by a hundred failors, commanded by Lieuts. Muckle and Campbell, the detachment was divided into three columns, agreeably to the following difpofition.

LEFT COLUMN,
Lieut. Col. Trigge.

	O.	S.	D.	R.& F.
72d Grenadiers	4	5	0	101
72d Lt. Infantry	4	5	0	101
Sailors, with an Engineer }	3	3	0	100
Artillery - -	1	4	0	35
12th Regiment	26	28	2	430
58th Lt. Infantry	3	3	0	57
	41	48	2	824

CENTRE COLUMN,
Lieut. Col. Dachenhaufen, and Major Maxwell. The Referve.

	O.	S.	R.& F.
39th Grenadiers	3	3	57
39th Lt. Infantry	3	3	57
73d Grenadiers	4	5	101
73d Lt. Infantry	4	5	101
Engineer with Workmen	6	14	150
Artillery -	2	4	40
56th Grenadiers	3	3	57
58th Grenadiers	3	3	57
	28	40	620

RIGHT COLUMN,
Lieut. Col. Hugo.

	O.	S.	D.	R.& F.
Reden's Grenadiers }	3	7	0	71
La Motte's Grenadiers }	3	7	0	71
Engr with Workmen	4	6	0	50
Artillery	1	2	0	25
Hardenberg's Regiment }	16	34	2	296
56th Lt. Infantry	3	3	0	57
	30	59	2	570

IN the total of the columns, Brigadier Rofs, with feveral officers who accompanied him as Aide-de-camps, are not included.

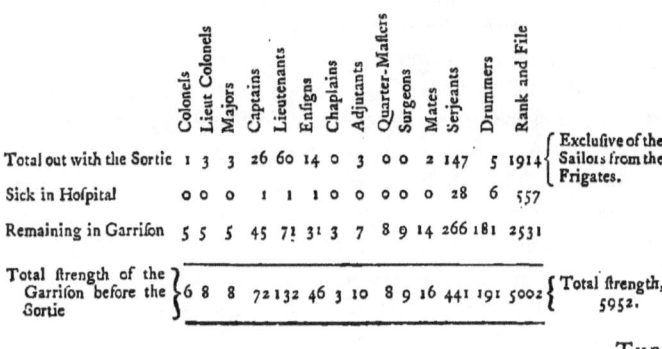

	Colonels	Lieut Colonels	Majors	Captains	Lieutenants	Enfigns	Chaplains	Adjutants	Quarter-Mafters	Surgeons	Mates	Serjeants	Drummers	Rank and File	
Total out with the Sortie	1	3	3	26	60	14	0	3	0	0	2	147	5	1914	{ Exclufive of the Sailors from the Frigates.
Sick in Hofpital	0	0	0	1	1	1	0	0	0	0	0	28	6	557	
Remaining in Garrifon	5	5	5	45	71	31	3	7	8	9	14	266	181	2531	
Total ftrength of the Garrifon before the Sortie	6	8	8	72	132	46	3	10	8	9	16	441	191	5002	{ Total ftrength, 5952.

THE

THE detachment being formed in three lines, the right column in
the rear, and the left in the front, tools for demolifhing the works
were delivered to the workmen, and the following directions for their
deftination communicated to the principal officers.

" THE right column to lead and march through Forbes's barrier,
" for the extremity of the parallel; keeping the eaftern fences of
" the gardens clofe on their left.   The centre immediately to fol-
" low, marching through Bay-fide barrier, and directing their route
" through the gardens for the mortar-batteries.   The left column
" to bring up the rear, marching along the Strand for the gun-bat-
" teries.   No perfon to advance before the front, unlefs ordered by
" the officer commanding the column : and the moft profound
" filence to be obferved, as the fuccefs of the enterprife may depend
" thereon.   The 12th and Hardenberg's regiments to form in front
" of the works, as fuftaining corps; and are to detach to the
" right and left, as occafion may require.   The referve to take
" poft in the fartheft gardens.   When the works are carried, the
" attacking troops are to take up their ground in the following
" manner.   The grenadiers of Reden's and La Motte's behind
" the parallel ; the 39th and 73d flank companies, along the
" front of the fourth branch ; and the 72d grenadiers and light-
" infantry, with their right to the fourth branch, and left to the
" beach."

By the time the deftination of the columns was made known to
the different officers, and other arrangements had taken place, the
morning of the 27th was far advanced ; and as the moon had then
nearly finifhed her nightly courfe, the detachment, about a quarter
before three o'clock, began its march, by files from the right of
the rear line, for the attack.   Although nothing could exceed the
filence and attention of the troops, the Enemy's advanced fentries
                                                    difcovered

discovered the right column before they passed Forbes's barrier, and after challenging, fired upon them. Lieut. Col. Hugo, finding they were alarmed, immediately formed the attacking corps, and pushed on at a brisk pace for the extremity of the parallel; there finding no opposition, he took possession, and the pioneers began to dismantle the works.   Part of Hardenberg's regiment, which was attached to this column, mistook the route of the grenadiers, owing to the darkness of the morning; and in pursuing their own, found themselves, before they discovered their error, in front of the St. Carlos's battery.   In this dilemma, no other alternative offered but pressing forwards, which they gallantly did, after receiving the Enemy's fire.   Upon mounting the parapet, the Enemy precipitately retreated, and with great difficulty they descended the stupendous work, forming with their left to the Tower.   They were thus situated, when Lieut. Col. Dachenhausen, at the head of the 39th flank companies, entered the St. Carlos's battery, and naturally mistaking them for his opponents, fired, and wounded several. Further mischief was however prevented by the countersign; and the Hanoverians joined the remainder of their corps, which now formed *en potence*, in front of the parallel.   The 73d flank companies were equally successful in their attacks; and Lieut. Col. Trigge, with the grenadiers, and light company of the 72d regiment, carried the gun-batteries with great gallantry.   The ardour of the assailants was irresistible.   The Enemy on every side gave way, abandoning in an instant, and with the utmost precipitation, those works which had cost them so much expence, and employed so many months to perfect.

WHEN our troops had taken possession, the attacking corps formed, agreeably to their orders, to repel any attempt which the Enemy might make to prevent the destruction of the works, whilst the 12th regiment took post in front of the St. Carlos's battery, to
sustain

suftain the weftern attack; and the referve, under Major Maxwell, drew up in the farther gardens. The exertions of the workmen and artillery were wonderful. The batteries were foon in a ftate for the fire-faggots to operate; and the flames fpread with aftonifhing rapidity into every part. The column of fire and fmoke which rolled from the works, beautifully illuminated the troops and neigh-bouring objects, forming all together a *coup-d'œil* not poffible to be defcribed.

In an hour the object of the Sortie was fully effected; and trains being laid to the magazines, Brigadier Rofs ordered the advanced corps to withdraw, and the fuftaining regiments to cover their retreat: but, by fome overfight, the barrier at Forbes's was locked, after the flank companies had returned; which might have proved of ferious confequences to Hardenberg's regiment, as they were, from that circumftance, under the neceffity of following the 12th regi-ment through Bay-fide.*

Several fmall quantities of powder took fire whilft the de-tachment was on its retreat; and juft as the rear had got within the Garrifon, the principal magazine blew up with a tremendous explofion; throwing up vaft pieces of timber, which, falling into the flames, added to the general conflagration. Although the Enemy muft have been early alarmed, not the fmalleft effort was made to fave or avenge their works. The fugitives feemed to com-municate a panic to the whole; and, inftead of annoying our troops from the flanking forts, their artillery directed a ridiculous fire towards the Town and our upper batteries, whence we continued a

D d   warm

---

* It was not a little fingular, that thefe two regiments, which at the memorable battle of Minden had fought by each other's fide, and, according to the natural courfe of events, could never expect to meet again, fhould be employed a fecond time on the fame occafion, and be the only entire regiments out.

warm and well-ferved difcharge of round fhot on their forts and
barrier.   Only two officers and fixteen privates were taken prifoners;
and little oppofition being made, very few were killed in the works.
The guard, from the beft information, confifted of one captain,
three fubalterns, and feventy-four privates, including the artillery.

THUS was this important attack executed beyond the moft fanguine expectations of every one.   The event challenges greater
admiration, when we reflect that the batteries were diftant near three
quarters of a mile from the Garrifon, and only within a few hundred
yards of a befieging Enemy's lines, mounting one hundred and
thirty-five pieces of heavy artillery.   The detachment had four privates killed; Lieut. Tweedie, of the 12th regiment, with twenty-
four non-commiffioned and privates, wounded; and one miffing,
fuppofed to be left wounded in the batteries.   Of this number,
Hardenberg's regiment had two killed and twelve wounded.   The
ordnance fpiked in the Enemy's works amounted to ten thirteen-
inch mortars, and eighteen twenty-fix-pounders.

GENERAL ELIOTT's anxiety on the occafion would not permit
him to wait the iffue within the Garrifon; but acquainting the Lieutenant Governor with his intention, he accompanied the Sortie, and
expreffed the higheft approbation of their behaviour by the following public orders: that " the bravery and conduct of the whole
" detachment, Officers, Sailors, and Soldiers, on the glorious occa-
" fion, furpaffed his utmoft acknowledgements."

ALTHOUGH the attack was not totally exempted from thofe little
derangements which naturally attend night expeditions of this
nature, yet, to the honour of the whole, neither mufquet, working-
tool, nor other implement, was left behind: a volunteer indeed of
                                                                    the

the 73d regiment loft his *kelt* in the attack, which the Governor being acquainted with, promifed him a fubftitute in return; and not long afterwards prefented him with a commiffion in an eftablifhed corps. When our troops entered the batteries, the written report of the commanding officer was found in one of the fplinter-proofs, which, when the guard was relieved, was intended to have been fent to the Spanifh General. The report expreffed that " nothing extraordinary had happened;" which, it muft be acknowledged, the captain had been a little premature in writing. The annexed Plan, with the references, will explain whatever may be deficient in the narrative.

REFERENCES to the PLAN of the SORTIE.

A. Mortar-batteries in the Enemy's Lines.

B. Gun-batteries.

C 1. C 2. C 3. C 4. C 5. The different branches of their Line of Approach to the advanced works; with traverfes.

D. The Parallel, or eaftern branch.

E. The St. Martin's batteries, mounting twelve twenty-fix-pounders.

F. The St. Pafchal's battery, mounting two thirteen-inch mortars and fix twenty-fix pounders, elevated on frames, to annoy our camp.

G. The St. Carlos's, or Mill-Battery, mounting eight thirteen-inch mortars; with two *places d'armes* on its flanks.

H. The pofition of the 72d flank companies, after taking poffeffion of the gun-batteries.

I. The 39th flank companies, after ftorming the St. Carlos's battery.

K. The position of the 73d grenadiers and light-infantry, when the former had driven the Enemy from the centre guard-house, and the latter had obliged them to evacuate the St. Paschal's battery.

L. The division of Hardenberg's regiment, which mistook their route, and entered the Enemy's works.

M. Reden's and De La Motte's grenadiers formed, after taking possession of the eastern parallel.

N. Queen's battery (Willis's).

O. Princess Anne's, ditto.

P. Princess Amelia's, ditto.

Q. Princess Caroline's, ditto.

R. Catalan batteries, ditto.

S. Queen Charlotte's, ditto.

T. Tower-battery.

V. Farringdon's battery.

W. Green's lodge, with the Terrace batteries below it.

X. Royal battery.

Y. Rock mortar, and Levant Royal batteries.

Z. Two battalions, under Brigadier Picton, ready to support the sortie if necessary.

Before the detachment returned from the Neutral ground, Lieut: Col. Tovey, of the artillery, died. He was succeeded by Major Lewis in the command of that department.

The night of the 27th, the Enemy were alarmed with an explosion in the ruins of their batteries ; and immediately directed a smart discharge of musquetry, with ground and grape shot, towards the spot. We imagined they suspected that we had made a second sally, to finish the destruction of what remained; and their error probably would have continued some time, had they not been

                                                                undeceived

K. The pofition. of the 73d grenadiers and light-infantry, when
 the former had driven the Enemy from the centre guard-
 houfe, and the latter had obliged them to evacuate the St.
 · Pafchal's battery.

L. The divifion of Hardenberg's regiment, which miftook their
 route, and entered the Enemy's works.

M. Reden's and De La Motte's grenadiers formed, after taking
 poffeffion of the eaftern parallel.

N. Queen's battery (Willis's).

O. Princefs Anne's, ditto.

P. Princefs Amelia's, ditto.

Q. Princefs Caroline's, ditto.

R. Catalan batteries, ditto.

S. Queen Charlotte's, ditto.

T. Tower-battery.

V. Farringdon's battery.

W. Green's lodge, with the Terrace batteries below it.

X. Royal battery.

Y. Rock mortar, and Levant Royal batteries.

Z. Two battalions, under Brigadier Picton, ready to fupport the
 fortie if neceffary.

BEFORE the detachment returned from the Neutral ground, Lieut.
Col. Tovey, of the artillery, died. He was fucceeded by Major
Lewis in the command of that department.

THE night of the 27th, the Enemy were alarmed with an explofion in the ruins of their batteries ; and immediately directed a fmart
difcharge of mufquetry, with ground and grape fhot, towards the
fpot. We imagined they fufpected that we had made a fecond
fally, to finifh the deftruction of what remained; and their error
probably would have continued fome time, had they not been

               undeceived

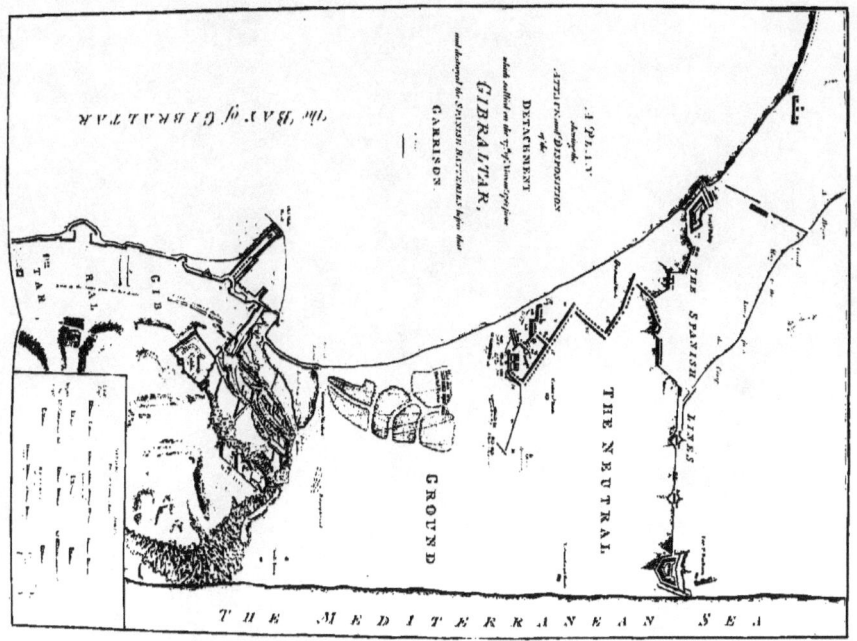

A PLAN
shewing the
ATTACK and DISPOSITION
of the
DETACHMENT
which sallied on the 27th of November 1781 from
GIBRALTAR,
and destroyed the SPANISH BATTERIES before that
GARRISON

the BAY of GIBRALTAR

THE SPANISH LINES

THE NEUTRAL

GROUND

THE MEDITERRANEAN SEA

undeceived by our throwing a fhell amongft the ruins ; after which they inftantly ceafed. By the number of lights feen in their camp, we had reafon to conclude that their army affembled on the alarm. The Enemy had not yet thought proper to take any meafures towards extinguifhing the flames, but avenged themfelves by a brifk cannonade upon the Town. In their camp feveral men were executed, who probably might be fome of the unfortunate actors in the late difgrace. The 30th, their batteries continued burning in five different places : when they ceafed to fmoke, the works feemed completely deftroyed, nothing but heaps of fand remaining. Five difmounted mortars could be feen in the St. Carlos's battery from the fummit of the rock ; one gun alfo in St. Pafchal's, and three in the St. Martin's. At night we fired feveral rounds of grape at their horfe-patroles, which, fince their late misfortune, appeared more numerous than before.

CHAP-

CHAPTER VI.

The Spaniards determine to restore their batteries.—Establish several defensive posts.—Repair their works; but are considerably retarded by the Garrison.—Description of a new-invented depressing gun-carriage.—Gallant behaviour of the Mercury, ordnance-ship.—The Vernon store-ship arrives with several gun-boats, in frames; also the Cerberus and Apollo frigates, with a reinforcement of men.—Singular quality of quick sight in two boys belonging to the Garrison.—Spaniards resolve to make a vigorous attack upon Gibraltar, under the command of the Duke de Crillon.—Begin to convert large vessels into BATTERING-SHIPS at Algeziras.—A party of Corsicans arrive, and offer to act as volunteers in the Garrison during the siege.—Enemy's army reinforced.—Unfortunate accident in a magazine at Willis's.—A strong reinforcement of French troops joins the Enemy's army.—The Duke de Crillon assumes the command of the Combined Forces; and the Besiegers batteries for some time are silent.

1781, Dec.

THE Spaniards, for several days, appeared totally at a loss how to act after their recent disgrace. Their batteries continued in flames; nor were any attempts made to extinguish the fire. In the beginning of December, however, they seemed as if suddenly roused from their reverie; upwards of a thousand men were at work, making fascines, &c. for which purpose large quantities of brush-wood were collected from the country. From these operations we concluded that they were resolved to restore their works, when sufficient materials were prepared.

THE

THE 1ft of December, a flag of truce brought letters from the
Englifh prifoners lately captured in the cutters bound to the Garrifon. Not a fyllable was mentioned, by the Spanifh officer, of the
late tranfaction; nor did he even enquire whether we had taken
any prifoners. As we had obferved the Enemy to poft ftrong
guards in the ftone guard-houfes on the neutral ground, particularly in the centre one, the Governor ordered the artillery to
endeavour to diflodge them. Anfwers were returned, on the 2d,
to the letters brought the preceding day: letters alfo were fent
from the prifoners taken in the fortie, to their friends in camp.
The Spanifh officer, on receiving the letters, appeared much furprifed, put them in his pocket, but was filent; and the boats
parted. One of the officers taken prifoner was the Baron Von
Helmftadt, an Enfign in the Walon guards, with the rank of
Captain: the other was Don Vincente Freefe, a Lieutenant of artillery. The Baron was dangeroufly wounded in the knee, and not
without many intreaties fubmitted to amputation. When the furgeons firft informed him that an operation was abfolutely unavoidable, he refolutely oppofed it: amputation, he faid, very feldom fucceeded in Spain; befides, he was then betrothed in marriage to
a lady, and would rather rifk his life than prefent himfelf before
her with only one leg. The Governor, being told this determination, immediately vifited the Baron, and ufed every argument to
perfuade him to comply. His Miftrefs, the General faid, muft
undoubtedly efteem him the more for the honourable wound
which he had received in the fervice of his country; and, as to
the operation being fatal, he might almoft affure himfelf of a
certain recovery, fince, in the many fimilar cafes which had
occurred in the Garrifon during the fiege, our furgeons had been
generally fuccefsful; and to convince him by ocular proof, ordered
feveral mutilated convalefcents into the room. This generous
attention of the Governor had a powerful effect on the Baron, who,

no

no longer able to refift his importunities, at length confented to the operation. The Enemy, the night of the 3d, repaired the damage done to the third branch of approach; and did fome trifling work at the fourth branch. The next day, a flag of truce from the Enemy brought letters of thanks from the Spanifh General, Don Martin Alvarez, and the Walon guards, to the Governor, for the humanity fhewn to the prifoners taken in the batteries. In the boat came fome poultry for the wounded Baron; alfo clothes and money for the officers. Their guards in the lines now appeared to be about eight hundred infantry, with a hundred artillery; befides fixty or feventy cavalry for patroles. The Governor, on the 5th, ordered that " no Officer of the line, commanding at a poft, fhould inter-
" fere in the mode of loading, pointing, or firing the cannon. If
" at any time he judged it neceffary to fire upon the Enemy, he was
" to point out the object to the artillery, and fubmit it to their
" opinion, whether it was practicable or not." The morning of the 7th, a cutter appeared from the weft, and, after an obftinate action with the Enemy's gun-boats, was obliged to ftrike. In this engagement we obferved that the Enemy had made fome alterations in the conftruction of their boats, which before would not allow the guns to be depreffed.

NOTWITHSTANDING our fire, the Enemy feemed determined to eftablifh themfelves at the Centre ftone guard-houfe, round which, on the night of the 7th, they made a trench, and alfo lined with fafcines part of the fourth branch of approach. Our firing continued to vary, as their operations were more or lefs noticed: in the day we directed it principally to parties obferved near the Tower, and at night to the Centre guard-houfe; againft which they had heaped up fand, and continued every evening to make other additions. —The Garrifon at this period was fo extremely fickly, that a hundred men were curtailed from the working parties; and the officers fervants,

vants, with others who ufually were exempted from thefe duties, ordered to affift, to leffen the fatigue of their comrades. Near feven hundred were at this time on our hofpital lifts.—The Unicorn cutter failed, in the night of the 12th, with difpatches for England; and the following evening, the Phœnix, with duplicates.

THE operations of the Enemy feemed now entirely defenfive. The Weftern ftone guard-houfe, on the beach, was unroofed in the fame manner as the Centre guard-houfe, and ftrengthened with fand; with a trench dug round at fome diftance in the front. We imagined that ftrong guards were ftationed every night at thefe pofts, to protect their remaining works. The evening of the 16th, about ten o'clock, one of the Enemy's advanced fentries, near Bay-fide, fired his mufquet; which was taken up by others in the gardens, and the alarm fpread to the Lines, and thence to the camp. Lights were immediately obferved moving about, and the drums beat to arms. After fome hours confufion they were calm and quiet. Their works, particularly the St. Pafchal's battery, continued to fmoke in feveral places, on the 18th. No ordnance could now be feen in any of the batteries: their fire was rather fmart, but no particular object feemed to engage their notice.

BRIGADIERS Rofs and Green were appointed, in the orders of the 20th, to be Major Generals in the army; and the next evening General Rofs failed in a boat for Faro, on his return to England. General Green fome time afterwards received a letter of fervice, and Lieutenant Holloway, his Brigade Major, was appointed his Aide-de-camp. The fame day a flag of truce brought over feveral letters, with money and clothes for the prifoners. At night the Enemy extended the fourth branch, in the fame direction, towards the Weftern ftone guard-houfe; and feveral pickets were driven, and fafcines laid in the ruins of the batteries, in order to retain the fand,

E e , and

and prevent it being wafhed down by the rains.   The night of the
23d they raifed an epaulement on the top of the Centre guard-
houfe, and finifhed the firft line of the new approach from the
fourth branch.

Two foldiers of Hardenberg's, and the 72d regiment, on the
25th, attempted to defert by a rope from Mount Mifery : the former
got down, though the rope broke ; which accident was the caufe of
the latter being retaken.   A few days after, a ferjeant of the artificers
was ordered to reconnoitre the place where this deferter defcended ;
and he got down far enough to difcover the unfortunate man dafhed
to pieces at the foot of the precipice.   The night of the 27th, the
Enemy made feveral additions to the Centre guard-houfe.   The
Baron Von Helmftadt being dangeroufly ill about this period, (not
in confequence of the operation he had undergone, but from fome
inward malady) flags of truce were daily paffing and repaffing, to
inform his friends of his dangerous fituation.   The 28th, the Baron
died ; and the following day his body was carried to the New mole,
accompanied by the grenadiers of the 12th regiment, with the
ufual honours of war, where two barges waited to convey it to the
Enemy's camp.   The Governor, and principal officers in the Garrifon, with Don Vincente, attended the ceremony.   The fowls and
other refrefhments fent by his friends, with the money not ufed
by the Baron in his ficknefs, were alfo returned, to the moft
minute article.

The Enemy, on the night of the 30th, added to the trench in
front of the Centre guard-houfe, which, a few evenings before, they
had altered from its original form.   Our engineers the fame night
erected a blind of canvas, &c. in front of Princefs Anne's battery
(Willis's) which the engineers afterwards caiffoned, when their fire
became lefs warm on this new object.   Another was afterwards
                                                              placed

placed before the Princefs Amelia's, for the fame purpofe. The materials with which the works at the northward were now repaired, were collected from the coal-fhips that had been run afhore in the New mole after Admiral Darby's departure. The fides of thefe veffels were cut up, under the direction of the engineers, into large folid pieces, of fuch form and dimenfion as the purpofe dictated to which they were to be applied. Of thefe materials the batteries at Willis's were at this time formed; the angles being connected and fecured by ftrong knees and bolts, having tranfverfe pieces within, which were alfo kneed. When the caiffons for the merlons were thus framed, they were filled in the front with layers of junk, and fand-bags behind. The height of the merlons were between ten and eleven feet; and the upper parts were fupported by ftrong beams acrofs the embrafures, forming *hoods* (as the engineers called them) over the muzzles of the cannon: thefe hoods were three feet deep, and extended about fix feet in length over the embrafures; by which improvements the guns were preferved from being broken by the fhells in their defcent, and the artillery-men on duty were well covered. The folid conftruction of thefe new works, and the adoption of a fimilar mode in repairing the other defences of the Garrifon, will account, in a great meafure, for the general cafualties of the troops not being fo numerous as might otherwife be expected; and, to evince the permanence of them, no other proof, I imagine, need be adduced, than that upwards of one hundred fhot-holes have been plugged up in the front of one merlon, and yet the battery was not materially damaged.*

E c 2   Two

---

* When the Enemy's proceedings afterwards rendered fome alterations neceffary in the works at Willis's, the fhip-timber was found very ufeful in further fecuring the upper batteries, and in protecting our artillery. The height of the parapets permitted the engineers to erect fplinter-proofs between the guns, of curved pieces of timber cut from the bottom of a fhip, which were placed againft the breafts of the merlons, and made bomb-proof by layers of fand-bags, which alfo formed a traverfe acrofs the battery. By thefe additions the communications between the ordnance were covered, and the batteries well traverfed againft the Enemy's eaftern enfilade-fire.

1781,
Dec.

Two ordnance-ships arrived in the courfe of December. As we are now arrived at the clofe of the year, it may not be impertinent to infert a return of cafuals, from the 12th of April to the 31ft of December, 1781, that the Reader may have an idea of our general lofs in that period.

	Officers.	Serjeants.	Drums.	Rank and File.	Total.
Killed and dead of wounds, —	3	10	1	108	122
Difabled, —— ——	2	7	1	36	46
Wounded, — ——	13	22	6	359	400

1782,
Jan.

THE New Year's day of 1782 was remarkable for an action of gallantry which is worthy of being refcued from oblivion. An officer of artillery at Willis's, obferving a fhell falling towards the place where he ftood, got behind a traverfe for protection; which he had fcarcely done, ere it fell into the traverfe, and inftantly entangled him in the rubbifh: one of the guard, named Martin, obferving his diftrefs, generoufly rifked his own life in defence of his officer, and ran to extricate him; but finding his own efforts ineffectual, called for affiftance; when another of the guard joining him, they relieved the officer from his fituation; and almoft at the fame inftant the fhell burft, and levelled the traverfe to the ground. Martin was afterwards promoted, and rewarded by the Governor, who at the fame time told him " he fhould equally " have noticed him for relieving his comrade." Several fimilar inftances of heroifm occurred during the fiege, all of which were equally honourable to the Garrifon.

THE Enemy perfevered in carrying on their works: the Centre guard-houfe now began to affume a regular figure. The ditch
formed

formed three fides of an hexagon, extending to the rear in obtufe angles with the front; and the fafcine-parapet, joining the building, was lengthened each way. Materials continued to be daily brought down to the lines, and advanced works. Their workmen were however confiderably annoyed, in repairing the fourth and fifth branches of the approach, from the Old-mole head and Montague's baftion. The fhip, St. Philip's Caftle, in Government fervice, arrived on the 4th from Mahon, with difpatches from General Murray: on board her came feveral prifoners taken by that General in a fally made from Fort St. Philip's. The Enemy endeavoured to cut her off from the Bay, but could not accomplifh it. She returned to Minorca on the 10th. Since their army had landed at Minorca, the Enemy's attention to the eaftward was vifibly abated; nor did they make fo many fignals from the tower on the Queen of Spain's chair, as had been their cuftom formerly. The fubfequent evening our prames made the fignal for the approach of the gun-boats : an eafterly wind however fpringing up, they threw up their rockets, and retired. We could not otherwife account for their not firing in an eafterly wind, than by imagining they were apprehenfive of fome accident in their magazines, which, being in the ftern of the boat, might run fome danger of being blown up by the fparks from the difcharge of their ordnance. The night of the 7th, befides making additions to the Centre guard-houfe, the Enemy *debouched* from the fifth branch, and dug a trench about fifteen or twenty yards towards the eaft. A Court of Enquiry, on the 8th, fat on Antonio Juanico, the fpy who was difcovered in the Faro boat; and fome time afterwards he was ordered to prepare for execution. The Governor however at laft pardoned him.

THE Enemy, about this time, removed feveral guns from the camp to the lines, taking others back. Moft of their cannon (we had

had reafon to imagine for fome time paſt) had been greatly damaged
by the firing; as the ſhot, at periods, were obſerved not to fly with
the ſame velocity as at firſt.   The laſt deſerter ſaid they had ſpoiled
three ſets of guns from the commencement of the bombardment.
In the night of the 9th, they raiſed the epaulement joining the
Centre guard-houſe; and opened four embraſures, two on each ſide
of the building.   They were all maſked with faſcines, and appeared
ſolely for defence.   The night of the 12th, the Enemy formed a
trench from the *débouchure* of the fifth branch, to the front of the
ruins of the St. Carlos's battery, towards the weſtern beach: part
of it was lined with faſcines.   They alſo raiſed a *place d'armes* on
the eaſt flank of the St. Carlos's battery, joining the fifth branch.   At
night ſailed the Henry and Mercury ordnance-ſhips to the weſtward.
Don Vincente Freeſe went paſſenger in the former for England, with
the priſoners taken in our ſortie, and thoſe ſent by General Murray.
About the 14th or 15th, the Enemy raiſed another *place d'armes*
on the weſt flank of the St. Carlos's battery, and joining the ruins
of the St. Paſchal's battery; and the ſubſequent evening ſtrengthened
and capped it with faſcines.   In the night, ſignals were made in
the Gut, and at day-break two cutters appeared at the entrance of
the Bay; but the wind blowing ſomewhat northerly, and dying
away, they were driven to leeward by the current: a frigate and
eleven gun-boats from Algeziras immediately gave chace, and ſoon
after they were joined by a frigate and xebeque from Ceuta.   The
cutters finding it impoſſible to make the Bay, and obſerving the
force of their purſuers, prudently crowded ſail to the eaſtward.   In
the afternoon ſome of the gun-boats got within range, and a few
rounds were exchanged; but the wind freſhening towards ſun-ſet,
the cutters evidently left the Enemy conſiderably aſtern.   When
night prevented us from continuing our obſervations, they had
indeed gained ſuch a diſtance, that we did not in the leaſt doubt but
they would eſcape.

THE

THE Enemy had made, for feveral preceding evenings, confiderable additions to the Centre redoubt; and on the night of the 17th, they raifed a work embracing each extremity of the fafcine-ditch which was in the front of it : this poft now appeared finifhed. They likewife raifed and threw fand in front of the *place d'armes,* and brought vaft quantities of different materials to their advanced works. Their firing was not at this period remarkable ; but, as they directed their ordnance principally among our working parties on the hill, we experienced a few cafuals. Our batteries in return were well ferved; and the fire pointed to all quarters. In the morning of the 18th, juft after gun-firing, fignals were made from the Enemy's advanced works, which were repeated to their camp. The batteries at the fame time kept up a brifk fire, all in a low direction. This gave us reafon to think they were apprehenfive of another fortie : and the following morning the four embrafures in the Centre redoubt were unmafked, and *animated* with four howitzers; and a confiderable number of troops left the lines foon after day-break : all which circumftances ferved to countenance our conjecture. In the evening of the 20th, the artillery at Willis's difcovered a party of the Enemy erecting a line of communication from the fourth branch to the Centre redoubt. The Old-mole head and Montague's were immediately opened on them, in addition to the upper batteries ; and we plied them fo brifkly, that the party were obliged to retire about midnight, leaving the work, as the morning evinced, in great confufion. The fubfequent night, notwithftanding our fire, they raifed and ftrengthened the new communication. In this duty they were well covered by a brifk fire from their lines; and which, from the repeated vollies difcharged, afforded room to think that their workmen had fuffered materially the night before.

THE night of the 23d, they repaired the parapet of the St. Carlos's battery nine fafcines in height, and began to rebuild the magazine

in

in the rear. Great quantities of fafcines, &c. were in and about the battery. The fucceeding afternoon, about four o'clock, the Governor opened the lower batteries on this work, and our fire was exceedingly well ferved for fome hours. The carcaffes feveral times fet fire to the fafcines, but the Enemy as frequently extinguifhed it. At firft their batteries returned our fire fparingly; but receiving a reinforcement of artillery-men from the camp, the cannonade became warm on both fides. Our lower batteries ceafed in the evening. The next day, the Governor renewed his endeavours to burn thefe works. The carcaffes were equally fuccefsful as the preceding day, but their guards and workmen foon extinguifhed the fire. The Spanifh lines returned the cannonade with great vivacity, having in the twenty-four hours difcharged one thoufand and forty-five fhot, and eighty-three fhells: our batteries diminifhed their fire about four in the afternoon. The carcaffes ufed by the artillery on this occafion were made of the Enemy's blind fhells, in which were perforated three large holes, and the cavity filled with compofition. They were found to anfwer extremely well; fome of them burning frefh a quarter of an hour after the Enemy had fmothered them with fand, which was the mode they adopted to put them out.

WE obferved, on the 27th, four large piles of fafcines at the eaftern extremity of the parallel. We were not at all at a lofs to guefs their meaning in placing thefe fafcines to the eaftward; as it was evident, that they wifhed to draw off our attention as much as poffible from the St. Carlos's battery. The manœuvre did not however anfwer. The following evening, about ten o'clock, arrived the two cutters which had been purfued by the Enemy's cruifers to the eaftward: the largeft of them, called the Viper, was of four hundred and fixty tons burthen, mounted twenty-eight guns, and was efteemed the largeft veffel of her kind ever built; the other was the Lively, of fourteen guns; both laden with ordnance-ftores.
They

They informed us that the evening of the day they were chaſed through to the eaſt, ſeveral of the gun-boats got up and engaged them, 'but were ſoon beaten off : at length the wind freſhening, the boats were left aſtern. The breeze, they ſaid, increaſed to a briſk gale, which, as the gun-boats were ſome leagues from land, might greatly diſtreſs them. This conjecture appeared confirmed, by none of them being obſerved to have returned to the Bay. The night of the 28th, the Enemy took down half of the old tower, or windmill, which they probably thought was too conſpicuous an object of direction for our artillery in the night : they added alſo conſiderably to the St. Carlos's battery, and made ſome alterations in the Centre redoubt, which they paliſaded in the rear, and within it hung a barrier-gate. The ſame night, arrived the Dartmouth Tartar cutter with ſtores. The night of the 30th, our opponents were obſerved very buſy to the eaſtward of the Centre redoubt. We inſtantly opened upon them, and drove them from the place. At day-break we found they had traced out a work of five ſides, with a large opening in the rear, and erected before it a ſcreen ſimilar to ours at Willis's, but ſo injudiciouſly placed, that the workmen behind were not at all concealed from our upper batteries. This work was never carried on ; and the ſcreen ſome time afterwards was knocked down, and removed. . Our engineers, of whom little has been mentioned for ſome time, were indefatigable in repairing the ſplinter-proofs, magazines, traverſes, and communications, along the north front, which were damaged by the Enemy's fire : the King's, Queen's, and Prince's lines, had likewiſe a ſhare in their attention. Parties were alſo engaged in ſecuring and repairing the *ſkeleton* traverſes, formed of timber and ſand-bags in front of the doors, windows, &c. of the powder-magazines near the New mole ; and depoſits of faſcines, ſand, and other materials, were collected in different parts of the Garriſon.

F f

In the beginning of February, great numbers of mules continued bringing fafcines, &c. to the Enemy's lines; and by the number of gabions miffing from their fafcine-park, it was thought they had concealed them in different parts of the approaches for new works. The St. Carlos's battery appeared nearly completed: it confifted of an epaulement with two fhoulders; five dodging traverfes were erected in the rear, and behind them two larger ones for magazines: the latter, however, were not of the fame form as thofe erected before. A gate was alfo hung at the opening of the fifth branch, and the *places d'armes*, on each flank of the battery, feemed finifhed. Part of the parallel joining the fifth branch, in extent about forty yards, was likewife lined with fafcines, and repaired. In this ftate were their works near the tower, when, on the night of the 2d, they reftored the weftern part of the St. Martin's battery, making only five embrafures to open upon the Town and Water port. Our firing was pretty fmart at this period; but their artillery did not exceed a hundred, or a hundred and fifty rounds in the twenty-four hours.

In this tedious and uninterefting manner affairs proceeded; every night the Befiegers making fome trifling addition to their advanced works. The afternoon of the 7th, one of their fhells fet fire to a magazine-box on the Queen's battery (Willis's), in which were a few loaded fmall fhells and cartridges. Thefe inftantly blew up, and fired an adjoining gun, but did not the fmalleft injury to the officers, or any of the guard, though the former were clofe to it when the accident happened. On hearing the explofion, the Enemy immediately increafed their fire, and continued it the remainder of the evening. The Enemy added, on the night of the 10th, another embrafure to the new battery; and two nights following, they prolonged the parallel about forty yards to the eaftward. Vaft quantities of materials were at this time fcattered in various parts of their works.

THE

THE afternoon of the 15th, fome practice was made from a gun mounted upon a new-conftructed depreffing-carriage, the invention of Lieut. Koehler, of the Royal Artillery, which was highly approved of by the Governor and other officers prefent. The Gun was fixed in a bed of timber, the under fide of which was a plane parallel to the axis of the piece : from this bed, immediately under the centre of gravity, projected a fpindle eight inches in diameter. This fpindle paffed through a groove formed for its reception in a plank, the upper fide of which was alfo a plane : upon this under piece the bed and gun recoiled, being attached to it by a key paffing through the fpindle. The bed and gun by thefe means were at liberty to move round upon the axis of the fpindle, and when fired, flided upon the under plank in the line directed by the groove. The under piece was then connected, by a ftrong hinge in front, to two cheeks of a common garrifon-carriage, cut down to be little higher than the trucks. The gun could be laid to any degree of depreffion under twenty degrees, by a common quoin refting upon the cheeks of the carriage; but when greater depreffion was neceffary, two upright timbers, with indented fteps, were fixed to the cheeks ; by which, with the affiftance of a moveable plank, to flide in upon the fteps, and a quoin, the back part of the plank, upon which the gun flided, was elevated at pleafure by iron pins in the uprights ; and the gun depreffed to any angle above twenty and under feventy degrees.

MANY advantages, befides that of immediate depreffion, refulted to the artillery from this invention. The carriage, when the gun was depreffed, feldom moved ; the gun fliding upon the plank to which it was attached by the fpindle, and returning to its former place with the moft trifling affiftance. When the fhot was difcharged, and the bed with the gun had recoiled to the extremity of the groove; the matrofs, by turning round the gun to lie horizontally acrofs the carriage, (which was done with the greateft facility) was alfo

enabled

enabled to load under cover of the merlon, unexpofed to the Enemy's fire, and avoided the difficulty of ramming the fhot upwards. It equally allowed the gun to be fired at point blank; and (by turning the muzzle to the back part of the carriage) at every elevation, to forty-five degrees, but in that ftate did not particularly excel. As to the accuracy of the depreffing fhot, no farther proof need be adduced, than that, out of thirty rounds, twenty-eight fhot took place in one traverfe in the St. Carlos's battery, at the diftance of near one thoufand four hundred yards. If the arrangements in the engravings for this work had not been previoufly eftablifhed, I fhould have been happy, by adding a plan of elevation, to have further explained this carriage, which has refleƌed fo much credit on the ingenious Inventor.

A POLACRE had arrived on the 15th; and on the 17th, came in the Flying-fifh cutter, with ordnance-ftores: the latter was oppofed, and engaged in the Bay by a frigate, a xebeque, and three gun-boats; but got in by perfeverance and fuperior fkill, without a fingle man killed or wounded. At night, a party of the Enemy was difcovered at the eaftern extremity of the parallel; and a brifk fire was immediately pointed to the fpot. At day-break, we remarked they had traced out with fafcines a work (of five fides, leaving the gorge open), at the weft return from the parallel. It appeared to be for another redoubt. About the morning gun-fire, a brig was hailed from Europa, and anfwered, from Cork: finding fhe was a friend, the Captain was direƌed to anchor at the Mole; but imagining the fhips, as before the war, remained at Water port, he paffed our prames, and did not difcover his error till he had gone too far to return: he was confequently obliged to put about, and the veffel grounded at the back of the *Old* mole. When the Enemy obferved her in the morning, the Black battery, and Fort St. Philip, direƌed a fmart fire upon her; but, though it was continued the whole day, not a fhot ftruck

the

the hull. Captain Curtis brought away the crew, and at night
went with feveral boats, and cut away her mafts : part of her cargo
was alfo removed; but the greater portion of it was damaged by
the fea-water. In the evening, Water-port guard was reinforced
with a picquet.

THE Enemy, on the night of the 18th, added five embrafures to
the gun-battery, and left a fpace, feemingly for two others. This
addition made it appear as if they intended the whole for one battery, which before was divided into two. Great quantities of materials were difperfed in various parts of their works, and brufh-wood
continued to be brought into their camp from the country. The
fucceeding night they erected an epaulement of thirty-nine cafks
long, faced with fafcines, within the hexagon figure, at the extremity of the parallel. The front work was alfo raifed, and a ditch,
extending along the front of the parallel to the eaft flank of the
St. Carlos's, lined with fafcines. They worked alfo on the platforms of the new battery. The morning of the 20th, ten gun-boats
returned to Algeziras from the eaft : they were fuppofed to be the
fame which had chafed the Viper and Lively cutters. Intelligence
from Portugal mentioned, that feveral of them had been loft in the
gale which fprung up the fame evening : we were rather difappointed
therefore to fee fo many return. In the evening the Viper, Lively,
and Dartmouth—Tartar cutters, failed for England. About the
time of their departure, a traverfe in the St. Carlos's was fet on fire
by our artillery, which produced a fmart cannonade for fome hours.
The fucceeding day another traverfe was fet on fire, and burnt for
fome time. The Enemy always behaved with great fpirit on thefe
occafions. The night of the 21ft they completed their Gun-
battery, which now prefented to us thirteen embrafures : they likewife repaired the damage done by the fire.

ABOUT

ABOUT noon on the 23d, feveral fignals were made at Cabrita point, which brought out a frigate and a xebeque from Algeziras. Soon after, we obferved a veffel ftanding into the Bay with a flowing fail. The xebeque paffed her aftern; but the frigate bore down, and appeared as if fhe intended to board. The veffel, however, in coming abreaft, threw in fo well directed a broad-fide, that the Spaniard was greatly confufed, and fell aftern. The frigate afterwards wore, and returned the falute; but the veffel was at fuch a diftance, that no damage was received. On her arrival at the New mole, to our furprife we found her to be the Mercury ordnance-fhip, which had left the Bay in January, and, as we imagined, was bound to England. Several inhabitants, fuppofing the fame, had taken their paffage on board her for England; and never difcovered their miftake, till, to their great mortification, they found, on their entrance into the Straits, the unpleafant fhores of Spain and Barbary, inftead of the exhilarating coaft of Britain. Captain Heington, who commanded her, on leaving the Garrifon, had fecret orders to put into Lifbon, where he was to take in a cargo of various articles, and return; which orders he had directions not to divulge to any perfon, left the Enemy by their emiffaries fhould get information of the plan, and way-lay him in his return. He accordingly put into Lifbon, and took in his cargo of wine and fruit. When every thing was completed, he pretended fome further bufinefs would ftill delay him, and preffed the paffengers to embrace the opportunity of the packet, and fail for England. They however approved of their accommodation too well to remove; and Captain Heington was reluctantly obliged to bring them back to the Garrifon. The Governor did not fuffer this gallant conduct of Captain Heington to pafs unrewarded, but generoufly prefented him with a handfome *douceur*, and ftrongly recommended him to the Admiralty for promotion; which accordingly fucceeded. On the afternoon in which the Mercury arrived, the Enemy fired a grand *feu-de-joie* in camp,

commencing

commencing with a falute from the lines. They repeated the fire
a fourth time; which led us to imagine they had gained fome
advantage at Minorca; and we afterwards found that our apprehenfions had been too well founded.

THE Enemy's fhips in the Bay were reinforced on the 24th
and 25th with a frigate, four or five xebeques, and feveral armed
fettees; part of which probably had been employed to block up the
port of Mahon. The morning of the 25th, arrived the St. Ann,
ordnance-fhip, with a fupply of powder, and two gun-boats, on a
new conftruction, in frames. We were informed by her, that the
Vernon ftore-fhip, under convoy of a frigate, was on her paffage for
Gibraltar, with ten other gun-boats on board. The following
morning we obferved the Enemy had entirely new-faced the eaftern
epaulement, and raifed it to the height of eight fafcines. They alfo
worked on the magazine of the St. Martin's battery, and *debouched*
from the centre of the parallel, throwing up a trifling line, extending towards the fouth-weft. The 27th, four rows, of ten tents
each, were pitched in the rear of the Catalonian camp. We
imagined they were occupied by the artillery cadets. At night the
Enemy added feveral traverfes to their thirteen-gun battery. Befides
the arrivals already noted, three other veffels and feveral boats came
in, in the courfe of the month.

THE 1ft of March a flag of truce went to the Enemy, in anfwer
to one from them fome days before. The Spanifh officer who
received the packet informed us, that Fort St. Philip, in Minorca,
had furrendered on the 5th of February. The fucceeding day, a
carcafs fet fire to the thirteen-gun battery, which continued blazing
for two hours. On their attempting to extinguifh the fire, we
plied them fo brifkly, that feveral were killed, and moft of them
driven from the work; but their ufual gallantry at laft prevailed.

                                                      At

At night they raifed a *place d'armes* at the weftern extremity of the thirteen-gun battery. Thefe defenfive works demonftrated that they were determined to provide as much as poffible againft another fortie. The following night they repaired the damage done by the fire. The carpenters of the navy, on the 4th, laid the keel of one of the new gun-boats. The 6th, fix rows of tents, ten in each row, were pitched in the rear of the fecond line of the Enemy's camp, near the horfe-barrack. A large party was alfo employed in making a road from the beach to the barrack; and others were engaged in landing fhells, and different ordnance. Thefe, with other appearances, befpoke a determined refolution to profecute the fiege. Our Governor, on the other hand, with unwearied attention employed the Garrifon in repairing, and putting in the beft order of defence, the upper batteries, and other works, which had fuffered from the continued bombardment of the Enemy. The bridge, in the ditch at Land port, was likewife pulled down; and other alterations took place in that quarter. The Enemy, on the 8th, raifed one face of the Eaftern redoubt, feveral fafcines in height: and from the noife heard the preceding night, we imagined they alfo finifhed platforms in their batteries. The day following, Lieut. Cuppage, of the Royal Artillery, was dangeroufly wounded on the Royal battery, from a fplinter of a fmall fhell, which burft immediately after being difcharged from the Rock-gun. This was the fecond accident of the fame nature. The 11th, a frigate and xebeque paffed to the weft, with fix top-fail veffels; fuppofed to be part of the late Minorca garrifon. The night of the 13th, the Enemy traced out a work within the weftern *place d'armes* of the St. Carlos's battery; apparently with an intention of extending the epaulement. The firing on both fides was now confiderably increafed: that from the Enemy amounted on an average to about three hundred rounds in the twenty-four hours.

THE

THE operations of the Befiegers ftill continued tedious. On the 16th they palifaded the gorge of the Centre redoubt; and on the 18th began to pitch a new camp, near the Grand magazine, on the beach. At night they erected the epaulement of St. Pafchal's mortar-battery, and raifed three traverfes in the rear. Lieut. White, of the 56th, was flightly wounded on the 16th. On the night of the 20th, the St. Pafchal's battery was raifed three fafcines. At night the wind blew fo ftrong a gale, that the new windmill, on Windmill-hill, took fire from the violence of the friction, and was burnt to the ground. The 22d, the Enemy made fome trifling additions, and fixed a barrier-gate at the extremity of the fourth branch of approach. The fubfequent evening, a little before midnight, we were gratified with the fafe arrival of the Vernon ftorefhip, having on board the remaining ten gun-boats, and other materials for the Garrifon. Some hours after, the Cerberus and Apollo frigates, Captains Mann and Hamilton, with four tranfports, having the 97th regiment on board, anchored under our guns.

THE Vernon's arrival may be confidered as truly fortunate, fince no lefs than *thirty* Spanifh men of war, of different force, were out purpofely to intercept her and the Succefs frigate, Captain Pole, her convoy. Some leagues to the weftward of the Straits they fell in with a forty-gun frigate, which had left our (blockade) ftation, and was one of the above-mentioned cruifers. A warm action confequently commenced; but the Spaniard, finding the Vernon well armed, and that fhe boldly bore down to fupport the Succefs, after an engagement of feveral glafies, in which the Vernon had a confiderable fhare, thought proper to fubmit. On board the prize were found papers defcribing the Vernon, to the moft minute part of her rigging; at the fame time mentioning the officers names who were paffengers, and every particular article of her cargo: and from the prifoners we learned the number of fhips

G g   which

which were cruifing to intercept her. Captain Pole afterwards burned the Santa Catalina, and feparated from the Vernon on the appearance of the Cerberus, with her convoy, which he miftook for the Enemy's cruifers. The Vernon therefore proceeded alone for the Garrifon, and at the entrance of the Straits, in the evening, fell in with, and indeed was furrounded by, the Enemy's fhips : but happily the fky prognofticating a rough night, and fhe tacking at the fame time they did ; they, fuppofing her a friend, ftood in for the high land ; and at dufk fhe altered her courfe, and was foon fafe in her deftined port. Lieut. Col. Gledftanes, of the 72d regiment, and other officers, came in her as paffengers, with recruits for the different regiments in the Garrifon. The next day, the 97th regiment, commanded by Col. Stanton, difembarked feven hundred complete, and were immediately quartered in Scud hill and Rofia barracks. This regiment foon after became very fickly ; and though they were attended to with the greateft care by the Governor and Officers, in a few months many of them died ; and the reft were of little affiftance to the Garrifon before September.

THE Enemy, on the night of the 24th, were difcovered, from Willis's, at work in the front of the epaulement, at the eaftern extremity of the parallel : a few rounds of grape, however, quickly drove them under cover. They made feveral attempts to proceed, but were as conftantly obliged to retire. The fucceeding morning, we obferved they had employed parties in other parts of their works. The communication to the Centre redoubt was raifed ; many traverfes were erected behind the fourth approach, and a confiderable quantity of fafcines and other materials brought down to their works. In the forenoon of the 25th, the Spanifh officers belonging to the Santa Catalina, who were brought to the Garrifon in the Vernon, were fent by a flag of truce into Spain on their parole. In the courfe of the day, a fhot came through one of the capped

embrafures

embrafures on Princefs Amelia's battery (Willis's), took off the legs of two men belonging to the 72d and 73d regiments, one leg of a foldier of the 73d, and wounded another man in both legs : thus *four* men had *feven* legs taken off and wounded by one fhot. The Boy who was ufually ftationed on the works where a large party was employed, to inform the men when the Enemy's fire was directed to that place, had been reproving them for their carelessness in not attending to him; and had juft turned his head toward the Enemy, when he obferved this fhot, and inftantly called for them to take care : his caution was however too late; the fhot entered the embrafure, and had the above-recited fatal effect. It is fomewhat fingular, that this Boy fhould be poffeffed of fuch uncommon quicknefs of fight, as to fee the Enemy's fhot almoft immediately after they quitted the guns. He was not, however, the only one in the Garrifon poffeffing this qualification; another boy, of about the fame age, was as celebrated, if not his fuperior. Both of them belonged to the Artificer company, and were conftantly placed on fome part of the works to obferve the Enemy's fire : their names were Richardfon and Brand; the former was reputed to have the beft eye.

THE night of the 25th, the Enemy extended their parallel in a continued direction with the old work about one hundred yards, with cafks and fafcines, banked up with fand in front. The fucceeding evening, we perceived feveral guns in the St. Martin's battery; and it was imagined, that ordnance were brought forward for the other batteries. The night of the 26th, they began merlons for fix embrafures in the Eaftern redoubt, two in each face opening on the Devil's tower, Lines, and Old mole : they alfo lengthened the parallel, and ftrengthened that part which was raifed the pre-ceding night. The 28th, they fcaled feveral guns and mortars in the advanced batteries; and the following day, we concluded, they

mounted

mounted all their ordnance, as their working parties gave a general
huzza, and then withdrew for the day.

OUR Opponents at this time scarcely expended more than two
hundred rounds in the twenty-four hours; but we frequently saluted
them, with double that number in that period. The night of the
28th and 29th, the Enemy lined with fascines the prolongation
of the parallel, and erected five traverses in the Eastern redoubt.
Their batteries near the tower now appeared to be completed; the
fourth month being just expired since they had been destroyed.
The 31st, being a grand festival, our batteries were double-manned,
expecting the Besiegers would open their advanced batteries; but
not firing, the reinforcement was remanded at noon. In the evening, about six o'clock, a shell set fire to the flank of the Eastern
redoubt, and, the flame being assisted with a brisk discharge, burnt
rapidly for some hours: at last, however, the Enemy extinguished
it. The succeeding morning, we perceived that they had covered
with sand the part which had taken fire, and a number of fascines
were lying in great confusion about the work. The same night, a
boat came in from Portugal with sheep, oranges, lemons, and fowls;
two others also arrived in the course of the month.

April.
ON the evening of the 1st of April, a soldier of the 39th regiment
deserted from Land port: several hundred rounds of musquetry and
grape were discharged at him, some of which it is imagined took
place, as he dropped just before he got to the St. Carlos's battery,
and was carried into the work by seven of the guard. At dusk, a
Volunteer of Arragon came over to us: he brought his arms and
some necessaries, which, with other circumstances, occasioned a
suspicion of his being a spy. He reported that the Enemy had
suffered considerably in restoring their batteries; upwards of four
hundred being killed, and nearly as many more wounded. The
Eastern

Eaftern redoubt, he informed us, was called the Mahon battery. The Enemy, on the 2d, began to pitch tents in rear of the Walon guards : they were afterwards increafed to fix double rows, capable of quartering a battalion of infantry.

As GRATES for heating fhot were diftributed on the different northern batteries in the beginning of this month, we imagined the Governor intended applying red-hot fhot againft the Enemy's works, which appeared now complete. We were however difappointed : they were ftill referved as a *bonne bouche*, for the clofing of the fcene.

THE night of the 5th, the Enemy erected, at the extremity of the parallel, a *place d'armes* of four fides, one of which was the parallel lengthened, the other three extending in obtufe angles to the rear. The 6th, Colonel Stanton was appointed a Brigadier-general ; and Capt. Blanckley, of the 97th regiment, his Brigade-major. The 8th, we perceived fome tents pitched upon the plain beneath the ruins of Carteia ; and the following day this camp was increafed with five double rows of tents : a regiment in white took poffeffion in the evening. The 9th, a regiment in blue marched into the new camp, pitched the 2d of this month. The fame day all the carpenters of the regiments in garrifon (thofe of the 97th regiment excepted) were ordered, with a hundred additional real-men, into the King's works. At night the Enemy made fome alterations near St. Pafchal's battery, and ftrengthened the *place d'armes* at the extremity of the parallel. The 10th, Lieut. Wetham, of the 12th regiment, was killed by a fplinter of a fhell, marching at the head of the fpur-guard up the ramp, from Land-port ditch. His fervant alfo loft his arm, and the drummer had his drum broken to pieces : but the reft of the guard efcaped. The death of this young Officer was much regretted ; and it feemed particularly unfortunate, as the Enemy only fired that fatal fhell, and one fhot, in the earlier part of the day.

A FARO

A FARO boat arrived on the 11th from Portugal, with difpatches for the Governor. A private letter fent from Lifbon by this boat, mentioned, that great preparations were making at Cadiz, and in the Mediterranean ports, for a moft vigorous attack on Gibraltar; and that the Duke de Crillon, who had lately taken St. Philip's, was to command with twenty thoufand French and Spanifh troops, in addition to what were at prefent before the Garrifon; with Monfieur D'Arçon, a French engineer of great eminence and abilities; and Admiral Don Bonaventura Moreno, with ten fail of the line, befides floating-batteries, gun and mortar boats, &c. &c. The truth of this intelligence we little doubted, as many circumftances now occurred daily that ferved to confirm it. The Enemy's cannonade, in the courfe of the 12th, was fingular indeed: from fix in the morning to fun-fet, they fired every two or three minutes a fingle gun or mortar; and being the *anniverfary* of their bombardment, it appeared ftill more extraordinary. Some jocular perfons in the Garrifon remarked, that perhaps they were commemorating the day with fafting and prayer, and by their *minute-guns* expreffing their forrow, that fo many thoufand barrels of powder, and rounds of ammunition, fhould have been expended to fo little purpofe. Their firing from the 12th gradually decreafed, for about a week; when, for a few nights, they fired brifker than ufual. It afterwards diminifhed to about a hundred rounds on an average in the twenty-four hours, and fcarce exceeded that number during the remainder of the month. Their fafcine-parties continued to be actively employed preparing materials in their parks; and long ftrings of mules were conftantly removing them to the Lines and advanced batteries. Throughout their camp new life feemed to be infufed into the troops: inftead of that inactive languor which had fo long prevailed in all their operations, every perfon now appeared in motion.

THE

THE morning of the 16th, we remarked that the Enemy had repaired the eastern part of the Mahon battery, burnt down the latter end of the preceding month. Some other trifling additions were also made to this work. The 20th, arrived the Antigallican ordnance-ship from England. The nights of the 21st and 22d, the Enemy's parties added some further repairs to the Mahon battery: they also raised a small work near the tower, and erected several traverses in various parts of the parallel. The 24th, one of our new gunboats, which had been launched on the 18th, was tried with an eighteen-pounder on board; and the practice met with the approbation of the Governor and Officers of the Navy. As a person was sent out in the Vernon to superintend their construction, the keels of several other boats after his arrival were immediately laid on the stocks; and the carpenters, being now acquainted with the marks, proceeded with confidence and expedition: four or five more therefore were in great forwardness. We observed, about this time, numbers of boats passing and repassing, between Algeziras and Point Mala, and two ships in the river Palmones, which we imagined were fitting out as fire-ships: precautions were therefore taken to render them ineffectual, in case they resolved on *another* attempt to burn our frigates. The 25th, a little after day-break, a deserter came in from the Enemy: he was a native of Arragon, and comrade to the last: he confirmed our information from Lisbon, respecting the intended attack, under the command of the Duke de Crillon; adding, that they had resolved to make the principal attack by sea; for which purpose large ships were to be fitted up with cork, &c. The new camp, near Rocadillo point, he said, was occupied by the regiment of Cordova infantry, lately arrived from Ceuta.

THOUGH their camp had been considerably reinforced within the preceding six weeks, yet we could not observe that they had made any addition to their guards, which continued to be about the same number

as

as mentioned fome months before. The 28th, they raifed the merlons of the Mahon battery with fand-bags. In the courfe of the day, they brought down two guns from their artillery-park to Fort Tonara, whither they had carried four the preceding day. The 30th, they began laying platforms in the Mahon battery : on the fame day we launched our fecond gun-boat. Seven more were on the ftocks.

May.

In the beginning of May, the Enemy repaired the weft branch of the St. Carlos's, which fell down fome time before, and made fome alterations in the Black battery. Several hundred mules came likewife with clay to the lines. From feven in the evening of the 4th, to the fame hour the fucceeding afternoon, both the Garrifon and the Enemy were filent. This was the firft *twenty-four hours* in which there had been no firing for the fpace of nearly THIRTEEN MONTHS.

The evening of the 7th, the Cerberus and Apollo frigates, with four tranfports and four ordnance-fhips, failed for England. The fucceeding morning we obferved that three of the tranfports were captured, and in company with the Enemy's cruifers were then turning to windward. In the afternoon of the 9th, a line-of-battle fhip, with feven large veffels and a few polacres and tartans, arrived in the Bay from the weft, and anchored at Algeziras. At dufk, the large veffels, which appeared to be old men of war, or galleons, hauled clofe in fhore. The Governor, at night, ordered a picquet to reinforce Waterport guard. The Enemy ftill continued difcharging about a hundred rounds every twenty-four hours; and their parties as well as ours were employed in making trifling additions and repairs. The arrival of the above-mentioned fhipping at Algeziras, occafioned various conjectures: from many circumftances, we had reafon to imagine they were intended for the attack by fea, which was medi-
tating

tating againſt the Garriſon. The Governor and Chief Engineer's
attention conſequently became engaged towards the ſea-line : the
beach behind the Old mole was fortified with a row of ſloping paliſades ; Water-port gateway was well barricaded, and a *chevaux-de-
friſe* ordered to be got ready to place at the foot of Land-port glacis : the ramp in the ditch was likewiſe removed ; and thoſe batteries on the ſea-line, which they conceived might probably be
oppoſed to the Enemy's attack, were inſpected, and put in the beſt
order of defence.

THE Enemy, about the 12th, removed, and made a new arrangement of their ordnance in the forts and batteries along the coaſts :
we ſuppoſed they were changing them for others of a larger calibre.
The 14th, ſeveral of the large ſhips at Algeziras ſtruck their yards
and top-maſts, and a great number of men appeared on board them ;
which movements left us no longer to doubt, that they were intended
to be fitted up as FLOATING BATTERIES for the grand attack :
this opinion was confirmed in the afternoon, by their beginning
to cut down the poops of two of them. The ſubſequent day, three
ſtore-ſhips, the Queen Charlotte, Leonora, and Charles, arrived
from England, with powder, ſhells, bedding, and timber. Three
gun-boats, on their appearance in the Gut, went from the point
to ſpeak them ; but the ſhips hoiſting French colours, and ſtanding
for Algeziras, the boats were deceived, and returned : the falſe
colours were ſoon after ſtruck, and Britiſh diſplayed ; and they
arrived without oppoſition. The new gun-boats which were
launched, were, on this occaſion, of particular ſervice ; and before
night, nineteen hundred barrels of powder were ſecured in our
magazines. The Enemy, on the 17th, opened thirteen large port-
holes in the larboard ſide of one of the ſhips at Algeziras, and ſeven
in another.

H h   THEIR

THEIR operations now in the advanced works almoſt totally ceaſed; their whole attention ſeemed occupied by the ſhips at Algeziras, and by arrangements in their camp. Cannon and variety of military ſtores were landed beyond Point Mala, and a ſtrong party was employed in erecting a large building near the landing-place, which we conjectured was for an hoſpital. The firing on both ſides varied as circumſtances directed. Three men of the 58th regiment were miſſing on the 19th; and a party being immediately ſent in queſt of them, their bodies were found daſhed to pieces behind the rock; the rope by which they were to have deſcended being many yards too ſhort. The Enemy were very active about their ſhips; eleven port-holes were opened in the ſide of a third; and on the 21ſt, they began to ſtrengthen their larboard ſides with ſome materials which appeared like junk. The elaſticity and reſiſtance of this article rendered it very eligible for the purpoſe. On the land ſide they continued collecting bruſh-wood from all parts of the country, and had ſtrong parties at work, making faſcines. At the landing-place, ſtores of every ſpecies were daily diſembarked. On the other hand, the Garriſon, with unwearied aſſiduity, made various diſpoſitions to repel their attack. The ſloping paliſades at Water port by this time were finiſhed, and the gateway barricaded, excepting a ſmall paſſage for the wicket. To this poſt the Governor ſeemed particularly to attend. The intentions of the Enemy were no longer myſterious: every preparation was therefore made to give them a warm reception: an additional number of grates for heating ſhot, were made and diſtributed along the Line-wall; and the Navy lowered their yards and top-maſts, to be in readineſs to act on ſhore at a moment's notice.

A PRIVATEER xebeque arrived on the 25th from Leghorn, with a Corſican officer and twelve privates, who came to offer their ſervices as volunteers during the approaching attack; which the
Governor

Governor accepted, and ordered them to be entertained by different regiments till the others arrived, who, they informed us, were on their paſſage. In the evening, a large building, to the eaſt of the Catalonian camp, took fire, and was totally confumed: it had formerly been a barrack, but was now, as the deferters informed us, a granary for forage and corn. We numbered at this time upwards of a hundred pieces of cannon in the artillery-park of the Enemy. The 25th, the engineers began to mine a gallery from a place above Farringdon's battery (Willis's), to communicate through the rock to a notch or projection of the rock, below Green's Lodge, in which the Governor propoſed to make a battery. The 26th, another veſſel arrived from Algiers, and brought letters, acquainting us that it was univerſally believed in Spain, that the Garriſon, from the magnitude of the preparations for the attack, inevitably muſt be taken before the end of July. The fame day about noon, a large fleet appeared from the eaſt, upwards of a hundred fail of which we obſerved in the evening enter the Bay, and anchor between the river Palmones and Algeziras. The ſucceeding morning we were enabled to make our obſervations on them: three were large and armed, one of them with a flag at her mizen: the reſt were ſhips with troops on board, and ſmall polacres and ſettees, ſuppoſed from their appearance to be laden with ſtores. In the courſe of the 27th, 28th, and 29th, they landed, it was imagined, about twelve battalions; which, calculating at about ſeven hundred and fifty to each battalion, amounted to about nine thouſand men, if the regiments were complete. As the troops diſembarked, they encamped in the rear of the ſecond line, extending towards the horſe-barrack now called *Buena-Viſta*, which, we underſtood from the laſt deferters, had been fitted up for the Commander in Chief's quarters: others of them occupied the ground on the left of the firſt line, and on the right of the Catalonians, in an obtuſe direction up the hill towards the Queen of Spain's chair. Large parties were detached to land the military ſtores.

H h 2   A FLAG

1782,
May.

A FLAG of truce came from the Enemy on the 28th, with a letter from Mr. Anderfon, a merchant who had left the Garrifon fome days before; and had been taken on his paffage to Faro. Before the purport of the flag was known, the Governor, fpeaking to the officers near him, faid " he fuppofed the Duke was arrived, and had fent to " fummon the Garrifon; but he fhould give him a fhort anfwer, " No,—No,—and hoped the gentlemen" (addreffing himfelf to the Officers prefent) " would all fupport him." He had not, however, an opportunity of being fo fpiritedly laconic. The day following, we perceived a new encampment between the Catalonians and the left of the firft line, and great additions were made to thofe mentioned before. Six of their battering-fhips were now in hand, and an univerfal activity was obferved throughout their camp. The firing on both fides varied very little: if there were any difference in the number of rounds, the Garrifon had the advantage. Our Engineers at this time were employed in repairing the damaged and uneven platforms on the fea-line batteries, and the Artillery in difpofing of the heavy ordnance, where they would act with greater execution and effect. Scarce a day now paffed but veffels of all denominations, arrived in the Bay, at the Enemy's camp; the generality of which feemed laden with military ftores and materials for the fiege.

June.

JUNE did not commence with any thing extraordinary. The 2d, Brigadier Stanton died of a *coup de foleil*. The Enemy, the following day, pitched feveral large tents to the fouthward of Algeziras, for the accommodation of the workmen employed in fitting up their fhips. The 4th, being his Majefty's birth-day, the laft of our new gun-boats was launched; and at noon the whole fired a falute, commencing with a falvo of forty-four guns *fhotted*, from the north front of the Garrifon: the Enemy's batteries inftantly returned our land-fire, and in fo fmart a manner as to

convince

convince us, they had prepared to retaliate. The following are the
names of the gun-boats, and ships from which they were manned.

From the Brilliant frigate	Revenge	one 24 pr.	21 Men		From the Porcupine frigate	Europa	one 24 pr.	21 Men
	Defiance	one 24 do.	21 do.			Terrible	one 18 do.	21 do.
	Resolution	one 18 do.	21 do.			Fury	one 18 do.	21 do.
	Spitfire	one 18 do.	21 do.			Scourge	one 18 do.	21 do.
	Dreadnought	one 18 do.	21 do.			Terror	one 18 do.	21 do.
	Thunder	one 18 do.	21 do.		From the Speedwell cutter	Vengeance	one 18 do.	21 do.

On the 5th, three rows of double tents, ten in each row, were
pitched near Barcelo's battery, at Algeziras. Mr. M'Gregor, a
volunteer in the 73d, was wounded the same day by a shell; of
which article the Enemy's artillery, within a day or two, had been
more profuse than usual. The 6th, Captain Wideburg of Reden's
was wounded in the Queen's lines. On the 7th, our artillery
practised from the King's bastion, with *red-hot shot*, against the
Irishman's brig, which was stranded at the back of the Old mole.
In the first round, one of the artillery-men putting in the shot,
the fire by some means immediately communicated to the cartridge,
and the unfortunate man was blown from the embrasure in some
hundred pieces: two others were also slightly wounded with the
unexpected recoil of the carriage. The practice after this accident
was discontinued. In the evening, a shell fell into a quarter in
town, and carried away part of a chair, in which Ensign M'Kenzie,
of the 73d, was sitting: it immediately burst in the room below,
and lifted him and the chair from the floor, without farther injury.

The Enemy's inactivity in their advanced batteries was suffi-
ciently compensated by their diligence and celerity at Algeziras:
six ships were now in great forwardness, and on the 10th they began
upon another. Of this interval of tranquillity, as we may call it,
(though the Enemy had not quite discontinued their fire) the

Governor

Governor took advantage, and employed it with indefatigable zeal
in completing the works of the Garrifon. New batteries bearing
on Water port, which appeared to be his grand object of defence,
were opened in the Moorifh caftle : a caiffoned battery was alfo
erected at upper Forbes's, and fome alterations made in the lines :
moveable palifades, with cafks of earth, fand, &c. were diftributed
in various parts along the line-wall, to be ready in cafe a breach
fhould be effected ; and the outworks at Land port underwent fome
advantageous alterations. Two or three men about this time attempted to defert ; but they were all retaken.

On the 11th, between ten and eleven o'clock, an unlucky fhell
from the Enemy fell through the fplinter-proof, at the door of the
magazine on Princefs Anne's battery (Willis's), and burfting, communicated to the powder, which inftantly blew up. The explofion
was fo violent as to fhake the whole rock, and throw the materials
on both fides an almoft incredible way into the fea. Three merlons on the weft flank of the battery, with feveral unfortunate men
who had run behind them for fhelter, were forced down from
the level of the platforms into the Prince's lines, which, with the
Queen's below, were almoft filled with rubbifh. The magazine
near it happily efcaped, though the door was thrown open by the
explofion. Our lofs by this dreadful accident was chiefly among
the workmen who were employed on the flank of the battery : one
drummer, and thirteen rank and file, were killed ; three ferjeants,
three drummers, and nine rank and file, wounded. Immediately
after the report of the explofion, and on the appearance of the large
column of fmoke, the Enemy gave a loud huzza : their drums
beat to arms in the camp ; and fome perfons aver, that their firft
line affembled, and were actually on their march towards Fort St.
Philip, but afterwards returned. As the engineers, after the accident, got together the remains of the party, to effectually fecure
the

the magazine which had fo miraculoufly efcaped, the Enemy continued the cannonade the remainder of the day; and, as if fate was
refolved at that particular time to fport with our anxiety, in the
courfe of this firing, two other fhells fell upon the remaining magazine, and one into the very fplinter-proof in front of the door:
happily the latter did not go through; for, if it had, this magazine might have fhared the fate of its neighbour, and the whole of
the batteries at Willis's have probably been *materially* injured.
Princefs Anne's battery, the flank of it excepted, was not confiderably
damaged: the caiffoned merlons were much fhaken, and the battery
filled with rubbifh; however, before night the whole was cleared
away, and feveral rounds fired from that battery, as well as from
the other batteries, to convince the Enemy that the misfortune was
not of fo much importance as they probably imagined: indeed, from
fo dreadful an accident, it was wonderful that the injury was not of
greater confequence.

THE Navy, on the 13th, under the direction of the Engineers,
began to caiffon the weft face of the New-mole fort. About fun-
fet, a foldier of the 58th regiment, who had lately joined in the
Vernon, deferted from Land port: at night a picquet was ordered
to reinforce that guard. The 14th, a French frigate, with eighteen
or nineteen polacres, &c. arrived in the Bay. The fame afternoon,
a xebeque, returning to Algeziras, from the eaft, ftood in fo clofe
to the Garrifon, that fhe was perplexed by the eddy-winds, and
remained a confiderable time ftationary: the Garrifon fired upon
her, and the gun-boats were manned, and rowed out to attack her;
but two of the Enemy's boats, coming to her affiftance, towed her
head round; and foon after, a breeze carried her out of all danger.
If our boats had got out a little earlier, fhe might have been roughly
handled; and fome were fanguine enough to think fhe might have
been taken.

As

As BOATS were conſtantly detached by the Navy at night-fall, to row guard at ſome diſtance from the Garriſon, and give information of the approach of the gun-boats, or any other veſſels, curioſity often prompted them to approach the Enemy's ſhore; and for ſome preceding nights they reported, that they heard, at Algeziras, a noiſe like that of men hard at work; whence we concluded, their impatience to finiſh their battering-ſhips made them embrace all opportunities, both by day and night. The 16th, a new camp was obſerved between the Grand magazine and the Orange-grove. The battalion which occupied it were ſuppoſed to be diſembarked from the ſmall convoy which arrived on the 14th. At night, a noiſe of boats was diſtinctly heard from our prames, at ſome diſtance in the Bay: it however ceaſed on a gun being fired towards that quarter. This circumſtance occaſioned new ſignals to be appointed for the prames. The 97th regiment, on the 17th, for the firſt time, gave a picquet of forty men. The following day, Hardenberg's regiment was ordered, in caſe of an alarm, to act with the 58th at Europa, inſtead of marching to town. In the afternoon, a French convoy, of upwards of ſixty ſail, under three frigates, anchored in the Bay, off the Guadaranque, from the eaſt. As moſt of the ſhips had troops on board, we concluded it was the French reinforcement, of which we had received previous information. The following evening, ſeveral Spaniſh and *French* general officers, with their ſuites, viſited the lines; where they remained, excepting one General, who, accompanied by an an artillery officer and an engineer, came forward to the advanced works, and ſtood ſome time in front of the St. Martin's battery. At this time, a groupe of thoſe who remained in the lines were aſſembled on the glacis: our artillery thought proper to give them a ſhot, which the General in the advanced works probably took as a hint to retire; for he immediately pulled off his hat, and returned into the battery. This circumſtance ſerved to confirm us in our conjectures, that the reinforcement was French; and it was computed

puted

puted to be about five thousand men. Soon after the above fleet arrived, five gun-boats approached very near the town, apparently out of bravado, to demonstrate to their new friends how contemptuously they considered us; but a few rounds taking effect, they retired in great confusion, and most likely paid dear for their arrogance. The 20th and 21st the French troops disembarked, and encamped to the east of the Stone quarry, immediately under the Queen of Spain's chair.

As AFFAIRS were daily becoming more serious, the serjeants, and such drummers of the Garrison as were able, were ordered, in case of alarm, to turn out with firelocks and accoutrements; which were accordingly delivered to the different regiments from the grand store. The Governor seemed determined to have no idle hands in the place at such a critical time. Muficians, who before had been exempted from duty, also returned to the use of the firelock and shovel.

THE morning of the 21st, two Genoese, formerly inhabitants of the Garrison, who had been taken by the Enemy in a settee bound for Gibraltar, made their escape in a boat from a prison-ship at Algeziras. They informed us that the grand attack was fixed to be in September; but that all, both failors and soldiers, were much averse to the enterprise. In the afternoon, two General officers again visited the lines; and we remarked, their guards did not relieve at their ufual hour, but probably came down after twilight. From the 19th to the 21st, the Enemy's fire daily diminished; and on the 22d, about five in the evening, their batteries were totally filent. This sudden cessation induced us to conclude that the Duke de Crillon had assumed the command of the COMBINED ARMY.

I i   CHAPTER

CHAPTER VII.

Spaniards very active in completing their battering-ships.—The nephew
    of the celebrated Corsican general, Pascal Paoli, arrives at Gibraltar,
    and offers, with others of his countrymen, to act as a volunteer during
    the siege.—Enemy after great preparations commence the additional
    works on the Isthmus.—Letters between the Duke de Crillon and
    General Eliott.—Enemy's works are by accident set on fire, which
    induces the Duke to protect them by a temporary cannonade.—The
    British seamen landed and formed into a Marine Brigade.—Active
    operations of the besiegers.—Some of the battering-ships remove to
    the Orange-grove, where the Enemy begin to assemble their maritime
    force.—Lieut. General Boyd recommends an immediate trial of hot
    shot, the success of which provokes the Enemy to open their new
    batteries before they are completed.—The Combined fleets of France
    *and Spain arrive in the Bay of Gibraltar.—*THE GRAND ATTACK.
    —The battering-ships destroyed, and the Enemy rescued from inevi-
    table death by the gallantry of the Marine Brigade.—Conduct of
    the besiegers after their defeat, till their small craft disperse.

1782,
June.

THE Court of Madrid, whose whole attention seemed bent upon
the recovery of Gibraltar, had hitherto found all her attempts,
whether by sea or land, totally ineffectual; and the repeated disgrace
which her arms had suffered, could not fail to mortify her pride.
The cruel and wanton destruction of the town had tended to no
other purpose, than to reflect dishonour on her measures, in the eye
of Europe. Pride and revenge therefore now urged her to the utmost
exertions of her power and skill, so that no means were neglected,

no

no expence was fpared, to infure fuccefs.   Her treafures were lavifhly   expended; the labour of the nation was exhaufted in the magnitude of the preparations; and her whole naval and military force now appeared directed to the recovery of that natural and ancient appendage of the Crown.

THE Duke de Crillon, lately returned from the conqueft of Fort St. Philip, who had formerly commanded at the Spanifh lines before Gibraltar, and was perfectly acquainted with the fituation of the Garrifon, was appointed to conduct the military force to be employed in this arduous and interefting enterprife.   With him were joined Monfieur d'Arçon, (a French engineer of great repute,) and Admiral Moreno.   The former had projected a plan, which had met with the approbation of his Moft Catholic Majefty, for attacking the place with battering-fhips, conftructed upon fuch principles, that they were equally confidered as *impregnable* and *incombuftible*; and from the prodigious powers of which, little elfe was expected than almoft the annihilation of the Garrifon : the latter had rendered himfelf equally eminent with the General in the preceding conqueft of Minorca.   Under commanders of fuch diftinguifhed ability, aided by every combination of force which human invention could devife, we need not in the leaft wonder at the flattering idea, univerfally formed by the nation, of the event.

GENERAL ELIOTT, on the oppofite fide, unawed by the impending ftorm, provided for every circumftance which might occur : though furrounded on every hand with Enemies, and far diftant from any hopes of relief and affiftance; yet he repofed fuch confidence in the vigorous and united exertions of the little army under his command, whom he had already found fuperior to the greateft hardfhips, that he was not apprehenfive of trufting the event to the

I i 2   decifion

1782,   decifion of that fortune, which had been fo often favourable to the
June.   interefts of the Garrifon.

THE 24th of June, the Garrifon began to practife parapet-firing,
with ball, at cafks placed at different diftances in the Bay. Two
days following, the Enemy's cannon were all *under metal*; and
their advanced fentries and guards were reinforced. At Algeziras
they ftill continued to work on feven fhips; and in camp numerous
parties were employed in landing great quantities of ftores, and in
ranging ordnance, &c. in their artillery-park. Early on the morning of the 27th, the Captain of the Queen's-lines guard challenged
two perfons who had approached to Forbes's barrier; one of whom,
finding they were obferved, cried out in French, " Don't fire !"
after which both inftantly ran away towards the lines. In their
retreat one of them fell; and his cloak coming unfolded, our fentries
could diftinguifh that his uniform was white; which circumftance,
added to that of their fpeaking French, induced us to conclude they
were Officers of that nation. A perfon of diftinction, fuppofed to
be the Duke de Crillon, on the 30th, vifited the lines and advanced
works. Our artillery fired a fhot over him and his fuite, to fhew
them that they were obferved. At night, a foldier of the 56th,
attempting to defert from the Signal-houfe guard, was dafhed to pieces
in his defcent. The next day his body was expofed as a public
fpectacle, to intimidate others from provoking a fimilar fate.

July.   IN the beginning of July, the TENTH fhip had been in hands
two or three days; and the Enemy's artificers were at work on the
tops of thofe which were in the greateft forwardnefs, placing ftrong
timbers, in form of a *dos d'âne*, to ferve as bomb-proofs. At night
they raifed their parallel feveral fafcines in height, and banked it up
in front with fand. Though the Enemy's batteries had continued
filent fince the 22d of June, the Garrifon perfevered in a brifk difcharge,

charge, directing their fire to all parts of the lines, as well as the advanced works. The evening of the 2d, a party of the Enemy advanced to Bay-fide barrier; but feveral rounds of grape, which were fired from Willis's, foon forced them to retire. The fucceeding evening they again attempted to take poft there, and met with a fimilar reception. Our Navy, under the direction of an engineer, about this time repaired the boom of Water port, and funk anchors in the fhallow water at the back of the Old mole. The Enemy, though we expected it, never molefted them in this duty: indeed they feemed too intent upon their own operations, to pay attention to any of ours.

THE fuccefs attending our progrefs in the gallery above Farringdon's battery, produced the idea of making a communication from the extremity of the King's, to the Queen's lines; and on the 6th, a party of miners began this new fubterranean paffage. Early the day following, a brig, coming in from the weft, was taken by a xebeque, and carried into Algeziras. If the mafter of this veffel had acted prudently, he might probably have efcaped. On his firft appearance he coafted under French colours; but being abreaft of the point, and obferving a felucca ftanding out to fpeak him, he hoifted Britifh, and fired a fhot. This circumftance fpread the alarm: four or five gun-boats immediately rowed out, and oppofed her paffage, till a xebeque came up and ran her aboard.

THE afternoon of the 18th, an extraordinary inftance of gallantry and prefence of mind occurred at the laboratory adjoining the South baftion. An artillery-man (named Hartley) was employed in the laboratory, filling fhells with Carcafs compofition, and driving fufes into five and a half and fix-inch fhells: one of them, by fome unaccountable accident, took fire in the operation; and although he was furrounded with unfixed fufes, loaded fhells, compofition, &c. with the

the moſt aſtoniſhing coolneſs he carried out the *lighted* ſhell, and threw it where it could do little or no harm ; and two ſeconds had ſcarcely clapſed before it diſploded.   If the ſhell had burſt in the laboratory, it is almoſt certain the whole would have been blown up ; when the loſs in fixed ammunition, fuſes, &c. &c. would have been irreparable, excluſive of the damage which the fortifications would have ſuffered from the exploſion, and the lives that might have been loſt.   He was handſomely rewarded by the Governor.   The night of the 10th, a ſoldier of De la Motte's, who had been miſſing from the 5th, was diſcovered by the quarter-guard of that regiment ſtealing bread from the men's tents : he was inſtantly purſued, but could not be overtaken : the next day however he was found concealed in a cave.   Two others had alſo been retaken within a few preceding days.   Such attention had been paid to ſcarping the back of the rock, that it was little ſhort of madneſs in theſe wretches, at this period, to attempt deſertion.

Some experiments were made, in the beginning of this month, with large ſtones, cut to fit the calibre of a thirteen-inch mortar.   The ſtones had a ſmall hole drilled in the centre, which being filled with a ſufficient quantity of powder, they were fired with a ſhort fuſe, to burſt over the Enemy's works ; and the fragments were expected to do ſome damage, as well as alarm their workmen.   It was an unuſual mode of annoyance, and for its novelty was uſed for ſome time, but was ſoon laid aſide.   The 11th in the afternoon, four ſailors, under pretence of viſiting ſome fiſhing-pots, deſerted to the Enemy.   Two of them were concerned in the conſpiracy to run away with the Speedwell cutter, as mentioned, ſome months before.   The following evening, a ſerjeant of the 72d regiment, who had abſented himſelf ſeveral days from his corps, and who, previous to his abſence, had left a letter ſignifying his intention to deſert, was retaken half way down the rock, between Charles the Vth's wall and Mount Miſery.

He

1782.
July.

(An East View of Gibraltar)

He was fo fituated as to be unable to defcend or return, and was at length obliged to cry for affiftance; which being heard by the guard at the former poft, fearch was made for the unhappy man, and he was afterwards executed.

A DESERTER from the regiment of Bechart came in on the 14th : he acquainted us, that the Duke de Crillon had affumed the command of the fiege, and that General Don Alvarez had quitted the Camp ; that the Combined Army confifted of forty-five battalions of infantry, including eight French battalions, two battalions of Spanifh, and four companies of French artillery, befides cavalry; but, owing to defertion, their numbers were confiderably diminifhed.   The battering-fhips, he faid, were to have on board French artillery; and it was reported they would be completed in about fix weeks, the time we had calculated, ourfelves, from obfervations on their progrefs.   About this period, additional forges for heating fhots were eftablifhed in different parts of the Garrifon, with all the proper apparatus.   The 15th, the Enemy laid a boom of fpars from the breakers north of the ifland at Algeziras towards the northward : fome few days afterwards it was confiderably lengthened, and the gun-boats were ranged in front of it : a boom was alfo placed between the ifland and the main land.   We concluded thefe obftructions were intended to defend their battering-fhips from any attempts we might make (before they were completed) to deftroy them.   The fame day, an embrafure was opened in the face of the rock, communicating with the gallery above Farringdon's : the mine was loaded with an unufual quantity of powder, and the explofion was fo amazingly loud, that almoft the whole of the Enemy's camp turned out at the report : but what muft their furprife be, when they obferved whence the fmoke iffued !—The original intention of this opening, was to communicate air to the workmen, who before were almoft fuffocated with the fmoke which remained after blowing
                                                                    the

the different mines; but on examining the aperture more clofely, an idea was conceived of mounting a gun to bear on all the Enemy's batteries, excepting Fort Barbara : accordingly orders were given to enlarge the inner part for the recoil; and, when finifhed, a twenty-four-pounder was mounted.*

THE 18th, a foldier of the 56th regiment, who had efcaped from the quarter-guard fome days before, and who, it is imagined, had endeavoured to defert, furrendered himfelf voluntarily to the main guard. One of the 58th, and another of the 97th regiment, had got off in the former part of the month : the difcouragement, how-ever, which had of late attended thefe deluded wretches, we were in hopes would now deter others from attempting to abandon their colours at this critical juncture.

OUR Artillery, as the firing was very inconfiderable, were now chiefly engaged in preparing fhells and carcaffes to be ufed againft the Enemy's fhips. The Engineers were alfo equally indefatigable in their department. On the part of the Befiegers, multitudes of mules were conftantly employed in different duties in their camp, and large parties continued to land military ftores and powder at the Orange-grove. The 25th, the St. Philip's Caftle and Hector cutter arrived from the eaftward, and communicated the agreeable news of the entire defeat of the French fleet in the Weft-Indies, by Admiral Sir George Rodney, with the capture of the Ville de Paris, and the French Admiral the Count de Graffe. In confequence of this

victory,

---

* This work was profecuted with fuch fuccefs, that four, if not five guns were mounted in the Gallery, before the fubfequent September : and in a little more than twelve months from the day the Engineers commenced, it was advanced to the projection of the Rock, where the Governor purpofed to make a battery; which afterwards was effected, and is now diftinguifhed by the name of St. George's Hall. As this wonderful work was not however finifhed during the Author's refidence in Gibraltar, he will not pretend to give the Reader any further parti-culars concerning it.

victory, a grand falute was fired at noon ; and in the evening a *feu-de-joie*, by the troops drawn up from the Grand battery to the New-mole fort. Signor Leonetti, nephew to Pafcal Paoli, the celebrated Corfican General, with two officers, a chaplain, and fixty-eight volunteers, came as paffengers in thefe veffels, to offer their fervices to the Governor. In the courfe of the fame day, our Engineers began to fix a *chevaux-de-frife* from the foot of Land-port glacis, adjoining Water port, to the floping palifades on the caufeway ; and thence to be continued acrofs the Inundation to the advanced covert-way, leading to Lower Forbes's barrier. The Enemy did not moleft the party on this duty ; which to us appeared very extraordinary.

A BOAT arrived, on the 26th, with two packets from Faro, which mentioned, that the Enemy's preparations for the attack would be complete by the middle of Auguft, and that all the boats along the coaft in the vicinity of Cadiz were already engaged to embark troops for the expedition. A private letter by this boat gave us fome general information of the immenfe preparations which were making, and fome idea of the conftruction of the new-invented veffels, which had infpired the Enemy with fuch confidence of fuccefs. It recited,
" That ten fhips were to be fortified fix or feven feet thick, on the
" larboard fide, with green timber bolted with iron, cork, junk,
" and raw hides ; which were to carry guns of heavy metal, and be
" bomb-proof on the top, with a defcent for the fhells to flide off :
" that thefe veffels, which they fuppofed would be impregnable, were
" to be moored within half gun-fhot of the walls with iron chains ;
" and large boats with mantlets were to lie off at fome diftance,
" full of troops, to affift, and be ready to take advantage of occur-
" rences : that the mantlets of thefe boats were to be formed with
" hinges to fall down, to facilitate their landing : that they were
" to have forty thoufand men in camp, and the principal attack was
" to be made by fea, to be covered by a fquadron of men of war,

K k   " with

" with bomb-ketches, floating-batteries, gun and mortar boats, &c.
" and that the Count d'Artois, brother to the King of France, with
" other great perfonages, was to be prefent at the attack."

Towards the conclufion of the month, our attention was engaged
for feveral nights fucceffively by a great noife on the Ifthmus, like
that of a large body of men at work : a few light balls were thrown
in different parts, to difcover whence it proceeded; but we could
never difcern any men, except their patroles : it was therefore
imagined thefe parties were employed within the lines. The 29th,
the wooden buildings in the navy-yard, at the New mole, were
taken down, and removed to Rofia, where they were afterwards
re-eftablifhed on an enlarged plan. As the communications along
the line-wall, &c. to the Northward, were expected to be much
expofed to the Enemy's fire when the fhips were brought before the
walls, the Engineers, about this time, began a covert-way along
the rampart, from Orange's baftion to the Grand parade, and thence
to be continued to South port : this was done by clearing away the
rubbifh from the old houfes immediately under the works, and
filling others up, which alfo ferved as traverfes againft the land-
batteries. Another covert-way was likewife made, to communicate
from the Princefs of Wales's lines with the South barracks. The
31ft, upwards of a hundred covered waggons came to the Enemy's
lines from the camp, fuppofed to be laden with ammunition and
ftores for the batteries.

Auguft.   Appearances became daily more important, in the month of
Auguft. The Enemy's artificers were remarkably diligent at Algeziras, and the cruifers became more attentive to the blockade.
They were particularly fufpicious of every veffel that came in fight
from the weft ; and the gun-boats were ftationed out as night-
cruifers; which probably was the reafon why we had not been for
fome time vifited by them. In their camp every perfon feemed
employed;

employed; and their dépôts of faſcines and pickets were very conſiderable, notwithſtanding the quantities continually removed to
the lines. Nor were we leſs active in taking advantage of this interval: large and lofty traverſes were raiſed along the line-wall; new
communications were made at Willis's; the flank of the Princeſs
Anne's battery was rebuilt, and heavy metal mounted, to bear over
Water port. The 4th, the Corſican Volunteers were formed into
an independent corps, under Signor Leonetti, who was appointed
Captain Commandant. The company conſiſted of a Captain, and
Captain Lieutenant, Firſt and Second Lieutenants, one Adjutant,
one Chaplain, four Serjeants, four Corporals, two Drummers, and
ſixty-eight Privates. They were armed with a firelock and bayonet,
each a horſe-piſtol ſlung on the left ſide, and two cartridge-boxes.
The Governor quartered them on Windmill-hill, and committed
that poſt to their charge.

As THE completing of the ſubterranean communication from the
King's to the Queen's lines appeared (from the difficulty at that
time attending the reinforcing of the latter, in caſe of an alarm) to
be an object of great importance, the Governor, on the 5th, ordered
all the miners in the different regiments into the King's works, to
proſecute it with greater diligence, and aſſiſt in the gallery above
Farringdon's, which now extended a hundred and forty feet in the
ſolid rock. The ſame day, the Enemy removed the old maſts out of
ſeveral of the battering-ſhips, ſubſtituting jury-maſts in their places.
Three hulls now appeared nearly finiſhed. The evening of the 6th,
the Governor thought proper to detach a truſty ſerjeant, with four
men, from Land port, to a receſs in the rock under the Queen's
lines, near Lower Forbes's, with orders to advance a ſentry to the
barrier, who was to liſten attentively to what was tranſacting upon
the neutral ground; but by no means to fire, except in his own

defence,

defence.   This party was to withdraw at the grey of the morning, that they might not be obſerved by the Enemy.

THE 7th, came in a deſerter who had been formerly in our ſervice at Minorca.   He ſwam from behind Fort Barbara, and landed at the. Devil's tower ; near which place he met a patrole of cavalry, but, throwing himſelf on the ground, was not obſerved.   He ſaid the Duke was reſolved to fire the 25th inſtant ; and from the prodigious number of mortars mounted in the lines, reports were induſtriouſly propagated in the camp, that our ordnance would ſoon be ſilenced by their ſuperior fire, and the batteries *beaten to powder*.   He further acquainted us, that there were thirty-four thouſand men in camp, and but little intercourſe between the Spaniards and their Allies, who were principally new levies, and very little diſciplined ; concluding with a confirmation of the laſt intelligence, that the ſoldiers in general ſo diſreliſhed the buſineſs, that many daily deſerted with their arms into the country.   We continued to fire a few light balls at night, for fear the Enemy ſhould make any addition to their advanced works, which, from the immenſe quantity of materials brought to the lines, we ſuſpected would be commenced very ſoon ; and as it was apprehended their advances would be made to the eaſtward, the guns at Willis's and the heights bearing towards that quarter, were loaded with grape, to be more effectual in the execution, in caſe they were diſcovered.   On the 11th, the 72d regiment, which was quartered in the baſtions in town, independent of their quota towards the other duties of the Garriſon, voluntarily offered to aſſiſt in making the new covered-way from the Grand parade to Orange's baſtion ; and a hundred of them were immediately employed.   The Governor however, as a compenſation for their zeal, ordered them to be paid as real-men, (that is, to receive two reals each *per day* ; which is equal, *at par*, to about 9*d*. ſterling). with the addition, to each man, of a pint of grog.

THE

THE Enemy, on the 13th, got up the maſts and yards in ſeveral ſhips, and bent the ſails of two : but from the appearance of the whole, we did not think they could be finiſhed by the 25th.   Some few days before, they lined the upper port-holes of the two-deckers with tin ; to protect, as we imagined, the cheeks of the ports from being burnt by the conſtant firing of the cannon.   In the evening, the 97th regiment furniſhed, for the firſt time, a working party of a hundred and twenty men, to remove ſhip-timbers from the New mole, to Montague's baſtion, where the engineers intended to erect a cavalier for two guns.

ABOUT this time, a ſpecies of influenza made its appearance on board the frigates in the Mole, and ſoon communicated with the Garriſon.   Its general ſymptoms were ſudden pains, accompanied with a dizzineſs in the head ; though others were affected in a dif-ferent manner.   For ſeveral days near a hundred men were daily taken to the Hoſpital ; but bleeding, and a night's reſt, uſually removed it.   It was attributed, at that time, to the extraordinary heat of the atmoſphere, which was unuſually warm, owing to the prodigious fires made by the Spaniards on the neighbouring hills, and the ſtagnant ſtate of the air : but we have ſince learned that it was univerſal over Europe ; and we had reaſon, at that time, to think the Enemy were not leſs affected by it.

A GENERAL OFFICER, ſuppoſed to be the Duke, viſited, on the 15th, the advanced works ; which, we afterwards ſuppoſed, was to reconnoitre the ground, previous to entering upon the ſucceeding additions which were made to the parallel ; for the ſubſequent morning at day-break, to our great aſtoniſhment, we diſcovered that they had raiſed, during the preceding night, a very ſtrong and lofty epaulement, in extent about five hundred yards, connecting the parallel to the eaſtern breach, with a communication, near a thouſand

three

three hundred yards long, extending from the principal barrier of the lines to the east end of the epaulement. Their works now embraced each shore of the isthmus, and fully completed the first parallel. The communication, or *boyau*, (as it was distinguished by our engineers) consisted of casks filled with sand, which was also thrown up in front, having traverses at equal distances in the rear, made of casks and fascines: but the epaulement appeared to be raised entirely with sand-bags, from ten to twelve feet high, with a thickness proportionable; and all together was a most stupendous work. Its purpose however was not immediately pointed out. To erect these new additions in so short a time, we computed, at a moderate calculation, must have employed ten thousand men; which was afterwards confirmed to us by their officers: and for so numerous a party to be at work within eight hundred yards of the Garrison, and not be discovered, must appear, to a person not present, almost incredible. We threw a few light balls whilst they were at work, one of which, we afterwards learned, greatly alarmed them; but, finding they were not discovered, they resumed their occupation, and withdrew in the morning unobserved. The Spanish gazette described this parallel as of two hundred and thirty toises* in length; and added, that *a million six hundred thousand sand-bags* were used in raising it. The communication it mentioned to have been in length six hundred and thirty toises, and formed of fascines and casks. The Governor at night did not order an increase of firing on the new works: a few rounds were discharged, with several carcasses and light balls; but the latter were almost immediately extinguished.

THE night of the 17th, the Enemy brought a great number of casks, pickets, and fascines, to the rear of the eastern communication, which was raised some little near the barrier. They also erected three epaulements with shoulders, of sand-bags, for mortar-batteries,

---

* A toise is equal to our fathom, or six feet.

batteries, in the parallel. Two were to the weftward, and the
third to the eaftward of the Mahon battery.

THE morning of the 18th, we obferved one of the battering-
fhips at anchor off Barcelo's battery. About noon, the men of war
at Algeziras were decorated with flags, as was cuftomary on the
celebration of a feftival; and, what did not efcape our obfervation,
the Englifh enfign was at the main-top-gallant maft-head of the
Admiral's fhip, with the Spanifh enfign flying triumphantly over it.
Soon after, feven barges with crimfon awnings rowed from Algeziras
to the Orange-grove, where they received on board fome great
perfonages, and returned to Algeziras, efcorted by fifteen gun-
boats, which repeatedly fired falutes, as did the men of war: on
their return amongft the fhipping, the battering-fhips hoifted their
enfigns, and falutes were again fired by the men of war. The
barges then proceeded to the battering-fhip which was anchored
apart from the reft, where they remained fome time; and on the
company's quitting the fhip, fhe fired a falute of eight guns, and
the boats went along-fide the Admiral. About three, the battering-
fhip got under way, and failed to the northward, paft the flag-fhip:
fhe endeavoured to fail back, but in vain; and was obliged to be
towed to her ftation by ten gun-boats. At fix o'clock, three barges
only returned from the Spanifh Admiral to the Orange-grove, and
were faluted and reconducted with the fame ceremony as before.
We now imagined that the Count d'Artois was arrived, and thefe
compliments were paid in confequence of his dining with the
Spanifh Admiral. Our firing at night was very brifk. The fucceeding morning we perceived that the Enemy had conftructed nine
traverfes adjoining the eaftern part of the epaulement, and had raifed
the boyau with fafcines. The epaulement for another mortar-battery
was likewife erected in the parallel oppofite the Centre redoubt.
At night the Enemy were heard hard at work: our firing was
consequently

conſequently increaſed by the addition of the lower batteries: the Enemy did not return a ſhot.

ON the 19th, a ſmall magazine blew up in the Enemy's camp, near Buena-Viſta, which ſet a hut on fire. About noon, a flag of truce came from the Duke: the officer appeared to be a perſon of rank, as the boat had a crimſon awning, and the rowers were in uniforms. After paſſing and repaſſing ſeveral times, our boat returned with a preſent from the Duke to the Governor, of ice, fruit, vegetables, &c. The officers informed us that the ſalutes fired the preceding day were in compliment to the Count d'Artois, &c. The following was handed about as a genuine tranſlation of the Duke's letter on this occaſion; therefore, without vouching for its authenticity, it is here inſerted, to gratify the curioſity of the Reader.

" SIR,   *Camp of Buena-Viſta*, 19th *of Auguſt*, 1782.

" HIS Royal Highneſs Count d'Artois, who has received per-
" miſſion from the King his brother to aſſiſt at the ſiege, as a
" volunteer in the Combined Army, of which their Moſt Chriſtian
" and Catholic Majeſties have honoured me with the command,
" arrived in this camp the 15th inſtant. This young Prince has been
" pleaſed, in paſſing through Madrid, to take charge of ſome letters
" which had been ſent to that capital from this place, and which
" are addreſſed to perſons belonging to your Garriſon: his Royal
" Highneſs has deſired that I would tranſmit them to you, and
" that to this mark of his goodneſs and attention I ſhould add the
" ſtrongeſt expreſſions of eſteem for your perſon and character.
" I feel the greateſt pleaſure in giving this mark of condeſcenſion
" in this auguſt Prince, as it furniſhes me with a pretext, which I
" have been anxiouſly looking for theſe two months that I have
                                                " been

" been in camp, to aſſure you of the higheſt eſteem I have conceived
" for your Excellency, of the ſincereſt deſire I feel of deſerving
" yours, and of the pleaſure to which I look forward of becoming
" your friend, after I ſhall have learned to render myſelf worthy
" of the honour, by facing you as an enemy. His Highneſs the
" Duke de Bourbon, who arrived here twenty-four hours after the
" Count d'Artois, deſires alſo that I ſhould aſſure you of his parti-
" cular eſteem.

" Permit me, Sir, to offer a few trifles for your table, of which
" I am ſure you muſt ſtand in need, as I know you live entirely
" upon vegetables: I ſhould be glad to know what kind you like
" beſt.   I ſhall add a few game for the Gentlemen of your
" houſehold, and ſome ice, which I preſume will not be diſagreeable
" in the exceſſive heat of this climate at this ſeaſon of the year.
" I hope you will be obliging enough to accept the ſmall portion
" which I ſend with this letter.

" I have the honour to be, &c.

" B. B. Duc de Crillon."

" *His Excellency General* Eliott, *&c.*"

The barge which brought the letter and preſent, ranged at a ſhort
diſtance along the town, from off the Old-mole head to Ragged-
ſtaff, where ſhe was ſtopped by our flag ; but being thought rather
too near, as they might thence make what obſervations they choſe on
our batteries, a ſhot was fired over her from the Repulſe prame ; upon
which ſhe rowed further out in the Bay, and waited at a conſiderable
diſtance for the return of our flag. The night of the 19th, the Enemy
raiſed the ſemicircular parapet of the *place d'armes* joining the eaſt
flank of the St. Carlos's battery, with ſand-bags eight or nine feet
L l   high,

high, apparently for a battery: they alſo made ſome conſiderable additions to the eaſtern works. The day following, a flag of truce went from the Garriſon with an anſwer to the Duke's polite letter of the preceding day: the Governor's letter was reported to be to the following purpoſe.

      " SIR,   *Gibraltar, Auguſt the 20th*, 1782.

    " I FIND myſelf highly honoured by your obliging letter of yeſter-
" day, in which your Excellency was ſo kind as to inform me of
" the arrival in your camp of his Royal Highneſs the Count
" d'Artois, and the Duke de Bourbon, to ſerve as volunteers at the
" ſiege. Theſe Princes have ſhewn their judgement in making
" choice of a maſter in the art of war, whoſe abilities cannot fail to
" form great warriors. I am overpowered with the condeſcenſion
" of His Royal Highneſs, in ſuffering ſome letters for perſons in this
" town to be conveyed from Madrid in his carriages. I flatter
" myſelf that your Excellency will give my moſt profound reſpect
" to His Royal Highneſs, and to the Duke de Bourbon, for the
" expreſſions of eſteem with which they have been pleaſed to honour
" ſo inſignificant a perſon as I am.

    " I RETURN a thouſand thanks to your Excellency for your hand-
" ſome preſent of fruits, vegetables, and game. You will excuſe
" me however, I truſt, when I aſſure you, that in accepting your
" preſent I have broken through a reſolution to which I had faith-
" fully adhered ſince the beginning of the war; and that was, never
" to receive or procure, by any means whatever, any proviſions or
" other commodity for my own private uſe: ſo that, without any
" preference, every thing is ſold publickly here; and the private
" ſoldier, if he has money, can become a purchaſer, as well as the
                                                  " Governor.

"Governor. I confefs, I make it a point of honour to partake both
"of plenty and fcarcity in common with the loweft of my brave
"fellow foldiers. This furnifhes me with an excufe for the liberty
"I now take, of entreating your Excellency not to heap any more
"favours on me of this kind, as in future I cannot convert your
"prefents to my own private ufe. Indeed, to be plain with your
"Excellency, though vegetables at this feafon are fcarce with us,
"every man has got a quantity proportioned to the labour which he
"has beftowed in raifing them. The Englifh are naturally fond
"of gardening and cultivation ; and here we find our amufement in
"it, during the intervals of reft from public duty. The promife
"which the Duke de Crillon makes, of honouring me in proper time
"and place with his friendfhip, lays me under infinite obligations.
"The intereft of our Sovereigns being once folidly fettled, I fhall
"with eagernefs embrace the firft opportunity to avail myfelf of fo
"precious a treafure.

" I have the honour to be, &c.

" G. A. ELIOTT."

"*His Excellency the* DUKE de CRILLON, *&c.*"

OUR Artillery, on the night of the 20th, fired with great vivacity
from the upper and lower batteries, in all directions ; for the objects
now were fo divided, the parallel being upwards of half a mile in
extent, that we could not always be certain where they were employed. In the morning we found they had raifed the boyau, and
made fome alterations in the Weftern works. The Enemy's operations were not now carried on in the fame flow manner as formerly :
the Duke feemed determined to act with vigour, and aftonifh us by
the rapidity with which he raifed his batteries. His army was numerous, and his orders (if we may credit report) with refpect to materials, unlimited. Every exertion was therefore ufed to complete

L l 2

them

them with expedition. Whilſt our opponents were ſo active, we were not on our parts indolent, or inattentive to the defence of the Garriſon. The late additions of the Enemy made conſiderable alterations neceſſary in the works at Willis's, &c. Our parties were therefore augmented, and employed in ſtrengthening the communications, repairing the ſplinter-proofs, and on other important duties of the ſame nature. Green's lodge and the Royal battery were ordered to be caiſſoned with ſhip-timber: the intrenched covert-way from the Princeſs of Wales's lines was continued, and ſloping paliſades placed under thoſe parts of the line-wall, from the Eight-gun baſtion to the New mole, which were not well flanked from above. A boom of maſts was likewiſe laid from the former to the head of the watering-tank, and anchors ſunk in the ſhallow water between that Baſtion and Ragged-ſtaff.

THE afternoon of the 21ſt, a carcaſs from Willis's ſet fire to ſome looſe faſcines in the rear of the Eaſtern boyau, which ſoon communicated to the work itſelf; and the line for a conſiderable extent was involved in the flames. On the appearance of the ſmoke our lower batteries immediately opened, and a moſt animated cannonade was directed from the Garriſon. A party of the Enemy endeavoured to extinguiſh the fire; but finding their efforts to ſtop its progreſs in vain, they gallantly pulled down the line on each ſide, to prevent the flames from ſpreading; which they at length effected, but not without conſiderable loſs from our artillery. For ſome time we imagined the Enemy would remain _ſilent_ ſpectators of the conflagration; but an Officer arriving at the lines about ſix o'clock, their batteries inſtantly returned the fire, ſeconded ſoon after by the new thirteen-gun battery near the Tower: the latter, however, after four or five diſcharges, was ſilenced by the Oldmole-head howitzers. Our fire was ſo briſk, and ſo well ſerved, that it exceeded theirs by four to one. About half paſt ſeven

the

the flames burnt out: and our additional ordnance, as well as the
Enemy's batteries, ceafed.   In this fhort firing they returned feven
hundred and forty-three fhot, and thirty-eight fhells; and we
expended in the twenty-four hours, including what were difcharged
on this occafion, ninety barrels of powder. We had three men
flightly wounded. In the prior part of the day, thirteen feluccas
arrived in the Bay from the eaft : fome imagined they were intended
for additional gun-boats; others, for debarking troops. . The 22d,
the Enemy had repaired the damage done by the fire the preceding
day; but in the afternoon a fimilar accident had nearly happened :
a carcafs was thrown into the St. Martin's battery, and took effect ;
but the guard exerted themfelves with fuch activity and bravery,
that it was foon extinguifhed, although our lower batteries were
again open to fupport it. The Enemy were on this day totally
filent. The fucceeding night, they dreffed and raifed the new
communication, and made fome additions to the eaftern part of
the parallel : they were alfo at work in their new mortar-batteries ;
and great quantities of materials were brought down to the lines, and
into the advanced works. .

THE 24th, the inhabitants in Hardy-town began early to remove
their bedding, &c. towards Europa : they were confident, from
the information of the laft deferters, that the Enemy would again
open their batteries the fucceeding day, being the anniverfary of
St. Louis ; and no perfuafions could banifh their apprehenfions.
They were however convinced, the following day, that the Duke
was not prepared, whatever his intentions might have been fome
weeks before.

THE Enemy being heard at work, on the night of the 24th,
drew a warm fire from our batteries. In the morning we found
they had raifed additional traverfes to the fand-bag epaulement, which
now

now prefented a formidable battery of SIXTY-FOUR embrafures, divided into four batteries of fourteen embrafures each, and one of eight; leaving a fpace at the eaftern extremity, as we concluded, for mortars. The original epaulement remained entire, the additional merlons joining at proper intervals the front work, which ferved to mafk the embrafures till the batteries were finifhed. Several embrafures of the eight-gun battery they had already lined with fafcines. Some additions were alfo made to the St. Carlos's battery, the parapet of which was lengthened towards the weft. The following night, the Enemy, notwithftanding a warm fire from the Garrifon, erected three large magazines, and began a fourth, in the rear of the fixty-four-gun battery: they likewife lined many of the embrafures with fafcines, and raifed a fand-bag traverfe to cover the communication from the weft flank of the fixty-four-gun battery to the parallel.

THE 26th, the Queen Charlotte, Leonora, and Charles ordnance-fhips, with the St. Philip's Caftle, were ordered into the Mole to be run afhore till the attack was decided. The feamen belonging to the frigates were employed alfo, about this time, in carrying fails and yards to erect tents for a camp at Europa, where they were to be ftationed when the Governor fhould think proper to order them on fhore. In the evening about ten o'clock came in a deferter, an Irifhman who formerly had been in our fervice: he fwam from the beach beyond Fort St. Philip, and attempted to land at Bay-fide, but was fired upon by their advanced fentries. He informed us it was reported that the Duke had intended firing on the 25th, but was prevented from finifhing his batteries fo foon as he expected, by the heavy fire from the Garrifon; that in their endeavours to extinguifh the flames on the preceding 21ft, the party had fuftained very confiderable lofs: a colonel and feventeen men of the regiment to which he belonged were killed. He corroborated the intel-ligence,

ligence, by the laſt deſerter, concerning the number of men in camp, and reſpecting the prevalence of deſertion.

WE did not diſcover any material additions the morning of the 27th : a fifth magazine was erected; alſo ſeveral traverſes in the rear of the parallel. Another of the battering-ſhips anchored the ſame day off Barcelo's battery, apart from the reſt : as ſhe ſwung round with the tide, we had an opportunity of viewing with glaſſes the ſtarboard-ſide, which we perceived was not finiſhed like the oppoſite; the bomb-proof only extending about three parts over, leaving conſiderable openings between the ſtrong uprights which ſupported it from the deck, for the convenient reception of men, proviſions, and ammunition. We obſerved, the ſame day, a great number of boats ranged along the ſhore at Algeziras. In the afternoon, the Repulſe prame came into the New mole; and the ſucceeding morning the Fortune and Vanguard were likewiſe withdrawn from the Bay. At night the Enemy erected a number of traverſes in rear of their parallel and battery, and finiſhed ſome interior work, as they had done the preceding night, though we kept up our uſual fire.

THE Enemy's ſquadron was reinforced on the 28th' with ſix Spaniſh line-of-battle ſhips and a xebeque, under a Commodore from the weſt. In the courſe of the day, two twenty-four-pounders were taken up the hill to the gallery above Farringdon's, for the embraſures already opened; and four hundred additional workmen were ordered into the works. Upwards of ſix hundred men were at this time daily employed at Willis's, covering and ſtrengthening the flanks; likewiſe in forming new communications, with ſplinter-proofs, traverſes, &c. as the new battery *enfiladed* moſt of the old covered ways, and rendered a thorough change neceſſary in thoſe works, before the artillery could be properly covered. The com-

munications in town and at the ſouth were therefore diſcontinued,
till the above were put in the beſt ſtate of defence and ſecurity.   At
duſk, three ſerjeants were poſted upon the NORTH, KING's and
SOUTH baſtions, to obſerve and report the Enemy's ſignals in camp,
and along the coaſt.   At night, a deſerter from the Walons came
over in the ſame manner as the laſt.   He reported, that a very ſtrong
party was ordered for work that evening; which induced the Governor to increaſe the firing from Willis's, the lines, and lower
batteries.   He further acquainted us, that we killed numbers of
their workmen; and that the 15th of next month was fixed for
opening upon the Garriſon; but that all, even the volunteers, were
diſheartened at the very thoughts of the attack.   Ninety pieces of
cannon, he likewiſe ſaid, were brought into the ſixty-four-gun
battery; which number was to be increaſed, to ſupply the place of
thoſe which might be damaged, or over-heated.   The night of the
28th, the Enemy raiſed more traverſes, and began communications
to their magazines: a hundred and fifty-three of the former were
erected behind the long boyau.   They alſo worked upon the mortar-
batteries.

IT was about this period, that the Spaniſh twenty-ſix-pounders,
with other guns of the ſame heavy nature, were diſtributed on the
ſea-line in room of ordnance of ſmaller calibre, which were mounted
in their places againſt the Enemy's batteries.   By this diſpoſition,
the Duke would not have it in his power to return any of the ſhot
we fired, as his cannon were all twenty-ſix-pounders; and the
Governor was enabled to retaliate on their ſhipping, thoſe ſhot which
he had received from the land; *annoying* them by this means with
their own weapons.   Towards the concluſion of the month, the
influenza had almoſt diſappeared: the working-parties were therefore reinforced, though the heavy duty of the guards would with
difficulty permit it: on the 29th, the Engineers paraded upwards of
seventeen

seventeen hundred workmen, including non-commissioned officers. The Enemy, on the night of the 29th, raised merlons for four embrasures, joining the semicircular sand-bag epaulement, east of St. Carlos's battery. Six battering-ships were at anchor off Barcelo's battery on the 30th. The same day, our seamen were ordered on shore, to encamp at Europa. At night, the Artillery, in addition to their former fire, opened the Grand battery : it did not however prevent the Enemy from platforming the sixty-four-gun battery, and making further additions to the mortar-batteries. They also lined with fascines the embrasures of the semicircular four-gun battery. Many hundred mules were still employed in bringing clay and fascines to the parallel. Our fire was very destructive amongst these animals, as well as their workmen ; two, three, and sometimes more of the former, being frequently seen dead on the sands at day-break.

Our Engineers, by the close of the month, had extended Landport *chevaux-de-frise* to the causeway, and begun the other across the Inundation. Carpenters were also engaged in caissoning the Royal and Green's-lodge batteries, and raising new traverses at those posts. The Enemy's squadron in the Bay at this period was as follows : four line-of-battle ships, and one of fifty guns, (on board of which was the flag) two frigates, three cutters, four bombketches, and smaller armed vessels, were at Algeziras : two ships of the line were at anchor off the Orange-grove ; and a frigate, with an armed brig, was at Cabrita. To these we may add the battering-ships and gun-boats. Since two of the men of war had removed nearer the Enemy's camp, boats full of soldiers were frequently observed going on board them ; and as the guns were seen to be drawn back from the ports, and suddenly run out again, whilst the troops were on board, we suspected that they were practising to work the guns, previous to their embarking on board the battering-ships.

AFFAIRS

AFFAIRS feemed now drawing to a crifis: and, as every appearance indicated that the attack would not long be deferred, the inhabitants, apprehenfive of the confequences, were wonderfully active in fecuring themfelves and their property. The Befiegers wrought hard the night of the 31ft: two crofs-communications, lined with fafcines, were thrown up from the long boyau, leading to the parallel; one to the weftern flank of the fixty-four-gun battery, the other to the weftward of the Mahon battery. Five traverfes were alfo erected within each of the new mortar-batteries, and magazines for ammunition begun near them, joining the parallel. We imagined they were likewife employed in bringing down ordnance to the advanced works. Our artillery amufed them with a brifk fire; but the Governor rather objected to fuch a quantity of powder being at this time expended, as he was of opinion they were now too well covered in their batteries to be much annoyed; and we might afterwards have more occafion for the ammunition. The evening of the 1ft of September, a fmall boat, manned with Englifh failors, failed for Portugal. Lieut. Campbell, of the navy, failed in her with difpatches from the Governor for England. At night, the Enemy erected an epaulement of fand-bags, apparently for two guns, adjoining the weft flank of the Mahon battery; and raifed, feveral fafcines in height, the new communications. Some additions were likewife made to the magazines. Long ftrings of mules ftill continued bringing down fafcines and other materials, which were depofited in different parts of their works. We imagined thefe animals alfo brought down fhot and fhells, as their piles in the artillery-park were confiderably diminifhed. In the Garrifon, our engineers were indefatigable in raifing defences againft thefe formidable batteries; and coals were diftributed to the grates and furnaces for heating fhot.

WE perceived very little alteration in the operations of our opponents on the 3d: they lined the embrafures of the new two-gun battery,

battery, and added to the crofs-communications. In the courfe of the day, their fquadron was reinforced with two French men of war from the eaftward; which were conducted into the Bay by a Spanifh frigate. The 4th, the Enemy removed the guns from the two fourteen-gun batteries in the lines, and difmounted moft of the ordnance in the mortar-batteries; probably to repair the beds and platforms. The removing of the cannon from the former gave us no fmall pleafure, as we had experienced more fatal effects, during their late wanton bombardment and cannonade from thofe batteries, than from any other in their lines. The guns, we fuppofed, were brought forward to the parallel; for we obferved ten in the eaftern extremity of the fixty-four-gun battery. In the forenoon, fixteen boats, with mantlets or barricades in the bow, came from the river Palmones, and anchored off the landing-place beyond Point Mala: thefe, we concluded, were for the fea-attack. About fun-fet, thofe battering-fhips which were finifhed, removed from Algeziras to the Orange-grove: they failed rather heavily, and ufed fweeps, notwithftanding the breeze. About the fame time, two grand falutes were fired by the French men of war.

During the night of the 4th, the Enemy's parties mafked the fix weftern embrafures of the St. Martin's battery, and raifed the parapet with fafcines, intending, as we imagined, to convert it into a mortar-battery, as fix mortars were feen, the preceding day, lying in the rear. The howitzers were alfo removed from the Centre redoubt, and fome additions made to the epaulement, in front of the St. Pafchal's battery, which was now completed for eight mortars. They likewife funk four deep excavations behind the eaftern boyau, as refervoirs for water, in cafe of fire. At night, another battering-fhip joined the others at the Orange-grove: foon afterwards, the Enemy fhipped powder on board them from the pier. Early on the 5th, a large body of men marched in a very

irregular

irregular manner from Algeziras to the camp. We imagined they were the artificers who had been employed upon the ships, and were encamped south of the tower; half of which camp was now struck. During the day, twenty-nine square-sailed boats arrived, (under convoy of an armed brig from the west) and, with upwards of a hundred and twenty from Algeziras, assembled in a line off Rocadillo Point, at the mouth of the Guadaranque. A large floating battery was also towed out, and anchored at the entrance of the Palmones. Towards evening, about five hundred men, escorted by a body of cavalry, embarked from the pier, on board the battering-ships: the singular mode of conducting them to the beach could not fail to attract our notice, and to cause in us some degree of surprise. About eight in the evening, a deserter came in from the regiment of Naples: he reported that the 8th was named for the grand attack, and that all hands were actively employed in completing every thing in the several departments.

Few additions were perceived on the 6th: some sand-bags were placed on the mortar-battery of the St. Martin's. In the forenoon, more boats joined the others at Rocadillo, from the west: the floating-battery was likewise towed to the pier near Point Mala. The Governor, the same day, made some new arrangements in the Garrison detail. An additional field-officer was ordered to mount in the lines, to be independent of the field-officer in town; and the field-officers of the day, in future, were directed to make such disposition of the guards, picquets, and ordnance in their several districts, on every occasion, as appeared to be most for the benefit of the service. A subaltern was added to the New-mole guard, who was at night to be detached with twenty men to the Mole-head; and the picquets in future were ordered to mount fully accoutred, with ammunition complete. The 39th regiment was also ordered to town: the battalion companies to encamp in South-

port

port ditch, and the grenadiers and light infantry to be quartered
in the picquet-yard bomb-proofs, before occupied by part of the
72d regiment, who on this difpofition joined the reft of their
regiment in Montague's and King's baftions.

THE Enemy's works on the land fide were now every hour
advancing to perfection; but the Duke's attention towards completing them feemed fo entirely to engage him, as in a great
meafure to prevent his taking the prudent precautions neceffary
for their defence. The advanced batteries in the parallel were either
unfinifhed (though nearly completed), or undergoing fuch alterations, that the materials in their vicinity greatly obftructed the ufe
of the ordnance which were mounted; and their batteries in the
lines (except the forts) were in a fimilar fituation; the cannon, to
permit the neceffary repairs, being totally removed from fome, and
the mortars drawn back or difmounted in others. The forts, and
fome few mortar-batteries, were therefore the only defences left
to protect thefe immenfe works from infult and attack. This
ftate of their works prefented an opportunity, in fome refpects
not unlike that which General Eliott had embraced in the preceding year, when by an unexpected fally he glorioufly deftroyed the
labours of fo many months. The honour, however, of caufing
a fecond difgrace, was referved for Lieutenant General Boyd, the
Lieutenant Governor, who, in the forenoon of the 6th, recommended, by letter to the Governor, the immediate ufe of red-hot
fhot againft the land-batteries of the befiegers. General Eliott
acquiefced in the propofal, and immediately ordered Major Lewis,
the Commandant of the artillery, to wait on Lieut. General Boyd
for his inftructions and commands, fubmitting entirely to him the
execution of the attack which he had projected. In confequence of
the Governor's affent, preparations were inftantly made; and in a
fhort time every thing was properly arranged for the fervice. In

the

the interval, we muft not however omit to take notice of the Enemy's
operations.

EARLY the morning of the 7th, feveral gun-boats were difcovered
off the Old-mole head, retiring from the Garrifon; which we
imagined had been founding under cover of the night. The Garrifon orders of this day contained the following arrangements.
" The marine brigade (which compofed a corps of about nine hun-
" dred men) to take rank on fhore according to the King's regu-
" lations; Captain Curtis as colonel with the rank of brigadier,
" Captain Gibfon as lieutenant-colonel, Captain Bradfhaw as major,
" eight lieutenants as captains, eighteen midfhipmen as enfigns; and
" the brigade to mount Europa-advance, and Little-bay guards.
" A picquet of the line to be detached every evening to the Prince's
" lines, and an additional fubaltern at the fame time to Land port.
" One captain and eight privates to be added to Water-port guard,
" whence a detachment of a fubaltern and thirty men was to be
" fent, at fun-fet, to the Old-mole head; which at fecond gun-fire
" was to be joined by one of the captains. Twelve privates to
" the main guard. One ferjeant, nine privates, and a gunner, to
" Ragged-ftaff; detaching a ferjeant and fix men, with the gunner,
" at retreat-beating, to the Wharf-head." The alarm-pofts were alfo
fixed as follows: " The 39th flank companies, to take poft on the
" North-baftion town: three battalion companies of the fame regi-
" ment, the South baftion; the remaining five, at Ragged-ftaff;
" extending towards the eight-gun baftion. The 72d regiment:
" right, the North-baftion town; left, Orange's baftion, extending
" as far further towards the King's baftion as poffible. The 73d
" regiment, (which was quartered at the fouthward,) to take poft
" on the left of the 72d, towards the South baftion. Captain Mar-
" tin's company of artillery, the Grand battery and Water port. Cap-
" tain Lloyd's company, the King's and South baftions. BRIGADIER
" GENERAL

" GENERAL PICTON to command the corps in town. The Hano-
" verian brigade, from the eight-gun baftion fouth, to Prince
" Edward's battery inclufive, under the command of Lieut. Colonel
" Dachenhaufen. The 56th regiment, South parade. The 12th
" regiment, New-mole parade. The 97th regiment, Rofia parade.
" The 58th regiment, in front of their encampment, detaching
" a flank company through the hole in the wall upon Windmill-
" hill, to reinforce Europa-advance guard." (This regiment was
to receive orders from Brigadier Curtis.) " The engineers and
" artificers in two divifions, one to affemble at the Efplanade town,
" the other at the Efplanade fouth." It was recommended at the
fame time to the commanding officers, to have a fufficient referve in
cafe of deficiencies, and to pay particular attention to the flanks and
redans which commanded the front of the Line-wall.

As THE above exhibits the Governor's difpofition of the troops,
it will not be improper to infert in this place a detail of the guards
which mounted in the Garrifon at this period, with the ftrength of
the Garrifon, and men daily on duty. The ftrength of the Garrifon,
with the marine brigade, (including the officers) in September, was
about feven thoufand five hundred men; upwards of four hundred
of whom were in the hofpital. The number daily upon duty is
fhewn in the following abftract..

Guards, - - - - - - - - - - - - - - 1091 Men including Officers.
Picquets, (including the Additions of the 12th) 613 ditto
Working-parties, under the Chief Engineer   } 1726 { exclufive of the Engineers
   and the Quarter-mafter General,   }   { and Overfeers.

Total 3430

befides many who were conftantly employed as orderlies and affiftants
in the hofpital, and in other departments in the Garrifon.

GUARDS.

1782,
Sept.

GUARDS.	Field Officers	Captains	Subalterns	Serjeants	Corporals	Drummers	Privates	Artillery N.Com.	Artillery Privates	DETACHMENTS TO
Town District.	1	0	0	0	0	0	0	0	0	
Governor's, or Convent-gd.	0	0	0	1	1	0	6	0	0	N.B. Grenadiers.
Lieut. Governor's,	0	0	0	1	1	0	9	0	0	N.B. Lt. Infantry.
Willis's, &c.	0	1	2	0	0	0	0	6	58	
Flag-ftaff,	0	0	1	0	0	1	0	2	15	
Land port,	0	1	4	5	12	2	86	1	4	- - - - the Spur & Flèche.
Grand Battery,	0	0	1	1	4	1	26	0	0	
Water port,	0	2	2	4	6	2	88	0	2	- - - { the Lunette, & Mole head.
Main,	0	1	1	2	4	2	40	1	3	
South port,	0	0	1	2	4	1	29	0	1	
Caftle,	0	0	0	1	2	0	12	0	0	
North Line-wall,	0	0	0	1	2	0	15	0	0	
South Line-wall,	0	0	0	1	2	0	9	0	0	
Artillery-magazine,	0	0	0	1	1	0	6	0	0	
Middle-hill,	0	0	0	0	0	0	12	2	0	
Signal houfe,	0	0	0	1	1	0	6	1	0	- - - - Cha. Vth's wall.
Victualling-office,	0	0	0	1	1	0	9	0	0	
Patroles,	0	0	0	9	0	0	18	0	0	
Orderlies,	0	0	0	13	0	1	2	0	0	
Lines,	1	0	0	0	0	0	0	0	0	
Prince's,	0	1	1	3	6	2	50	1	1	- - - { Upper ... &c.
King's,	0	0	1	1	4	1	50	0	2	
Queen's,	0	1	1	1	2	1	30	0	1	
South District,	1	0	0	0	0	0	0	0	0	
Europa,	0	1	1	1	3	2	32	1	8	
Europa-advance,	0	0	1	1	1	1	20	1	4	} N.B. Marine
Little Bay,	0	0	1	1	1	1	18	0	1	} Brigade.
Ragged-ftaff,	0	0	1	2	2	1	30	0	1	- - - - the Wharf.
Rofia,	0	0	1	1	2	1	30	0	2	- - - - Victualling-tent.
New mole,	0	1	2	3	3	2	59	0	3	- - - - New-mole head.
Buena-Vifta,	0	0	0	0	0	0	6	2	0	
Camp,	0	0	0	1	1	0	9	0	0	
Hofpital,	0	0	0	1	1	0	12	0	0	
Magazine,	0	0	0	1	1	0	15	0	0	
South Shed,	0	0	0	1	2	0	21	0	0	- - - - The Provoft-fhip.
Princefs of Wales's Lines,	0	0	0	1	1	0	6	0	0	
Windmill-hill,	0	0	0	0	1	0	9	0	0	N.B. Corficans.
General De la Motte's,	0	0	0	0	1	0	3	0	0	
Orderlies,	0	0	0	1	0	1	0	0	0	
Total	3	9	22	64	73	23	773	18	106	

IN the evening of the 7th, a little before midnight, two large lights appeared on the shore west of the Orange-grove, forming a right line with our Grand battery; and at the same time, two similar fires were seen behind Fort St. Philip; whence, if a line was produced, it would to appearance have interfected the former, about eight or nine hundred yards to the north-west of the Old-mole head. These unusual signals made many conjecture that the Enemy were founding in that quarter. A few rounds were accordingly fired at intervals in that direction from the North bastion.

BY the morning of the 8th, the preparations, in the department of the artillery, under General Boyd's directions, were completed; and the success of the attack in a great measure depending upon embracing the favourable moment, it was no longer deferred. At seven o'clock, the town-guards being relieved, the firing commenced from all the northern batteries which bore upon the western part of the parallel, and was supported through the day with admirable vivacity. The effect of the red-hot shot and carcasses exceeded our most sanguine expectations. In a few hours, the Mahon battery of six guns, with the battery of two guns on its flank, and great part of the adjoining parallel, were on fire; and the flames, notwithstanding the Enemy's exertions to extinguish them, burnt so rapidly, that the whole of those works before night were consumed. The St. Carlos's and St. Martin's batteries however on this occasion escaped the fate which they had formely experienced. They were nevertheless so much *deranged* by the breaches made to obstruct the effects of the carcasses, &c. that the Enemy were under the necessity of taking down the greater part.

THE Enemy, for near an hour, continued silent spectators of our cannonade. About eight, they fired a few guns from the St. Martin's battery; and between nine and ten, returned our fire from Forts

N n St.

St. Philip and Barbara, with the seven-gun battery in the lines, and soon after from eight new, mortar-batteries in the parallel. This tardiness in returning our fire, in some degree we attributed to the works being confused with materials, and some of the batteries being deficient in ammunition. It might however be owing to want of discretionary orders, as an Officer of rank was observed to enter the lines about the time when their cannonade became general : a reinforcement also marched down from the camp.

THE astonishing bravery displayed by the Enemy in their repeated attempts to extinguish the flames, could not fail to attract our particular notice. Urged on most probably by emulation, they performed prodigies of valour; so that their loss, under so well-directed a fire, must have been very considerable. The French Brigade, we afterwards understood; had a hundred and forty killed and wounded. If the Spanish casuals bore an equal proportion, their united loss have greatly exceeded our calculations.

ABOUT four o'clock in the afternoon, the cannonade abated on both sides, and the Enemy soon after were totally silent, though we continued our usual fire. The Garrison had two or three killed, and several wounded. Lieut. Boag, of the Artillery, and Ensign Gordon, of the 58th regiment, were of the latter number. The former Officer had been wounded before : on this occasion he was pointing a gun from Hanover battery in the lines, when a shell fell in the battery. He had scarcely time to throw himself down in an embrasure, when the shell burst, and fired the gun under the muzzle of which he lay. The report immediately deprived him of hearing, and it was some time before he recovered a tolerable use of that faculty. Major Martin, of the same corps, had likewise a very fortunate escape from a twenty-six-pounder, which shot away the cock of his hat close to the crown. I insert this anecdote,

dote, becaufe it is commonly believed, that if a cannon-ball of this
diameter paffes fo near the head of a perfon, it is generally fatal.
The Major was confiderably ftunned with the wind of the fhot,
but experienced little further injury. In the forenoon of the 8th,
two more fhips of the line removed to the Orange-grove, followed
fome time afterwards by twenty-two gun and mortar boats; and
in the evening, one of the French men of war joined them from
Algeziras. In the courfe of the day, a number of troops were
embarked on board fuch of the battering-fhips as were finifhed;
and at night, our Artillery replaced the ammunition in the expence-
magazines, which had been ufed to fuch good purpofe in the
morning.

This unexpected infult, undoubtedly precipitated the Duke's
meafures; and by provoking him to the attack, before the preparations in the other departments were ready to combine with
him in a general and powerful effort againft the Garrifon, ferved
greatly to fruftrate the enterprife. Apprehenfive, probably, that,
elated by our good fortune, we might renew our attempts finally
to deftroy thofe works which had efcaped, the Duke determined
to avoid the blow (which alfo might be in other refpects fatal in
its confequences) by opening his batteries, even in their unfinifhed
ftate. Actuated, moft probably, by thefe motives, the embrafures
of the new batteries were unmafked during the night of the 8th;
and the fucceeding morning, at day-break, we were furprifed to
find every appearance in their works for firing upon the Garrifon.
Two rockets from the forts in the lines were the fignals to begin;
and the cannonade commenced at half paft five o'clock, with a
volley of about fixty fhells from all their mortar-batteries in the
parallel, fucceeded by a general difcharge of their cannon, amounting,
in the whole, to about a hundred and feventy pieces of ordnance, all
of large calibre:—a Difcharge, I believe, not to be paralleled! Their

firing

firing was powerful, and entirely directed against our works; but was not, after the first round, altogether so tremendous as we had reason to expect from such a train of artillery. At intervals, from ten to twenty shells were in the air at the same moment; their effects though were not equal to the numbers expended. The town, southward of the King's bastion, was little affected; but the northern front, and line-wall leading from the Grand parade to the North bastion, were exceedingly warm; and the lines and Land port were greatly annoyed by the shells from the howitzers, which were distributed in various parts of their parallel. Montague's and Orange's bastions seemed to be the centre of the Enemy's cross-fire; whilst the line-wall in their vicinity was taken *à revers*, by the shot which passed over the lines from the sixty-four-gun battery.

Not imagining, from the rough appearance of the Enemy's works, that they could possibly retaliate so soon, the guards and picquets at the north end of the Garrison were for some time exposed, and some casuals occurred: but we soon discovered whence we were chiefly annoyed, and consequently became more cautious. Lieut. Wharton, of the 73d regiment, was dangerously wounded at Land port.

Whilst the land-batteries were thus pouring forth their vengeance upon the northern front, nine line-of-battle ships, including those under the French flag, got under way from the Orange-grove, and, passing along the Garrison, discharged several broadsides at the works, and particularly at a settee which had just arrived under our guns from Algiers. When this squadron had got round Europa point, they suddenly wore, and, returning along the Europa, Rosia, and New-mole batteries, commenced a heavy fire upon the Garrison. The marine brigade and artillery returned the salute till they passed, when the men of war returned to the eastward. About the same time that the Enemy were thus amusing us at the southward, fifteen

gun

gun and mortar boats approached the town, and continued their
fire for some time; but the artillery giving them a warm reception
from the King's baftion, two of them were towed off with precipitation, and the reft retired in great diforder.   One was thought to
be very confiderably damaged; and fome imagined that her gun was
thrown over-board to fave her from finking.

THIS mode of annoying us on all fides exactly correfponded with
the accounts which we had received of the plan of attack dictated
by Monfieur D'Arçon, the French engineer, who fuperintended the
Enemy's preparations.   They hoped probably to confound and
overwhelm us, by prefenting to us deftruction under fuch various
forms, and by the enormous quantity of fire which they poured in
upon the Garrifon.   The Governor however did not approve of his
troops being thus fubjected to be haraffed at their pleafure, and
refolved therefore, if poffible, to put a ftop to their fea-attacks.
For this purpofe, the furnaces and grates for heating fhot, at the
New mole, were ordered to be lighted; and fome arrangements took
place in the ordnance upon Windmill-hill.   Towards dufk, the
Enemy abated in the fire from their cannon; increafing however
in the expenditure of fhells, which, being generally fired with fhort
fufes, broke in the air.   This practice feemed well calculated for
the purpofes in view.   In the day, they could obferve with greater
certainty the effect of their fhot, and alter as circumftances directed:
the firing at night muft unavoidably be lefs depended upon; fhells
were therefore burft over the heads of our workmen, to prevent them,
if poffible, from repairing at night the damage received in the day.
It did not neverthelefs obftruct the duties in the department of the
engineers; and the artillery were not hindered from further completing the expence-magazines with ammunition.   The 97th regiment was now fo far recovered, as for fome time to affift in the
fatigue and duties of the Garrifon; and this day the officers, with
a hundred

a hundred men, were added to the general roster. The town guards were also ordered to assemble in South-port ditch.

The Enemy's men of war (as we expected) repeated their attack very early on the morning of the 10th. Each ship carried a light at her mizen-peak; but they did not approach near enough to produce much effect. We received them with a well-supported fire; and the next morning observed one of them at anchor, with her bowsprit unshipped, at Algeziras. The remaining eight renewed their cannonade about nine in the forenoon, and killed two of the marine brigade, and wounded a serjeant of artillery and two others. After they had passed as before, they wore ship, apparently with an intention of continuing their visits, but suddenly put about, and anchored off the Orange-grove. We were afterwards informed, that the discovery of a red-hot shot on board one of the ships, was the immediate cause of this hasty manœuvre.

The Enemy continued their firing from the Isthmus, recommencing at morning gun-fire on the 10th from their gun-batteries. At seven o'clock, including the expenditure on the 8th, they had discharged five thousand five hundred and twenty-seven shot, and two thousand three hundred and two shells, exclusive of the number fired by the men of war and mortar-boats. The Garrison, on the contrary, took no further notice of them, than to return a few rounds from the terrace-batteries at their working-parties, who were repairing the damage done on the 8th, and completing the rest of their works. In the course of the day, the Brilliant and Porcupine frigates were scuttled by the navy in the New mole; and at night the engineers, with a working-party, cleared the lines of rubbish, and restored those traverses which had been demolished. At night, the Enemy's fire was under the same regulation as the preceding evening.

THE

THE next morning, when our guards were relieving, a signal was made at the Tower, near the quarry, under the Queen of Spain's chair; and the Enemy's cannonade became excessively brisk: fortunately few casuals occurred. Their firing, when this object ceased to amuse them, seemed to be principally directed against the obstructions at Land port, and in that part of the Garrison. Many of the palisades in the covered way were destroyed, and the *che-vaux-de-frise* considerably injured : artificers were however constantly detached to repair those breaches; so that the whole were kept in a better state than might be expected. In the afternoon, we began to conclude, that the attack with the Battering-ships was no longer to be deferred. Several detachments of soldiers embarked from the camp, and others were standing on the neighbouring eminences; which, with the appearance, in the evening, of signals like those which we observed on the night of the 7th, led us to imagine that every preparation was complete; and the wind at that time blowing gently in the Bay, from the north-west, favoured our conjecture. Land-port and Water-port guards were immediately reinforced, the furnaces and grates for heating shot were lighted, and the artillery ordered to man the batteries.

THUS prepared, we waited their appearance (for it seemed to be the general opinion, that the Battering-ships would advance, and be moored in the night, that they might be less exposed to annoyance in this duty, and open with greater effect together at day-break). Our attention was however called off from the Bay to the land-side, where the Enemy had set fire to the barriers of Bay-side and Forbes's; and the whole of those palisades, to the water's edge, were instantly involved in flames. The northern guards and picquets were immediately under arms, and a smart discharge of musquetry was directed upon several parties, which, by the light of the fire, were discovered in the meadows. The Enemy increasing their bombardment, and

nothing

nothing new happening in confequence of the conflagration, the picquets and guards were remanded under cover; but the Artillery continued upon the batteries. We had fcarcely recovered from this alarm, before the gun and mortar boats, with the bomb-ketches, began to bombard the Northern front, taking their ftations off the King's baftion, extending towards Fort St. Philip. They commenced about an hour after midnight; and their fire, added to that of the land-batteries, exceedingly annoyed Water port and its vicinity. The out-picquets were again under arms, but providentially our lofs was trifling. We returned a few rounds from the Sea-line, but ftill difregarded the batteries on the Ifthmus; excepting when their workmen appeared, or were thought to be employed. Major Lewis, Commandant of the Artillery, was unfortunately amongft the wounded. The confinement of this active officer at this critical juncture, might have been highly prejudicial to the fervice, had not his Seconds been of confirmed ability and experience: owing to their united exertions, the feveral duties in that complicated and important department were conducted with harmony and fuccefs.

WHEN the gun-boats retired, nothing new occurred till the morning of the 12th: their firing continued to be fupported at the average of four thoufand rounds in the twenty-four hours. About eight o'clock, reports were received from Europa guard, that a large fleet had appeared from the weftward. The wind was brifk, and we had fcarcely time to form any conjectures concerning them, ere they approached the Bay; and proved to be the COMBINED FLEETS of FRANCE and SPAIN, confifting of feven three-deckers, and thirty-one fhips of two decks; with three frigates and a number of xebeques, bomb-ketches, and hofpital-fhips.; the whole under the command of ten Admirals, and a broad pendant.

In

In the afternoon, they were all at anchor between the Orange-grove and Algeziras.

THIS great accumulation of force could not fail to surprise, if not alarm the Garrison. It appeared as if they meant, previous to their final efforts, to strike, if possible, a terror through their opponents, by displaying before us a more powerful armament than had probably ever been brought against any fortress. Forty-seven sail of the line, including three inferior two-deckers; ten battering-ships, deemed perfect in design, and esteemed invincible, carrying two hundred and twelve guns; innumerable frigates, xebeques, bomb-ketches, cutters, gun and mortar boats, and smaller craft for disembarking men; these were assembled in the Bay. On the land side were most stupendous and strong batteries and works, mounting two hundred pieces of heavy ordnance, and protected by an army of near forty thousand men, commanded by a victorious and active General, of the highest reputation, and animated with the immediate presence of two Princes of the Royal Blood of France, with other dignified Personages, and many of their own Nobility. Such a naval and military spectacle most certainly is not to be equalled in the annals of war. From such a combination of power, and favourable concurrent circumstances, it was natural enough that the Nation should anticipate the most glorious consequences. Indeed their confidence in the effect to be produced by the battering-ships passed all bounds; and in the enthusiasm excited by the magnitude of their preparations, it was thought highly criminal even to whisper a doubt of the success.

IN drawing these flattering conclusions, the Enemy, however, seemed entirely to have overlooked the nature of that force which was opposed to them; for, though the Garrison scarcely consisted of more than seven thousand effective men, including the Marine brigade,

O o   they

they forgot that they were now veterans in this fervice, had been a long time habituated to the effects of artillery, and were prepared by degrees for the arduous conflict that awaited them. We were, at the fame time, commanded by OFFICERS of approved courage, prudence, and ability; eminent for all the accomplifhments of their profeffion, and in whom we had unbounded confidence. Our fpirits too were not a little elevated by the fucccefs attending the recent practice of firing red-hot fhot, which in this attack, we hoped, would enable us to bring our labours to a period, and relieve us from the tedious cruelty of a vexatious blockade.

BEFORE the Garrifon had well difcovered the force of their new vifitors, an occurrence happened, which, though trifling in itfelf, I truft, I fhall be excufed for inferting. When the van of the Combined Fleet had entered the Bay, and the foldiers in *town* were attentively viewing the fhips, alledging, amongft other reafons for their arrival, that the Britifh fleet muft undoubtedly be in purfuit; on a fudden, a general huzza was given, and all, to a man, cried out, the Britifh Admiral was certainly in their rear, as a flag for a fleet was hoifted upon our fignal-houfe pole. For fome moments the flattering idea was indulged; but our hopes were foon damped by the fudden difappearance of the fignal. We were afterwards informed by the guard at that poft, that what our creative fancies had imagined to be a flag, was nothing more than an *Eagle*, which, after feveral evolutions, had perched a few minutes on the weftern-moft pole, and then flew away towards the eaft. Though lefs fuperftitious than the ancient Romans, many could not help fancying it a favourable omen to the Garrifon; and the event of the fucceeding day juftified the prognoftication.

IN the morning of the 12th, the Governor reinforced the picquets of the line; nine of which, in future, were ftationed in town,

town, and diftributed as follows ; two at Water port, two at Land
port, two in the Lines, and the remaining three in the picquet-yard,
with the field-officer of the town diftrict. The other picquet of
the line was ftationed at the fouthward. The following return
fpecifies the ftrength of the picquets at this period.

	Sub.	S.	D.	R.F.
The Artillery, and Hanoverian brigade, each corps	1	1	1	39
The 12th, 39th, 56th, and 58th regiments . .	1	1	1	54
The 72d and 73d regiments	1	1	1	76
The 97th regiment	1	1	1	56
Total four Captains { one of the Artillery } { and three of the Line }	11	11	11	580

In the evening, about dufk, a number of men were obferved
to embark from the Orange-grove, on board the battering-fhips ;
which, with the prefence of the fleet, and the wind blowing
favourably, induced us to conclude that the important attack was
not long to be deferred.

The Enemy's cannonade was continued, almoft on the fame fcale
as the preceding days, during the night of the 12th. The next
morning, we obferved the Combined Fleet had made fome new
arrangements in their pofition, or moorings, and that the remaining
two battering-fhips had joined the others at the Orange-grove,
where their WHOLE force feemed to be affembled. About a quarter
before feven o'clock, fome motions were obferved amongft their
fhipping ; and foon after, the BATTERING-SHIPS got under way,
with a gentle breeze from the north-weft, ftanding to the fouthward, to clear the men of war ; and were attended by a number of
boats. As our Navy were conftantly of opinion that the Ships
would be brought before the Garrifon in the night, few fufpected

that

that the prefent manœuvres were preparatory to their finally entering on the interefting enterprife : but obferving a crowd of fpectators
on the beach, near Point Mala, and upon the neighbouring eminences, and the fhips edging down towards the Garrifon, the
Governor thought it would be imprudent any longer to doubt it.
The Town-batteries were accordingly manned, and the grates and
furnaces for heating fhot ordered to be lighted.

Thus prepared for their reception, we had leifure to notice the
Enemy's evolutions. The ten Battering-fhips, after leaving the
men of war, *wore* to the north ; and a little paft nine o'clock,
bore down in admirable order for their feveral ftations ; the Admiral
in a two-decker, mooring about nine hundred yards off the King's
baftion ; the others fucceffively taking their places to the right and
left of the flag-fhip, in a mafterly manner ; the moft diftant being
about eleven or twelve hundred yards from the Garrifon. Our
Artillery allowed the Enemy every reafonable advantage, in permitting them, without moleftation, to choofe their diftance ; but
as foon as the firft fhip dropped her anchors, which was about
a quarter before ten o'clock, that inftant our firing commenced.
The Enemy were completely moored in little more than ten minutes.
The cannonade then became in a high degree tremendous. The
fhowers of fhot and fhells which were directed from their land-
batteries, the battering-fhips, and, on the other hand, from the
various works of the Garrifon, exhibited a fcene, of which perhaps neither the pen nor the pencil can furnifh a competent idea.
It is fufficient to fay, that FOUR HUNDRED PIECES of the heavieft
artillery were playing at the fame moment : an inftance which
has fcarcely occurred in any fiege fince the invention of thofe
wonderful engines of deftruction.

AFTER

AFTER some hours cannonade, the Battering-ships were found to be no less formidable than they had been represented. Our heaviest shells often rebounded from their tops, whilst the thirty-two-pound shot seemed incapable of making any visible impression upon their hulls. Frequently we flattered ourselves they were on fire; but no sooner did the smoke appear, than, with the most persevering intrepidity, men were observed applying water, from their engines within, to those places whence the smoke issued. These circumstances, with the prodigious cannonade which they maintained, gave us reason to imagine that the attack would not be so soon decided, as, from our recent success against their land-batteries, we had fondly expected. Even the Artillery themselves, at this period, had their doubts of the effect of the red-hot shot, which began to be used about twelve, but were not general till between one and two o'clock. The Enemy's cannon at the commencement were too much elevated; but about noon their firing was powerful, and well directed. Our casuals then became numerous; particularly on those batteries north of the King's bastion, which were warmly annoyed by the Enemy's *flanking* and *reverse* fire from the land. Though so vexatiously annoyed from the Isthmus, our Artillery totally disregarded their opponents in that quarter, directing their sole attention to the Battering-ships, the furious and spirited opposition of which served to excite our people to more animated exertions. A fire, more tremendous if possible than ever, was therefore directed from the Garrison. Incessant showers of hot balls, carcasses, and shells of every species, flew from all quarters; and as the masts of several of the ships were shot away, and the rigging of all in great confusion, our hopes of a favourable and speedy decision began to revive.

ABOUT noon, the mortar-boats and bomb-ketches attempted to second the attack from the ships; but the wind having changed to

the

1782, the 'fouth-weft, and blowing a fmart breeze, with a heavy fwell,
Sept. they were prevented taking a part in the action.   The fame reafon
alfo hindered our gun-boats from flanking the Battering-fhips from
the fouthward.*

FOR fome hours, the attack and defence were fo equally well fupported, as fcarcely to admit any appearance of fuperiority in the
cannonade on either fide.   The wonderful conftruction of the fhips
feemed to bid defiance to the powers of the heavieft ordnance.   In
the afternoon, however, the face of things began to change confiderably.   The fmoke which had been obferved to iffue from the
upper part of the flag-fhip appeared to prevail, notwithftanding the
conftant application of water; and the Admiral's Second was perceived to be in the fame condition.   Confufion was now apparent on
board feveral of the veffels ; and by the evening their cannonade was
confiderably abated.   About feven or eight it almoft totally ceafed,
excepting from one or two fhips to the northward.   rrom
their diftance, had fuffered little injury.

WHEN their firing began to flacken, various fignals were made
from the foutherniioft fhips ; and, as the evening advanced, many
rockets were thrown up, to inform their friends (as we afterwards
learned) of their extreme danger and diftrefs.   Thefe fignals were
immediately anfwered, and feveral boats were feen to row round the
difabled fhips.   Our artillery, at this period, muft have caufed
dreadful havock amongft them.   An indiftinct clamour, with
lamentable cries and groans, proceeded (during the fhort intervals of
ceffation) from all quarters ; and a little before midnight, a wreck
floated in, upon which were twelve men, who only, out of three-
                                                                    fcore

* A View of the Attack at this period is annexed.   The drawing was copied from a fketch
taken by an ingenious officer of the 12th regiment, who, being quartered at the fouthward,
had an opportunity of embracing this interefting period.

. A View of

A View of the Grand Attack upon Gibraltar September 13th 17.

score which were on board their launch, had escaped. These circumstances convinced us that we had gained an advantage over the Enemy; yet we did not conceive that the victory was so complete as the succeeding morning evinced. Our firing was therefore continued, though with less vivacity: but as the Artillery, from such a hard-fought day, exposed to the intense heat of a warm sun, in addition to the harassing duties of the preceding night, were much fatigued; and as it was impossible to foresee what new objects might demand their service the following day; the Governor, about six in the evening, when the Enemy's fire abated, permitted the majority of the officers and men to be relieved by a picquet of a hundred men from the Marine brigade, under the command of Lieut. Trentham; and officers, and non-commissioned officers of the artillery, were stationed on the different batteries, to direct the sailors in the mode of firing the hot shot.

ABOUT an hour after midnight, the Battering-ship which had suffered the greatest injury, and which had been frequently on fire the preceding day, was completely in flames; and by two o'clock, she appeared as one continued blaze from stem to stern. The ship to the southward was also on fire, but did not burn with so much rapidity. The light thrown out on all sides by the flames, enabled the artillery to point the guns with the utmost precision, whilst the Rock, and neighbouring objects, were highly illuminated; forming, with the constant flashes of our cannon, a mingled scene of sublimity and terror. Between three and four o'clock, six other of the Battering-ships indicated the efficacy of red-hot shot; and the approaching day *now* promised us one of the completest defensive victories on record.

BRIGADIER CURTIS, who was encamped with his brigade at Europa, being informed that the Enemy's ships were in flames, and
that

that the calmness of the sea would permit his gun-boats to act, marched, about three o'clock, with a detachment to the New mole; and, drawing up his boats in such manner as to flank the Battering-ships, compelled their boats to abandon them. As the day approached, and the Garrison-fire abated, the Brigadier advanced, and captured two launches. These boats attempted to escape; but a shot killing and wounding several men on board one of them, they surrendered, and were conducted to Ragged-staff. The Brigadier being informed by the prisoners, that many men were through necessity left by their friends on board the ships, he generously determined to rescue them from the inevitable death which seemed to impend. Some of these infatuated wretches nevertheless (it is said) refused at first the deliverance which was tendered to them, preferring the chance of that death which appeared inevitable, to being put to the sword; which they had been persuaded would be the consequence, if they submitted to the Garrison. Being left however some moments to the horrors of their fate, they beckoned the boats to return, and resigned themselves to the clemency of their Conquerors.

Whilst the Navy were thus humanely relieving their distressed Enemy, the flames reached the magazine of one of the Battering-ships to the northward, which blew up, about five o'clock, with a dreadful explosion. In a quarter of an hour following, another, in the centre of the line, met with a similar fate. The wreck from the latter spread to a vast extent, and involved our gun-boats in the most imminent danger. One was sunk, but the crew were saved. A hole was forced through the bottom of the Brigadier's boat, his coxswain killed, and the strokesman wounded; and for some time they were obscured in the cloud of smoke. After this very fortunate escape, it was deemed prudent to withdraw towards the Garrison, to avoid the peril arising from the blowing-up of the remaining ships. The Brigadier however visited two other ships in his return, and

landed

landed nine officers, two priefts, and three hundred and thirty-
four private foldiers and feamen, all Spaniards; which, with one
officer and eleven Frenchmen, who had floated in the preceding
evening, made the total number faved amount to three hundred and
fifty-feven. Many of the prifoners were feverely, and fome of them
dreadfully wounded. They were inftantly, on being brought on
fhore, conveyed to our Hofpital, and every remedy adminiftered
neceffary for their different cafes.

During the time that the Marine Brigade were encountering every
danger in their endeavours to fave an Enemy from perifhing, the
batteries on the Ifthmus (which ceafed the preceding evening, moft
likely for want of ammunition, and which had opened again upon
the Garrifon on the morning of the 14th) maintained a warm fire
upon the town, which killed and wounded feveral men; and
three or four fhells burft in the air, over the place where their countrymen were landed. This ungenerous proceeding could not efcape
the obfervation of the fpectators in their camp; and orders probably
were fent to the lines for the batteries to ceafe, as they were filent
about ten o'clock.

Notwithstanding the efforts of the Marine Brigade in
relieving the terrified victims from the burning fhips, feveral unfortunate men could not be removed. The fcene at this time exhibited
was as affecting, as that which had been prefented in the act of hofti-
lity, had been terrible and tremendous. Men crying from amidft
the flames for pity and affiftance; others, on board thofe fhips where
the fire had made little progrefs, imploring relief with the moft
expreffive geftures and figns of defpair; whilft feveral, equally expofed
to the dangers of the oppofite element, trufted themfelves, on
various parts of the wreck, to the chance of paddling to the fhore.
A felucca belonging to the Enemy approached from the Orange-

P p   grove,

1782, Sept.

grove, probably with the intention of relieving thefe unfortunate perfons; but, jealous of her motives, the Garrifon fufpected that fhe came to fet fire to one of the battering-fhips which appeared little injured, and obliged her to retire. Of the fix fhips which were ftill in flames, three blew up before eleven o'clock; the other three burnt to the water's edge, the magazines being wetted by the Enemy before the principal officers quitted the fhips. The Admiral's flag was on board one of the latter, and was confumed with the veffel. The remaining two Battering-fhips, we flattered ourfelves, might be faved as glorious trophies of our fuccefs; but one of them unexpectedly burft out in flames, and in a fhort time blew up, with a terrible report; and Capt. Gibfon reprefenting it as impracticable to preferve the other, it was burnt in the afternoon, under his directions. Thus the Navy put a finifhing hand to this fignal defenfive victory.

DURING the hotteft period of the Enemy's cannonade, the Governor was prefent on the King's baftion, whilft Lieut. General Boyd* took his ftation upon the South baftion, animating the Garrifon by their prefence, and encouraging them to emulation. The exertions and activity of the brave ARTILLERY, in this well-fought conteft, deferve the higheft commendations. To their fkill, perfeverance, and courage, with the zealous affiftance of the Line, (particularly

---

* It will not be improper in this place to repeat, that General Boyd was the founder of the King's baftion, as it will be an apology for introducing a remarkable fpeech of the General on that occafion. In 1773, General Boyd, attended by Colonel Green, the Chief Engineer, and many Field-Officers of the Garrifon, laid the foundation-ftone of that work, with the ceremony ufual on fuch occafions. Upon placing the ftone, " This," faid the General, " is " the firft ftone of a work which I name the KING's BASTION: may it be as gallantly " defended, as I know it will be ably executed; and may I live to fee it refift THE UNITED " EFFORTS OF FRANCE AND SPAIN!"

cularly the corps in town, the 39th and 72d regiments), was Gibraltar
indebted for its safety againſt the Combined Powers, by ſea and land, of France and Spain; and the Marine Brigade, though they had not ſo conſiderable a ſhare in the duties of the batteries, yet merit the warmeſt praiſes for their generous intrepidity in reſcuing their devoted enemies from amidſt the flames.

WHILST the Enemy were cool, and their ſhips had received little damage, their principal objects were the KING's baſtion, and LINE-WALL, north of Orange's baſtion. Their largeſt ſhips (which were about fourteen hundred tons burthen) were ſtationed off the former, in order to ſilence that important battery, whilſt a breach was attempted by the reſt, in the curtain extending from the latter to Montague's baſtion. If a breach had been effected, the priſoners informed us, that " their grenadiers were to have ſtormed the " Garriſon under cover of the Combined Fleets." The private men complained bitterly of their officers for deſcribing the Batter-ing-ſhips to be invulnerable, and for promiſing that they were to be ſeconded by ten ſail of the line, and all the gun and mortar boats. They further told us, that " they had been taught to " believe the Garriſon would not be able to diſcharge many rounds " of hot balls: their aſtoniſhment, therefore, was inconceivable, " when they diſcovered that we fired them with the ſame preciſion " and vivacity as cold ſhot." " Admiral Moreno," they ſaid, " quitted the Paſtora, which was the flag-ſhip, a little before " midnight; but other officers retired much earlier." The loſs ſuſtained by the Enemy could never be aſcertained; but from the information of the priſoners, and the numbers ſeen dead on board the ſhips, we eſtimated it could not be leſs than two thouſand men, including the priſoners. The caſuals of the Garriſon, on the con-trary, were ſo trifling, that it will appear almoſt incredible, that ſuch a quantity of fire, in almoſt all its deſtructive modes of action,

ſhould

fhould not have produced more effect, with refpect to the lofs of men. The return ftands thus:

SEPTEMBER 13th, 1782.

REGIMENTS.	Killed.				Wounded.			
	O.	S.	D.	R.&F.	O.	S.	D.	R.&F.
Royal Artillery	1	.	.	5	3	.	.	21
12th Regiment	.	.	.		.	.	.	2
39th ditto	.	2	.	2	.	.	.	5
56th ditto	.	.	.	2	.	.	.	2
58th ditto	.	.	.	1	1	.	.	4
72d ditto	.	.	.	2	.	.	.	12
73d ditto	.	.	.	.	1	.	.	8
97th ditto	.	.	.	.	.	.	.	2
Hardenberg's	.	.	.	.	.	.	.	1
Reden's	.	.	.	.	.	.	.	.
De la Motte's	.	.	.	.	.	.	.	1
Engineers, with the Artificer Company	.	.	.	.	.	.	.	.
Marine Brigade	.	.	.	1	.	.	.	5
Total	1	2	0	13	5	0	0	63

Officers killed and wounded
{
Artillery. Captain Reeves killed; Captains Groves and Siward, with Lieut. Godfrey, wounded.
58th regiment. Lieut. Wetham, (who had permiffion to act as an Artillery officer) wounded.
73d regiment. Captain M'Kenzie wounded.
}

THE diftance of the Battering-fhips from the Garrifon was exactly fuch as our Artillery could have wifhed. It required fo fmall an elevation, that almoft every fhot took effect; and the cannon thus elevated did not require the fhot to be wadded :—a circum-ftance not unimportant; as the time, which at point-blank would have been expended in doubly wadding, was employed in keeping up the cannonade with greater brifknefs. The damage done to our works held no proportion with the violence of the attack, and the exceffive cannonade which they had fuftained. The merlons of the different batteries were difordered, and the flank of Orange's baftion was a little injured; but the latter was chiefly done by the land-fire,

and

and was not of such consequence as to afford any room for apprehension. The ordnance and carriages were also damaged; but by the activity of the Artillery, the whole sea-line, before night, was in serviceable order.

THE Enemy, in this action, had more than three hundred pieces of heavy ordnance in play; whilst the Garrison had only eighty cannon, seven mortars, and nine howitzers in opposition. Upwards of eight thousand three hundred rounds, (more than half of which were *hot shot*) and SEVEN HUNDRED AND SIXTEEN barrels of powder, were expended by our Artillery. What quantity of ammunition was used by the Enemy, could never be ascertained. The following was handed about as an authentic list of the Battering-ships; and the Reader is referred to the annexed Plan, for a further explanation of this memorable attack. In a compartment of the plan, he will also observe a representation of a two-decked Battering-ship. A section, to show the interior construction of these extraordinary vessels, was intended to have been added; but no opportunity occurred of making further observations than what were cursory and superficial.

Names of the Battering-ships	Guns in use	Guns in reserve	Men	Commanders
Paftora	21	10	760	Rear Admiral Buenaventura Moreno
Talla Piedra . .	21	10	760	Prince of Naffau
Paula Prima . .	21	10	760	Don Cayetan Langara
El Rofario . . .	19	10	700	Don Francifco Xafier Munos
St. Chriftoval . .	18	10	650	Don Frederico Gravino
Principe Carlos .	11	4	400	Don Antonio Bafurta
San Juan . . .	9	4	340	Don Jofeph Angeler
Paula Secunda . .	9	4	340	Don Pablo de Cofa
Santa Anna . . .	7	4	300	Don Jofeph Goicochea
Los Dolores . .	6	4	250	Don Pedro Sanchez
	142	70	5260	

N. B. About thirty-six men to each gun in use, besides sailors, &c. to work the ships.

REFERENCE

REFERENCE to the Plan of the GRAND ATTACK.

The ENEMY'S WORKS.	WORKS in the GARRISON.
No.	21 The Extremity of the Prince's lines
1 The Black battery	22 The Communication from the King's to the
2 The Infanta's battery	Queen's lines
3 The Prince's, or Well battery	23 Crouchet's and other batteries at the en-
4 The Princess's, or Eastern Fourteen-gun	trance of the lines
battery	24 The Land-port Flêche
5 Mortar-batteries in their lines	25 The North bastion and Cavalier
6 The Old Approach made by General Don	26 The Grand magazine, (Moorish castle)
Alvarez	27 The Queen's battery, (Willis's)
7 The St. Martin's battery	28 The Tower battery
8 The St. Paschal's battery	29 The Princess Anne's battery
9 The St. Carlos's battery, with another	30 The Magazine which blew up
Mortar-battery on its Western flank	31 The Princess Amelia's battery
10 A battery of four Howitzers	32 The Princess Caroline's battery
11 Magazines along the parallel	33 The Catalan batteries
12 Places d'armes for Musquetry	34 Farringdon's battery
13 A Fascine-ditch in front of the works	35 The entrance to the new gallery leading to
14 The ruins of the Mahon redoubt, with a	St. George's Hall
two-gun battery; both destroyed on the	36 Green's-Lodge battery
8th of September	37 The Corsican post
15 Mortar-batteries along the parallel	38 The Royal battery and Rock-gun
16 The New Approach and communications	39 The Rock-mortar and Levant Royal
made by the Duke de Crillon	40 The Esplanade and Galley-house
17 The Sixty-four-gun battery	41 The White Convent
18 Wells for watering the gardens	42 The Fountain
19 The New Boyau, erected after the defeat	43 The 39th regiment encamped in South-
on the 13th of September	port ditch
20 The cave under the rock near the Devil's	44 Anchors sunk in shallow water, with sloping
tower, where the Enemy formed the	palisades placed upon the beach to ob-
chimerical idea of making a mine	struct a landing.

THE

REFERENCE to the Plan of the GRAND ATTACK.

The ENEMY's WORKS.	WORKS in the GARRISON.

No.

1 The Black battery

2 The Infanta's battery

3 The Prince's, or Well battery

4 The Princess's, or Eastern Fourteen-gun battery

5 Mortar-batteries in their lines

6 The Old Approach made by General Don Alvarez

7 The St. Martin's battery

8 The St. Paschal's battery

9 The St. Carlos's battery, with another Mortar-battery on its Western flank

10 A battery of four Howitzers

11 Magazines along the parallel

12 Places d'armes for Musquetry

13 A Fascine-ditch in front of the works

14 The ruins of the Mahon redoubt, with a two-gun battery; both destroyed on the 8th of September

15 Mortar-batteries along the parallel

16 The New Approach and communications made by the Duke de Crillon

17 The Sixty-four-gun battery

18 Wells for watering the gardens

19 The New Boyau, erected after the defeat on the 13th of September

20 The cave under the rock near the Devil's tower, where the Enemy formed the chimerical idea of making a mine

21 The Extremity of the Prince's lines

22 The Communication from the King's to the Queen's lines

23 Crouchet's and other batteries at the entrance of the lines

24 The Land-port Flêche

25 The North bastion and Cavalier

26 The Grand magazine, (Moorish castle)

27 The Queen's battery, (Willis's)

28 The Tower battery

29 The Princess Anne's battery

30 The Magazine which blew up

31 The Princess Amelia's battery

32 The Princess Caroline's battery

33 The Catalan batteries

34 Farringdon's battery

35 The entrance to the new gallery leading to St. George's Hall

36 Green's-Lodge battery

37 The Corsican post

38 The Royal battery and Rock-gun

39 The Rock-mortar and Levant Royal

40 The Esplanade and Galley-house

41 The White Convent

42 The Fountain

43 The 39th regiment encamped in South-port ditch

44 Anchors sunk in shallow water, with sloping palisades placed upon the beach to obstruct a landing.

THE

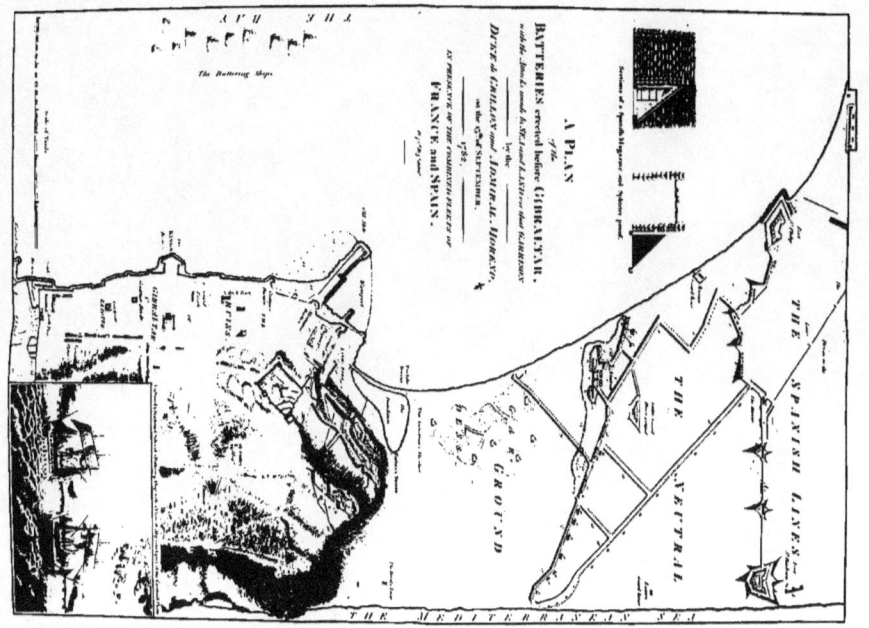

A PLAN
of the
BATTERIES erected before GIBRALTAR,
with the Attack made by the Combined FLEETS on that Fortress,
by the
DUKE de CRILLON and Admiral MORENO,
on the 13ᵗʰ of SEPTEMBER,
1782,
IN PRESENCE OF THE COMBINED FLEETS OF
FRANCE and SPAIN.

THE BAY

The Battering Ships

THE SPANISH LINES

THE NEUTRAL
GROUND

THE MEDITERRANEAN SEA

THE afternoon of the 14th, feveral thoufand men marched with
colours from the Enemy's camp to their lines ; and many fhips in
the Combined Fleet loofed their top-fails.   Thefe motions, and the
circumftance of many of their boats being manned, caufed various
fpeculations in the Garrifon.   Whatever their future operations
might be, it was prudent to be on our guard : the Artillery were
ordered therefore to remain upon the batteries, and the furnaces
for heating fhot to be continued lighted, left the Enemy fhould
be prompted to put all to the ftake, and attempt the Garrifon by a
general attack.   It was indeed afterwards rumoured, that fuch a
defign had been in contemplation, but was over-ruled by the Duke,
who was of opinion, it would be expofing the fleet and army to
immediate deftruction.

1782,
Sept.

NOTWITHSTANDING this recent defeat, the Enemy re-commenced their cannonade from the Ifthmus ; expending, during the
remainder of the month, from one to two thoufand rounds in the
twenty-four hours ; diminifhing gradually, and confining their
fhells to the night.   Their operations on the land fide were ftill
carried on ; and if we were able to form any conjectures at this period,
from their motions to the northward, their late misfortune did not
feem at all to damp their hopes of fucceeding againft the Garrifon.
A flag of truce went on the 15th with letters from our prifoners to
the camp ; and about two o'clock in the afternoon, the Combined
Fleet handed in their top-fails.   Some hours afterwards, they manned
their yards, and fired a grand falute.   We were at a lofs to account
for thefe *fingular* rejoicings.   Lieut. M'Namara, of the 72d regiment,
was wounded the fame day at Willis's, where our working-parties
were employed clearing away the rubbifh from the batteries.

THE Garrifon having experienced the powerful efficacy of
red-hot fhot, and the Governor thinking it expedient to have a
                                                        continual

continual supply of them, the Engineers erected kilns (similar to those used in burning lime, but smaller) in various parts of the Garrison. They were large enough to heat upwards of one hundred in an hour and a quarter; and by this invention hot shot were, if thought necessary, kept continually ready for use. Our former method of heating the shot, was either in the grates and furnaces made for that purpose, or by piling them in a corner of some old house adjoining the batteries, (as was principally the practice on the 13th) and surrounding them with faggots, pieces of timber, and small-coal. By those means, the artificers were enabled to supply the Artillery with a constant succession for the ordnance. Answers were received, in the afternoon of the 16th, to the prisoners letters. At night, a great number of signals were made by the Combined Fleet. Shot were therefore again ordered to be heated, and the Artillery cautioned to be ready to man the batteries. The 39th and 72d regiments also lay fully accoutred. The same night, the sailors recovered the gun-boat which had been sunk on the morning of the 14th. As the prisoners informed us, that intelligence had been received, previous to the attack of the Battering-ships, that Lord Howe, with the British fleet, was preparing to sail for the relief of Gibraltar, the Navy began to prepare to raise the Brilliant and Porcupine frigates, which had been scuttled in the New mole; but their efforts, for some time, were not attended with success.

The Spanish officers, prisoners, with the Frenchmen who were taken up from the wreck upon the night of the 13th, were sent to the camp on the evening of the 17th. The remaining Spanish privates were encamped upon Windmill-hill, and given in charge to the Corsicans. Of the number who had been saved from the Battering-ships, were an officer, a Captain of Marines, and twenty-nine privates, who were wounded. Most of these recovered in our
Hospital;

Hofpital ; but the officer, notwithftanding every affiftance and attention, died on the 17th. He was buried, the fucceeding day, with all military honours, attended by the grenadiers of the 39th regiment.

WHEN we reflected of what vaft importance this grand enterprife was efteemed, and what immenfe fums had been expended in the ingenious and formidable preparations, it was obferved, with no fmall furprife, by many who were prefent when the prifoners were landed, that the majority of them feemed to be paft that age when the vital powers are fuppofed to be in their greateft vigour. In an expedition where youth and ftrength beft promifed a favourable iffue, this impolitic arrangement certainly could not pervade the whole! The Spaniards, from their dark complexion and fcanty diet, have naturally, even when young, an aged look : and yet our obfervations feemed confirmed by other indubitable facts. Several bodies were thrown afhore, all of which feemed advanced in years ; and one in particular appeared, from his grey beard and lean vifage, paft fixty. This corpfe was horribly mutilated, and, with the miferable objects then under the care of our furgeons, convinced us, by ocular proof, of the dreadful havock which our Artillery muft have made in the latter part of the day.

THE wefterly wind, which had caft up thefe unfortunate men, threw alfo on fhore many trifling curiofities, and fome things of value, which had floated on the furface of the Bay, after the Battering-fhips had blown up. Large wax candles, fuch as are ufually burnt by the Romifh priefts before their altars ; falt provifions ; and a great number of ammunition-boxes, containing ten rounds of powder in linen cartridges, were collected by the Garrifon the morning fucceeding the defeat. Confiderable pieces of mahogany, and fome cedar, were faved from the wrecks of thofe fhips

Q q   whofe

whofe magazines did not blow up, which were afterwards converted into various ufeful articles, ferving as memorials of our
victory.   The Governor had a handfome fet of tables made for the
Convent, (the holes in the cedar, where the fire had penetrated,
being filled up with found wood, cut in various figures, forming a
beautiful contraft with the burnt part) which will ferve as a
ftanding monument, to the guefts, of the tranfactions of that
glorious day.

THE Enemy's fire on the 19th was warmer than the few preceding days; and what was rather extraordinary, it was continued
whilft a flag of truce went from the Governor, and another returned
in anfwer.   The officer who brought the Duke de Crillon's anfwer
was one of his Aide-de-camps, the Count de Rufigniac, Colonel
of the French Regiment de Chartres.   He preffed much to deliver
his packet *perfonally* to the Governor, and offered to fubmit to be
blind-folded, provided he could be admitted into the Garrifon.   He
was even fo urgent as to put his foot on board our boat, but was
informed by the Aide-de-camp that his requeft could not be com-
plied with.   Not content with this anfwer, our flag was obliged to
return, to acquaint the Governor with this extraordinary circumftance, who politely excufed himfelf the honour which the Count
intended him, as the ftate of affairs would not then permit it.   We
fhall have occafion again to mention the Count before the clofe
of this work.   The wind changed to the eaft in the night of the
19th; but the Combined Fleet ftill remained at anchor in the Bay.
The 20th, the mortar-boats, which had remained inactive for fome
time, bombarded the Garrifon.   They feemed to be attended by
only four or five gun-boats, and were extremely cautious in directing their fire.   Three fhells fell in South-port ditch, amongft the
39th regiment.

SOME changes took place in the Governor's fuite on the 21ft: Town-major Capt. Foulis was appointed Aide-de-camp to the Commander in Chief, and Capt. Delhofte, of the 72d regiment, Town-major. A flag of truce, the fame day, brought over a letter from the Duke, in anfwer to one from the Governor, of the preceding day. Their boat alfo brought clothing for the Walon prifoners. In the evening, about eight o'clock, reports were received from the Northern guards, that the Enemy were in motion in their camp, and that troops were marching down to the lines. About the fame time, fome extraordinary fignals were made by the Spanifh Admiral. The three picquets remaining with the Field-officer in town were immediately detached to reinforce the Captain of Land port, the Lines, and Water port, who, befides their ufual guards, had each two picquets with them before. The 39th and 72d regiments were again ordered to lie accoutred, and the Artillery cautioned to be alert. By this difpofition it was evident, the Governor ftill expected a further attack upon the Garrifon; and that evening it was moft to be apprehended, as it was poffible that the Duke by that day might receive an anfwer from Madrid, indicating his future operations. Upwards of twelve hundred men being thus diftributed in the vicinity of the Grand battery, with two regiments at hand to act as corps de referve, we waited the further movements of the Enemy. A little before midnight, a foldier of the 73d regiment, removing rubbifh from the Prince's lines, fell from the extremity, and was killed. An officer with a fmall detachment was immediately ordered from Land port, to bring in the body. This was difcovered by the Enemy's advanced parties, who oppofed it by a brifk difcharge of mufquetry in regular platoons. Queen's-lines guard protected our party, who returned with the body without any cafualties. The fteady and animated fire fupported by the Enemy, convinced us of the ftrength of their advanced pofts.

Nothing.

Nothing extraordinary, however, happened during the night after this occurrence.

THE Governor ſtill continued the party at Lower Forbes's under the Lines. On the night of the 23d, they diſcovered two men near the ſtone ſentry-box, within the ruins of the old barrier. The Serjeant's orders (the Reader may remember) were, not to fire but in his own defence, or in caſe of an alarm; but, obſerving them meaſuring, with a chain, the diſtance between the foot of the Rock and the Inundation, and thinking they might be perſons of ſome conſequence, and probably poſſeſſed of memorandums which might diſcover the motives of their manœuvres, he determined in this caſe to fire: they, in return, alarmed at his preparations, ſuddenly appeared on the defenſive; but the Serjeant was ſo lucky as to kill the principal perſon, and the other ran off. The body was inſtantly brought in, but no papers of conſequence were found about him. He was thought to have been a volunteer. The Serjeant, who was a *Cadet* in General Reden's regiment, was ſoon afterwards promoted to a commiſſion; but whether for this ſervice, or in his *tour*, I cannot inform my Reader.

THE Enemy's firing ſeemed now to be directed under the follow- ing regulations. About five or ſix in the morning, when the night- picquets were retiring from their poſts, the cannonade commenced, and continued pretty briſk till noon. From twelve to two o'clock there was the uſual intermiſſion; for, as I have remarked before, they would not be deprived of their cuſtomary nap, or *ſieſta*. In the decline of the day, they diſcharged more or leſs, as their caprice dictated. About ſeven in the evening, their cannon ceaſed, and their mortars took up the fire, continuing it till day-break of the ſucceeding day. The ammunition now expended was generally from four to five, and ſometimes ſix hundred ſhells in

the

the twenty-four hours, with from fix hundred to a thoufand fhot.
The profufion of the former had greatly diminifhed the immenfe
piles in their artillery-park, and their howitzers were not fo lavifh
of their troublefome fhells as they had been.

THE 24th, the Brilliant frigate was raifed after much trouble.
The fame day about noon, upwards of fifty boats, which had
been affembled for the attack, returned to the weftward, and the
mantlet boats retired up the river Palmones. The departure of
the former, with others which had left the Bay the two preceding
days, reduced their fmall craft to a very trifling number.

CHAPTER

CHAPTER   VIII.

The Combined Fleets remain in Gibraltar Bay, being determined to oppose the relief of the Garrison.—Captain Curtis visits the Enemy's Camp to establish a cartel.—Enemy raise additional works.—The Combined Fleets greatly distressed by a hurricane.—A Spanish line-of-battle ship is driven under the walls of Gibraltar, and submits to the Garrison.—At this juncture the British Fleet appear in the Straits, but the convoy unfortunately pass the Rock to the eastward.— Letters received from the British Ministry by the Governor.—The Combined Fleets, after making repairs, follow the British Fleet, but avoid an action.—Lord Howe conducts the convoy safe into the Bay, sails to the westward, and is followed by the Combined Fleets.—Enemy's cannonade diminishes, and the fire from the Garrison increases.— Enemy establish a post under the rock near the Devil's tower.—Repeat their attacks from the gun-boats.—The Duke de Crillon acquaints General Eliott that the preliminaries of a GENERAL PEACE had been signed.—Hostilities in consequence cease.—The Emperor of Morocco sends a present of cattle with a letter to General Eliott, who soon afterwards receives from England official accounts of the peace.— Interview between the Duke de Crillon and the Governor.—The Governor views the Spanish batteries, and dines at San Roque.—The Duke returns the visit, in the Garrison.—Ceremony of investing the Governor with the Order of the Bath.—Sir George Augustus Eliott's speech to the Garrison, upon communicating to them the THANKS of the King and Parliament for their DEFENCE of GIBRALTAR.

1782,
Sept.

Notwithstanding we might naturally infer from the dispersion of their small craft, that the Enemy had at length relinquished the hope of taking Gibraltar by force of arms; yet the continuance of their cannonade, and the presence of the Combined Fleets,
(though

(though frequent opportunities had offered for their return to the westward) rendered their conduct so ambiguous, that we could form no idea what line they purposed to pursue in their future operations. We knew a relief was intended by the British Fleet; but we could never imagine, if there was any thing of an equality, that the Enemy would venture an opposition, even though a victory might make them masters of Gibraltar.   We waited therefore a few days to observe the movements of our adversaries, and by their actions expected to solve the difficulty.

THE evening of the 26th of September, the whole of the Combined Army were under arms, formed in one line (which extended about four miles and a half) from the river Guadaranque to very near Fort Tonara.   Some persons of high rank, attended by a numerous suite of cavalry, passed along the front; and they were not dismissed till after sun-set.   In the evening, Major Horsfall, of the 72d regiment, was wounded by a splinter of a shell.   At night, another of our workmen in the Prince's lines fell from the extremity, and was killed.   A party was detached from Land port to bring in the body, and the Queen's-lines and other guards ordered to protect them : the Enemy however remained quiet.   The 27th, their parties began to collect brush-wood for fascines.   This circumstance served the more to increase our doubts relative to their future conduct.   The same day, our Navy got up the Porcupine frigate; the Engineers also finished the Royal and Green's-lodge batteries.   The former is thirteen hundred, and the latter nine hundred feet above the level of the Isthmus; yet, notwithstanding this elevation, the Enemy's fire, during Don Alvarez's bombardment, was found to be so galling, that the Engineers were under the necessity of covering them with caissoned merlons.   Several launches full of troops were observed, on the 29th, going on board the Combined Fleet.   They were supposed to be Marines who had been landed from the men of war

previous

previous to the Grand Attack. A flag of truce, the fame day, brought clothes for the prifoners. Early on the morning of the 30th, a foldier of the 72d regiment deferted from the ferjeant's party at Lower Forbes's. His own brother was one of the guard. The fame day, the Combined Fleets were joined by a line-of-battle fhip. The Enemy's cannonade ftill continued to be about a thoufand, or eleven hundred rounds of fhot and fhells in the twenty-four hours. Willis's batteries, and the extremity of the Prince's and Queen's lines, were much damaged from the fixty-four-gun battery. A flag of truce went from the Garrifon with a letter, and two parcels, which had been fent on the 29th, directed for perfons who could not be found amongft the prifoners. In the evening of the 30th, the mortar-boats bombarded our camp. At firft we imagined they were alone, but the gun-boats foon afterwards fired upon the town from the northward. Two fhells fell in the Hofpital, and wounded feveral of the fick. Other cafualties alfo happened in the Garrifon. The prifoners upon Windmill-hill were alarmed on two or three fhells falling near their camp; and it was not without fome feverity, that their guards could keep themfelves within the boundaries.

Oct.　　EARLY on the firft of October, a boat came into Little Bay, with a Corfican on board, who had efcaped from Algeziras. He had been mate of a neutral veffel; but hearing that fome of his relations were in the Corfican corps, he was determined to join his countrymen. The intelligence which he brought was, that Lord Howe only waited fome reinforcements to fail for the relief of Gibraltar, and that the Combined Fleet were refolved to oppofe him. Thus confoled with the hope of preventing the intended fuccours, the Enemy ftill flattered themfelves that Gibraltar muft of neceffity fubmit, through the mere failure of provifions. In the courfe of the day, the corpfe of a Spanifh Officer was wafhed afhore under our walls: a purfe of piftoles, and a gold watch, were found in his
pockets.

pockets. He was buried with respect, two Navy Officers attending the funeral; and the following day, a flag of truce delivered the watch and money, to be returned to his friends. The 2d, several men were wounded by the Enemy's shot, in the gallery above Farringdon's, which continued to be prosecuted with diligence; and Serjeant Harrop, of the 72d regiment, (a man universally admired for his gallantry and conduct in the works) was killed at Willis's. We observed, the same day, several boats, which formerly had mantlets in the bow, returning from the river Palmones; having, as we imagined, undergone some alterations, to enable them to act as gun-boats. In case of a visit from the latter, signals were now determined upon, to intimate when the Artillery were to man the batteries. Two guns quick, and a red flag hoisted upon a flag-staff erected on the South bastion, was to be the day-signal; two guns quick, and a light, the signal for the night. In the evening, we had an opportunity of practising our new signals, by the approach of the mortar-boats, which bombarded the Garrison for about two hours. The gun-boats, though perhaps attending them, did not fire. Previous to their visit, some musquets were discharged, and some signals made amongst the Fleet; but we could not observe any particular movements.

In the forenoon of the 3d, a Spanish frigate, with a flag of truce at her fore-top-gallant mast-head, anchored within gun-shot of the Old-mole head, and immediately Capt. Curtis went on board her. In the forenoon Capt. Curtis returned, and the frigate sailed back to the fleet. The wind at the time was so strong, that she was obliged to leave her anchor behind; which being mentioned to the Governor, orders were sent, not to fire upon the boats when they returned to fish it up. The following day, Capt. Curtis, accompanied by the Governor's secretary and a Naval officer, went in his barge to the Orange-grove; where a carriage waited, and conducted

R r   them

them to Buena-Vista, the Duke's quarters. The intention of this visit, we afterwards understood, was to establish a cartel with the Spaniards for the exchange of prisoners. Capt. Curtis was introduced, by the Duke de Crillon, to His Royal Highness the Count d'Artois, who thanked him, in very handsome terms, for his humanity and gallantry in relieving the unfortunate prisoners from the burning Battering-ships; requesting Capt. Curtis at the same time to inform the Governor, that he entertained the highest esteem and respect for him, for his benevolence and liberality to the prisoners upon the same occasion. Before Capt. Curtis returned, which was in the evening, the kilns for heating shot were lighted, and other preparations made, as if some attack was expected. During this correspondence, the Enemy's batteries observed a proper silence, in respect to the flag. Capt. Curtis informed us, that Lord Howe, with the British fleet, was on his passage to the Mediterranean. The Garrison did not however feel that indescribable satisfaction and pleasure on this intelligence, which we had experienced when Admirals Rodney and Darby were announced in 1780 and 1781. A French Rear-Admiral, in a three-decker, with a frigate, and several smaller armed vessels, joined the Combined Fleet on the 3d. The man of war had many signals flying when she entered the Bay, which were answered by the Spanish Admiral.

The Enemy's cannonade was still continued, with such variation as their caprice dictated. The number of rounds of shot and shells usually exceeded eight hundred in the twenty-four hours, and sometimes amounted to eleven or twelve hundred. We amused them with a trifling return, directed chiefly to their parties, who, to our astonishment, were still forming considerable dépôts of fascines and materials in the lines. Lieut. Kenneth M'Kenzie, of the 73d, was wounded on the 4th, in the communication from the King's to the Queen's lines. Two days afterwards, agreeably to a flag of truce of

the

the preceding day, the Spanish prisoners (excepting ten sick in the Hospital, and fifty-nine Walons and foreigners who requested to stay behind) were sent to the Combined camp. The Walons who preferred staying in the Garrison were embodied into those corps which chose to receive them. The 39th and 58th regiments entertained ten each; and the remainder were incorporated with the Corsican company.

Two of the Enemy's engineers had been observed, on the 4th, picketing out a work, extending from the ruins of the Mahon battery to the western beach, crossing the north-west angle of the fartheft gardens. We were at a loss what to conclude from this appearance of a determination still to prosecute the siege. They did not however let us remain long in suspense; for, on the morning of the 6th, we discovered that they had erected a strong boyau of approach, extending, in the line before mentioned, about four hundred and thirty yards—near a quarter of a mile. It was raised with sand-bags; and from its resemblance to the original epaulement of the SIXTY-FOUR-gun battery, some imagined it was intended for the same purpose; though the Engineers were of opinion, it was only a communication to some additional works in embryo. Although the Enemy, by throwing up this extensive work, gained by stealth a second advantage upon the Garrison, yet the Governor was determined, if possible, to prevent them completing it. The Old-mole head howitzers, with a warm fire from the heights, were opened at night upon this new object; and, as the former almost entirely enfiladed it, the Enemy were so much annoyed, that it was never finished. The night of the 6th, they made good the communication to the parallel, from the extremity of the boyau, near the ruins of the Mahon battery, which was left imperfect the preceding night.

THE

THE following day, the St. Martin's battery took fire from the wadding or difcharge of their own cannon. One merlon was deftroyed, and another confiderably damaged before the flames were extinguifhed. We threw a few fhells from below to difturb them in this duty; but otherwife no particular notice was taken of the accident. The Enemy found their fituation fo extremely warm in their new boyau, that on the night of the 7th they threw up a ftrong fhoulder at the extremity near the beach, to protect them againft the howitzers of the Old-mole head. The fhells were neverthelefs fired with fuch judgement and dexterity, as juft to clear the traverfe, and feemed to do as much execution in the interior part as before. Great quantities of fafcines, &c. were fcattered in the rear; whence we concluded they purpofed working in the night, but had been prevented by the vivacity of our fire. They alfo repaired the St. Martin's battery. A flag of truce brought over letters for the Governor and Capt. Curtis on the 8th; and at night, a boat failed for Leghorn with a midfhipman and fix failors, bearing home difpatches from the Governor. This was the firft boat or veffel which left the Garrifon after the victory of the preceding month.

THE Enemy, about the 8th or 9th, adopted a new plan for the regulation of their bombardment during the night: every ten or fifteen minutes they difcharged five, feven, and fometimes ten mortars at the fame time, directing the fhells principally to the fame object. After a filence of the above period, they faluted us with a fecond volley, and fo on till morning gun-fire. The number of rounds continued variable, from four to fix hundred fhots, with almoft the fame proportion of fhells, in the twenty-four hours. They were enabled to expend thefe immenfe quantities of ammunition by receiving conftant fupplies. The parties in the fafcine-park appeared now to be confiderably increafed, and an univerfal

activity

activity feemed ftill to prevail through. the different departments. 1782, Oct.
A perfon ignorant of what had paffed, and fuddenly brought to view
their proceedings, might therefore naturally conclude from their
operations, that they were elated with. fome fuccefs, rather than
depreffed by a defeat. On the night of the 9th, fome fignals were
made at Cabrita point, which were anfwered by the Combined
Fleets, each fhip fhowing a light.

The wind blew frefh wefterly on the 10th; and two frigates and
a cutter joined the Combined Fleets from that quarter. In the
evening, a number of fignals were made by the Spanifh Admiral,
which were anfwered by various fhips in the fleet. After fun-fet, the
gale increafed, and at midnight it blew a hurricáne, with fmart
fhowers of rain. Signal-guns were repeatedly fired by the Combined Fleets; and from their continuance, and the violence of the
wind, we concluded fome of them were in diftrefs. At day-break,
a Spanifh two-decker was difcovered in a crippled ftate, clofe in
fhore off Orange's baftion : fhe was under clofe-reefed courfes, and
had loft her mizen-top-maft. Obferving her danger upon an
Enemy's lee fhore, fhe fuddenly luffed up, and endeavoured to
weather the Garrifon : as fhe paffed, feveral fhot were fired through
her from the King's baftion, which killed two, and wounded
two others ; and foon afterwards fhe grounded near Ragged-ftaff,
and ftruck to the Garrifon, hoifting an Englifh jack over her own
colours. A boat from the Speedwell cutter immediately took poffeffion of the San Miguel, or St. Michael, of feventy-two guns, commanded by Don Juan Moreno, a *Chef d'Efcadre*. The officers
and men, to the number of fix hundred and thirty-four, (many
of whom were difmounted dragoons), were immediately landed,
and conducted to the quarters before occupied by their friends
upon Windmill-hill. The Governor was prefent when they were
brought afhore, and generoufly permitted them to take their baggage
unfearched,

unsearched, and the officers their stock of fresh provisions. When the morning cleared up, so as to admit of our observing the state of the Combined Fleets, we discovered the whole in great disorder. One was on shore near the Grand magazine: a French ship of the line had lost her foremast and bowsprit: one, a three-decker, was missing, supposed to be driven from her anchors to the eastward; and three or four were forced half-bay over (two within range of the Garrison) where they all seemed to be in a very precarious situation. Many of the parapet-boats, and other small craft, were also driven on shore near the Orange-grove. If the storm had continued a few hours longer, it is not improbable that a three-decker, with several other ships, would have suffered the fate of the St. Michael. The wind, however, abated as the day advanced; and, when the swell would permit them to assist the disabled ships, the boats were busily employed in carrying out anchors and cables to those which appeared most in distress. The Garrison were not idle spectators of these movements: several sea-mortars were soon brought to bear on the nearest ships, and one was in a short time obliged to move; but anchoring again off Point Mala, we continued annoying her with shells and red-hot shot, till she warped out of our range.

THE prisoners were no sooner landed from the prize, than the seamen began to lighten the vessel, by removing her powder ashore, and cutting away the mizen-mast: but remaining still aground, they carried out anchors to prevent her going further ashore, intending to renew their exertions to warp her off at high water. The St. Michael was esteemed one of the best sailers in the Spanish navy. She was a new ship built at the Havannah; very lofty between decks, which were of mahogany, and her beams of cedar. When the Combined Fleets appeared in the English channel, the St. Michael was one of the leading ships, and was also in the squadron which

which fired upon the Garrison the 9th of September, when the 1781.
Oct.
Duke de Crillon opened his batteries. The Spanish officers informed
us they had received intelligence, the preceding day, of the approach
of the British Fleet; which had induced Admiral Cordova to order
the Combined Fleets to lie at single anchor, and prepare to weigh at
the shortest notice: that they were thus situated when the gale came
on; and, the hurricane still increasing, a three-decker, early in the
morning, ran foul of the St. Michael, and forced her from her
anchor: that she immediately set sail, but, as the event had evinced,
found it impossible to weather the Rock.

THE intelligence of Lord Howe being so near, now, for the first
time, gave us sensible pleasure; not so much on account of our
personal situation, as of the advantage which the Enemy's recent
misfortunes would give his Lordship over his Opponents, as well
towards accomplishing the object of his orders, as affording him
a further opportunity of acting as his Lordship's well-known abilities might dictate. We were so elated by our Enemy's distress,
that some were so sanguine as to anticipate the most glorious conclusion of the war, and our own sufferings. Our hopes however
were soon depressed by intelligence of Lord Howe's great infe-
riority in number. Thirty-four sail to oppose forty-two, which still
remained at anchor in the Bay, gave us reason to be apprehensive for
the safety of the British Fleet. The navigation of the Straits was so
precarious, that, if his Lordship once entered the Mediterranean,
he might probably be prevented from returning for a considerable
time; and the Enemy, though now distressed, might, by the
assistance of the camp, soon refit, and attack him under every
advantage. By this digression I am however anticipating the regular narrative. In the afternoon, a French two-decker sailed to
the eastward; and soon after, a settee came in from the west, and
fired several guns as she entered the Bay. At this time it was so
very

1782,
Oa.

very hazy in the Straits, that we could not fee the oppofite coafts. About fun-fet, feveral large fhips were difcovered through the haze; and foon after, the Latona frigate, Capt. Conway, anchored under our guns, and informed us, that the fhips in the Gut were the Van of the Britifh Fleet, commanded by Lord Howe, confift-ing of thirty-four fail of the line, including eleven three-deckers, with fix frigates and thirty-one ordnance tranfports, and a reinforce-ment of upwards of fixteen hundred men for the Garrifon. Capt. Conway further told us of the anxiety which prevailed at home, relative to the fituation of Gibraltar; and that it was only off the fouthern coaft of Portugal that Lord Howe had his doubts removed, by receiving intelligence of the Enemy's late defeat. This welcome information, he faid, was accompanied by advice, that " the Com-" bined Fleets had taken their ftation in the Bay of Gibraltar, refo-" lutely determined to prevent, if poffible, the intended relief." We learned, that upon receiving the latter intelligence, the Admirals and principal Officers were fummoned on board the Victory; where par-ticular inftructions and orders were communicated, in expectation of an engagement, which was confidered as unavoidable.

ALTHOUGH the Enemy's fignals for the approach of the Britifh Fleet were made early in the afternoon, yet the Spanifh Admiral exhibited not the leaft appearance of oppofition to any reinforcements being fent into the Bay. This favourable opportunity was however loft; owing, as Lord Howe expreffes in his official letter, " to the " want of timely attention to the circumftances of the navigation." Only four or five tranfports reached the Bay; the reft, with the Fleet, paffed to the eaftward into the Mediterranean. At night, or early on the 12th, Capt. Curtis failed in the Latona, to inform Lord Howe of the calamity which had befallen the Enemy's fleet. At noon, the Britifh Fleet appeared in good order off Eftepona or Marbella; and the tranfports, with the frigates, were working to
windward

windward to gain the Bay. As they approached the Iſthmus, the
Enemy ſaluted them from their mortars, and fired upon them from
behind the eaſtern advanced Guard-houſe.

WHILST the Britiſh fleet, with the tranſports, were thus critically ſituated, the Combined Fleets were very active in repairing
their damages, and in forming a line of battle along the ſhore.
In the evening, a number of troops were embarked on board
them from the camp. Their xebeques, cutters, armed brigs, and
gun-boats, alſo aſſembled in Sandy-Bay, with an intention probably of picking up our ſtraggling tranſports. In the cloſe of the
day, however, this fleet of craft returned to their main fleet. At
night, the Panther man of war, and ſeveral tranſports, anchored
in the Bay.

THE Enemy on the land-ſide perſevered in their cannonade, and,
obſerving that the St. Michael had run aground within the range
of their batteries, threw great numbers of ſhells, with an intent
to deſtroy her. Many burſt over her, and ſome fell very near;
but, as their artillery could only be directed by her maſts, none
fell on board. They pointed their uſual weight of fire againſt our
works, which the Governor (now that a proſpect of ſupplies appeared) returned with unuſual vivacity. Their new boyau ſeverely
felt the effect of our ordnance. It was conſiderably deranged, and
the *enfilading* howitzers at the Old-mole head prevented them from
ſtrengthening it with any additions of conſequence. In the Gar-
riſon-orders of the 12th, the following extracts were inſerted:

G. O.

G. O. " *Extract from a Letter to the Governor, from the Right*
" *Hon. the Earl of* Shelburne, *principal Secretary of*
" *State to His Majesty. Dated St. James's, July* 10*th,*
" 1782.

" I AM alfo honoured with His Majefty's command to affure
" you in the ftrongeft terms, that no encouragement fhall be want-
" ing to the brave Officers and Soldiers under your command.   His
" Royal approbation of the paft, will no doubt be a powerful incen-
" tive to future exertions ; and I have the King's authority to affure
" you, that every diftinguifhed act of emulation and gallantry, which
" fhall be performed in courfe of the fiege, by any, even of the
" loweft rank, will meet with ample reward from his gracious pro-
" tection and favour.   Thefe His Majefty's intentions you will com-
" municate to every part of your Garrifon, that they may be perfectly
" fatisfied their Royal Mafter feels for the difficulties they are under,
" admires their glorious refiftance, and will be happy to reward
" their merit."

" *Extract from a Letter to the Governor, from the Right Hon.*
" *General* Conway, *Commander in Chief of His Majefty's*
" *Forces.   Dated Auguft* 31*ft,* 1782.

" I AM now to add, that I have the King's command to inform
" you, that he is in the greateft degree fatisfied with the brave and
" fteady defence made by your Garrifon ; and His Majefty is de-
" firous of fhowing them every mark of His Royal Approbation.
" It is in this light that His Majefty has been gracioufly pleafed to
" confent to granting bât and forage-money, as a proper indulgence
" to your Officers."

THESE

THESE extracts were perused by the Garrison with great satisfaction, as they demonstrated, that the safety of Gibraltar was esteemed a matter of the first importance; and flattered us with the agreeable hopes, that our late services would be acceptably received by our Friends and Countrymen.

THE British Fleet, at day-break on the 13th, was still off Marbella, with the wind at west., About nine o'clock A. M. the Spanish Admiral made the signal for the Combined Fleets to weigh anchor. By one o'clock the whole were under way. At three, a French Rear-Admiral, being the last of the rear division, cleared the Bay. Their number in all amounted to eighty sail, of which the following, I believe, is an accurate account: six three-deckers, thirty-eight two-deckers, including several fifties (total forty-four men of war); five frigates; twenty-nine xebeques, cutters, armed ships, and brigs; also two, imagined to be fire-ships. Notwithstanding little doubt was to be entertained of the Enemy's intention of leaving the Bay, the Panther man of war remained at anchor with several officers of the Garrison on board, whom the Governor had permitted to act as volunteers in the engagement. When the Combined Fleets had cleared the Bay, they stood some time to the southward, and leaving a line-of-battle ship and two frigates to prevent the Panther from joining her Admiral, drove with the current some leagues to the eastward. They then appeared to edge down towards the British Fleet, which was in close line of battle upon a wind, with their heads to the southward; the transports, with the frigates which had been beating up, falling behind them to leeward. Thus were both fleets situated at the close of the evening. Before the Enemy had totally quitted the Bay, Captain Curtis landed in a small boat from the Latona frigate, with twenty thousand pounds in specie for the Garrison, having narrowly escaped being cut off by the Combined Fleets. He told

us

us the Britifh Fleet were in high fpirits, and impatient to engage
notwithftanding the Enemy's great fuperiority.   When the Combined Fleets firft appeared in motion, the Spanifh prifoners who
had been landed from the St. Michael, were fo overjoyed, that they
could not forbear expreffing their ecftacies in fo riotous a manner,
as to call for fome feverity, to confine them within the limits of
their camp.

As our obfervations on the manœuvres of the fleet were interrupted foon after fun-fet, we impatiently waited for the fucceeding
day to be fpectators of the action; which was now confidered as
impoffible to be avoided; and orders were therefore given for preparing feveral wards in the Navy Hofpital for the reception of
the wounded : but on the dawn of the 14th, the Fleets, to our
aftonifhment, were fome leagues diftant from each other; the
Britifh being to leeward in the fouth-eaft quarter, whilft the Combined Fleets appeared off Eftepona.   In the evening, the Britifh
Fleet could only be difcovered from the fummit of the Rock.   It
feemed to the Garrifon, that the Spanifh Admiral, by having the
weather-gage, had it in his option to bring the Britifh Fleet to
action if he pleafed.—The Fleets being thus feparated, the Panther,
about noon, endeavoured to join Lord Howe, but put back for want
of wind.   Seventeen gun-boats came from Algeziras, apparently to
prevent her leaving the Bay; but, obferving her caft anchor, they
returned.

The Enemy's cannonade on the land fide was continued with
great vivacity.   A few days, nay, probably hours, were to turn the
balance for or againft their future hopes of obtaining the grand
object of their wifhes : they were not therefore economical in their
ammunition; nor was the Garrifon in the leaft behind with them
in the brifk ufe of their ordnance.   Lieut. Gromley, of the Royal
                                                                  Artillery,

Artillery, was mortally wounded in the evening, at Willis's, and died
foon after he was brought to the Hofpital.

PART of the Combined Fleets, in the morning of the 15th, were
feen, though the weather was very hazy, off Marbella. The Britifh
Fleet was out of fight; the Panther neverthelefs attempted to join
them. About eight A. M. the wind came about to the eaftward.
In the forenoon, nine polacres failed from the Spanifh camp, with
troops on board, for Ceuta. This brought to our recollection the
critical ftate of that Garrifon, both as to men and provifions, when
Admiral Rodney was in their neighbourhood in 1780; and the
Enemy, from embracing this opportunity of fending fupplies,
appeared not entirely to have forgotten it. About noon, the Britifh
Fleet was difcovered in the offing, to the fouth-eaft of Ceuta,
ftanding under an eafy fail towards the Rock. At night the Latona,
with eight or ten tranfports, anchored in the Bay. They informed
us, that the Buffalo man of war, with the remaining twelve fhips, had
feparated (by order) from the Fleet, but had not afterwards joined.
This intelligence gave us fome uneafinefs for their fafety; but we
flattered ourfelves they were gone, agreeably to inftructions, to the
Zafarine Iflands, the place of rendezvous in cafe the fleets engaged.
Capt. Conway, after a fhort conference with the Governor, returned
in the morning of the 16th to the Britifh Fleet, which were cruifing
to the eaftward of the Rock, with the wind at eaft. The Combined Fleets were not in fight: we concluded therefore that they
were gone into Malaga to make further repairs, and join thofe fhips
which had left the Bay on the 11th. Since the arrival of the firft
tranfports, the Garrifon had been bufily employed in difembarking
the fupplies. The former fleets had principally brought us provifions; this brought us only men and ammunition, which probably
might, without this fupply, have become as fcarce articles as the
former had been.

THE

THE exertions of the navy not being fuccefsful in floating the St. Michael, a hundred foldiers were detached on board, on the 17th, to their affiftance; and not long afterwards, fhe was anchored off the New mole. It was peculiarly fortunate that fhe grounded on a bank of fand, though fhe was furrounded with rocks: her bottom was therefore little injured. Sir Charles Knowles, Bart. who had been formerly on this ftation, was appointed to command her. The wind had now changed to the fouth-weft.; and in the forenoon of the fame day, a Britifh frigate appeared from the weft. She made a fignal when off Europa, which being anfwered by our Fleet, fhe immediately joined them. At night, the gun-boats being heard in the Bay, our batteries were manned to receive them; but, upon a gun being fired from the St..Michael, they threw up their rockets, and returned. Some were of opinion that they meditated an attempt to cut her out. The 18th, the wind again came about to the eaft; and the Buffalo, with eleven of the miffing tranfports, arrived in the courfe of the day. Thefe fhips, as we had conjectured, had feparated from the Fleet, and were proceeding to the place of rendezvous, when, not hearing the engagement, and the wind veering about, they returned, and were very near joining the Combined Fleets, but difcovered their error time enough to rectify it. The miffing veffel, they informed us, had been taken by the Enemy, fome days before, off Malaga; and having on board, the wives and baggage of the two regiments which were on board the Fleet, and were intended for our reinforcement, her capture greatly diftreffed thofe corps, and the Garrifon heartily condoled with them. The Latona, in her return to the Fleet, chafed and boarded a veffel, which proved to be a Spanifh fire-fhip. The crew deferting her, were conducted, by two gun-boats attending, to a xebeque at fome diftance, which afterwards went into Ceuta. The prize was fent into the Bay. About noon, four or five men of war arrived from the fleet, with the 25th and 59th regiments. Lord Mulgrave, who

who commanded the difembarkation, landed the troops with the greateft expedition under the line-wall at the New mole, Rofia and Camp bays, and returned to Lord Howe off Tetuan. The two regiments were encamped before ten o'clock at night; the former behind the Barracks, the latter upon Windmill-hill. We now learned that the Admiral, having accomplifhed the object of the expedition, intended to embrace the favourable opportunity of the wind, and immediately return to the weftward. In the courfe of the night, the fire-fhip brought in by Capt. Conway was purpofely fet on fire, and being anchored apart from the fhipping, blew up without doing any damage. The Latona foon afterwards joined the Britifh Fleet. Capt. Vallotton, the Governor's firft Aide-de-camp, embarked in her to bear home the public difpatches. Capt. Curtis alfo went in her, to communicate a meffage from the Governor to Lord Howe; and did not return.

At day-break on the 19th, both Fleets, to our great aftonifh-ment, were in fight; the Combined Fleets being fome leagues to windward. When the Britifh Fleet was a-breaft of Europa, Lord Howe difpatched the Tifiphone fire-fhip, with a further fupply of powder collected from the Fleet. The Britifh Fleet afterwards put before the wind, and ftood, under an eafy fail, in clofe order to the weftward. The van of the Combined Fleet, compofed of French fhips, followed with a prefs of canvas at fome diftance. By two o'clock P. M. Lord Howe was out of fight; but the Spanifh fhips failing heavily, it was night before they difappeared. Though fully convinced of the prudence of his Lordfhip's conduct, it was no very pleafing profpect for a Britifh Garrifon to behold a Britifh Fleet, though inferior in force, lead the Enemy. At night, the wind changed to the fouth-weft; and the fucceeding day, a brifk can-nonade was heard from that quarter. This however could not proceed from the action which afterwards took place between the fleets, as the firing was heard early in the morning. Some time on

the

the 19th, a guard of two fubalterns, and ninety-fix men, was ordered from the 25th and 59th regiments on board the St. Michael, where they remained till fhe was completely repaired.

SEVERAL large fhips were obferved, on the 20th, to be anchored at fome diftance from Algeziras; and as fix or feven were conjectured to be fire-fhips, precautions were accordingly taken, and the batteries from South baftion to Europa ordered, in cafe of alarm, to be doubly manned. The Enemy, the fame day, got off the man of war which ran afhore near their grand magazine. In the evening, fome movements were obferved in the French camp; and on the fucceeding day moft of the tents were ftruck. In the afternoon, the Spanifh Prieft was confined to his houfe, for holding converfation with fome of the prifoners on Windmill-hill. The Enemy's cannonade was ftill continued, upon an average of about five or fix hundred rounds in the twenty-four hours. They lined fome part of the new boyau with fafcines, and raifed a few traverfes in the rear, notwithftanding our brifk fire: they were, however, prevented from making any additions of confequence. On the 22d, a polacre arrived from Algiers, with intelligence from the Britifh Conful, that Lord Howe had failed for the relief of Gibraltar. Happily his Lordfhip had effected that bufinefs, and probably before they at Algiers were informed of the Britifh Fleet having left England.

THE extreme diftrefs which the Garrifon had experienced in the clofe of the years 1779 and 1780, and the great profits which from the exigencies of thofe periods had arifen to the adventurers who ran the hazard of a voyage with provifions for our relief, were, by this time, pretty generally known at home. The favourable opportunity of a fafe convoy under the Britifh Fleet, prompted, therefore, many mafters of tranfports (fome of whom had been in the Garrifon before during the war) to lay in a ftock of various
articles,

articles, with the profpect that the diftreffes of their *friends* might afford thefe *truly humane and generous patriots* an occafion to fell them, on their arrival, at their own price.   Although thefe fupplies were moft highly acceptable, yet the Garrifon was not at this time in fuch abfolute need of their affiftance, as to purchafe them at thofe enormous prices which before had been given with pleafure; nor in juftice did we think, from the little rifk the adventurers ran, that they deferved fuch immenfe profits.   A Committee of officers from every corps affembled on the 23d, to confider what meafures to purfue in order to prevent fuch impofitions in future; and, as every article brought to the Garrifon was fold at public auction, it was unanimoufly agreed, that a certain price fhould be fixed upon each article, allowing fuch profit as might reafonably be thought adequate to the hazard; and when the eftimate was publifhed, every officer (I believe) pledged his honour not to exceed the terms therein fpecified.*

THE prudent and manly regulation of the Committee was ftrictly attended to for about a fortnight, but it had not that immediate effect we expected : many of our *generous* countrymen, rather than difpofe of their ventures for a profit of a hundred and fifty, and in fome inftances three hundred per cent. very liberally determined to fell them for a *trifling* advantage at Lifbon, or elfewhere, in their way home. We fhould neverthelefs have foon got the better of their obftinacy, had we continued determined and confiftent ourfelves : but fome individuals, who preferred felf-gratification to the public good, beginning to evade the agreement, the WHOLE was cancelled, and the demands of the adventurers became afterwards equally as exorbitant, if not more fo than before.   So little dependence is there upon the adherence of a multitude to any fumptuary regulations, however effential to their real intereft.

T t   THE

* See Appendix.

THE mortar-boats, on the night of the 23d, paid us a visit, and did confiderable damage. Their fhells were chiefly directed towards the New mole. The Hector cutter, in Government's service, was funk by a fhell, and every thing on board loft. Several other veffels narrowly efcaped the fame fate. We fired upon them from Willis's and the Old mole; but their gun-boats were filent. The 24th, we obferved that the Enemy had ftruck the tents of four or five battalions, and two regiments were feen this day marching along the beach. The day following, fome baggage was obferved removing from the Duke's quarters; which gave us great hopes that his Grace was preparing to leave the camp, and that matters were verging towards a conclufion. In the evening a deferter came in, a native Catalonian. He informed us there had been an engagement between the Britifh and Combined Fleets, but could give us no particulars. He further told us that their camp was breaking up: fixteen battalions had already marched away, and others were preparing to decamp: that they had ceafed to work in their approaches; and that their night-guards confifted of four thoufand men, under the command of two brigadier generals: concluding with acquainting us, that the winter-camp before the Garrifon was to confift of twenty thoufand men: that additional gun-boats were building to conftantly harrafs us; and that a corporal and twelve men were ftationed in the Gardens to prevent defertion. The 26th, the tents occupied by the Duke's corps encamped before Buena-Vifta were ftruck; which ferved to increafe our hopes, that the profpect was not far diftant of an end to our fatigues. Don Juan Moreno left the Garrifon the fame day, with a flag of truce. Our boat could not learn any further account of the engagement; but the officers were informed, that a general peace was expected, as the Americans had been acknowledged independent by Great-Britain.

MORE

MORE battalions left the Enemy's camp on the 27th : their cannonade neverthelefs was continued, and feveral fhot ranged as far as the entrance of Windmill-hill ; a diftance of about five thoufand yards. Their camp was ftill decreafing on the 28th and 29th ; and we judged from our obfervations, that about twenty-three battalions, with a brigade of artillery, had marched into the country. The laft deferters faid many had taken the route to Cadiz. The 30th, we obferved the Enemy had ftationed a guard under the Rock near the Devil's tower. They were taken fome notice of by our Artillery, who endeavoured to annoy them with fmall projectiles from the fummit of the Northern front. The Tifiphone, Captain Sandys, with five or fix ordnance-fhips (having a hundred and fixty Jews on board) failed for England early in the morning of the 31ft. The fame day, a foldier of the 97th regiment *was killed at Rofia*, by a long-range fhot from the Ifthmus.

THREE deferters came in on the 2d and 4th of November, but Nov. could give no fatisfactory information relative to the action between the Fleets. They faid the French troops had quitted the camp with the Royal Volunteers. The Enemy's camp continued to break up on the 7th and 8th, though fome of the regiments, it was imagined, took poffeffion of the large building eaftward of Point Mala, which had been built for a hofpital. On the 7th, two men of war and a floop (fuppofed to be French, from the Weft-Indies) paffed to the Eaftward. The Spanifh gun-boats feemed to fufpect they were enemies, and intended to come in ; as they were in motion, and appeared to be preparing for an attack. The 8th, twenty-three gun-boats paraded at a fhort diftance from the Garrifon, extending in a line a-head to the fouthward. We expected an attack upon the St. Michael ; but an eafterly wind fpringing up, they returned. They had fcarcely got back, when a fignal was made at Cabrita Point, and they again put about. Our attention

was

was engaged by this manœuvre; and upon inveſtigating the cauſe, we diſcovered a ſloop ſtanding towards the Garriſon from the eaſtward. If this veſſel had continued the courſe ſhe then ſteered, ſhe might undoubtedly have reached the Rock : whether, however, it was owing to the weſterly current off Europa, or the ignorance of the crew, we could not determine; in the courſe of an hour ſhe drove ſo conſiderably to leeward, as to be out of the protection of our guns, and after receiving ſeveral diſcharges of round and grape from the gun-boats, was boarded by the Enemy. Sir Charles Knowles, Bart. (who ſince Captain Curtis's departure commanded in the Bay) ordered ſeveral barges out to her aſſiſtance, but to no purpoſe. A boat, with five of her crew, eſcaped to the Garriſon, and informed us ſhe was laden with ſugar and tea from Falmouth. Soon afterwards, a Daniſh dogger was brought to an anchor in the Bay, by a gun from Europa : ſhe was laden with rice and pilchards from England. A flag of truce, on the 9th, went with a letter to the Duke; and in the evening, another brought over Enſign Lewis, of the 58th regiment, with a Quarter-maſter and a Volunteer of the 25th, who had been taken in the Minerva brig, with the baggage, &c. of the 25th and 59th regiments. This flag alſo brought over other priſoners. By theſe gentlemen, we learned that an engagement had taken place between Lord Howe and Admiral Cordova, and that the latter was returned into port with his fleet much ſhattered.

After the departure of the fleets, little attention was paid by the Enemy to the blockade. Not one cruiſer was now to be ſeen in the Straits, or to the Eaſtward ; and few veſſels of force were ſtationed at Cabrita Point. The idea of gaining Gibraltar, either by force or ſtratagem, ſeemed at length to be totally relinquiſhed. Their cannonade from the land nevertheleſs was continued ; but as it gradually diminiſhed, and ſcarce exceeded at this
time

time two hundred and fifty rounds in the twenty-four hours, we imagine! it would in a short time totally cease. The St. Philip's Castle, and several ordnance-ships, had left the Bay the evening of the 8th; and on the 10th and 12th, two light vessels came to Algeziras, which from their appearance were thought to be of the. latter. On the 12th, a flag of truce went with a letter to the. Duke : whilst it was out, the Enemy's gun-boats commenced a smart cannonade upon the St. Michael, (which was now refitted) whilst their mortar-boats bombarded our camp. We returned their fire; and two of the mortar-boats retired very early, the others following them in about an hour. Three or four shot were fired through the St. Michael, but no other damage was received. Our flag returned just as the cannonade ceased. As it appeared probable that the Enemy might renew their attacks upon the Prize, Colonel Williams, who commanded the Artillery, ordered more mortars to be distributed along the sea-line, from the King's bastion to the New-mole fort. The 15th, a regiment quitted their camp; and at night their workmen raised about twenty traverses in the rear of their advanced boyau, extending from the parallel about half the length of the work. Our fire at this period was variable. The day following, between twenty and thirty transports, with troops on board, sailed under convoy of two frigates for the westward. Their artillery also about this time removed most of the ordnance from their park to the landing-place; where we numbered thirty cannon and five mortars, with a great quantity of shot and shells ready for embarkation. The 17th, a xebeque, and several armed vessels and gun-boats, anchored at Cabrita Point, as if they had determined to renew the blockade. Three days after, all the Spanish prisoners taken in the St. Michael, excepting a few who chose to remain behind, were sent to the camp. The Spanish officers, on this occasion, informed us that there had been an engagement between the British and Combined Fleets, which had

ended

ended to the advantage of the *former*. In the evening of the 20th, a party of about a hundred men were feen to go from the eaftern part of the Enemy's parallel to the back of the rock. We could not at that time account for the marching of thefe troops. The fmall craft continued at Cabrita Point, the men of war and larger veffels being at anchor off the Orange-grove. Four fail of the line and three frigates, befides xebeques, &c. were now in the Bay. The Enemy, on the 21ft and 22d, embarked a vaft quantity of powder from their grand magazine on board the men of war. Moft of the fpare ordnance had already been fhipped on board, and others were removing daily toward the beach.

Two boats arrived on the 23d from Portugal: they brought certain intelligence of the preceding action between the Fleets. The particulars of this intelligence were, that a partial action had taken place between the Britifh, of thirty-four fhips, and the Combined Fleets of forty-fix fhips of the line; that, though the latter had the weather-gage, they ftudioufly avoided a clofe engagement; and after a cannonade of feveral hours, hauled their wind, and directed their courfe to Cadiz. The fame day, Lieut. John M'Kenzie, of the 73d, was dangeroufly wounded at Willis's. The Enemy's fire now fcarcely exceeded a hundred and fifty rounds. Two more boats got in from Faro the night of the 26th. Our fuccefs, in obtaining thefe welcome fupplies, rendered the Enemy more vigilant and active to intercept them: every boat, even friends, which approached the Rock, raifed their fufpicion.

THOUGH every appearance in their camp indicated that they had given up all hopes of fubduing the Garrifon by force, their parties on the Ifthmus continued to be very bufy, and fome evenings they made additions of traverfes to their works. Heavy timber was alfo brought forward to the parallel, but for what purpofe we could not then

then imagine. Their advanced parties had likewife the audacity frequently to approach half way upon the caufeway from Bay fide; but the Artillery having orders to *fcower* the Gardens, and the neighbourhood of Bay fide, with grape from the Old mole, their curiofity in a fhort time was pretty well cooled. Towards the clofe of this month, the Enemy's fire became more faint, and ill directed, whilft ours was more animated and effectual. Our Engineers continued to be conftantly engaged. The rebuilding of the whole flank of the Prince of Orange's baftion, a hundred and twenty feet in length, with folid mafonry, (which was now nearly finifhed,) in the face of fuch powerful Artillery, can fcarcely be paralleled in any fiege.

In the beginning of December, the Achilles ordnance-fhip, with two or three boats, arrived from England and Portugal. The 6th, a Venetian fhip was driven by the current under the guns of Europa: we fired to bring her to, and the mafter inftantly came afhore, and informed us fhe was bound to London; but, before he could return, his veffel was boarded by three gun-boats, which towed her to Algeziras. The mafter then came into the Garrifon, and at night was permitted to follow his veffel. The following evening, a German deferted to us from the Walon guards. He informed us, that the Enemy ftationed every evening a guard of three hundred men near the Devil's tower, where they had miners at work in a cave; hoping to form a mine, to blow up the north part of the Rock. We paid no kind of attention at firft to this intelligence; fo ridiculous, and even chimerical, the fcheme appeared. Recollecting however that a party had been obferved to march that way fome evenings before, and remarking, upon a clofer infpection, that every evening a numerous body of men approached along the eaftern fhore towards that quarter, we began to give fome credit

to

to this fingular information.*   The above deferter alfo informed us,
that the Enemy had removed fome ordnance from the parallel, and
that their guards and advanced parties were ftill very ftrong. .

By this period, our Engineers had penetrated a confiderable diftance in the gallery above Farringdon's battery, and had opened five
embrafures to the front of the Rock; and to have a more fecure communication to this fingular work, a covered way was funk, by blafting
the rock from the above battery, to the entrance of the gallery. The
fuccefs with which this work had been profecuted, and the confiderable advantages which promifed to refult from it when finifhed,
induced the Governor to order that a fimilar battery, but only for two
guns, fhould be made in the rock near Crouchett's battery, above the
Prince of Hefle's baftion; and the workmen had now made fome
advances therein.   On the 12th, a guard-boat of the St. Michael,
with two officers and feven failors, went over to the Enemy.   We
afterwards learned from the Officers, who returned in a flag of truce,
that the failors rofe upon them, faying they were refolved to go over
to the Enemy: that Lieut. Small, who commanded the boat, drew
his hanger, and attempted a ftroke at the man who was fpokefman
upon the occafion; but that he was knocked down by the coxfwain
with the tiller of the rudder: that, whilft he was thus fenfelefs,
they had it in debate to throw him overboard; but, by the interceffion of the young midfhipman, he was preferved, and, when taken
afhore, was fome time before he recovered.

The Enemy's parties under the rock, near the Devil's tower, began
now to engage our curiofity.   Every part of the north front was
explored,

---

* In 1727, the Befiegers formed the defign of blowing up Willis's batteries by a mine;
but it is imagined they found it impracticable, as they never attempted to fpring the mine,
though the Journal of that Siege mentions it was loaded.

explored, to endeavour, if poſſible, to diſcover what they were about.
At length, on the 15th, a place was found above Green's-lodge,
whence we could diſtinguiſh a part of their work. The communication with this poſt, being along a level beach, was greatly expoſed
to our fire. When their parties were diſcovered advancing from the
eaſt flank of the ſixty-four-gun battery, our Artillery at Willis's
and on the heights prepared to ſalute them. They were permitted
to approach unmoleſted within two or three hundred yards, when a
general volley was diſcharged of cohorn-ſhells, with grape, ſeconded
by the mortars on the Levant battery, loaded with hand-ſhells, or
grenades, quilted together. *A chance,* or mine, was ſometimes
ſprung upon them from the top, when they had nearly got under
the rock; the ſtones from which added not a little to their confuſion
and loſs. Notwithſtanding they were in this manner obliged every
evening to paſs the gantlope of our fire, they continued to bring
materials, and maintained their poſt with ſurpriſing obſtinacy. Some
of the guard were ſeen frequently, in the day, to advance from their
cover : a party of Corſicans, who hitherto had done no other duty
than guard the priſoners on Windmill-hill, were ordered therefore
to the poſt above Green's-lodge, to fire wall-pieces upon thoſe that
appeared from below.

A FLAG of truce went from the Garriſon on the 17th. The
Spaniſh Aide-de-Camp informed us, that preliminaries of a General
Peace were expected to be ſigned in the courſe of the month.
The ſucceeding day another flag went from the Governor with letters to the Duke : it had ſcarcely returned, when twenty-nine gun
and mortar-boats commenced a ſpirited attack upon the St. Michael,
and other ſhips, at anchor off Buena-Viſta. Since theſe boats had
made a cuſtom of firing upon the Garriſon, we never remarked
them to be arranged with more judgement, or to behave with greater
gallantry, than they did on this occaſion. The mortar-boats com-

U u   poſed

poſed the centre diviſion, and a diviſion of gun-boats was arranged
on each flank; their line of battle extending about two miles. They
got their diſtance the firſt round, and retained it with ſuch preciſion,
that almoſt every ſhell fell within fifty yards of the St. Michael,
which was the chief object of their attack. The ſeventy-fourth
ſhell fell on board, about mid-ſhip; pierced the firſt, and broke on
the lower deck; killed four, and wounded eleven ſailors, three of
them mortally. After this accident, Sir Charles Knowles, being
apprehenſive of the moſt fatal conſequences if a ſhell ſhould fall into
the magazine, removed the powder, through the oppoſite port-holes,
into a launch, which was immediately towed under the rock: eighty
barrels, which could not be removed, were thrown into the ſea. The
Enemy ſtill maintained a warm fire, but, it is imagined, did not
obſerve that any had fallen on board. Several ſhells carried away
ornaments and parts of her rigging: fortunately however ſhe received
no further injury. Not one ſhell came aſhore from the boats.
Captain Gibſon, at the commencement of the action, rowed out
with eight gun-boats from the New mole, and very warmly attacked
their northern diviſion. On his appearing in motion, three parapet-
boats advanced from the Orange-grove to take our boats in flank.
One of this number was however ſoon diſabled by the Garriſon,
and the other two joined the main body. When the Enemy had
expended their ammunition, the mortar-boats retired, and the gun-
boats covered their retreat in a moſt beautiful manner. They
ſtood towards the Orange-grove, and embarked ſome of their crews
on board the men of war. Three of the line-of-battle ſhips,
two frigates, and a xebeque, with ſeveral bomb-ketches and other
veſſels, which were all laden with military ſtores, ſailed to the
weſtward. The Enemy's land-batteries, as is mentioned before,
were gradually diminiſhing in their fire; but upon this occaſion,
they ſupported the boats from the Bay with a very animated
additional cannonade.

THE

THE remainder of the Enemy's ships, laden with military stores, sailed on the night of the 19th from the Orange-grove to the westward. The wind continued easterly; and on the succeeding night, or rather the morning of the 21st, blew so strong a gale, that the St. Michael was driven from her anchors more than half-bay over: every exertion was made to recover her station, but all proved ineffectual; when fortunately an eddy wind brought her about, and Sir Charles Knowles was happy to run her aground within the New mole on a sand-bank south of the tank. The gale was so powerful on Windmill-hill, that the tents of the 59th regiment were torn from the pickets, and carried a considerable distance from the camp-ground. To obviate the like disagreeable circumstances in future, that regiment was removed to encamp in South-port ditch, opposite Sydow's (formerly Hardenberg's) regiment. This arrangement obliged the town parade to be changed; and the guards afterwards assembled on the Red sands, which continues at this time to be the general parade. In the course of the day, the St. Michael was warped into deep water, and moored in the New mole. At night a deserter came in: he informed us that the Enemy had twenty miners at work near the Devil's tower, protected by a strong guard; that we annoyed their communication with that post very much, and every evening killed and wounded many men. In consequence of this intelligence, our fire towards that quarter was increased. A flag of truce, on the 20th, had informed us that the women belonging to the 25th and 59th regiments were at the Enemy's camp, waiting more moderate weather, to be sent by water into the Garrison. The 22d, they were received, but upon their landing were conducted to the Naval hospital, where some few of them were detained by the faculty as exceptionable. Lieut. Small, of the Navy, came over on the 23d in a flag of truce. He told us the Enemy's small craft had materially suffered from the storm which had so greatly endangered the St. Michael. The Duke de

Crillon,

Crillon, the day following, vifited the parallel, and was prefent in the weftern boyau, whilft an engineer picketed out a work at the extremity of it, near the beach. At intervals, we could now diftinctly hear the explofion of the mines in the Enemy's cave or gallery at the Devil's tower. Few men were however to be feen in that neighbourhood; though at night they continued the reliefs, and brought materials as ufual.

In the afternoon of the 25th, we obferved the gun and mortar-boats in motion; and about four o'clock, eighteen of the former, and eleven of the latter, advanced from Algeziras, apparently with an intention of renewing their attack upon the unfortunate St. Michael; but eleven of our gun-boats oppofing them, the centre divifion of mortar-boats, and the fouthward divifion, ftood towards Europa, and began a warm bombardment upon our Camp; throwing their fhells indifcriminately from Windmill-hill to South fhed. Our gun-boats in this action behaved with great gallantry, directing their oppofition entirely againft the mortar-boats; the fire of which they in a great meafure diverted from the fhipping. A blind fhell neverthelefs fell into the ward-room of the St. Michael; and another fhell carried away the mizen-maft of the Porcupine frigate, and burft in the ftate-cabin. Seven or eight fhells fell within the hofpital-wall: one difploded in a ward, and killed and wounded feveral of the fick. Several houfes and fheds were alfo deftroyed, and others confiderably injured. In fhort, it was thought to be the warmeft attack we had ever experienced from the gun-boats; and our men, being moftly in fpirits after their Chriftmas dinner, were confequently lefs upon their guard. One was killed, and feven were wounded, in the camp. As our Artillery had time to prepare, the Enemy's cannonade was returned with great vivacity; but the mortar-boats and fouthward divifion had taken fo judicious a ftation, that few ordnance could be brought to bear upon them.

We

We had neverthelefs fome reafon to conclude their lofs was fuperior to our own. Their land-batteries (with the addition of Fort St. Philip and the Black battery, which had been filent fome time) upon this occafion, as upon the laft, increafed their fire upon the Town. We therefore had the Enemy upon our whole front, from Europa Point to Land-port. At a quarter paft fix o'clock, the mortar-boats retired, and were covered in their retreat by the gun-boats as before.* This difhonourable and cruel mode of profecuting the war, we had reafon to think, would be continued till a peace fhould put an end to all hoftilities. The Enemy had been very induftrious in impreffing this *pleafing* information on the memories of the women, who had been lately detained by the weather in their camp. They were told *for their comfort*, that, as the befieging army had been reluctantly compelled to relinquifh the idea of recovering Gibraltar, they were determined to harrafs and alarm the Garrifon by fucceffive attacks from the gun and mortar-boats, which, for the purpofe of having regular reliefs, were to be increafed in number : thus, by being expofed to a revengeful Enemy, the profpect before us promifed to be more irkfome and vexatious than the more interefting period which had paffed.

Although the Enemy's fire from the Ifthmus was almoft difcontinued, the Governor, towards the conclufion of December, made up for their deficiency by a more animated difcharge than ufual : every night the whole North front appeared a continued line of fire. The Devil's tower chiefly engaged his attention : their guard at

this

* It was during this attack, that the materials from which this work is compiled, were in the moft imminent danger of being entirely deftroyed.—A thirteen-inch fhell from the Enemy's mortar-boats, falling above the Camp-guard, rolled along the road leading from Buena Vifta, and entered the Author's marquée : though lighted when it entered, and though its force muft have been greatly fpent upon the ground, the fufe luckily broke as it lodged within, and the marquée, with the furniture, by that fortunate circumftance was preferved.

this poſt generally relieved about ſeven or eight o'clock in the evening, if not prevented by our fire. The work (which we could diſcover) of ſand-bags was totally deſtroyed ; and the floping timbers which they had placed againſt the rock to protect them from the *over-head* fire, were much ſhattered by the weighty fragments of rock which were hurled upon them from above. The night of the 27th, the Enemy opened three embraſures in the epaulement at the eaſt end of the ſixty-four-gun battery. The embraſures were then maſked, and, the ſucceeding evening, were faced with faſcines. The night of the 29th, they raiſed a work of ſand-bags, of about a hundred feet in extent, at the weſtern extremity of the new boyau. It was picketed out when the Duke was preſent, and extended to the rear at right angles with the epaulement. The 30th, nineteen gun and mortar-boats came out of the river Palmones, where they generally retired to repair, after firing upon the Garriſon. The evening of the ſucceeding day being very calm, and ſome movements being obſerved amongſt them, we expected they would commence the new year with another viſit : but we were happily diſappointed. Since we were ſufficiently perſuaded of the conduct which the Enemy had determined to purſue for the remainder of the war, the Governor again adopted the idea of retaliation : the gun mounted on Col. Williams's elevated carriage was removed to the Old-mole head, and other preparations were made to annoy their camp, when the boats ſhould renew their attack. In the courſe of December, ſeveral veſſels and boats arrived with ſtores and ſupplies. Others likewiſe left the Bay, and flags of truce frequently paſſed between the Governor and the Duke. Their purport was not however publickly known.

The laſt day of December, a party of the Navy fiſhed up one of the guns from the wreck of the Battering-ſhips ; and the following day, the firſt of JANUARY, 1783, the gun, which was of iron, and

a twenty-a twenty-fix pounder, was drawn in proceffion by the Britifh tars, with a Spanifh enfign which had been taken from on board one of the fhips, difplayed over it, and attended by a band of mufic, playing *God fave the King.**

Our obfervations made upon the Enemy's proceedings at the Devil's tower were as yet very unfatisfactory; though, by the enterprifing activity of a ferjeant in the artificers, we knew that they were in reality at work in a cave : for he had defcended, by means of ropes and ladders, fo low as to fee the mouth of the cave, and hear the people converfe. Early, therefore, on the morning of the 4th,. three of the Governor's Aide-de-camps went in a barge, protected by two gun-boats, to reconnoitre this poft. Their curiofity prompted them to approach nearer than was perhaps prudent, as the guard fired mufquetry upon them, and a gun or two were difcharged from Fort Barbara. Soon after they returned, the new three-gun battery,. at the eaft end of the fixty-four-gun battery, was unmafked, though the guns were *under metal.* In the afternoon of the fame day, the gun and mortar-boats advanced in two divifions from Algeziras, and, when half-bay over, were joined by a third divifion of five from Cabrita Point, confifting in all of thirty-three. The centre divifion of fixteen, principally mortar-boats, was warmly attacked by Sir Charles Knowles, with eleven of ours, whilft the northern divifion was as brifkly annoyed from the King's baftion. This divifion of twelve gun-boats had the boldnefs to approach within the range of grape, and fuffered very confiderably. One was undoubtedly funk by an howitzer fhell, and others were greatly damaged. Two of the

---

* Many more of thefe guns were afterwards recovered from the wrecks ; and moft of them, being of brafs, were fold, and the fums, with other monies arifing from the head-money granted by Parliament for the Battering-fhips, and the fale of the St. Michael prize, were proportioned in fhares to the Garrifon and Marine Brigade.—See Appendix.

the mortar-boats were alfo driven from the line, and feveral others were obferved to be in confufion. The land-batteries, which had been filent fince the Duke had vifited the lines on the 2d of January, feconded the attack by fea with a very animated fire. The Bay being calm, and little wind blowing to carry off the fmoke, the appearance of this attack all together, from the extent of the front engaged, was tremendous. Lieut. Holloway, of the Engineers, Aide-de-camp to General Green, was wounded by a fplinter of a fhell, which fell oppofite to General De la Motte's quarters at the fouthward, where the ftaff at the fouthward ufually affembled upon thefe occafions. Two men were killed, and one wounded, in the Garrifon; but the feamen had no cafuals. The St. Michael alfo on this occafion efcaped; and it was remarked, not one fhell fell near the Hofpital. When the boats had expended eighty-three fhot, and two hundred and fix fhells, they retired: from the Ifthmus five hundred and feventy-eight fhot, and a hundred and two fhells, were difcharged in this fhort period.

WHEN our Artillery had put the batteries in order, a party was detached, about eight in the evening, to the Old mole; and upwards of a hundred rounds of *red-hot* fhot, with large and fmall fhells, were thrown into the Enemy's camp: all appeared to anfwer, except the heavy fhells, the fufes of which were too fhort for the range. The following morning, feveral pieces of a gunboat, an oar, with fome bread, garlick, &c. were feen floating in the Bay, and gathered by our boats. This ferved to ftrengthen our conjecture of the preceding evening, that one of the gun-boats had been funk in the action. In the evening, about nine o'clock, our northern guards were furprifed with a fudden difcharge of mufquetry on the caufeway, and in the neighbourhood of Bay fide: it was immediately returned from Land-port, and the
lines,

lines, with a few rounds of grape from Covert-port battery; after which there was a dead filence. The next morning, a bloody hat, with feveral fhot-holes through it, was taken up near Bay fide. We could not otherwife account for this firing, than by fuppofing that fome fentries, attempting to defert, had been obferved and purfued. One or two of our own men in the Flêche were wounded by the fcattered grape-fhot from the Covert-port battery.

THE evening of the 9th, the Enemy paraded with only twenty-three boats, feemingly with an intention of renewing their attack upon the fhipping and Garrifon; but Sir Charles appearing with his fmall force, his opponents thought proper to retire. We were however alarmed, early the next morning, by their firing upon the Garrifon: they approached very cautioufly, and directed their fire towards the New mole. Sir Charles Knowles had his boats foon manned; but had not been long out, before one of them was unfor-tunately funk by a fplinter from one of our fhells which burft in the air. The crew were inftantly taken up by their friends, and the boat towed in. The land-batteries opened as before, and continued firing until the boats retreated. Our fhipping received no damage, nor were any feamen hurt; but in the Garrifon, we had one killed, and fifteen or fixteen wounded, befides a Jew, an inhabitant. One of their fhells fell into the north pavilion of the South barracks, and burft upon the fecond floor: the officers were luckily out; for the rooms, above and below, were totally deftroyed. When the fmoke had fufficiently difperfed, we numbered thirty-eight boats, but could not diftinguifh (as their fterns were towards us) how many carried mortars. The Governor faluted their camp in the evening from the Old mole. A boat arrived on the 11th from Faro, with difpatches to the Governor. The Brilliant frigate was ordered foon afterwards to be prepared for fea.

THE Enemy's cannonade from the land, except when the gun-boats fired, was at this time so trifling, that it scarce deserved the name of a continuation. Our Engineers were therefore employed in repairing the curtain of the Grand battery, the north face and flank of Montague's bastion, with the adjoining curtain ; and though the men were much exposed in this duty, the Enemy seldom if ever molested them. Their parties continued bringing various materials from the parallel to the post at the Devil's tower: We never allowed them to pass; or even appear, without a tremendous volley of shells, and grape, and fragments of stones, discharged from the summit of the rock. But our Artillery were not solely engaged with the Enemy in this quarter; every annoyance that could be devised was directed against them in all quarters. The ordnance, since the arrival of the last dispatches from Faro, were kept in as quick action as the metal would permit. A party of Corsicans were also stationed in the lines, to punish their patroles, who frequently had the audacity to approach within a few yards of the extremity. The evenings of the 18th and 19th, the Enemy played off a number of rockets and other fire-works at Algeziras, accompanied with several discharges of cannon. They likewise saluted us from the lines with a volley of shells, and twenty-one rounds of shot. We could not divine the cause of these rejoicings. On the 25th, some sparks of fire communicating to an ammunition-box at Middle-hill guard, the contents blew up, and carried away great part of the wall and guard-house, bruising and burning several of the guard. The engineers were immediately ordered to repair the breach, and not quit the post till the works were in their original state. A reinforcement of a subaltern from the line, with a drum and twenty-one rank and file, was ordered likewise to join that guard every evening; and other regulations relative to it were established.

ON

ON the 29th, Lieut. Angelo Raffaeli, of the Corsican company, was slightly wounded in the lines. In the evening, the gun and mortar-boats, in number twenty-eight, fired upon our shipping and the camp. They took their stations off Europa and Rosia, apparently determined to avoid the fire from the KING's BASTION, (which they had found so *fatal* to their enterprises) and directed their fire principally against the Brilliant frigate, which was then at anchor off Buena-Vista, and the St. Michael in the New mole. Their land-batteries opened at the same time, directing a furious cannonade into the Town, and along our northern front. The Garrison returned their fire with great vivacity, though not with their usual success. Our gun-boats were also unfortunate, one of them being damaged very early in the action, and obliged to be towed in. We had three men killed, and eleven wounded; six of whom were of the 59th regiment. The Enemy discharged from their boats two hundred and thirty-six shot, and two hundred and twenty-five shells; and from the Isthmus, five hundred and fifty-five shot, and two hundred and forty-five shells; after which, the former retired, and the latter were silent. The next day, four gun-boats fired upon the Brilliant, *en passant*, but soon retired. At night, a soldier of the Artillery, who had been punished some time before, threw himself down the precipice from the Queen's battery at Willis's: he passed so quickly by the men on duty, that he was scarcely seen; and was not known till he was missing the next morning. In the course of the month, one of the 25th regiment deserted, and another of the 58th (who had been entertained from the number that remained behind of the prisoners, who were taken in the battering-ships) was retaken in attempting to get off. Two boats came in also from Faro, and a third was intercepted in her passage.

FEBRUARY was introduced by an animated fire from the Garrison. Every part of the Enemy's works felt the effects of our artillery. Thus affairs were proceeding, when on the 2d, letters from the Duke de Crillon informed the Governor, that *the preliminaries* of a general PEACE had been figned between GREAT-BRITAIN, FRANCE, and SPAIN. When the boats met, the Spaniards. rofe up with tranfports of joy, and cried out, " *We are all friends* ;" delivering the letters with the greateft apparent fatisfaction: They could not inform us what were the terms of the peace; which occafioned fome anxiety in the Garrifon relative to the fate of Gibraltar. Previous to the boats meeting, the Enemy difcharged about thirty rounds, but never, after the letters were delivered, fired upon the Garrifon. Our artillery alfo ceafed in the evening. The Spaniards, the fucceeding day, advanced from their works, and converfed with our fentries in the lines, expreffing their fatisfaction that we were no longer at variance. This intercourfe was however forbidden by the Governor, who ordered the guards to inform thofe who approached our works, that all correfpondence of this nature was to be fufpended till official accounts were received from England of the peace. General Eliott anfwered the Duke's letter on the 3d, and ordered the Captain of Artillery to fire an elevated fhot, from Willis's, over any parties which might pafs between their parallel and the Devil's tower. The Duke, on the 5th, informed the Governor that the BLOCKADE by fea was difcontinued ; in confequence of which, a placart was publifhed in the Garrifon, fignifying that the *port of Gibraltar* was again OPEN. About noon, an elevated gun was wantonly fired *over* their works, which was the laft fhot fired in this fiege.

THIS return of tranquillity, this profpect of plenty, and relief from the daily vexations of fo tedious a fiege, could not fail to diffufe a general joy throughout the Garrifon. Indeed fuch feelings

are

are feldom experienced; they baffle all attempts to defcribe them: far beyond the pleafure refulting from private inftances of fuccefs or good fortune, ours was a focial happinefs; and the benevolent fentiments acted upon the heart with additional energy, on the profpect of meeting thofe as friends, with whom we had been fo long engaged in a fucceffion of hoftilities.

THE Duke, on the 6th, informed the Governor that the pre-liminaries had been figned the 20th of January at Paris, and that GIBRALTAR was to remain in the poffeffion of GREAT-BRITAIN. From this period, operations on both fides were fufpended; each party anxioufly waiting official accounts from England of the Peace. Towards the clofe of the month, the Duke began to withdraw fome of the ordnance from the advanced batteries, and to remove materials from the parallel to the camp. The Garrifon, on the other hand, were employed in making repairs, and in arranging various matters, which could not before be attended to. Several fhips, and a number of boats, arrived from England and Portugal; fo that provifions became every day more abundant, and confequently the prices of articles more moderate.

IN the beginning of March, a fchooner arrived from Barbary, with a letter accompanying a prefent of bullocks for the Governor. We were ignorant of the contents of the letter; but it was ima-gined the fubject was, to requeft a renewal of our friendfhip. Two officers and twenty-four Corficans, who in their paffage to Gibraltar had been chafed afhore on the coaft of Barbary by the Spaniards, arrived alfo in this boat. The former informed us, that upon the commencement of the attack of the Battering-fhips on the pre-ceding 13th of September, the Moors at Tangier repaired to their mofques, imploring Heaven in behalf of their *old allies*; and that, on receiving accounts of the defeat of the Enemy, they made public rejoicing,

rejoicing, and gave every demonstration of their affection for the English Nation.

WHEN the cessation of hostilities took place, parlies were almost daily passing between the Governor and the Duke; and the Spanish Aide-de-camps never omitted expressing their surprise that the Governor had not yet heard from England. Their patience as well as ours was nearly exhausted, when the long-expected frigate arrived on the 10th of March: but for some time, even when she had got into the Bay, she kept us in suspense, by steering close along the Spanish shore, and showing no colours. At length, however, the British ensign was displayed, and the anxious Garrison saluted her with a *general huzza*. She was the Thetis frigate, Captain Blankett; and soon after she anchored, Sir Roger Curtis (who had been knighted for his conduct on the 14th of September) landed with dispatches for the Governor. The Duke de Crillon sent a parley to the Garrison in the evening, which was answered the succeeding day. The subject of this correspondence probably was to appoint an interview between the Generals, as on the 12th his Grace, attended by his suite, came down to the extremity of the western boyau, and sent an Aide-de-camp to inform the Governor he was arrived. General Eliott, attended by Lieut. Koehler, his Aide-de-camp, soon afterwards rode out by Lower Forbes's, and was met by the Duke on the beach, half-way between the works and Bay-side barrier. Both instantly dismounted and embraced. When the salutations were over, they conversed about half an hour, and then returned to their respective commands. The cannon in the Spanish batteries were now all dismounted; and large parties were daily removing them, with ammunition, also various materials, from their post at the Devil's tower, to the lines and camp. As their guards were now considerably diminished, numbers of deserters were daily coming over to the Garrison. They were principally foreigners; and the reason they gave, was a dislike to the service.

THE

343

rey
led
1g,
er,
s :
er-
ith
ft,
1ce
:he
er-
1n,
nd
ers
as
d,
he
ce
ce

1e
re
d
:e
"
d
s
,
t
s
-

s

A View from Gibraltar of the Spanish Lines &c.is erected in the late Siege before that Garrison

THE Duke, the 18th, fent the Governor a prefent of a grey Andalufian horfe. The 22d, the St. Michael man of war failed for England, where fhe happily arrived fafe. The day following, the Governor, accompanied by General Green the chief Engineer, with their Aide-de-camps, met the Duke in the Spanifh works: they were conducted by His Grace through the whole, and afterwards to the cave at the Devil's tower. The Governor dined with the Duke at San Roque, and returned in the evening. The 31ft, the Duke de Crillon, accompanied by the Marquis de Saya, Prince de Mazarano, Counts de Jamaïque and de Serano, Don ——, the Intendant, and Captain Tendon, returned the vifit. The Governor received his Grace near Forbes's; and on entering the Garrifon, a falute was fired of feventeen pieces of cannon from the Grand battery. When the Duke appeared within the walls, the foldiers faluted him with a general huzza; which being unexpected, it was faid, greatly confufed him. The reafon however being explained, he feemed highly pleafed with the old Englifh cuftom; and, as he paffed up the main ftreet, where the ruinous and defolate appearance of the town attracted a good deal of his obfervation, his Grace behaved with great affability.

THE officers of the Garrifon were introduced by corps to the Duke, at the Convent. When the Artillery were mentioned, he received them in the moft flattering manner: " Gentlemen," faid his Grace, addreffing himfelf to them, " I would rather fee " you here as friends, than on your batteries as enemies, where," added he, " you never fpared me." The Duke afterwards vifited the batteries on the heights. At Willis's he made fome remarks on the formidable appearance of the lower defences; obferving, whilft he pointed towards the Old-mole battery, that, " had not " his opinion been over-ruled, he fhould have directed all his efforts " againft that part of the Garrifon." The good ftate of our batteries

teries in so short a period produced some compliments to the Chief Engineer; and, when conducted into the gallery above Farringdon's battery*, his Grace was particularly astonished, especially when he was informed of its extent, which at that time was between five and six hundred feet. Turning to his suite, after exploring the extremity, " These works," he exclaimed, " are worthy of the Romans." After dinner, (at which were present the Generals and Brigadiers in the Garrison, with their suites) he passed through the camp to Europa, each regiment turning out without arms, and giving three cheers. The youth and good appearance of the troops much engaged his attention. When his curiosity was gratified in that quarter, he returned, and was conducted about eight o'clock without Land-port, being saluted with seventeen cannon on his departure. His horse startled at the flash of the guns, and almost, if not entirely unhorsed him; but he escaped without being hurt. The Duke, in the course of the conversation at dinner, paid many handsome compliments to the Governor and Garrison for their noble defence. "He had exerted himself (he said) to the utmost of his " abilities; and, though he had not been successful, yet he was happy " in having his Sovereign's approbation of his conduct."

Before the Duke de Crillon entered the Garrison, the Count de Ruffigniac, Colonel in the French service, (who, the Reader may remember, was very pressing for admittance into the Garrison some few days after the defeat of the Battering-ships, and who, for the sole purpose of seeing the place, had remained behind) was admitted into the Garrison without the Duke's knowledge; and being in the flèche at Land-port when the Duke was approaching from Forbes's, his Grace could not avoid seeing him. As he had entered without the Duke's permission, his Grace requested he might not see him at the Convent; and the Count being informed, withdrew

* Now called Windsor.

withdrew into the Garrison, apparently much chagrined at the Duke's particularity. When his Grace returned, it was said, orders were given, not to permit the Count to go back by way of the lines. The following evening, however, after satisfying his curiosity in the Garrison, he returned.

THE 2d of April, the Duke de Crillon quitted the camp in his route to Madrid. He was succeeded in command by Lieut. General the Marquis de Saya, who had accompanied his Grace into the Garrison, and (what was very singular) had served as an officer at the preceding siege of Gibraltar in 1727. Deserters still continued coming over to us, and the Spaniards were employed in removing materials from the neutral ground to the lines. Letters often passed between the Marquis and General Eliott; but though the latter requested to pay his compliments at San Roque, the etiquette observed by the former (orders having been received from Madrid to prevent all intercourse) would not, for some time, permit him to receive the Governor. The 15th of April, Sir Roger Curtis sailed in the Brilliant frigate on an embassy to the Emperor of Morocco: he took with him, as a present, four brass twenty-six-pounders (which had been weighed from the wreck of the Battering-ships) with proportionable ammunition.

His Majesty having been pleased to confer upon the Governor the Most Honourable Order of the Bath, as a mark of His Royal approbation for the defence of Gibraltar; and having signified his pleasure by Sir Roger Curtis, that Lieutenant General Boyd should act as His Majesty's representative in investing General Eliott with the insignia of the order, which ceremony was to be performed in as splendid and magnificent a manner as the state of the Garrison would permit; the Engineers, soon after the arrival of the Thetis, began to erect a COLONNADE upon the rampart of THE KING'S BASTION,

that

that the honours might be conferred where the VICTORY was gained. By the 23d of April (St. George's day) the colonnade was finifhed; and every preparation for the ceremony being completed, the Governor commenced by communicating to the troops the thanks of their King and Country for THEIR defence of Gibraltar. Detachments from all the regiments and corps, with all the Officers not on duty, were affembled in three lines on the Red fands at eight o'clock in the morning; and the Governor taking poft in the centre of the fecond line, and the ufual compliments being paid, his Excellency addreffed himfelf to the Garrifon as follows :.

'GENTLEMEN;

'I HAVE affembled you this day, in order that the Officers and Soldiers may receive, in the moft public man-
'ner, an authentic declaration tranfmitted to me by the Secretary of State, expreffing the high fenfe His Majefty entertains of your meritorious conduct in defence of this Garrifon. The King's fatisfaction upon this event was foon divulged to all the world, by His moft gracious Speech to both Houfes of Parliament.
'The Houfe of Lords and the Houfe of Commons not only made the fuitable profeffions in their addreffes to the Throne, but have feverally enjoined me to communicate their unanimous thanks by the following refolutions :"

"Die Veneris, 13 Decembris, 1782.

"RESOLVED, nemine diffentiente, by the Lords Spiritual and
"Temporal, in Parliament affembled, that this Houfe
"doth highly approve and acknowledge the fervices of the
"Officers, Soldiers, and Sailors, lately employed in the
"defence of Gibraltar; and that General Eliott do fignify
"the fame to them."

"Die

" *Die Jovis,* 12 *Decembris,* 1782.

" RESOLVED, *nemine contradicente,* that the thanks of this
" Houfe [Commons] be given to Lieut. General Boyd,
" Major General De la Motte, Major General Green
" Chief Engineer, to Sir Roger Curtis, Knt. and to the
" Officers, Soldiers, and Sailors, lately employed in the
" defence of Gibraltar."

THE Governor then proceeded :—' No army has ever been
' rewarded by higher national honours; and it is well known how
' great, univerfal, and fpontaneous were the rejoicings throughout
' the kingdom, upon the news of your fuccefs. Thefe muft not
' only give you inexpreffible pleafure, but afford matter of triumph
' to your deareft friends and lateft pofterity. As a farther proof
' how juft your title is to fuch flattering diftinctions at home, reft
' affured, from undoubted authority, that the Nations in Europe,
' and other parts, are ftruck with admiration of your gallant beha-
' viour : even our late refolute and determined Antagonifts do not
' fcruple to beftow the commendations due to fuch valour and
' perfeverance.

' I now moft warmly congratulate you on thefe united and bril-
' liant teftimonies of approbation, amidft fuch numerous, fuch
' exalted tokens of applaufe : and FORGIVE ME, FAITHFUL COM-
' PANIONS, IF I HUMBLY CRAVE YOUR ACCEPTANCE OF MY
' GRATEFUL ACKNOWLEDGEMENTS. I ONLY PRESUME TO
' ASK THIS FAVOUR, AS HAVING BEEN A CONSTANT WIT-
' NESS OF YOUR CHEERFUL SUBMISSION TO THE GREATEST
' HARDSHIPS, YOUR MATCHLESS SPIRIT AND EXERTIONS,
' AND ON ALL OCCASIONS, YOUR HEROIC CONTEMPT OF EVERY
' DANGER.'

A GRAND

A GRAND *feu-de-joie* was then fired by the line, each difcharge commencing with a royal falute of twenty-one guns. Three cheers clofed the ceremony. The Commander in Chief, General and Field Officers, afterwards withdrew ; and the detachments (formed two deep) marched into town, and lined the ftreets leading from the Convent, by the Spanifh church and Grand parade, to the King's baftion. About half paft eleven o'clock, the proceffion began in the following order : ALL uncovered, and two deep, except the troops under arms.

MARSHAL.

Mufic, 12th Regiment,

Playing, " *See the conquering Hero comes.*"

ARTILLERY.

QUARTER-MASTER-GENERAL, and ADJUTANT-GENERAL, TOWN-MAJOR, and DEPUTY;

With other STAFF OF THE GARRISON.

Firft Divifion of FIELD OFFICERS, youngeft firft.

Mufic, 58th Regiment,

THE COMMISSIONER's SECRETARY,

Bearing on a crimfon velvet cufhion the Commiffion.

THE COMMISSIONER's AIDE-DE-CAMPS.

LIEUT. GENERAL BOYD, THE KING's COMMISSIONER.

THE GOVERNOR's SECRETARY,

Bearing, on a crimfon velvet cufhion, the Infignia of the Order of the Bath.

THE

THE GOVERNOR's AIDE-DE-CAMPS,
AS ESQUIRES.

GENERAL ELIOTT,
THE KNIGHT ELECT;

Supported by Generals DE LA MOTTE and GREEN.
Aide-de-camps to the Major Generals.

MAJOR GENERAL PICTON.
His Aide-de-camp.

THE BRIGADIER GENERALS, eldeſt firſt.
Their Brigade Majors.

Muſic, De la Motte's.
Second Diviſion of FIELD OFFICERS, eldeſt firſt.

Muſic, 56th Regiment.
The GRENADIERS of the Garriſon.

No COMPLIMENT was paid to the Knight Elect; but as the Commiſſioner paſſed, each Regiment, with the Officers, ſaluted. When the proceſſion arrived at the Colonnade, the General and Field Officers placed themſelves on each ſide of the Throne; the Artillery formed under the Colonnade, and the Grenadiers, fronting the baſtion, along the line-wall. The proper reverences being made to the vacant Throne, the Commiſſioner deſired his Secretary to read the Commiſſion: which being done, he addreſſed the Knight Elect in a ſhort complimentary ſpeech, taking the ribband at the concluſion,

and

and placing it over the Governor's shoulder, who inclined a little for that purpose : three reverences were then a second time made, and each took his seat on a crimson velvet chair on each side of the Throne, the Commissioner sitting on the right hand. The Governor was no sooner invested, than the music struck up, *God save the King*. The Grenadiers fired a volley, and a grand discharge of a hundred and sixty pieces of cannon was fired from the Sea-line. The procession then passed forwards through the colonnade, and returned in the same order. The detachments were afterwards dismissed, and each Non-commissioned Officer and Private received a pound of *fresh* beef and a quart of wine. The Generals, with their suites, and the Field Officers, dined at the Convent. In the evening, the Colonnade was illuminated with different-coloured lamps, and transparent paintings in the back scene : and Sir George Augustus Eliott, with the Lieutenant Governor, and principal Officers of the Garrison, assembling at the King's bastion about nine o'clock, there was a display of fire-works from the north and south bastions, and the Spanish church ; the principal of which were fired from the latter, being opposite to the Company.

THUS, in festivity and with honour, ended the labours of the Garrison of Gibraltar. During a period of THREE YEARS, SEVEN MONTHS, AND TWELVE DAYS (that is, from the commencement of the blockade to the cessation of arms) we had experienced a continued series of watchfulness and fatigue, the horrors of famine, and every harassing and vexatious mode of attack, which a powerful, obstinate, and revengeful Enemy could devise. On reviewing the transactions of this period, two circumstances cannot fail to strike the attentive reader ; viz. the very slow manner in which the Enemy proceeded in their operations, and the impossibility of maintaining so strict a blockade, as to prevent all communication by sea. To evince these, and other circumstances not unimportant to military

readers,

readers, I have been reduced to greater accuracy and minuteness than ordinary historians are obliged to observe ; and instead of the acuteness of investigation, or a splendid sententiousness, I have been necessitated to pursue the narrative, almost uninterruptedly, in the tedious form of a Journal. I have not presumed to intersperse many animadversions of my own : the only merit to which I can lay any claim, is that of a faithful narration of facts ; and I confess, I would at any time rather walk in the beaten track of truth, than mislead the judgement of my readers in the wilds of fancy and conjecture.

A RETURN of Casualties is annexed ; also the expenditure of Ammunition, both by the Enemy and the Garrison. These papers, as well as the Estimate of Provisions, I thought better to throw into the form of an Appendix, than to interrupt the narrative by their insertion.

APPENDIX.

A P P E N D I X.

A GENERAL RETURN OF CASUALTIES.

REGIMENTS.	KILLED.				DEAD OF WOUNDS.				DISABLED BY WOUNDS.				WOUNDED, BUT RECOVERED.				DEAD BY SICKNESS.				DESERTED.
	O.	S.	D.	R. & F.	O.	S.	D.	R. & F.	O.	S.	D.	R. & F.	O.	S.	D.	R. & F.	O.	S.	D.	R. & F.	R & F.
Royal Artillery	2	1	0	20	0	0	0	8	0	2	0	11	8	2	1	105	1	1	0	34	1
12th Regiment	1	3	1	13	0	0	0	10	1	0	0	10	2	4	7	89	0	3	0	32	3
25th ———	0	0	0	1	0	0	0	1	0	0	0	0	0	1	0	7	1	0	0	13	1
39th ———	1	3	1	16	1	1	0	6	0	0	0	10	3	5	1	44	0	1	0	37	5
56th ———	0	0	0	17	0	1	0	9	1	0	0	6	3	2	0	59	1	4	1	34	3
58th ———	1	1	0	11	0	1	0	5	0	0	1	8	2	2	2	61	0	1	1	53	11
59th ———	0	0	0	2	0	0	0	6	0	0	0	2	0	0	0	7	0	0	0	33	0
72d ———	0	2	0	31	0	2	0	21	0	1	1	21	3	11	5	109	0	1	0	47	9
73d ———	0	0	0	30	0	1	0	13	1	5	0	31	5	2	0	77	0	0	0	58	2
97th ———	0	0	0	7	0	0	1	5	0	1	0	4	0	3	1	33	1	6	0	106	1
Reden's Regt.	0	2	0	7	0	0	1	5	0	1	0	4	1	1	1	33	1	1	0	16	1
De la Motte's	0	3	0	16	0	0	0	6	0	1	0	0	0	2	0	42	2	2	0	10	1
Sydow's, formerly Hardenberg's	0	2	0	18	0	0	0	6	0	2	0	6	1	7	2	69	0	0	0	7	5
Soldier-Artificer Company	0	1	0	6	0	0	0	0	0	0	0	7	2	3	0	30	0	0	0	23	0
Marine Brigade	0	1	0	2	0	0	0	0	0	0	0	0	0	1	0	8	0	0	0	0	0
Corsican Comp.	0	0	0	0	0	0	0	0	0	0	0	0	1	0	0	0	0	0	0	0	0
Total	5	19	2	197	1	6	2	101	3	13	2	120	31	46	20	773	7	22	2	505	43

ABSTRACT OF THE TOTAL LOSS OF THE GARRISON.

Killed, and dead of wounds, - - - - - - - - - 333

Difabled by wounds, (Difcharged) - - - - - - - 138

Dead of ficknefs, exclufive of thofe who died of the fcurvy } 536
in 1779 and 1780, - - - - - - - - - - - -

Difcharged, from incurable complaints, - - - - - 181

Deferted, - - - - - - - - - - - - - - - 43

Total 1231

EXPEN-

EXPENDITURE of AMMUNITION from the GARRISON AND ENEMY.

Commencing the 12th of Sept. 1779, and ending the 3d of Feb. 1783. | Commencing the 12th of Apr. 1781, and ending the 2d of Feb. 1783.

MONTHS.	SHOT.	SHELLS.	GRAPE.	CAR-CASSES	LIGHT BALLS.	MONTHS.	Agreeable to the Laboratory Accounts.		
							SHOT.	SHELLS.	
1779.									
Sept.12—30	1767	201							
October	372	1116	1		6				
November	57	183	5						
December	82	63	6		4				
1780.									
January	88	131	38						
February	2	6	3						
March	17	7	3						
April	6								
May	8		6			Enemy silent			
June	123								
July	246								
August	56								
September	6								
October	85	243	73	1	160				
November	771	6004	510	63	64				
December	160	4242	250	79	54				
1781.									
January	33	875	63	22	8				
February	32	346	76	9					
March	23	221	17	13		**1781.**			
April	2672	2494	26	2		Apr.12, to } May 31	56760	20134	Computed
May	804	2782	23	6					
June	828	2250	104	35	3	June	8799	2643	
July	428	761	51	13	5	July	3036	698	
August	130	172	103	56	2	August	1350	184	
September	2614	6228	213	58	42	September	9320	750	
October	1722	11515	64	19	5	October	15754	2750	
November	509	3587	82	33	3	November	2430	1120	
December	632	7119	139	60	44	December	3378	1010	
1782.						**1782.**			
January	722	11052	132	60	23	January	4342	1012	
February	2617	7295	177	21	19	February	3046	566	
March	3657	10362	733	56	45	March	5828	1313	
April	2314	2768	370			April	3541	938	
May	2315	1669	352		14	May	2418	856	
June	2052	178	263	1	8	June	2190	653	
July	228	37	100		13	July			
August	5441	1781	1047	3	48	August	750	30	Computed, exclusive of the Battering-ships.
September	13557	3262	479	215		September	36432	16993	
October	2604	6881	735	12	14	October	11312	10673	
November	1937	5701	1157	74	17	November	2897	3243	
December	2596	12159	1422	26	3	December	1036	1958	
1783.						**1783.**			
January	2640	14176	3444	42	25	January	1067	680	
February	210	1047	414			February	55	144	
	57103	129151	12681	926	670		175741	68363	

Total 200,600 Rounds
British Gun-boats 4,728 Shot
205,328

Total 244,104 } Rounds, all of a heavy nature
Spanish Gun-boats 14,283 } Shot and Shells
258,387

The Garrison expended very near 8000 barrels of powder; and the number of ordnance damaged and destroyed during the siege, amounted to 53.

The number of barrels of powder expended by the Enemy could never be ascertained, nor what ordnance were destroyed.

An Estimate of the Prices fixed upon Provisions by a Committee of Officers, at Gibraltar, October the 23d, 1782.

To which is annexed the Price of various articles, as they were sold at different Periods of the Blockade and Siege.

The sums are turned into sterling, at the *average* exchange of 39*d.* the dollar; though the Garrison-exchange fluctuated betwixt 40*d.* and 42*d.*

PRICES LIMITED BY THE COMMITTEE.   PRICES DURING THE BLOCKADE.

	£	s.	d.			£	s.	d.		£	s.	d.
Fresh Beef, Veal & Mutton, per lb.	o	2	6	From	o	2	1	to	o	4	10½
Pork, ditto ———	o	1	3	From	o	2	1	—	o	4	1
Ducks and Fowls, per couple,	o	9	9	From	o	13	o	—	1	1	11½
A Goose, ——— ———	o	11	o						1	10	4
A Turkey, ———	o	14	7½						2	8	9
A pair of Pigeons, ———	o	3	3						o	9	9
Corned Beef, per lb.	o	1	3	Round of Bf. per lb.					o	2	11
Corned Pork, ditto	o	o	10	Salt Beef and Pork					o	1	3
Ham, ditto ———	o	1	10½	———					o	4	1
Bacon, and dried Tongues, ditto	o	1	3	———					o	3	3
Cheese, ditto ———	o	1	3	———					o	4	1
Salt Butter, ditto ———	o	1	10½	From	o	2	6	—	o	4	1
An Egg ———	o	o	2½	per dozen					o	4	10½
Pickled Tripe, per lb. ———	o	1	3						o	o	o
Potatoes, ditto ———	o	o	7½						o	2	6
Loaf-Sugar, ditto ———	o	2	6	Sold at an Auct. for					o	17	1
Powder Sugar, ditto ———	o	2	1	From	o	2	6	—	o	4	10½
Best Green Tea, ditto ———	1	1	11½	} ——— From	1	8	o	—	2	5	6
Bohea, or Souchong, ditto	o	13	o	}					o	5	9
Coffee, ditto ———	o	1	10½						o	5	9
Flour, ditto ———	o	o	7¼	From	o	1	3	—	o	2	1
Mould Candles, ditto ———	o	1	o½						o	o	o
Common, ditto ———	o	o	10	———					o	2	6
A Hogshead of Porter ———	5	13	9½						o	o	o
Bottled Porter (with bottles) per d.	o	14	7½						o	o	o
A Hogshead of Port Wine	24	7	6						o	o	o
Port Wine, (with bottles) per dez.	1	12	5½						o	o	o
Good common Wine, per gallon	o	4	11	Malaga Wine per B.					o	4	10½
Inferior ditto, ditto, ———	o	3	8						o	2	6
Claret, (with Bottles) per dozen	1	17	4½						o	o	o
Best Fish, per lb. ———	o	1	3	} These articles were ge-nerally sold, according to their size and quality, at most exorbitant rates.					o	o	o
Inferior kind, ditto ———	o	o	10						o	o	o
Small Fry, ditto ———	o	o	7½						o	o	o

This estimate afterwards underwent some small alteration by the Committee, the wines being fixed, they thought, at too low a price. Besides the articles mentioned under the head of the Blockade-price, the following sold in the course of the Siege for the sums annexed to them.

A Calf's

	£.	s.	d.
A Calf's Head and Feet	1	14	1½
A Calf's Pluck	0	14	7½
Hind quarter, with the Head and Tail of an Algerine Sheep	7	10	0
Head and Feet of a Sheep	0	14	7½
A Bullock's Head, without Tongue	1	3	4½
A Bullock's Heart	0	9	9
A Goat's Head	0	8	1½
Onions, per lb.	0	2	6
A Cabbage	0	1	7½
A bunch of Cabbage leaves	0	0	5
A bunch of Carrots and Turnips	0	1	0½
A small bunch of Radishes	0	0	5
A pint of Milk and Water	0	1	3
A Lemon	0	0	5
A Quill	0	0	6½
A live Pig sold for	9	14	9

A large Sow in pig sold for upwards of 29l. A Goat, with a young kid, both of which had been purchased in England for 15s. sold in the Garrison, when the latter was about twelve months old, for near 12l. An English Milch Cow was sold, in 1780, for fifty guineas; reserving to the seller a pint of milk each day whilst she gave milk: and another Cow was purchased by a Jew for sixty guineas; but the beast was in so feeble a condition, that she dropped down dead before she had been removed many hundred yards. If these *facts* were not thought sufficient to demonstrate the exorbitant prices of every article in the Garrison, others could be adduced, of equally as surprising a complexion.

The

The following are the proportions of the Prize-Money, as distributed to the Garrison of Gibraltar, from the sums arising from the Head-Money granted by Parliament for destroying the Battering-ships, and the sale of the St. Michael, man of war.

The subsequent Sums are proportions of 30,000 *l.*

Which was the Sum first divided.

	£.	s.	d.		£.	s.	d.
The Governor, 1-16th - -	1875	0	0	Captain - - - - - -	43	10	1
Lieutenant Governor - -	937	10	0	Lieutenant - - - - - -	25	5	6
Major General - - - -	468	15	0	Second Lieut. and Ensign -	22	0	6¼
Brigadier General - - - -	267	10	0	Serjeant - - - - - - -	3	6	9
Colonel - - - - - -	156	1	0	Corporal - - - - -	2	0	11½
Lieutenant Colonel - - -	80	16	0	Private - - - - - -	1	9	1
Major - - - - - -	57	15	6				

A second Act of Parliament afterwards passed, for granting to the Garrison whatever might be fished up from the wrecks of the Battering-ships; and those employed in this duty proceeded with such success, that brass and iron cannon, with other articles, were recovered to a considerable value.

Two divisions, of 16,000*l.* and 8000*l.* have since been distributed;—the latter of which, it is imagined, will be the last.

F I N I S.